Treason to Whiteness
Is Loyalty to Humanity

T0243638

Geert Dhondt cotaught with Noel Ignatiev at Massachusetts College of Art and John Jay College, the City University of New York where he is an associate professor of economics.

Zhandarka Kurti is an assistant professor of Criminology and Criminal Justice at Loyola University, Chicago.

Jarrod Shanahan is an assistant professor of Criminal Justice at Governors State University, Illinois, and the author of *Captives: How Rikers Island Took New York City Hostage*.

All three are editors of *Hard Crackers: Chronicles of Everyday Life*.

Treason to Whiteness Is Loyalty to Humanity

Noel Ignatiev

Edited with an Introduction by Geert Dhondt,
Zhandarka Kurti, and Jarrod Shanahan

With a Foreword by David Roediger

Afterword by John Garvey

VERSO

London • New York

First published by Verso 2022
© Noel Ignatiev 2022
Foreword © David Roediger 2022
Afterword © John Garvey 2022
Introduction and editorial notes © Geert Dhondt, Zhandarka Kurti, and Jarrod Shanahan 2022

1 3 5 7 9 10 8 6 4 2

Verso
UK: 6 Meard Street, London W1F 0EG
US: 20 Jay Street, Suite 1010, Brooklyn, NY 11201
versobooks.com

Verso is the imprint of New Left Books

ISBN-13: 978-1-83976-501-8
ISBN-13: 978-1-83976-505-6 (US EBK)
ISBN-13: 978-1-83976-502-5 (UK EBK)

British Library Cataloguing in Publication Data
A catalogue record for this book is available from the British Library

Library of Congress Cataloging-in-Publication Data

Names: Ignatiev, Noel, author. | Dhondt, Geert L., editor. | Kurti,
    Zhandarka, editor. | Shanahan, Jarrod, editor. | Roediger, David R.,
    writer of foreword. | Garvey, John, 1948– writer of afterword.
Title: Treason to whiteness is loyalty to humanity / Noel Ignatiev ; edited
    by Geert Dhondt, Zhandarka Kurti and Jarrod Shanahan ; with a foreword by
    David Roediger ; afterword by John Garvey.
Description: London ; New York : Verso Books, 2022. | Includes
    bibliographical references and index.
Identifiers: LCCN 2021055886 (print) | LCCN 2021055887 (ebook) | ISBN
    9781839765018 (paperback) | ISBN 9781839765056 (ebk)
Subjects: LCSH: Racism—United States. | Anti-racism—United States. |
    Social conflict—United States. | Working class—United States—Social
    conditions. | United States—Race relations. | United States—Social
    conditions.
Classification: LCC E184.A1 I36 2022 (print) | LCC E184.A1 (ebook) | DDC
    305.800973—dc23/eng/20211222
LC record available at https://lccn.loc.gov/2021055886
LC ebook record available at https://lccn.loc.gov/2021055887

Typeset in Minion by Hewer Text UK Ltd, Edinburgh
Printed and bound by CPI Group (UK) Ltd, Croydon CR0 4YY

To future generations of abolitionists, race traitors, and revolutionaries

Contents

Part I
THE WHITE BLINDSPOT

Part II
BLACK WORKER/WHITE WORKER:
THE SOJOURNER TRUTH ORGANIZATION

Part III
ABOLISH THE WHITE RACE:
THE *RACE TRAITOR* PROJECT

Part IV
DUAL POWER IS THE KEY TO REVOLUTIONARY STRATEGY

Foreword

My first memorable meeting with Noel came during the US bituminous miners' strike of 1977–78. We'd probably been around each other a few times before. I worked in the bookstore of a Chicago revolutionary collective, Red Rose Books, and much of the Chicago left periodically dropped in. I lived near the Stewart-Warner plant on the North Side, a site of Sojourner Truth Organization (STO) activity that Noel helped to lead, and friends sometimes asked for help leafleting on shift changes. As the Chicago Surrealist Group and the Charles Kerr Publishing Company became my political homes, I heard the praises of Noel sung, especially by Penelope and Franklin Rosemont. If some of my shallow earlier training on the Trotskyist left would have led to a temptation to dismiss STO as "Maoist," the surrealists connected with Noel as a fellow enthusiast for the work of C. L. R. James.

Nevertheless that first actually memorable meeting (memorable for me—I doubt it registered with Noel) made me less enthusiastic to know him. Surrealists and some others had organized a demonstration on behalf of the striking miners at Chicago's Museum of Science and Industry. The plan struck us as pure genius. The museum featured a mock-up of a working coal mine, corporate-sponsored and well-scrubbed enough to make extractive labor seem child's play, verging on an amusement park ride. By picketing it we got to talk to museumgoers, got into it with museum security, and made a little media splash. When we ran into Noel by chance afterward he greeted our account of our successes with "So you picketed on behalf of a white supremacist organization," meaning the United Mine Workers. The long-time surrealists were ready with a reflection: "That's Noel." But being twenty-five years old, from a union family, and at the time a more or less standard issue labor historian in search of a "usable past" and an ennobling, uncomplicated present, I was less forgiving.

That didn't last long. Seeing Noel at the bookstore and at demonstrations, I came to like him lots. Of all the revolutionaries who had left universities to enter industrial jobs, he had the best stories and seemed the best listener to fellow workers. *Acceptable Men*, his forthcoming memoir of life at US Steel Gary Works, offers a sampling of such stories.[1] It shows his capacity to be interested in how the shop floor empowered and immiserated and captures some of the wisdom distilled in his 1981 striking essay "The Backward Workers," included in this volume. I found him funny and revolutionary, a rare enough combination. He clearly loved intellectual exchanges among radicals in a way that left him genuinely excited, if fierce. So many of us became clenched during political arguments, but Noel often seemed more relaxed and in his element as things heated up. In some ways—this will seem odd in that he was twelve years older than I and pushing 40—Noel struck me as somewhat boyish, stretching to get comfortable, wise-cracking, provoking, and hoping for the best in the long run of the exchange no matter how tense it became.

Then, too, my own politics changed as I studied with my graduate school mentor, the great African American historian Sterling Stuckey, and with my informal teacher, George Rawick. With Sterling I read W. E. B. Du Bois systematically and with Rawick, James. I'd known Noel's writings on the white worker, with and without Ted Allen, from the 1960s (many of which are included in this volume), admiring them vaguely but without the need to take on the full import of their conclusions. That changed in reading Du Bois and in confronting Chicago's Nazis in the Marquette Park neighborhood. I did not come to think the miners organized for white supremacy but did come to know that their practice, heroic stories like those in the film *Matewan* notwithstanding, too often failed to break from it. By 1981, when Sojourner Truth Organization published a special issue of *Urgent Tasks* on James, I briefly wrote for it on *Mariners, Renegades and Castaways*. Noel also passed my rough litmus test for knowing if I'd like people on the Chicago left: He understood the genius of and loved the extraordinary black anarcho-pacifist poet Joffre Stewart.

By the mid-1980s, Noel and I both left Chicago, he for Harvard and a doctorate in history. We came to know each other, we later mutually lamented, too little. But scholarship and radicalism brought us together frequently later. In 1990, as those from different generations of the left converged on publishing around the issues of whiteness and class, Noel sent me his wonderful essay "Whiteness and American Character," published in Ishmael Reed's journal *Konch* (and reprinted in this volume under the title "Immigrants and Whites"). It was through that article that I and others discovered James Baldwin's seminal 1984 piece "On Being 'White,' . . . and Other Lies."[2] (Reed's Before Columbus Foundation later honored Noel and John Garvey with the American Book Award for their anthology *Race Traitor*.[3]) Following Baldwin and Allen—and indeed Reed as well—we both became interested in the transformation of racially suspect Irish immigrants to the antebellum United States, Noel with much more spirit and detail than I in his arresting 1995 book *How the Irish Became White*.[4] We shared some academic platforms, including the Making and Unmaking of Whiteness conference at Berkeley in 1995, a splashy announcement of critical whiteness studies that captured some of what would sustain that enterprise and much that would plague it. We spoke together with the novelist and historian Alexander Saxton at a textile factory museum in Lowell, before an aging but seeming ageless Saxton walked us into the ground in search of the best Portuguese food.

Noel took students seriously but academia far less so. Practically his first published words in a history journal mounted a fierce, completely righteous dissection of the deep differences between the approach of Du Bois to Reconstruction and that of Eric Foner, regarded on the liberal left as simply Du Bois's successor as the leading student of Reconstruction. Noel remained much more at home with older radicals and leftward moving youth. Among the latter were a number of my graduate students, especially in Minneapolis. Happily, he routinely set aside doctrinaire distinctions between anarchism and Marxism. The late and great Joel Olson, who worked with me at University of Minnesota, especially learned much from Noel, including how to disagree with Noel. At one point his younger interlocutors and Noel allowed me to join them in the late 1990s at the Phoenix home of Audrey Creed and Joel Olson. We discussed a useful provocation Noel had prepared asking for consideration of the possibility that race, in the ways that we had been speaking of it, would soon be over—that the "lowest white man" would no longer be made to hold racial privilege. He knew I'd object, both to the effect that such a framework had always been too rigid and also by observing that the very site of the gathering underlined the need to think about race through indigeneity and through immigration as well as through slavery and its legacy. It was a great evening.

On any spectrum of US political differences, Noel and I occupied the same tenth of a percent of space. That reality hardly guarantees that people get along. It is as easy to dwell on small differences as large, especially on issues we regard as life-or-death ones. Noel's own relations with Ted Allen suggest as much. We were proud, I think, of not exaggerating differences or heeding calls of "Let's you and him fight." I think our coming from such different microgenerations of the New Left helped to keep us from dividing irrevocably over any particular foundational split or event. We also profited from sharing the experience of getting calls and letters from young Irish Americans, including new migrants again fleeing misery in Ireland who were trying to understand and escape whiteness.

One needless strain between us hinged on a miscalculation on my part. In the early 1990s, as Noel and others launched the wonderful and important journal *Race Traitor*, they asked that I play a role. I was on a small crusade of emphasizing that critiques of whiteness have always come mostly from people of color and over-worried that the name too identified opposition to whiteness with whites. Would we really expect black radicals, I wondered, to identify with *Race Traitor* as a name? This bit of ultra-literalism on my part seemed especially dodgy when the exemplary black radicals John Bracey and Robin D. G. Kelley promptly joined the editorial board. But this misstep left me still writing for *Race Traitor*, especially in its spectacular special issue on surrealism and whiteness, and working on the production of Noel's book *The Lesson of the Hour*, a collection of Wendell Phillips's speeches.[5]

I especially loved the joy Noel took from being around older leftists. He hung on every word as Alex Saxton marched us through Lowell. In 1988 I collaborated with the St. Louis organization Workers' Democracy to organize the Conference on Workers' Self-Organization at Washington University. The event was to be dedicated to George Rawick but a stroke prevented the guest of honor from attending. We organizers were delighted that Noel came. His delight came from the number of veteran revolutionaries attending. These included Marty Glaberman and Stan Weir, themselves worker-revolutionaries with later lives as university teachers. Noel alternated between animated banter with them and, as James sometimes recommended, falling silent. Whatever their differences, Noel certainly revered Allen's contributions. My introduction to a new Verso edition of Saxton's *Rise and Fall of the White Republic* in 2003 offered the observation that Saxton's book represented the state-of-the-art among post–Du Bois historians writing on whiteness.[6] Knowing firsthand his deep regard for Saxton's work, I thought Noel might concur. "Oh no," he said, "that's Ted Allen's work." I am glad for him and for the world that Noel will long have his passionate advocates and those whom he taught to carry on his own very significant political and intellectual heritage, one that includes not only analyses of the world but personal examples of how to live in it.

David Roediger
Lawrence, Kansas
February 2021

Acknowledgments

We owe an enormous debt of gratitude to Noel Ignatiev's family, especially to his sister and executor, Amy Sanders, who supported our collection and publication of his political writings, and his children Rachel and John Henry.

We couldn't have put together this edited book without the guidance of Kingsley Clarke, John Garvey, Beth Henson, and David Ranney, who listened to our initial ideas, took the time to look at various drafts and offered their perceptive comments and suggestions. We also want to thank Audrey Creed and give a special shout out to our fellow editors at *Hard Crackers: Chronicles of Everyday Life*. Noel Ignatiev brought us all together and we soldier on without him, committed to exploring the contradictions of daily life and, within them, the possibility for a new world.

None of this would have been possible without the dedicated team at Verso, especially Ben Mabie who supported this project from the beginning and helped us navigate the entire process from start to finish, and Citlalli Aparicio who transcribed several articles from the original format. Finally, we wish to acknowledge the hard and important work of the Sojourner Truth Organization Electronic Archive (sojournertruth. net), where much of the work of Ignatiev and his comrades is preserved.

Introduction: An American Revolutionary

In a 2018 interview, Noel Ignatiev summed up his political orientation:

> After sixty years of political activism and study I can boil down what
> I have learned into three propositions: 1) Labor in the white skin
> cannot be free where in the black it is branded; 2) For revolutionaries,
> dual power is the key to strategy; 3) The emancipation of the working
> class is the task of the workers themselves.[1]

These three themes guided how we assembled this collection, and the
reader can see how they develop Ignatiev's writings across a great
expanse of time. As an agitator, he contributed to struggles spanning
over half a century, and in its course, he left behind a wealth of historical, theoretical, and practical interventions that are as relevant to the
struggles of today as they were when he first wrote them. To the very
end of his life, Ignatiev retained an undying faith in the ability of the US
working class to lead its own emancipation. On this point he was
intransigent.

Ignatiev was a revolutionary. He joined the Communist Party in the
1950s as a teenager and was subsequently involved with revolutionary
organizations and writing projects until he died. Ignatiev was in the
national leadership of Students for a Democratic Society (SDS); the
group split, and he emerged as an important intellectual leader in one
of those splits, Revolutionary Youth Movement II. He was one of the

founders of the Sojourner Truth Organization (STO) and worked with this group in the 1970s and 1980s, organizing and editing the STO journal *Urgent Tasks*. In the 1990s he was a co-founder of the New Abolitionist Society and the *Race Traitor* journal and briefly joined the Love and Rage Revolutionary Anarchist Organization while he was involved in Boston's Copwatch. In the 2000s he was closely linked with the revolutionary group Bring the Ruckus. In the last few years of his life, he started a new publication, *Hard Crackers*; the three editors of this volume are editors of that journal. Ignatiev was a comrade, collaborator, and friend. As a new generation of revolutionaries struggle to make sense of US society in order to overturn it, we are happy to offer the first sustained, though by no means exhaustive, collection of Ignatiev's considerable body of short works. These writings will help revolutionaries today navigate a moment that is pregnant with great promise and pitfalls.

A collection of Ignatiev's major essays hasn't come a moment too soon. The recent resurgence of right and left populism in the United States, and globally, has demonstrated the failure of traditional political parties to respond to the growing immiseration of the working class. The rise of redoubled racial chauvinism and nationalism has reinvigorated discussions about whiteness and white supremacy. And though the conflagrations of 2020 may have disappeared from America's streets for the time being, their defining issue—the enduring color line in US society—will continue to inspire resistance and rebellion so long as the capitalist order that it props up remains intact. Meanwhile, the tantalizing glimpses of revolutionary struggle seen on many US streets in 2020 have forced militants to grapple with the strategic lessons of the rebellion and imagine a future struggle that could be sustained and pushed all the way. The bourgeois response to the rebellion has been predictable: an ocean of ink has been spilled on America's long overdue reckoning with systemic racism, most of it amounting to restating empirical facts about racial disparities or repeating the shopworn platitudes of "diversity and inclusion" that now dress the windows of boardrooms and halls of power as they go about business as usual. Meanwhile, liberal anti-racism has done little to do away with the institutions that reproduce race and racial oppression or to transform in any meaningful way the daily conditions of work and life for millions of working-class black people. While Ignatiev's work offers no blueprint for the future—not in the least because he had little use for them—major currents of his work lend us guidance in the present.

Since the 2000s, the eruption of the immigration rights movement, Occupy Wall Street, Black Lives Matter, #NODAPL, and teacher strikes among others represent important flashpoints of struggle against the wretched status quo. The considerable presence of white people in these protest movements has challenged the stubborn belief that white people have no interest whatsoever in the larger project of human liberation. But given the relative advantages that white people have historically held, and continue to hold, how could they be trusted to participate in the struggle against racist injustices and exploitation of people of color? The answer to this perennial question has found a new home in a term that has become the source of considerable abuse: white privilege. Today this term has become a way of talking about the color line and race in movement work without having to unpack what it means. Instead, it is often deployed as a cudgel against opponents—deserving or other-wise—or else used to argue for a kind of political paralysis in which white people are not authentic or oppressed enough to undertake any political initiative of their own volition. In many leftist milieus, white people are taught to conduct internal self-diagnosis of their privileges, which often amounts to endless navel-gazing introspection and ulti-mately only reinforces white identity. It would certainly come as a surprise to many people engaged in such projects that the original "white privilege" theory arose from communist labor organizing in US factories and was pioneered in large part by Ignatiev himself, during the time when he was a factory worker battling white supremacy at the point of production.

The concept of white privilege grew out of W. E. B. Du Bois's *Black Reconstruction* and the concrete experiences Ignatiev and others of his generation had in their attempts to organize with white workers.[2] Du Bois emphasizes the tragedy of the white workers, whose wretched condition stood to be considerably improved by common struggle with African Americans, but who were bought off by the "wages of whiteness" afforded to them by the ruling class, in exchange for forswearing solidarity with their black counterparts. This framework made a considerable impact on Ignatiev and his political mentor Theodore Allen, who was the first to use "white skin privilege" in a 1965 essay on the life of anti-slavery revolutionary John Brown.[3] Two years later, Ignatiev and Allen cowrote "The White Blindspot," which explored the struggle against white supremacy as fundamental to anti-capitalist working-class struggles in the United States. The point of analyzing white privilege, they argued, was to understand the way it inhibited multiracial class struggle and to convince white workers that in embracing white identity, they had walked right into a trap set by the ruling class. Crucially, they argued, letting go of white privilege was not an act of sacrifice by the white worker, but a matter of farsight-edness, of seeing beyond the short-term benefits (often only imagi-nary) of their disastrous alignment with the ruling class. "To suggest that the acceptance of white-skin privilege is in the interests of white workers," Ignatiev subsequently wrote,

> is equivalent to suggesting that swallowing the worm with the hook in it is in the interests of the fish. To argue that repudiating these privi-leges is a "sacrifice" is to argue that the fish is making a sacrifice when it leaps from the water, flips its tail, shakes its head furiously in every direction and throws the barbed offering.[4]

Ignatiev had little interest in academia, even after leaving the Rust Belt to study at Harvard following over twenty years organizing at the point of production. For him, the concern with white skin privilege was always political—he wanted to understand how it hurt the struggle for human emancipation. This investigation began with the question of how to overthrow capitalism and establish a communist society. It led Ignatiev to the conclusion that the social compact of whiteness, which bound white workers to the white bourgeoisie in alliance against black workers, must be eliminated to achieve this aim. The concept of aboli-tion here is key. A student of history who understood that the white race has not always existed, Ignatiev decided that it must be brought to an end. This is not, as vulgar critics interpret, a call to do away with people of European descent, but to eliminate the social basis on which they aligned with one another at the expense of the rest of the world, and ultimately, their own futures.

"The reader will note that I have written a book about racial oppres-sion," Ignatiev wrote in the Afterword to How the Irish Became White, "without using the term 'racism.' I consider the term useless."[5] Racial oppression to Ignatiev was a concrete arrangement of political power under the capitalist division of labor that must be contested through mass struggle, not bad ideas that can be fought by education or raising awareness. Furthermore, Ignatiev never tired of pointing out that race *itself* was an inegalitarian power arrangement; he did not imagine racism could be ended in a world where race was still a meaningful concept. This conclusion led Ignatiev and John Garvey to co-edit the journal *Race Traitor*. Its slogan "treason to whiteness is loyalty to humanity" was certainly a provocation to those in academia who embraced endless privilege checking as an antidote to white supremacy. Borrowing from Marx's famous dictum, *Race Traitor* urged a new generation to not just study and interpret the white race, but to abolish it.

Though Ignatiev is primarily remembered as a historian, he didn't just furnish us the historical context to understand the needful tasks for realizing an emancipated future; he taught us *how to think* about them. Coming of age in the heady environ of postwar Marxism, Ignatiev learned the dialectical method as not just a means of combat—which he never shied away from—but as a means of attaining superior understanding of the world where he aimed to take deliberate action. For instance, he was deeply invested in understanding how race was made and remade in the period before and after the Civil War. He often remarked that US revolutionaries knew more about the Russian Revolution than the unique revolutionary tradition of their own country. By contrast, Ignatiev posited the Civil War and the emancipation of the slaves as America's true revolutionary moment. Most Marxist accounts of the Civil War emphasize economic factors that made conflict between two rival modes of production inevitable. In their reading, the architectonics of history made abolition a fait accompli—it was only a matter of time before the industrialists would supersede the supposedly age-old regime of slave-labor management. But following W. E. B. Du Bois, Ignatiev emphasized the political, subjective, and therefore contingent nature of abolitionist victory: an outcome snatched in the "general strike" of the slaves quitting work at Southern plantations and the influx of black soldiers into the Northern army, as well as the insurrectionary actions of John Brown and his band of militants, whose decisive minoritarian actions Ignatiev believed made emancipation possible. While he derived important lessons from revolutionary leaders like Lenin—often to the consternation of the more anarchist-inclined comrades who he accumulated over the years—Ignatiev understood runaway slaves and abolitionists as our real revolutionary forebears. He did not emphasize the subjective factors of this revolution because he believed the political–economic account of the war to be unimportant. Ignatiev simply did not pursue history for its own sake and valued the past as it furnishes lessons to those seeking to make revolution in the present.

In our own time the George Floyd Rebellion brought overnight popularity to the politics of "abolitionism," loosely defined as a movement to do away with the cops, the prisons, and other repressive institutions of society, and to instead provide everyone with the means to live a dignified life.[6] Today the meaning of abolition, and how it can be achieved, are daily contested by young people reflecting on the hottest year of struggle in the United States in a half century. Amid these ongoing debates, Ignatiev's work invites us to return to the militant and revolutionary visions of the nineteenth century black, Garrisonian, and revolutionary abolitionists who were not interested in gradual reform to end slavery. Instead, they burned down plantations, hatched slave revolts and uprisings, tore down the Southern economy—all in the name of creating a new society free of human bondage. Ignatiev never missed a chance to point out that there were plenty of reformist contemporaries of the abolitionists, who sought to regulate the social order of slavery and make it more humane. Shortly before his death he ran afoul of activists demanding a minimum wage for prison laborers by asking: why not demand to let them out instead?

Had he lived to see it, the George Floyd Rebellion would have excited Ignatiev immensely. He believed that the working class is not hopelessly backward and hence in need of education, uplifting, and leadership by its social betters. His life's work was driven by the belief that "every cook can govern," to borrow a formulation from one of his major influences, C. L. R. James.[7] In a 1981 essay entitled "The Backward Workers," Ignatiev chides the common leftist assumption that the conservatism or apolitical appearance of workers means they are in need of instruction and leadership, arguing instead that unlike revolutionary intellectuals, workers make choices based on what is possible. If they in fact believe *another world is possible*, and prefigured by their struggle, history tells us they will fight with great ferocity. If, instead, they are being asked to take risks and make sacrifices for piecemeal reforms that will not fundamentally alter their lives, workers remain aloof. But this is not the same thing as being backward. Returning, as ever, to the lessons of the Civil War, he argues: "It is evident that the slaves' perception of the futility of a general uprising before the Civil War, and the usefulness of one after the War began was accurate." Challenging those who speak of the backwardness of workers, he wonders: "Is it always the case that the oppressed people perceive with such scientific precision the possibilities of such a situation?"[8]

Despite the provocative hypothesis of this article, that workers and oppressed people always choose correctly, it is clear that Ignatiev had a more complicated relationship to the people he believed could bring a new society into being. It is rare to find a scholar so well versed in the historical drama and tragedy of the US working class—and in particular, the refusal of European workers to build meaningful solidarity with African Americans—who simultaneously retains faith that the world can be remade through the deliberate action of everyone in society. Through viewing the proletariat as capable of remaking the world, but also possessing the agency to fail spectacularly at this mission, Ignatiev cultivated a complex relationship to proletarian self-activity. His ambivalence is maybe best expressed in an anecdote he included in the introduction to *How the Irish Became White*. "One occasion many years ago," he wrote,

> I was sitting on my front step when my neighbor came out of the house next door carrying her small child, whom she placed in her automobile. She turned away from him for a moment, and as she started to close the car door, I saw that the child had put his hand where it would be crushed when the door was closed. I shouted to the woman to stop. She halted in mid-motion, and when she realized what she had almost done, an amazing thing happened: she began laughing, then broke into tears and began hitting the child. It was the most intense and dramatic expression of conflicting emotions I have ever beheld.[9]

And this Ignatiev compared to his own experience outlining the history of the great struggles of Irish proletarians in the New World, which culminated in their choosing to be white, thus making common cause with the US bourgeoisie, rather than embracing solidarity with African Americans. "My attitude toward the subjects of this study," he concluded, "accommodates stresses similar to those I witnessed in that mother."[10]

The *Hard Crackers* project, which Ignatiev spent much of his time and energy in his final years overseeing, was dedicated to pursuing these very contradictions, which explode so violently in US society, between the emancipatory striving of oppressed and exploited people and the often antisocial or downright flummoxing dimensions these strivings take, when given form in the toxic stew of capitalist society.

Taken in sum, the most consistent feature of Ignatiev's work is its grounding in the need for serious revolutionary strategy. In a moment when debates about reformist versus revolutionary approaches have been significantly sharpened by the George Floyd Rebellion and the emergence of demands like "defund the police," Ignatiev's work provides much-needed clarity and a model for what it could look like to orient our praxis toward a concrete revolutionary horizon. He once told us that when he began organizing with the Sojourner Truth Organization, he was aware of a handful of Steel Belt factories that could be seized as the basis for a revolutionary offensive; there was a straight line, at least in theory, between his day-to-day activity and a communist society. His subsequent studies of US history, popular culture, and the nature of the US color line were all investigations into the viability and proper methodology for making revolution in the United States. Ignatiev placed zero value in the self-congratulatory theatrics of "speaking truth to power." Instead, he understood political questions to stand and fall on the question of dual power: are we or aren't we building the power of the working class to take initiative on its own accord, through its own institutions, against the institutions of the bourgeoisie?

Speaking at the 2010 Baltimore Book Fair, Ignatiev remarked:

> No revolution has ever taken place without a period of dual power. The masses of ordinary people will not transfer their allegiance from the dominant institutions, an allegiance based largely on habit, to a new society unless the institutions of the new society already exist in tangible form. At the same time, every popular upheaval gives rise to institutions that prefigure the new society.[11]

He challenged the audience, many of whom he took to be engaged in the project of building "alternative institutions" on the margins of capitalist society, to consider the way such projects, while important to fulfill immediate needs, do very little to threaten or challenge the capitalist order. The task facing revolutionaries, he argued, was not to survive at the margins, but to take decisive action at the heart of society. Surely, to many listeners in the time between Barack Obama's victory and Occupy Wall Street, such talk of impending revolution in the United States must have seemed far-fetched. But Ignatiev believed that revolution would not slowly announce itself over a protracted period of months and years. "Every modern society," he told the crowd, "the US included, no matter how stable it appears, is but one step away from a general breakdown in which the existing institutions collapse and the issue of power is posed."[12] It is this scenario, Ignatiev argued, toward which we must orient our praxis, and stay prepared.

This edited volume is meant to introduce readers and future generations of revolutionaries to Noel Ignatiev's most important political writing. We have elected to divide his political writings chronologically into four main sections, which reflect the long trajectory of his political development and central political interventions.

The first section, "The White Blindspot," highlights Ignatiev's political development during a time when revolutionary communist groups in the United States were being reconstituted and challenged by larger global forces, such as the degeneration of the international communist movement toward accommodation with the misery of postwar capitalism, and the rapid rise of third world liberation movements. Ultimately the central questions of race, critiques of Stalinism, and a preoccupation with rank-and-file organizing would push him to leave the Communist Party, and together with Ted Allen and Harry Haywood, found the Provisional Organizing Committee, an ultra-left splinter group. It was during these years that Ignatiev was introduced to the concept of white privilege by Ted Allen. Together they would launch a critique of groups like the Progressive Labor Party for refusing to acknowledge the centrality of white supremacy to working-class revolutionary struggles in the United States. For Ignatiev, white supremacy at home remained an enduring blind spot of the American left even as it aligned with anti-imperialist struggles abroad. In the late 1960s, as political disagreements imploded Students for a Democratic Society, Ignatiev pushed its members and those of other New Left organizations to consider the fight against white supremacy as integral not only to building solidarity with third world liberation movements against US imperialism, but also as central to the lives and interests of

US workers. During these years of fervent debate about revolutionary tactics and strategies, Ignatiev sharpened his revolutionary critique of white supremacy, which he argued was a real material force within the working class movement that should be studied and challenged at the point of production.

The second section, "Black Worker/White Worker," delves into Ignatiev's involvement in the STO, a communist group established in the late 1960s. The group was composed of committed revolutionaries mostly employed in large-scale industries in the Midwest who tried to grapple with the changing material terrain of capitalism, including the strategic importance of an increasingly multiracial industrial workforce, the rise of black radicalism, and third world liberation movements to develop revolutionary strategies in response. Like many left groups at the time, STO sought to connect with large-scale industrial workers at the point of production. However, as Ignatiev later recounted to us, what distinguished STO was its political line on workplace organizing, which focused on fighting white supremacy among white workers and support- ing the self-activity of black and Latino workers against the union bureaucracy.[13] Ignatiev contributed greatly to the group's engagement with complex theoretical and political questions through organized study groups, writing and agitating for its newspaper *Urgent Tasks*, and participating in and supporting worker-led direct action and strikes. The excerpts we have included in this section will give the reader a deeper sense of the wider political context that gave rise to STO and Ignatiev's contributions to the lively debates that took place within the organization.

The third section, "Treason to Whiteness Is Loyalty to Humanity," deals with Ignatiev's contribution to *Race Traitor*, an independent jour- nal he co-edited with John Garvey that brought together various left intellectuals and revolutionaries to discuss what it would take to abolish white supremacy. *Race Traitor* was published in the 1990s, a time when liberals effectively embraced multiculturalism and racial identity as the main way to reform a system based on domination and control without addressing the origins of the racial order in capitalism. In response, *Race Traitor* raised the mantle of new abolition, a political vision developed from the lessons of the nineteenth revolutionary movement against slavery. The journal took seriously the ways in which whiteness was constructed both historically and in the present moment through an exploration of popular culture, current events, and everyday life stories. Over the span of twelve years that the journal existed, Ignatiev contributed incisive political thinking and analysis of race and its role in US society. Ultimately the journal's aim was not simply to understand white America but to abolish the system of white supremacy that held it together. This was a praxis that abjured soapboxing platitudes or tugging the heartstrings of guilty white people in favor of direct action that repudiates white privilege in the name of humanity.

Essays in the fourth and last section, "Dual Power Is the Key to Revolutionary Strategy," deal with Ignatiev's insistence on dual power as the necessary horizon of anti-capitalist movements, and his involvement in the *Hard Crackers* project. This work draws on the strategies, tactics, and lessons of past revolutionary movements and historical figures like Wendell Phillips, C. L. R. James, and John Brown to make sense of our contemporary moment. Ignatiev constantly sought ways to engage with the new generation of revolutionaries who were politicized by the last decade of struggles and interested in unpacking the relationship between race and class. In his short essay "Race or Class?" Ignatiev dismisses framing the discussion as an either/or question. Instead, he implores us to consider race as a critical mechanism through which class society is reproduced and defended. Ignatiev's commitment to the *Hard Crackers* project in the last years of his life was a reflection of his insistence on examining the contradictory consciousness of ordinary everyday people and their capacity to turn around the mess we are in through their actions and struggles for a liberated world.

As a new generation is called to fulfill its historic mission, we return to Ignatiev's political legacy to remind ourselves of the lessons learned along the way, the unique political terrain of the United States, and the struggles ahead. As we grapple with what our side stands for, Ignatiev's coordinates remain ours: the centrality of the struggle against white supremacy, the strategy of dual power, and the capacity of the working class to fight for and build a new world free of domination.

Geert Dhondt, Zhandarka Kurti,
and Jarrod Shanahan
June 2021

I

The White Blindspot

1

Passing

Ignatiev reflects on his early life and work experiences, and the nagging questions of authenticity that complicated his relationship to political work. This essay first appeared in Ignatiev's PM Press blog in 2015.

In the summer of 1961, I left the University of Pennsylvania and took a job at a factory in Philadelphia. I did so for two reasons: first, I wanted to be close to what I regarded as the revolutionary class of our age; and second, I wanted to help the class in its struggle for communism. Today I guess people would say I identified as a worker. I had been undecided about going to college in the first place, but after my third year decided I had had enough. (To be precise, I had got the job over the summer and when the fall term started, I simply didn't return to school.)

My background was lower (definitely lower) middle class. Throughout my growing-up years my father delivered the *Philadelphia Inquirer* door-to-door—seven days a week, eighteen years without a day off. From the time I was eleven years old I used to get up at 4 a.m. three or four mornings a week to help him; we would work for a few hours, then have breakfast, which he would cook, after which I would catch a little sleep before going to school. My mother and I helped with the collections on Saturday. On Sunday we would stop at the automat, which was a treat: to this day I can taste the sausages. One of the high points of breakfast was eating with the drivers who delivered the papers in bulk. I was fascinated by their conversation; one of them said to my father (speaking of me), "Good kid. Don't say much." (People who know me now may have a hard time believing that, but I have always been inclined to listen to working-class people.) The route was in a mostly black neighborhood in West Philly; my father used to say that there was not another white man in the city who could have handled it; many of the customers would stop and tell me what a fine man he was. I was proud to be doing a man's job.

My father had attended Penn but left after three years; my mother had no college. In his youth my father had hoped to become a writer, my mother a dancer; three kids ended those hopes. They were both former Communist Party members (my mother second generation: both of her parents had been socialists and later communists, part of the army of eastern European immigrants of Jewish background seeking to escape ghetto life who were the backbone of the party in the big cities of the east). By the time I became conscious of such things (around 1948), they called themselves Progressives. They were both largely self-educated, a testimony to their background and to the radical milieu in which they circulated. I grew up in a house full of books and classical music; our dinner table conversation consisted of discussions of ideas.

Unlike in the case of one recent high-profile person who chose to identify with a group to which she had not been born and whose parents were hostile (probably ashamed) and even "outed" her, both of my parents, while they thought I was mistaken in leaving college (and said so), respected my decision. I remember them smiling at each other when I reported that I was paid for the Labor Day holiday; they understood what it meant to me to be part of the tradition that had won paid holidays. And I remember when some of their friends criticized my decision, my father told them, He's doing what he wants to do—can you say the same? Their support made a big difference.

The factory employed a couple of hundred people making the lamps that were suspended over the city's streets. My first job was as an assembler. The pay was $1.35 an hour. Did I take the job from a "real" proletarian? Undoubtedly: every person's job is one that might have gone to someone else. Did I get the job because of my middle-class background? Hardly; I was hired because I went back a second time after having been told they were not hiring, and the plant manager happened to be in the office when I did and remembered that I had been there before. After a few months I was upgraded to the position of drill press operator, at ten cents per hour more. I did not get that promotion because of my verbal skills but because I came to work regularly and on time. There I learned my first lesson of factory life: it was my fellow workers who taught me how to run the machine and also how to sabotage it when I needed a break; they taught me what was a reasonable amount of work to turn out so that I neither broke the rate nor let my fellow workers down. I remember especially one coworker, about fifty, Joe, nicknamed "I'm-Hungry-Joe," and the time they sent the two of us to the basement to grind the rough edges off large lead-alloy castings, using a sanding belt. (Cough, cough.) We had eight of them to do, and after about six hours of fooling around and telling stories, we had done two, and Joe said, "I don't want to work on these tomorrow. What say we finish them off now?" which we did. He later joined our little communist cell, probably because he responded to my obvious sincerity and because he was lonely. Except for the couple of men who swept the floor, the workforce was all white. Did I take a job that might have gone to a black man (or woman)? I sure did, and so did every other worker in the place. One of my goals became to destroy that pattern, which a black comrade told me was typical of manufacturing plants in the city.

My first goal was to fit in with my fellow workers, most of whom lived near the plant, in what was then (for those who know Philadelphia) called Fishtown. In order to do that I thought it wise not to let them know I had three years at Penn. That was easy, since no one expected a Penn near-graduate to be working there, and therefore the question never came up. I also thought it wise, when I was asked, "What are you?" (what nationality—at the time I used the name Ignatin, which provided no ethnic clue) to not reveal that I was of Jewish background—not because I had anything against Jews as such but because it would have been a tipoff that I was from a different social class from theirs. (In my years as a worker in industry I encountered exactly three Jews, all skilled men, leadmen and foremen—not counting the dozens who, like me, left college to take jobs in industry for political reasons.) So I said I was Russian. It was the truth, and it may have even been the essential truth, but it was a different order of truth than if I had said I was a Jew, and it produced a different response—that is, no response, which was what I wanted.

So began my career "passing." It was made easier by class being the product of history and not biology, "an active process, which owes as much to agency as to conditioning . . . something which in fact happens (and can be shown to have happened) in human relationships . . . always embodied in real people in a real context"—no less than that other social construct, race, that has received such attention, with class membership (in the United States) as a rule less visibly marked than race.[1] (I could write a book on the comparative ease of pegging people by class or race, looking at Ireland, where it is impossible to tell a "Protestant" from a "Catholic" by sight, or at Israel, where it is impossible to tell an individual "Jew" from an individual "Arab" by sight, compared to countries in which the visible markers of class are more obvious than in the United States, where television, universal secondary education, and ready-to-wear clothing have made it difficult to tell a shopgirl from a lady by appearance alone. Just you wait, 'enry 'iggins. And don't get me started on gender.)

I do not intend to review the political work I did in my years in the shop. Certainly, I made mistakes: some would probably have been avoided by someone born to the proletariat; others were the result of stupidity, which cuts across class lines. Suffice it to paraphrase Shakespeare's Othello: I have done the movement some service, and they know it. No more of that. Instead, I propose to recount, as well as I am able, the complications of living as something I was not but also was.

In the first place, from the time I entered the factory I was on my own: no special assistance from my family, other than the normal Christmas and birthday gifts. In the second place, whatever "cultural capital" (an inaccurate term because, unlike the capital Marx wrote about, it cannot be alienated) I had managed to acquire at home and at college did me no good in industry; on the contrary, it added to my difficulties and on at least one occasion jeopardized my position: shortly after I started at US Steel as a motor inspector helper, the company announced that it was discontinuing the helper jobs and all the helpers would either have to enter the apprentice program (a measure I had resisted) or take a layoff. I chose the former; in order to do so I had to produce a copy of my high school diploma, which I did not have. So I wrote to my high school (Central High School, the "smart Jewish boys' school") and asked them to write to the personnel office at US Steel and assure them that I had, indeed, graduated high school. They did more than that: they wrote saying that I had finished near the top of my class, had been a National Merit finalist, and had won a prestigious scholarship to Penn—in short, they almost blew my cover. Fortunately, it did not set the personnel department's antennae to quivering, and I was able to enter the apprentice program. Once in the program, whatever verbal skills I possessed were outweighed by the skills of my fellow apprentices, most of whom had grown up working on cars, boats, and tractors and doing plumbing and wiring around the house—while I was learning to conjugate French verbs.

I can only imagine the loneliness of those who, born to a group they regard as unjust and oppressive and not wanting to be part of that group, are left on their own to figure their way out; it is tempting to try and join the group they identify with, even if that may not be the best for all concerned. So it was with me; but I had an advantage over those who are alone: I had a loving, supportive family, and I was part of a movement, more specifically an organization made up of people from all social classes (mainly the working class), who accepted me for who I was as well as for who I was trying to be—a good communist. (My first organization was a tiny Marxist-Leninist sect, but in it were proletarians of many nationalities experienced in class struggle, from whom I learned a lot. I wouldn't trade the experience for a million dollars; I wouldn't repeat it for a million either.)

I was laid off after a few months at the streetlamp factory but found another job in the Frankford district in northeast Philadelphia. I don't remember what they made there, but I remember an assembly line by a large door that for some reason was kept open even in winter, with the result that I would be freezing on one side of my body and sweating on the other. The foreman, named Howard, who stood well over six feet tall and weighed almost three hundred pounds, used to stand at the end of the line under an overhead heater and scream at us to work faster. One day Larry, an Italian kid about my age from Camden, New Jersey, who was maybe five feet six inches and one hundred forty pounds, couldn't stand it anymore and told Howard, "Come out on the street, you fat motherfucker, I'll kill you," but nothing came of it. He and Darryl, Afro-American (or as we said then, Negro) from North Philly, were close friends, on and off the job, and welcomed me as one of them.

I soon left that place and got another job assembling scales. It was extremely frustrating work, and I remember losing my temper and throwing some parts against the wall. The foreman told me to go home. I came back the next day and nothing was said. At another place I ran a turret lathe, making three hundred parts a day for something of which I had no idea. The pay was $1.15 an hour. The owner, foreman, and set-up man were brothers, named Herman, Moe, and Jake. I wrote a jingle about them which I crayoned onto the wall in the toilet: it began, "Herman and Moe and Jake, my ass they are trying to break." Most of the other workers there were young black men. Once a week or so we would cook hot dogs on the heat-treating furnaces and eat them on Wonder Bread; few meals have ever tasted as good.

To give an idea of how bad the place was, one of the workers punched his card out in April and didn't return until October; he had worked construction over the summer, for real money. On his return he took his card out of the rack, punched in and went to work. Nobody ever said anything. I quit that place to go to San Francisco. I told the owner on Wednesday that I was leaving in two days. He asked, "Is that all the notice you give"? I asked him how much notice he would give me if he was going to lay me off. He said it depended on what his reason was. I said I had a good reason. "What is it?" he asked. "I found a better job." "That's a darkie trick," he said. "Just for that," I said, "I'm leaving now," and I took off my apron, handed it to him, and walked out.

In San Francisco I got a job at Simmons Furniture Company at Bay and Powell. The man in the personnel office who hired me explained that they had a bonus system, ten cents for every hour worked. "If you work four hundred hours," he asked, "how much will your bonus be?" My answer satisfied him—all that cultural capital—and I was assigned to the inspection department to help the chief inspector, who had more work than he could handle. The two of us spent so much time shooting the shit and visiting the ladies in the sewing department—I was beginning to get the hang of this—that they hired another man to help us, and the three of us did less work than the inspector had done alone.

So many years, so many memories. How can I recall the specifics of my evolution? I know that my four years in the steel mills were important to me, because there I got to know a greater number of workers from a variety of backgrounds and to know them better than I had before. I learned that everyone had a story: there was Slick, who had stopped off in Gary on his way to the West Coast from Detroit (where he was in trouble with the law), intending to stay a few weeks to accumulate a stake—twenty years earlier—who had his clothes tailor-made from fine fabrics and was an authority on jazz. There was Monroe, who had come up from Missouri and raised five children and sent them all to college and who was a champion bridge player; there was the other guy whose name I forget who was working in the mill while pursuing a degree at the University of Chicago. One person liked opera, another was an expert on the space program, another bred dogs, another had published a book (with drawings) proving that the earth was flat, etc. Gradually I learned that if I didn't wear my education as a badge of superiority, I would be accepted as just another person with his own peculiarities.

Over time I relaxed and came to understand that "It ain't where ya been, it's where ya goin.'" But it didn't happen right away, and sometimes I fell back. I remember one time in the factory one of my fellow workers, a hillbilly, asking me what kind of music I liked, easy listening? I couldn't imagine a greater insult. On another occasion I had the good fortune to be at a dinner party at the home of Eleanor Burke Leacock, the anthropologist, and her husband, James Haughton, the Harlem activist. (Also present was Eleanor's father, Kenneth Burke, the philosopher.) To make conversation Eleanor asked me, "What's your line?" I replied, biting off the words in my best proletarian manner, "I have no line, I'm a worker." Another guest, who knew me, laughed and outed me, "He's a Jewish intellectual." I deserved it.

During the years of my proletarian journey, I slept on benches on the midnight shift alongside my fellow workers and went fishing with them in the morning; cursed the company and the foremen along with them; got drunk and had fistfights with them; got chased with them down a street by a mounted policeman during a strike; and attended their weddings, funerals, and the christenings of their children. It is my judgment that no one not born to the working class can ever absorb to the bone the reactions of someone "born one morning when the sun didn't shine, who picked up his shovel and walked to the mine" (although some may come close). I think I came close, but there was always present in me a certain self-awareness that led to the native hue of resolution being sicklied o'er with the pale cast of thought and prevented me from reacting as a born worker.

I worked in the steel mill with a black worker who, every time the foreman called him, would ask, "Who, me?" I asked him why he did that. He answered, "Two reasons: the first is to give myself a moment to think what I might have screwed up so I can get my story ready. The second is, I figure it's to my advantage if he thinks I'm stupid. It means he expects less from me." In spite of my politics, I was never able to achieve the total, visceral separation from bourgeois values he had; of all the things that offended me about my supervisors, probably the one that most got under my skin was being thought stupid; that attitude was a legacy of my class background.

I have told the following story elsewhere, but it can bear retelling: I once worked a midnight shift in a metalworking plant. There were two other workers in the department on that shift, Jimmy and Maurice. Maurice had been having money troubles, which caused him to drink more than he should, which led to missed days and more trouble on the job, which led to troubles at home, etc. I came to work one night after missing the previous night, and Jimmy told me that Maurice had brought a pistol to the plant the night before, planning to shoot the general fore-man if he reprimanded him in the morning about his attendance. "Did you try to stop him?" I asked. "No, what for?" queried Jimmy. "What happened?" I asked. "When the foreman came in," explained Jimmy, "instead of stopping to hassle Maurice, he just said hello and kept going to his office. He doesn't know how close he came to dying."

I, of course, did not want Maurice to shoot the general foreman because I did not want him to spend the rest of his life in prison for blowing away an individual who was no worse than the generality of his type. Jimmy looked at matters differently: for him, Maurice's life was already a prison that could be salvaged by one dramatic NO, regardless of the consequences. Who was right? Well, I had read all the books and knew that ninety-nine times out of a hundred nothing would come of Maurice's action: the plant guards or the cops would take him away or kill him on the spot. But on the hundredth time, something different might happen: the workers would block the plant guards, fight the cops, and the next thing you knew you had the mutiny on the Potemkin. The new society is the product of those two kinds of knowledge, Jimmy's and mine, and neither could substitute for the other.

In 1984, after twenty-three years, I left the factory to pursue a master's degree at Harvard in education. My intention was to spend a year or so there, reading and taking a break from the factory, but I liked it, and did well enough at it that Harvard made me an offer I couldn't refuse, and so

I found myself pursuing a doctorate. I remember the first time I visited one of the undergraduate "houses" (dormitories), sitting in a leather chair with oriental rugs on the floor and bound volumes of *Punch* on the wall and looking out two-story windows onto the Charles River while listening to undergraduate music majors play a Schubert quartet, I said to myself, I sure hope the rest of the fellows back in Gary, Indiana don't find out how good I've got it here, or they'll all leave and there will be nobody left to make iron.

Did class privilege play a part in my admittance to Harvard? Without a doubt. I was able to get in because I knew someone who was enrolled there; like me, he had left college and worked in industry; we had done political work together in Chicago, and now he was going back to school; he wrote a letter to Admissions on my behalf. (The Harvard Graduate School of Education prides itself on admitting a small number of nontraditional students every year: the other one my year was an indigenous Australian.)

Adding the years at Penn to the years at Harvard and the years teaching at colleges, I have put in more time in the academy than I had in industry. Nevertheless, to paraphrase Melville, a blast furnace was my Harvard College and my Yale. When I applied for my present job, someone at the interview asked me how I happened to be there after the years in industry. (He had my CV in front of him.) I answered, "I was laid off from a steel mill, and decided to take a step down and go to Harvard." Sometimes I wonder what would have happened had I stayed in the mill: I would have had enough seniority to ride out temporary layoffs, and would have been retired long ago, with a good pension; on the other hand, I might be dead.

Some of what I regard as my best political work I did while I worked in industry. (Mike Staudenmaier recounted some of it in *Truth and Revolution*.[2] As Huck Finn said about Mark Twain, "He told the truth, mainly.") And some of it I did after I left industry; I refer mainly to the work I did with *Race Traitor*. Looking back at my life in radical politics, notwithstanding the mistakes I made and the things I would do differently, do I think I contributed to the subordination of the working class to capital, or, worse yet, to its erasure? Is the working-class movement worse off for my participation? I think not.

As Twain said, "Persons attempting to find a motive in this narrative will be prosecuted; persons attempting to find a moral in it will be banished; persons attempting to find a plot in it will be shot."

2

The POC: A Personal Memoir

Ignatiev reflects on the history, structure, and activities of the Provisional Organizing Committee to Reconstitute the Marxist–Leninist Communist Party, an anti-revisionist Stalinist sect of the Communist Party he joined in 1958, at age seventeen. This essay first appeared in 1979 in the journal Theoretical Review: A Journal of Marxist–Leninist Theory and Discussion.

When the Communist Party, USA, entered its period of crisis following the Khrushchev report to the 20th Congress of the Communist Party of the Soviet Union (CPSU) on the crimes of Stalin, there arose within the party in the United States at least four different factions. The first of these was the right wing, led by *Daily Worker* editor John Gates, Fred Fine, and others. The second was the center grouping, led by Eugene Dennis, the party's general secretary. The third was the "left," led by William Z. Foster, Bob Thompson, and Ben Davis. The fourth was the so-called "ultra-Left," which called itself the Marxist-Leninist Caucus.[1] It was this grouping, out of which grew the Provisional Organizing Committee to Reconstitute the Marxist-Leninist Communist Party (POC), with which I was associated.

I joined the Communist Party in Philadelphia in January 1958 (I was seventeen) after about a year of working with party people in youth activities. At the time, I considered myself in sympathy with Foster's left faction. I knew of the existence of the ultra-left through personal contacts with some of its leaders and was in general agreement with its criticisms of the current line and leadership, but felt that its illegal, factional approach was wrong and harmful.

Immediately after I joined the party, there was a realignment of factional forces on the national level. The center-right alliance, which had been in command of the party for over a year, broke up and in its place there arose a center-left coalition. The rights began to leave the party, and the new shift was hailed as a victory by the official "left."

The ultra-left refused to join in the grand realignment. Thus, in place of the four groupings which existed earlier, there were now two: the merged center-left and the extreme left. The extreme left caucus in Philadelphia counted in its ranks virtually the entire South Philadelphia section (mainly white working class) and a number of people from the North Philadelphia (black) section, mostly those who had been part of the black caucus, which had formed a few years earlier and maintained a precarious existence in a weakened party. The strength of the caucus in Philadelphia (20–25 people) was roughly equal to that of the dominant group, particularly if only activists were counted and not every card-carrying member.

There were several events which won me over from the legal left to the ultra-left caucus. The first was a forum on the Negro question, at which James Jackson of the center-left faction spoke. The caucus had earlier sponsored a talk by Harry Haywood, and Jackson was the official leadership's response. When he spoke, it was obvious that he had an integrationist, gradualist approach in contrast to Haywood's revolution-ary defense of the right of self-determination. The second event was the crisis that broke out in the summer of 1958 after the Iraqi revolution, in which US marines were sent to Lebanon. The party as a whole reacted lethargically. The ultra-left caucus came forward with an energetic program which called for leaflets and statements in the party's own name (a rarity at the time) as well as the usual resolutions in union meetings, churches, etc. The district leadership called a special meeting of party activists. At that meeting, the caucus proposals carried. There was one hitch, however: for some months, the South Philadelphia section had been withholding its dues from the party. A proposal was made that, in view of this situation, a special fund be established to carry out the agreed upon activities. This, of course, was unacceptable to the leadership and so the program of energetic struggle was undermined.

The third event was the official reaction to a proposal I made to the youth branch, of which I was a member. My proposal, very modest in terms, recommended that we do more in our own name instead of functioning simply as conscientious members of the Union, the NAACP, or whatever. It was met with extreme hostility, led by the branch secretary, Daniel Rubin (who is today the National Organizational Secretary of the party). These three events propelled me into the ultra-left caucus, and it was only a couple of months from my first meetings with the caucus that I found myself at its national convention, held on August 16–17, 1958, in a dingy hall on the lower east side of Manhattan. There were sixty-three delegates at the conference, comprising the caucus hard-core membership minus a few who for one reason or another could not be there.[2] They came from the two sections in Philadelphia I have already mentioned, from the waterfront[3] and Lower Harlem sections of New York (both largely Puerto Rican in composition), from Cleveland's Cedar Central district, from Williamsport, Pennsylvania, a steel town, and from the South Side of Chicago. Most of the delegates were working class; a high proportion were black or Puerto Rican. The most prominent individuals present were Harry Haywood; Ted Allen, author of one of the main caucus documents, "Two Roads"; Joe Dougher, coal miner and Spanish Civil War veteran; Lucille Bethencourt, Smith Act defendant; A. Marino, former maritime activist and New York state committee member; Admiral Kilpatrick, Spanish War veteran; and Armando Roman, Puerto Rican section leader and New York state committee member. Reports were heard on the crisis of the party, and there was discussion, most of it consisting of recounting of the party leadership's capitulation to the ruling class and stressing the impossibility of continuing the struggle from the inside.

The conference adopted a Declaration that stressed several points: uncompromising defense of the Soviet Union and a rejection of the critical stance which the party had begun to take toward the USSR at the time of Hungary; rejection of the line of peaceful transition to socialism and an affirmation of the proletarian revolution and proletarian dictatorship; defense of the revolutionary right of self-determination of black people in the Deep South as the cornerstone of policy on the black question; and a commitment to transforming the party thoroughly instead of making a few personnel changes at the top as a way to overcome the party crisis.

National officers were chosen for the new organization: Roman as general secretary, the highest post; Haywood as chairman; and Dougher as organizational secretary. A national committee of nineteen was elected, and it was decided to publish a monthly newspaper, the *Vanguard*. The POC was officially launched. The first few months following the conference were taken up mainly with establishing an apparatus, dues structure, defining the actual membership, etc. There were two important defections in this period, Haywood and Marino, each charging sectarianism and each taking a small group with him.

One of the first questions the new organization faced was whether to regard itself as a faction of the existing communist movement and therefore aim its efforts at those already in that movement or see itself as a new organization aiming to elaborate a general program and win over the working class. Typically, it was decided to do both. Thus, alongside conference reports and declarations of support from various party units, there appeared in the third issue of *Vanguard* (November 1958) an article about 300 Puerto Rican workers in the Bronx who went on strike against the company and the union.

As has been mentioned, a number of the POC leaders in New York were Puerto Rican. Shortly after the POC was founded, the Revolution came to power in Cuba, and this acted as a stimulus to the range of Latin movements which existed in New York. POC began having public forums together with the Movimiento Libertador de Puerto Rico, a group led by Pelegrin Garcia, one of the generation of revolutionaries spawned in the 1948 student strike in Puerto Rico.

Just at this time, the House Un-American Activities Committee (HUAC) decided to investigate Communist influence in the Puerto Rican movement. At the public hearings, the American Communist Party members who were called adopted a legal defense of pleading the fifth amendment. The POC members, on the other hand, used the hearings as a forum to denounce US imperialism and call for independence for Puerto Rico. Although the existence of POC never came up during the hearings (all the questions concerned membership in the party), when the hearings were published all those who had defied the committee were identified as members of the POC, "a hard-core, extremist group, etc." Those so identified included one party member who had deviated from the party line and acted in a militant fashion before the committee![4] The willingness of HUAC to distinguish so clearly between the party and the POC helped to expand POC's influence among Latin American revolutionary circles in New York.

At about the same time that the POC was splitting from the Communist Party, largely over the issue of defense of the Soviet role in Hungary in 1956, the Marcyites were leaving the Socialist Workers Party (SWP)[5] over the same issue, to constitute themselves as the Workers World Party. (This parallel should demonstrate the near uselessness of the labels "Trotskyism" and "Stalinism.") They addressed a letter to the POC, suggesting talks and joint work. The response of the POC was to denounce them, in terms reminiscent of 1938, as counterrevolutionaries, wreckers, saboteurs, etc. Thus, the classic view of Trotskyism was affirmed for the POC. This attitude would be a factor later on in determining POC's attitude toward the Fair Play for Cuba Committee, in which the SWP played a significant role.

Events themselves began to push the POC to reach out. This was especially so outside of New York, in areas where there was no large Communist Party and former party circle to aim at. In Philadelphia, between 1960 and 1962, the POC was involved in three areas of mass work. The first, and by far the most important, was the struggle against police brutality in the North Philadelphia ghetto. POC members took the initiative in forming the North Philadelphia Committee for Equal Justice. Committee members would hear of an incident of police brutality, either through personal contact or through the independent black press. They would visit the family, write and pass out leaflets, hold street corner rallies, and pack the courtroom, demanding acquittal for the victim and punishment for the offending cops. After a while, the committee was able to establish a real presence in the community, to secure a church in which to hold meetings, to discover a couple of lawyers who would work with the committee, and to develop relations with various black reporters. On one occasion—I think it was 1962—the committee actually had an important impact in the city for a short time. The cops had shot and killed a black youth who was an epileptic, and there was a tremendous protest from the black community, which forced the city to bring the cop to trial. During the trial, the committee passed out a leaflet calling for a march on the police station and demanding the death penalty for the cop. A copy of the leaflet found its way into the courtroom. When the cop saw it, he fainted. It nearly brought about a mistrial and made all the major papers. Out of this work, the POC was able to recruit three or four individuals who had no previous experience with communism or the left. Most of this work was done by the black comrades, but not all of it; I remember speaking on street corners in the black community.

POC realized correctly that the greatest well of support for the Cuban Revolution was among the Puerto Rican population rather than the liberals and intellectuals being targeted by the Fair Play for Cuba Committee. In Philadelphia, the POC founded, together with a few pro-Castro Cubans who had not yet returned to the island, the North American Cuban Solidarity Committee, which immediately went onto the streets in the small barrio there, attempting to link community issues with the struggle for Puerto Rican independence and against US imperialism in solidarity with the Cuban Revolution. I remember one fairly successful rally we had, where we attracted a good crowd by playing Cuban revolutionary songs on a car-top loudspeaker. One of the Cubans spoke, I spoke in broken Spanish, and one of the black comrades spoke of black–Latin unity. We were beginning to develop real ties; people came to us with cases of police abuse, they worked with us on leaflets for the community, etc.

A third area of work was the beginnings of some rank-and-file labor organizing. One comrade worked on the docks and wrote several leaflets attacking the International Longshoremen's Association leadership—the usual sort of leaflet—and from that came several contacts who worked with POC for a while. Also, we were able to pull together contacts in two different plants in one local of the International Brotherhood of Electrical Workers and put out one issue of a rank-and-file newsletter. One worker, with no previous movement experience, was recruited from that effort.

This work was carried on by about ten people, which was the average membership of the POC in Philadelphia during that time. It was not necessarily the same ten people; a number of the original members dropped out. But POC demonstrated that in those years—before the rise of the New Left—it was possible to recruit black and white workers to a communist organization, by going directly to them and engaging them in struggle.

Outside of Philadelphia, similar work was going on. In Chicago, POC organized the defense of a black youth who was framed for murder of a teacher at his school. Through street rallies, regular speaking in black churches, and leafletting, the Chicago Committee for Equal Justice was able to develop a significant defense campaign.[6]

Even in New York, where the outward turn was most limited, POC organized a defense campaign for Salvador Agron and Luis Antonio Hernandez, two Puerto Rican youths framed on a murder charge.[7]

During that same period, a group of lumber workers in Northern California and Oregon, led by Tom Scribner, who had dropped out of the Communist Party in 1947 along with Harrison George and Vern Smith (that was the real original anti-revisionist group!), made contact with and decided to affiliate with the POC.

In 1962, the POC had nationally about fifty members, with branches in New York, Philadelphia, Cleveland, Chicago, and the West Coast (the group in Williamsport had dropped out). It was in the fall of 1961, at the 22nd Congress of the Communist Party of the Soviet Union, where Khrushchev delivered his attack on the Albanian Party of Labor, that POC learned of the international dimensions of the fight against revisionism. Up until that time, we simply refused to accept all the speculation in the bourgeois press of a split between China and the Soviet Union. Of course, POC was aware of the differences in emphasis between the two parties in their literature and generally found the Chinese material more valuable, but it did not accept the reality of a split until Chou En-Lai walked out of the Soviet Party Congress.

I left Philadelphia in June 1962 for an assignment in a locality where there was no POC branch. When I returned at the beginning of 1963 I was struck by the changes that had taken place. Two of the three areas of mass work, the rank-and-file factory groups and the Puerto Rican work, had totally collapsed and the third area had lost its vitality. The time of the members was now occupied with refining the POC principles to a level of higher purity. This sectarianism was directly related to two new theoretical innovations which had been introduced in those six months.

The first of these was the theory of the bribery of the working class from US super profits, including black and Puerto Rican workers outside of their "national territories." Whatever merit there may be to the theory, it had a devastating effect on the POC, because it strengthened the tendency, already present, to withdraw from the reform movement.

The second innovation was the adoption of a conspiracy theory of the state, brought about particularly by the Cuban Missile Crisis. Instead of seeing that crisis as a normal part of US–Soviet bargaining, POC interpreted it as a joint plot of imperialism and revisionism to discredit the revolutionary movement in Latin America as the precondition for worldwide peaceful coexistence. This conspiratorial view of the world would later reach truly paranoid proportions. It is useful to see the fall of 1962, when these two new notions took root, as a dividing line between two periods of the POC. Not so much that they brought about a reversal of policy, but they solidified negative tendencies which already existed. Up until that time, POC was a legitimate communist organization—a bit sectarian, perhaps, but with real ties to the working class, able to draw upon the abilities and energies of its members to perform truly astounding quantities of work. Its national–racial composition gave it an important subjective advantage in assessing the world of which it was a part. After that time, the organization deteriorated into a pure sect—even worse than a sect, a comic opera version of a sect. One example of this was its attitude toward the black struggles that were growing.

The beginning of 1963 was a time of great ferment in the black community in Philadelphia. There were big demonstrations against police brutality, as well as a great mass struggle to open up Girard College, which was an endowed school for white male orphans. The latter took the form of mass blocking of new construction going on at the school. POC played no role in either of these struggles, in spite of being in an excellent position to do so.

The reason for this had largely to do with a mistaken estimate of the role of black nationalism. At that time, the teachings of Malcolm X were beginning to have an impact in the black community, and some of the key figures in those Philadelphia struggles regarded themselves as revolutionary nationalists, although they did not necessarily share the perspective of the struggle being centered in the South. POC adopted a sectarian stance toward them, in spite of their efforts to involve black POC cadre in the movement.

This was truly tragic, as some of these individuals would later become some of the most important figures in the black movement of the sixties; POC could have learned a great deal from them, and perhaps it could have contributed something to their development. The episode certainly demonstrates that holding a position in favor of the right of self-determination is no guarantee against underestimating the revolutionary potential of the autonomous black movement. (This blunder did not take place without opposition; several black comrades in Philadelphia were expelled for opposing the line.)

That experience in Philadelphia, instead of being recognized as sectarianism and corrected, set the pattern for future POC work in the black movement. The organization would play no role whatsoever in the upsurge to come and even went so far as to condemn Malcolm X and Black Power for "fostering illusions" about bourgeois democracy.

From that time on, POC degenerated in all areas. It abandoned any work of a united front character except with those in near total agreement with it. It retreated from its limited involvement in the reform movement in favor of propaganda about the evils of the system and the betrayals of the various reformists and revisionists, who included virtually every figure who came forward to articulate the demands of the fledgling movements. What then did its work consist of? It became inwardly oriented. There was a great emphasis on propaganda; leaflets were written which had to be gone over four or five times to eliminate any mistakes before they could be distributed. Major battles were fought over formulations, as if they really made a difference. The preparation of the newspaper, *Vanguard*, which appeared less frequently and devoted almost its entire space to analyses of revisionism on a world scale, occupied more and more of the organization's time.[8] More stress was placed on internal education, in the interests of "cadre training." Educationals were revised several times and repeated; this, of course, meant that the members never actually read and studied much. There were five different political economy educationals, yet we never got beyond *Wage Labor and Capital* and *Value, Price and Profit*. We read *Foundations of Leninism* a hundred times and *What Is to Be Done?* often enough, but never collectively read *State and Revolution*, or *Capital*, or even the entire *Communist Manifesto*. The various "united front" organizations were maintained, and there was even an "Equal Rights Congress," which brought together the POC front groups from the different cities where they existed, but these groups had no real existence apart from POC and their work was solely limited to propaganda.

Along with this sectarianism arose the conspiracy theory to which I referred earlier. POC had no notion of the relative independence of the superstructure. According to its doctrine, all the acts of the state were centrally orchestrated, even down to fairly small cases. Thus, POC believed that the slight repression directed its way and the lack of news coverage of its activities was deliberate bourgeois policy, to prevent knowledge of its work from reaching the masses, especially in view of the generous publicity received by the Communist Party and other misleaders.

Yet, it should be noted that throughout this period of incredible sectarianism, POC managed to recruit workers in small numbers (while continuing to lose members as well). How was this possible? It was achieved largely through the efforts of the members in selling the paper door-to-door in poor neighborhoods. This had a comical side, although I must admit I didn't see it at the time; here was this paper, whose lead article was likely to be entitled "Polarization on a World Scale," being used for outreach work. Yet to some degree it worked. There were always a few people who would be attracted by the members' obvious sense of purpose and dream of a better world. These recruits were of two categories: people from the lower depths of society and moreover people who had no previous independent political activity that would make them want something more than blanket denunciations of every form of struggle around them; and whites from the left who were masochistically drawn to POC's furious condemnation of intellectuals. I think the Jehovah's Witnesses are able to grow on much the same basis.

And this brings me to the point: how was the leadership able to stay in power? How was the original grouping of people, who had the independence of mind to break with revisionism four years before the Communist Party of China made it "legitimate" to do so, unable to prevent the degeneration of their organization into a cult?

POC had meetings and conferences, like any other organization. Proposals were put to a vote and ratified. Elections were held. It was clearly stated in the statutes that any member had the right to criticize any leader. Yet none of this made any difference. How was such a thing possible? The starting point is the view of Marxism as revealed truth, as a science whose mastery (or belonging to an organization possessing the mastery) eliminates the need for thought. Thus, critical thought becomes a vice, petit bourgeois weakness to be rooted out. Discipline becomes the greatest virtue—discipline and devotion to the final aim. Along with the notion of revealed truth comes the conception of those having it being a small band ranged against a hostile world. The willingness to subordinate one's doubts about policy in the interests of the groups' cohesion becomes the test of the faithful. And this is reinforced by a general anti-intellectualism which became the dominant tradition of the Comintern, where the model cadre was one who could take the policy (whatever policy) already adopted and express it in colorful "working class" terms. From its birth until the summer of 1962, POC went through at least five major political splits that I can recall. The first two, right after the organization's founding, were with Haywood and Marino. The third was with Joe Dougher in 1960. The fourth was with Ted Allen in 1962. The fifth was with the black grouping in Philadelphia. In each case, the oppositionists were identified as anti-organization and isolated. Others, seeing the futility of opposition, simply left.[9] Thus, none of the top leaders were left but the one person—Roman, the general secretary—who became the embodiment of the group.

After 1962, there was no political opposition left within the POC. There were few members with an independent history of struggle who might be capable of developing an opposition. Yet the splits and purges didn't end. They were invariably accompanied by personal slander and approved unanimously. As an organization loses touch with the outside world, its inner dynamic becomes more important to it; the internal struggles become the means by which the group's cohesion is maintained. In addition, as within any totalitarian structure, the leadership must surround itself not merely with loyal followers, but with individuals who have no possibility of ever becoming centers of opposition. That means it must surround itself with mediocrities.

After 1962, the process of purging POC took the form of eliminating all those who, however loyal they were to the line, were not perceived as mediocrities. I was an example of this: I was expelled in 1966, less than two months after having been "elected" to a high position. (I think that the first fish that managed to crawl up onto dry land from the ocean slime and discover a world of light and fresh breezes could not have been more shocked than I on being propelled from that cultish environment. Being expelled from the POC was the best thing that ever happened to me, surpassing in value being recruited to it originally.)

A more important example was Nelson Peery, today the leader of the Communist Labor Party. Nelson was a loyal member who had accepted all the purges and line shifts. He was expelled about a year after I was, not for failing to carry out the line, but for carrying it out too well. He had been sent to Los Angeles to build a branch and, largely due to the force of his own personality, had succeeded in doing so. This was enough to make Roman regard him as a potential center of opposition, and he, too, was accused of all kinds of bad behavior when he was kicked out, his expulsion unanimously approved by those who had praised his work a short time before.

So far as I know, the POC still exists, under a different name. (It is now the "American Workers Communist Party.") It has about fifteen members and thinks it is keeping alive the revolutionary tradition in a period when struggle is impossible. As for the former POC members, most have dropped out of politics. A few are trying to reconstitute a better POC, without the flaws of the last one. Occasionally, some of the former members, who shared an experience which touched them deeply, get together socially, but they have little in common beyond a bitterness toward Armando Roman. At one such gathering, someone suggested that the ex-members get together at the next conference and outvote him.

3

In My Youth

His work with the Provisional Organizing Committee fostered in Ignatiev a growing sense of disillusionment with the group, particularly around its untenable sense of self-importance, which was irrevocably shaken by an encounter he had with the police. This first appeared in Ignatiev's PM Press blog in 2015.

In my youth I belonged to a group called the Provisional Organizing Committee for a Marxist-Leninist Party (POC) that formed following Khrushchev's 1956 speech on the crimes of Stalin. The POC rejected Khrushchev's line of peaceful coexistence with imperialism and peaceful transition to socialism, identifying instead with the current, headed by the Communist Party of China, that looked to the national liberation movements in Asia, Africa, and Latin America and the upsurge of black militancy in the United States. Its leader was Armando Roman; among its founding members were Harry Haywood, Angel Torres, Nelson Peery, Joe Dougher, and Ted Allen.

It was an article of faith among us that we were the most dangerous communist group in the United States, and indeed we could have been—a group of sixty experienced proletarian militants, a majority black and Latin—but for a crippling sectarianism that prevented us from taking advantage of actual opportunities that arose to develop ties with Malcolm X, Max Stamford (Muhammad Ahmad) and the Revolutionary Action Movement, Robert Williams, Mohamed Babu (revolutionary leader in

Zanzibar), and with groups in the Dominican Republic and elsewhere—a tale for another day. As a result, the POC underwent several splits and defections and soon descended into irrelevance.

If, as Mao taught and we all believed, attacks by the enemy were the gauge of effectiveness, then how to explain the blanket of silence with which we were greeted, especially when compared with the official repression that was from time to time directed against other groups, even the Communist Party, which we "knew" to have long abandoned revolution? The answer was that the absence of repression was a deliberate policy to avoid drawing attention to us.

Get that: here we were, the most dangerous communist group in the country, and nobody in authority seemed to be paying any attention. Since the bourgeoisie was extremely class conscious and was therefore necessarily aware of the threat we represented, and since the state was the arm of the bourgeoisie, the policy of ignoring us must be deliberate. That is how ideology works: accept any improbability rather than question one's faith.

I am embarrassed to admit it, but that explanation satisfied me, a true believer (and moreover a youngster in awe of the leaders who promoted it) . . . until something happened that made it impossible for me to accept it any longer. The incident was as follows: I was passing out flyers about the world revolution under the 47th Street "L" station in Chicago when a cop arrested me and took me to the station. As I recall, I spent the night and was released on bail the next day.

In preparation for my trial, I went to the ACLU and found a lawyer to represent me. In the course of our conversations, he told me not to worry: the cops were always doing that sort of thing and the judges always dismissed the charges. What he predicted is exactly what happened: the judge dismissed the charge (disorderly or whatever), reprimanded the cop, and let me go. When I called Armando Roman in New York to report what happened, he said, "That proves it, they don't want to draw attention to us."

That was more than I could take. I had been in court, and it was obvious that I had been arrested by a dumb cop who didn't like communists passing out flyers on his beat and that the judge, who knew a little about the law, let me go, and that was all. It would take more faith than I had to believe that the judge had been acting on instructions from capitalist command central.

When I hear revolutionaries in 2015 talking as if every act taken by every agent of the state represents bourgeois policy, I feel as if I am in a time warp, back in the days of the POC and the certainty that the long arm of the ruling class reached from the highest authorities to a district court in Chicago.

4

Meeting in Chicago

Ignatiev's first encounter with Trinidadian revolutionary intellectual C. L. R. James was a key experience in his political development. Here he outlines James's unique understanding of the revolutionary potential of the proletariat, which shaped much of Ignatiev's later work. This essay first appeared in Sojourner Truth Organization's theoretical journal, Urgent Tasks, *Issue 12, 1981.*

I first encountered C. L. R. James and his ideas in 1968, when I attended, on the invitation of my friend Ken Lawrence, a public meeting on the South Side of Chicago at which James was the principal speaker. It was his first speaking tour following his readmission to the country after fourteen years away, and his comrades were happy and proud to be able to introduce him to the public. I myself was a Stalinist at the time, with several important reservations.

The first thing that impressed me about James and made me want to listen carefully and find out more about him was his style, which showed a mastery of his subject matter and a conviction that the ideas he was expressing were fresh and important. His topic that night was the self-activity of the working class, and he took for his text the next to last chapter of volume I of *Capital*, with its familiar words about the new mode of production, which has "sprung up and flourished along with, and under" the old. Familiar, yes, but how new was the reading he gave to them! Out of this chapter he drew a vision of the working class striving inexorably toward the socialist society, not out of loyalty to this or that political program but out of its position in capitalist society. In the question period, someone challenged James's notion of the inevitability of socialism and asked about state repression, "like the case of the tsar, who jailed the revolutionaries and used military force to suppress the movement." It was not a set-up question, although it might as well have been.

"You could hardly have picked a better example for my point," James said, with a chuckle. "The tsar had a large army, the tsar had a huge police force and a lot of prisons and (here James's accent grew stronger—that West Indian speech, most pleasing to the ear of all the tongues spoken on this green earth) . . . and wh' hoppened to de tsar?"

The second thing that impressed me about James was the complete absence of condescension on his part, his total unwillingness to play down to his audience. This was important to me, who came from a tradition that had produced more than a few "popularizers" whose translations were far inferior to the originals. James's talk was, as anyone who has ever read him knows, filled with concrete references, made to illustrate his point: clarify, yes; simplify, he would not do. He was dealing with difficult ideas (not so difficult, perhaps, but obscured by generations of "simplifiers") and he seemed to be saying, I will explain this as clearly as I can, but you must make some effort, too. It revealed an attitude toward people that I admired.

I had always been uneasy with the vague anti-intellectualism that prevailed among the Stalinists. Certain things I knew, for instance, that many of Shakespeare's characters were more real to me than people I passed daily in the street. What could be the role of culture in a movement which seemed to welcome intellectuals so long as they confined themselves to grinding out defenses of the party line (in the manner of Herbert Aptheker) but which placed them under immediate suspicion for their "doubtful" class background should they dare to advance a new idea? Was "culture" to be merely a private indulgence, tolerable if it didn't detract too much from the "real" movement? James, without sinking for a moment into academicism, exemplified a different view, which I sensed when I first heard him speak and which later became manifest to me when I read his book on Herman Melville. Here was a man, James, an extremely close observer of the details of working-class life, who argued straightforwardly that the struggle for the new society was a struggle between different philosophies as *they are lived out*. The role of the "thinker" was to make the ordinary citizen conscious of the process of which he or she was a part. And in *Mariners, Renegades and Castaways*, an essay which will live as long as *Moby Dick* itself, James shows how one great artist was able to present, in personified form, the central conflicts of his age.[1] Taken purely as literary criticism, *Mariners* is a masterpiece worthy of the novel it examines; it contains the most lucid explanation of the creative process to be found in the entire body of writing about literature. But it is more than that; it is a devastating blow to both academicism and anti-intellectualism, the presentation of a world view that links thought and action. To me it meant a great deal.

What was to be my attitude toward my own country? Like many US revolutionaries I faced a conflict, between my feelings of shame at the crimes committed by US imperialism and allowed by the American people and my own ties to this country, to its people, land, history, and traditions. (It is a conflict peculiar to revolutionaries; by no means do all socialists suffer from it.) In "Dialectical Materialism and the Fate of Humanity," James wrote of "the unending murders, the destruction of peoples, the bestial passions, the sadism, the cruelties and the lusts, all the manifestations of barbarism."[2] And then he added, "But this barbarism exists only because nothing else can suppress the readiness for sacrifice, the democratic instincts and creative power of the great masses of people." It was as if the writer had reached out, placed his hand on my shoulder, and spoken those words directly to me. Of course, they did not make the conflict go away; that would not have been proper. But they opened the door to a new concept of citizenship, one that allowed room for neither facile apologetics nor masochistic self-hatred. Curious that this gift should come from one who was himself not a native of the United States and who was officially denied the citizenship which he at one point sought. It is testimony to the universality of James's Marxism, that is to say, of Marxism.

I come from a family of intellectuals. When I left the university to work in industry, I was driven not by the whip of hunger but by the desire to associate myself as closely as possible with the revolutionary class of our age. I am acutely aware of the distinction and it is my conviction, after twenty years, that no individual who joins the proletariat for any reason but externally imposed necessity can ever acquire the instinctive responses of a worker (an outcome not necessarily desirable), although some may approach fairly close. I felt from the beginning that I had something to learn from the workers. That is a fairly commonplace notion on the Left, particularly among those who have been influenced by the Chinese Communist Party. But what to learn? The response of most Left groups to that question was that intellectuals should become "steeled" by contact with the oppressed. Upon further inquiry, "getting steeled" was soon revealed to mean learning how to suffer stoically. Now, that was one thing I didn't want to learn. It was James who provided an answer that met the needs both of my intuitive strivings and of reason. By repeatedly explaining and *demonstrating* the proposition (found in Marx but later obliterated by those who did such general violence to his, and Lenin's, teachings) that the new society comes into existence underneath and alongside the old, that the working class is not a "mass," open to socialist ideas, but is instead the revolutionary class in the literal meaning of the word, that its autonomous activities constitute socialism and that there is no other socialism, James gave me a point on which to keep my eyes fixed and transformed the hours I spent at work from a time of "misery, agony of toil, slavery," etc. into something . . . far more interesting. (I should mention that James was able to get my ear on this point in large part because of Marty Glaberman's old pamphlet "Punching Out," which was of course a product of James's group.[3] People with whom I worked and to whom I showed the pamphlet invariably responded in a way that showed it had touched them more deeply than the average Left tract, a fact which made no small impression on me. I figured that a group that could produce such a pamphlet—there are perhaps only a handful that compare with it today, thirty years later—deserved a serious hearing. I should also like to add that it was only several years later that I came across similar ideas in reading Gramsci, who writes, "The socialist State already exists potentially in the institutions of social life characteristic of the exploited working class."[4])

"Humble" is not a word one would apply to C. L. R. James; not for him the modest cough and lowered eyes. Yet when I finally met him for a face-to-face talk several years ago, his reaction, on learning what I did for a living, was to express regret that he had never had the opportunity to work in large-scale industry. I naturally replied that his writings had been extremely helpful to me in interpreting my own experiences there. He said, "Yes, people have told me that, but I am still sorry I never had the chance to experience it directly." All in all, one of the two most remarkable people it has ever been my privilege to see up close. (The other was Willie Mays, also the best in the world at his chosen occupation.)

5

The White Blindspot

Grounded in Ignatiev's close study of US history, this seminal essay, first published in 1967 for a debate within Students for a Democratic Society and coauthored with Theodore Allen, outlines Ignatiev's conception of "white-skin privilege" and the necessity for revolutionaries to challenge the color line. Originally written as an open letter to the Progressive Labor Party, this essay counters the tendency among the Marxist–Leninist left to simply subordinate race to class, thereby obscuring race's material, structural, and historical roots.

Author's 1967 Introduction

According to my calculations, this is the sixth printing of "White Blindspot"; it is reproduced here with no changes. I wrote the first part in the winter of 1966–67 as a letter of criticism to the Progressive Labor Party, which is today a near-forgotten sect, but which seemed formidable at the time. When Progressive Labor refused to publish it, it was printed privately by a group consisting of me, Hilda Vasquez, Esther Kusic, and Ted Allen.* The letter to

---

* The Progressive Labor Party was a Marxist-Leninist party established in the United States in 1962 following a split in the Communist Party USA. The organization followed the political line of the Communist Party of China and was considered a rival of Students for Democratic Society and the Revolutionary Youth Movement.

Progressive Labor together with one to me from Ted constitutes "White Blindspot."

The article, together with others developing and restating the theme (some of which are collected in this pamphlet), has provoked its share of controversy, both informed and uninformed. In general, I consider the article successful in that it said fairly precisely what I wanted to say. Nevertheless, looking back on ten years of controversy, and possessing a greater knowledge of my audience than I had ten years ago, I would today write it somewhat differently. There are a few points in my part of it on which I would lay greater stress, in order to avoid some misinterpretations by both opponents and supporters.

I would emphasize that what is being talked about is not some kind of a stage theory in any way comparable to the two stages of revolution in a semi-feudal nation oppressed by foreign imperialism. The article explicitly rejects such an interpretation, but not with sufficient force. Let me repeat here that the article is talking about only one struggle, the proletarian class struggle, in which the rejection by white workers of white supremacist ideas and practices is crucial to the emergence of the proletariat as a revolutionary class.

The second point I would stress is that the "white-skin privilege" line is not a general policy of lecturing white workers to alter their thinking and behavior. While some lecturing is necessary (and some fighting as well), the main thing involved is an approach toward strategy which is manifested in the choice of slogans and issues, the character of alliances, methods of organization—in all things which make up the total line of a revolutionary group.

The third thing I would underline is that "repudiation of the white-skin privilege" does not mean that our major work should consist of asking white workers, one by one, to give up their relatively good neighborhoods, jobs, and schools in favor of blacks and other Third World people (although individual actions are certainly appropriate and effective at times). The phrase in quotes refers to a policy of struggle, of which mass action is the decisive aspect, against the ruling class policy of favoritism for whites—a struggle which the article tries to demonstrate is in the class interests of the proletariat as a whole.

It is only the Blindspot in the eyes of America, and its historians, that can overlook and misread so clean and encouraging a chapter of human struggle and human uplift.
  W. E. B. Du Bois, *Black Reconstruction in America, 1860–1880* (p. 577)

The emancipation of man is the emancipation of labor and the emancipation of labor is the freeing of that basic majority of workers who are yellow, brown and black.
  W. E. B. Du Bois, *Black Reconstruction in America, 1860–1880* (p. 16)

Letter to Progressive Labor

In response to your request for comments from readers, I am writing this letter raising what I consider to be the fundamental error in your strategic outlook for the revolutionary struggle of the American working class.

In my opinion, this error consists of your failure to grasp and incorporate in your program the idea contained in the following statement by Marx:

In the United States of North America every independent movement of the workers was paralyzed so long as slavery disfigured a part of the Republic. Labor cannot emancipate itself in the white skin where in the black it is branded.
                                          Capital, Vol. I, Chapter 10, Section 7

While you pay a great deal of attention to the Negro liberation movement, and correctly recognize it as a part of the global struggles for national liberation, you fail to discover the specific role it plays in the proletarian revolution in the United States. Thus, in your strategy for the proletarian revolution, you place the Negro question outside of the class struggle.

In my opinion you do this in spite of the fact that you cite Mao's correct words that, "In the final analysis, a national struggle is a question of class struggle." In this letter, I shall attempt to demonstrate the truth of my criticism and, in the process, suggest what I consider to be the correct strategy for the American working class.

The Greatest Barrier to Class Consciousness

The greatest ideological barrier to the achievement of proletarian class consciousness, solidarity, and political action is now, and has been historically, white chauvinism. White chauvinism is the ideological bulwark of the practice of white supremacy, the general oppression of blacks by whites.

The US ruling class has made a deal with the misleaders of American labor and through them with the masses of white workers. The terms of the deal, worked out over the three-hundred-year history of the development of capitalism in our country, are these: you white workers help us conquer the world and enslave the non-white majority of the earth's laboring force, and we will repay you with a monopoly of the skilled jobs, we will cushion you against the most severe shocks of the economic cycle, provide you with health and education facilities superior to those of the non-white population, grant you the freedom to spend your money and leisure time as you wish without social restrictions, enable you on occasion to promote one of your number out of the ranks of the laboring class, and in general confer on you the material and spiritual privileges befitting your white skin.

Of course there are dislocations in this set-up. Contradictions between antagonistic forces cannot be resolved except by revolution. The masses of white workers produce vast quantities of value, and there is consequently an unceasing struggle over how this value shall be divided—within the pre-imposed limits of the deal.

The Original "Sweetheart Agreement"!

But in spite of this unceasing and often fierce struggle, what exists is an opportunistic "contract" between the exploiters and a part of the exploited, at the expense of the rest of the exploited—in fact, the original "sweetheart agreement."

Does this mean that the white workers have no revolutionary potential, that they should be written out of the ranks of the revolutionary forces? Does it mean that, as far as the white workers are concerned, communists must sit passively and wait until the ruling class, of its own necessity (e.g., loss of colonial holdings), moves to cut its losses at the expense of some of the white workers' racial privileges and attempts to reduce them to or near the level of black, brown, and yellow workers?

It does not mean either of these things. In spite of their privileges, the white workers (except for the aristocracy of labor) are exploited proletarians, victims of "the stupid system of violence and robbery which we call Law and Industry" (G. B. Shaw). In the struggle for socialism, as well as the struggle for immediate reforms, without which the working class will never achieve socialist consciousness, the white workers, like their black, brown, and yellow brothers, have a "world to win." But they have more to lose than their chains; they have also to "lose" their white-skin privileges, the perquisites that separate them from the rest of the working class, that act as the material base for the split in the ranks of labor.

The Progressive Labor Party deals with the struggle for the unity of the working class in the following manner, from your convention documents:

> The unity of black and white workers can be forged only in the course of winning the white workers to struggle against the common class enemy for their own class demands, and by combating racism and by supporting the cause of Black Liberation.

And in another passage, this time from the editorial on Watts in the October 1965 issue of *Progressive Labor*, we read the following:

> White workers today are generally better off than the black people, who are engaged in a militant struggle for more jobs, housing and full political rights. But even today, where white workers are fighting for the same demands, they are also ruthlessly wiped out, like the unemployed coal miners of Hazard, Kentucky or the 80,000 laid off white railroad workers, victims of the Johnson-bosses-union gang-up or the teamsters shot at in a recent Tennessee strike.
>
> They, too, meet up with violent repression at the hands of the ruling class.
>
> As more and more white workers lose their jobs due to automation and the inability of the capitalist war economy to grow along with the population, they too will have to fight for their economic and political demands, or go under.

The Johnson administration has only one answer for workers who struggle for a better life—armed terror and suppression. Just as it commits genocide in Vietnam and the Congo, the government does not hesitate to use its army against the black people at home. Similarly, the same thing is in store for white workers who fight back as soon as they feel the squeeze.

By rejecting the racist slanders of the press and the hysteria whipped up by the politicians who serve the bosses, by supporting the black people in their liberation struggle, white workers are protecting themselves and preparing their own defense for the attacks Johnson will unleash against them when he and his bosses cannot meet their demands.

The "Parallel Struggles" Fallacy

Both of these passages are representative of the general line of Progressive Labor Party; both avoid the central question of the struggle against white supremacy. Both explicit and implicit in the passages cited is the concept that white workers have "their own class demands" which are separate from the demands of Negro liberation (which you summarize as "more jobs, housing and full political rights") and that in the parallel struggles of two groups of workers for two sets of demands lies the path to the unity of black and white workers.

This is wrong on two counts: in the first place, it is not correct to reduce the demands of the Negro liberation movement to "more jobs, housing and full political rights." These are the demands of all workers. (Nor is it enough to toss in the demand for self-determination, as you do elsewhere, as a slogan for the Negro nation: the writings of Lenin on the national–colonial question make it abundantly clear that self-determination of an oppressed nation is a slogan directed toward the working class of the oppressor nation.) The fundamental demand of Negro liberation is and has been for one hundred years the ending of white supremacy, the granting to the Negro people of every bourgeois right held by every other sector of the American people, excepting the other oppressed national minorities.

In the second place, the ending of white supremacy is not solely a demand of the Negro people, separate from the class demands of the entire working class. It cannot be left to the Negro people to fight it alone, while the white workers "sympathize with their fight," "support it," "reject racist slanders" etc., but actually fight for their "own" demands.

The ideology of white chauvinism is bourgeois poison aimed primarily at the white workers, utilized as a weapon by the ruling class to subjugate black and white workers. It has its material base in the practice of white supremacy, which is a crime not merely against non-whites but against the entire proletariat. Therefore, its elimination certainly qualifies as one of the class demands of the entire working class. In fact, considering the role that this vile practice has historically played in holding back the struggle of the American working class, the fight against white supremacy becomes the central immediate task of the entire working class.

The incorrect formulations and evasions which abound in the two passages I have cited from Progressive Labor Party documents are not mere slips of the pen. For nowhere in your literature do we find a single appeal to the white workers to fight against white supremacy in the only way possible, by repudiating their white-skin privileges and joining in a struggle with the rest of the working class for the demands of the entire class.

Programmatic Error: A Hypothetical Case

Your wrong theoretical approach to this question expresses itself in a wrong program. Thus, in an article by Antaeus in *Progressive Labor* of October–November 1966, it is stated:

> It now remains for a revitalized labor movement, led by the rank-and-file, to fulfill one of its greatest inheritances from its glorious past: to fight the "national interest" squeeze of the Johnsons and the Kennedys, and their corporate masters; to raise the deteriorating standards of the working class, to curb unemployment, especially among black, Puerto Rican and Mexican workers, to fight all this by launching a nation-wide struggle for shorter hours at forty hours pay.

My, my. It seems that the shorter work week has more uses than aspirin, though it is probably true that the winning of the shorter work week would provide more jobs for the Negro, Puerto Rican, and Mexican workers.

One can easily compute the mathematics of it: in a factory presently operating with six toolmakers, sixty machine operators, sixty assemblers, six packers, and three sweepers, each working forty hours a week, if the work week were shortened to thirty hours the following changes, more or less, could be expected: in place of the present six toolmakers (all white), eight would be required to produce the same quantity of value in thirty hours that is produced in forty. However, since there is a shortage of toolmakers, they would continue on forty hours, drawing overtime pay. In place of the sixty machine operators (all white), eighty would be required; the additional twenty would be drawn from those assemblers with the greatest seniority (all white). We now have forty assemblers left but need eighty; their ranks would be filled by advertising in the "help-wanted, women" section, or from the ranks of the unemployed white men. For the increase of two packers required, the plant would hire one white and one Negro. And finally, to provide the additional sweeper (couldn't we do without him since we're now on thirty hours?), a Negro would be hired, in accordance with the traditional personnel policy.

Thus, we would have a net gain of two jobs for Negroes. Perhaps exaggerated, but not much. Of course, those who put forward the demand for the shorter work week as a partial solution to the problem of Negro oppression argue that Negroes would benefit from it to a greater extent proportionately than their numbers in the population, since they make up a disproportionate share of the unemployed. That is possibly so. One can concede the possibility (although not the certainty) that out of the sixty-two or sixty-three new workers needed in my example, maybe four, instead of two, would be recruited from the ranks of the Negro unemployed; perhaps even the lily-whiteness of the ranks of the assemblers might be tinted a little.

"Fair employment through full employment": A White Supremacist Slogan

But would this disturb the institution of white supremacy? I am not here opposing the "thirty for forty" slogan. But raising it the way you do, to "curb unemployment, especially among black, Puerto Rican and

Mexican workers," is merely an echo of the "Fair employment through full employment" argument of Secretary of Labor [W. Willard] Wirtz and other spokesmen of the "liberal" wing of the ruling class. Even at its best (which will never be), "fair employment through full employment" is just another way of excusing the practice of leaving the Negroes as the last hired. Under such a slogan we may be assured that the last unemployed man or woman hired—the one that makes it "full"—will also be the one that makes it "fair." In other words, "fair employment through full employment" is another way of saying that job discrimination against Negroes will be maintained as long as it is possible to do so.

The point is: raising the demand for a larger slice of the pie for the working class does not in itself alter the apportionment of the slice within the working class. In fact, the ruling class has always utilized every concession won from it to increase the gap between white and black, thus turning even a victory of the working class into a cause of greater division. The shorter work week, with the promise of more jobs for those last hired, does not challenge the pattern of who shall be last hired, and therefore does not alter the inequality of white and black workers.

Is it not a fact that there have been times when the average real income of the Negro worker has increased, while at the same time the gap between the Negro and white worker has also increased? Thus, while the living conditions of the Negro people may have improved for a time absolutely, relative to those of the white population they deteriorated. To accept the premise that the way to improve conditions for the Negro workers is by increasing the proportion of the value created that goes to all workers is equivalent to institutionalizing the split in the working class and accepting the inferior status of the Negro and other colored workers.

"If you want shorter hours, let me tell you what to do . . ."

I would go further: the working class will not be able to win the shorter work week, will not even be able to resist the growing offensive of the ruling class, unless it first comes to grips with white supremacy as the chief cause of the division within its ranks.

There is no easy way around this problem. The struggle against white supremacy cannot be replaced by the struggle for a larger portion of the pie to be parceled out unequally among the workers. The only way to overcome the division in the working class is by overcoming it.

Elsewhere in your literature you raise the demand that 8,000 of the jobs in the big industrial plants in the Watts ghetto should go to the Negro residents of Watts, since they make up 80 percent of the area's population. In my opinion, this demand contains some merit as well as some faults. But taking it for its merit, that it raises the need for a more equal distribution of the existing jobs instead of banking on the same unequal distribution of new jobs, let me place the question: for whom is this demand raised? For the Negro workers and unemployed alone? In that case it is a divisive slogan and should be dropped. For the entire working class? In that case it is, at least partially, a unifying slogan and should be supported. But then it is necessary to explain to the white workers, and especially those white workers at the big plants in Watts, why they should support such a demand, even though it apparently threatens some of them with the loss of their jobs.

It is the same with the slogan which I understand was raised in the election campaign of Wendy Nakashima (Progressive Labor Party candidate for state legislature in 1966 elections) in New York City last year. I am told that her demand for preferential hiring for Negroes and Puerto Ricans received quite a bit of support in the mainly Negro and Puerto Rican district in which she campaigned. It is easy to see why. But if that is a good demand—and I am convinced that it is—then it must be good also for the white workers, and the reasons why must be explained to them so that they may become active partisans of it.

For make no mistake about it: with the US imperialist economy stagnating or even contracting, the ending of white supremacy, the ending of the privileged position of white workers, means fewer jobs for white workers, fewer skilled jobs, poorer housing, etc., if it goes no further than that. For it is obvious that if the rate of unemployment among Negroes is lowered from around 25 percent where it now stands to about 8 percent (which is "normal" in this period of imperialist decline for workers not suffering from national oppression or "favored" by white supremacy) then the rate of unemployment among white workers must be increased from the 5 percent where it now stands (by virtue of their white-skin privileges) to the 8 percent, which is "normal." And likewise with the proportion of skilled and unskilled jobs held by Negro and white workers, and so forth.

If It Goes No Further Than That . . .

But please note the phrase in my last paragraph: "if it goes no further than that." The consequences of the ending of white supremacy, which can only be ended by mobilizing and raising the consciousness of the entire working class, would extend far beyond the point of spreading out the misery more equitably. The result of such a struggle would be a working class that was class conscious, highly organized, experienced, and militant—in short, united—and ready to confront the ruling class as a solid block.

The ending of white supremacy does not pose the slightest peril to the real interests of the white workers; it definitely poses a peril to their fancied interests, their counterfeit interests, their white-skin privileges.

As long as white supremacy is permitted to divide the working class, so long will the struggle of the working class remain on two separate planes, one concerned with their "own" class demands and the other, on a more elementary plane (but with a much higher degree of class consciousness) fighting first for the ordinary bourgeois rights which were won long ago for the rest of the workers. As soon as white supremacy is eliminated as a force within the working class, the decks will be cleared for action by the entire class against its enemy.

And what would be the outcome of such a struggle? Well, consider: if it were not for the ideology of white chauvinism, the American workers would by now have a labor party, which would represent a step forward in the class struggle. If it were not for the ideology of white chauvinism, the South would be organized, with all that that implies. If it were not for the ideology of white chauvinism, the American workers could see clearly the racist, imperialist, anti-working-class character of the US aggression in Vietnam, and oppose it from the only possible proletarian standpoint—opposition to US imperialism.

Communists (individually, this is the task primarily of white communists, although collectively it is the responsibility of the whole party) must go to the white workers and say frankly: you must renounce the privileges you now hold, must join the Negro, Puerto Rican, and other colored workers in fighting white supremacy, must make this the first, immediate, and most urgent task of the entire working class, in exchange for which you, together with the rest of the workers, will receive all the benefits which are sure to come from one working class (of several colors) fighting together.

This does not mean that the process will develop in clear stages, i.e., first the ending of white supremacy, then a massive struggle for reforms, then revolution. It is probable that Negro liberation will not take place without the conquest of power by the working class in our country as a whole. What it means is that, in the course of mobilizing the entire working class to fight white supremacy, some victories will be won and, most important of all, the ideology of white chauvinism will be widely exposed as the weapon of the oppressor, thus preparing the working class for the assumption of power. In this way the Russian workers, led by the Bolsheviks, made the liberation of their "own" colonies an integral part of their own class demands (now let us use your phrase without quotation marks) and thus were prepared to carry out their revolution.

"The real secret"—an Instructive Parallel

When we consult the writings of the founders of scientific socialism, we find a wealth of material on this question. In a *Resolution on Relations Between the Irish and the English Working Classes*, written by Marx in 1869 for the International Workingmen's Association, we read the following:

> On the other hand, the *English bourgeoisie* has not only exploited Irish poverty in order to worsen the condition of the working class in England, by the forced transplantation of poor Irish peasants, but it has moreover divided the proletariat into hostile camps. The revolutionary fire of the Celtic workers does not harmonize with the restrained force but slowness of the Anglo-Saxons. In all the big industrial centers of England a deep antagonism exists between the English and Irish workers.
>
> The average English worker hates the Irish as a competitor who lowers his wages and *level of living*. He feels national and religious antagonism towards him. He appears to him in much the same light as the black slaves appeared to the poor whites in the Southern States of North America. This antagonism between the proletarians of

England is artificially cultivated and maintained by the bourgeoisie. It knows that in this antagonism lies *the real secret of maintaining its power*.[1]

And in the same year, on November 29, in a letter to Kugelman, Marx wrote:

> I have become more and more convinced—and the only question is to bring this conviction home to the English working class—that it can never do anything decisive here in England until it separates its policy with regard to Ireland in the most definite way from the policy of the ruling classes, until it not only makes common cause with the Irish, but actually takes the initiative in dissolving the Union established in 1801 and replacing it by a free federal relationship. And, indeed, this must be done, not as a matter of sympathy with Ireland, but as a demand made in the interests of the English proletariat. If not, the English people will remain tied to the leading-strings of the ruling classes, because it must join with them in a common front against Ireland. Every one of its movements in England itself is crippled by the disunion with the Irish, who form a very important section of the working class in England.[2]

Please note the last phrase in the above citation. Now, if Marx could correctly observe that the Irish workers formed a "very important section of the working class in England" in 1869, what are we to say of the position of the Negro workers in the American working class in 1967?

Black Workers Are Proletarians—Not "Allies" of the Proletariat

This brings me to another error you make. For it follows logically from your first error of placing the national question outside of the bounds of the class struggle that you also isolate the Negro workers from the working class as a whole. In actuality, you relegate the Negro workers to a kind of limbo, peripheral to the main body of the working class, "allies" of the working class—anything but the integral part of it that they are.

The proof of this assertion lies in your underestimation of the importance of the Negro liberation struggle for the future of the American working class. Yes, I say underestimation, for that is in fact what you are guilty of in practice. I will give you some examples.

You correctly pose as one of the tasks before the working class that of building a third party, a labor party. But just such a party is being born under your very eyes, and you are blinded to it by your chauvinist (might as well speak plainly) lack of appreciation of the significance of the Negro liberation movement, such as the Black Panther Party in Lowndes County, Alabama, and the Freedom Democratic Party in Mississippi, as well as other stirrings in the same direction throughout the country. Of course, these movements differ in their degrees of clarity and maturity, but is there any doubt that they represent motion toward a breakaway from the two-party stranglehold? Suppose the Negro people succeed in launching such a party, will it not contain within it the essentials of a labor party program, in spite of its label as a Negro party? Will it not then be a prime task for those armed with Marxist-Leninist theory to take the program of such a party to the white workers and rally their support for it, whatever its name? And even if this party makes its appearance under less than ideal circumstances, for example under the auspices of a demagogue and opportunist like Adam Clayton Powell, as long as it is a real living party and not stillborn like the Freedom Now Party of 1963, the same thing will hold true—for let us not forget that the Congress of Industrial Organizations was born in 1935 by one labor faker, John L. Lewis, punching another, William Hutcheson, in the jaw!

If we are dialecticians, we base ourselves on what is new and look under the appearance of things to discover their essence. And one of the essential features of American history, which must be understood by everyone who hopes to apply Marxist-Leninist theory to the specific conditions of our country, is that traditionally the Negro people, for very real reasons, have carried forward the demands of the entire working class, cloaked in the garb of Negro rights!

This is true even now of the Black Power slogan, whose significance is not limited to the Negro people. As a white worker, I declare that I would a thousand times sooner live under the Black Power of Stokely Carmichael than under the "white" imperialist power of Lyndon Baines Johnson!

The Only Choice

And this is the choice which today, on one level or another, confronts every white worker. It can be seen most clearly in Sunflower County, Mississippi, where the only alternative to Black Power, for both black and white poor, is Eastland power. But the developing reality of the class struggle will soon bring forward in dramatic contrast everywhere the truth that there are only two paths open to the white workers: with the boss or with the Negro workers; abandonment of all claim to share in the shaping of our destiny, or repudiation of the white-skin privileges, for which we, in our very infancy, pawned our revolutionary souls.

Another example is the Mississippi Freedom Labor Union. In your trade union program, you praise it as a necessary response to the Jim Crow practices of the labor brass. Fine! But you treat it as a stopgap measure until such time as the racist unions change their policy. Why not instead recognize it as the kernel of a potential workers' controlled labor movement for all workers? You yourselves state that the union officials are now in the process of converting the unions into a fascist labor front. Instead of casting around for a way out of this by looking for some possible new alignments among the faction-ridden labor brass, why not recognize the importance of what is really new? In Mississippi we see the amazing (for the United States) phenomenon of workers organizing their own union to fight the bosses. Are you going to let the fact that these workers are black blind you to the fact that they are, first of all workers, and leave you standing on the sidelines with your mouths full of patronizing words of admiration, unable to see that these black workers are today the foremost representatives, not merely of the Negro liberation movement, but of the American working class?

Indeed, under present conditions, with the Negro liberation struggle moving into high gear while the rest of the workers remain backward and relatively quiescent, to speak of the white workers "supporting" the Negro liberation movement is something of impertinence. The Negro liberation movement today is doing more for socialism and the class demands of the proletariat than any "working class" movement outside of it and represents the firm and reliable support for any progressive struggles which may develop among white workers. Moreover, it represents a solid base from which to develop such struggles. But in order to draw upon the strength of the Negro people's movement, the white workers must, first of all, break the links which tie them to the bosses (to the "leading-strings of the ruling classes," as Marx wrote Kugelman) by repudiating the white supremacist contract.

If this is not done, we will see a repetition of what has transpired more than once in our history: The crisis arrives, conditions worsen, the working people are radicalized—and then—defeat, because the subjective factor was ignored and the white-skin privilege and its vile ideology were not specifically, directly, consistently, and courageously denounced and renounced in words and in deeds.

Up to now in my critical remarks, I have dealt only with the white chauvinism in your erroneous theoretical line. But you also exhibit its inevitable concomitant: serious deviations in the direction of bourgeois nationalism. Since I regard the battle against bourgeois nationalism as primarily the responsibility of those Negroes imbued with Marxist-Leninist theory, I will limit myself to pointing out one example from your literature. In the November–December 1966 issue of *SPARK*, your West Coast paper, you report the speech of John Harris, whom you identify as a Progressive Labor Party organizer, before a mass rally in Watts: "Harris talked about the war in Vietnam and said that Black men should not fight against their Vietnamese brothers, 'who look more like them than the white man who sent them there.'"

Such a statement does not require much comment. If made by a black nationalist, it would be a positive statement and could be supported, but when made by a responsible leader of an organization which claims to be guided by the science of Marxism-Leninism, and then reprinted in an official publication of that organization, it becomes nothing more than shallow opportunism.

The vanguard of the working class is the home of the internationalist workers; while bourgeois nationalism, outside the party, may on occasion play a positive role, within the party it has no more place than the white chauvinism which engenders it.

I would like to conclude this letter by referring to the words of old John Brown. For many years it has been the fashion in American left-wing circles to pay homage to old Osawatomie, while ignoring the lessons he taught us. Usually this is done by dismissing his use of armed struggle under the pretext that it was "appropriate for another era." But there was more to Brown than his determination and heroism; he was a serious and careful student of American social reality. In his last letter to his family, Brown wrote to his children to "abhor, with undying hatred also, that sum of all villainies—slavery."

The "Peculiar Institution"

John Brown clearly understood that all the social evils of our country were summed up in the "peculiar institution" of African slavery, without whose abolition progress in any field would be impossible.

So it was to old John Brown, and so it is to us, his children. All the evils of US imperialist rule in its dying days—the barbarous wars of extermination launched against colonial and semi-colonial peoples, the murder by starvation, the mass insecurity, the fascist clamp being tightened on the American people, the trampling on culture, and the contempt for the decent aspirations of humanity—all these are concentrated and summed up in the infernal theory and practice of white supremacy.

Therefore, the attack on white supremacy is the first order of business for all progressive forces in our country and the key to strategy for Marxist–Leninists.

6

Learn the Lessons of US History

Building on "The White Blindspot," Ignatiev makes a spirited defense for putting the color line front and center in organizing among working-class white people and theorizes the twin status of white workers: "exploited but privileged." This essay was published in New Left Notes, *a journal of the Students for a Democratic Society, in 1968.*

Many white radicals have begun to talk about the need to organize working-class whites. As one active movement figure put it, "We now see that the people we used to refer to as 'working-class fascists' are the very ones we have to reach."

As we all know, a large share of the credit for this new attention on the part of white radicals belongs to the Student Nonviolent Coordinating Committee (SNCC).* But even before SNCC took its stand on black power, there were some people, such as Southern Conference Educational Fund (SCEF) and Jobs or Income Now (JOIN), who felt that the main task for white radicals was organizing other whites.† But SNCC, by

---

* SNCC was a radical black youth-led civil rights group that emerged from the student-led sit-ins against segregation and played an important role to organize voting drives and Freedom Rides.

† SCEF started in the 1940s and used New Deal policies to address discrimination, poverty and disenfranchisement in the South during the Great Depression. In the 1950s and 1960s the organization survived red-baiting and focused its energies fighting racial

telling its white supporters that their role should be organizing whites for the black people to form coalitions with, pushed thousands of people into a new awareness.

In my opinion, this new awareness is healthy. However, along with this new and correct realization has come the baggage of old, unchallenged, and incorrect concepts which, if allowed to prevail, will certainly undo any positive work in this field.

Among many radicals who have begun to tackle seriously the task of organizing working-class whites, there is an approach which shows that we—the movement as a whole—have failed to learn the lessons of US history and specifically the lessons of past experiences in large movements of downtrodden whites. The approach I am criticizing I would summarize as follows: find the issues which immediately affect the people we are trying to reach and which they feel most keenly. Organize around these issues and, as the people are drawn more into struggle in their own interest, they will come to see, with our help, who are their friends and enemies. Specifically, coalitions between poor white and black will develop from each fighting for his own "self-interest" and coming to see that there is a common enemy, the rich white man.

I think there is no need to cite documents for the above, as everyone involved will recognize it as a fair summary of a very popular approach. I don't think it can succeed.

What is the greatest barrier to the development of working-class consciousness and solidarity in the United States? White supremacist thinking, both now and in the past. White supremacist thinking, while it is part of a mindset, is not a pure question of ideology. It has real roots in the practice of white supremacy, the general oppression of blacks by whites.

The Al Capones who run this country have made a deal with the labor officials and, through them, with the totality of white working people. The terms of the deal, which was a long time in the working out, are simply these: you white workers support us in our enslavement of the non-white majority of the earth's population, and we will reward you with a monopoly of skilled jobs, education, and health facilities superior

---

segregation in the South. SCEF had a good working relationship with SNCC. JOIN was an offshoot of Students for a Democratic Society whose work consisted of service and political education, primarily among working-class white people.

to those of the non-whites, the opportunity to occasionally promote one of your number out of the laboring class, social privileges, and a whole series of privileges befitting your white skin.

Exploited but Privileged

Thus, while the ordinary white workers are severely exploited, they are also privileged. White supremacy is a deal between the exploiters and a part of the exploited, at the expense of the rest of the exploited—in fact, the original sweetheart agreement!

Some may argue that it can't be called a deal, since most of those participating on either side are not conscious of where they fit in, that it is more accurate to consider white supremacy as the simple and determined result of the operation of certain blind laws, as something institutionalized, beyond the control, right now, of any sector of the people involved in its workings.

Those who argue thus should consider the following question: if the bosses are always screaming about high labor costs, why don't they simply hire the cheapest labor there is, namely black and brown labor? The reason is that, for the bosses, the few cents an hour they would save in wages would be far outweighed by the growth in working-class solidarity that would follow if all workers were on exactly the same footing. (For information on how the color line was erected in a single industry, in this case the cotton mill industry in the South, for the purpose of buying off the poor whites, see W. J. Cash's classic *The Mind of the South* or Broadus Mitchell's *The Rise of Cotton Mills in the South*.[1])

Certainly, national oppression goes hand-in-hand with imperialism, but that is not to say that it is an institution or that it should in any sense be considered too deeply entrenched to be challenged. White supremacy exists simply because sufficient numbers of white people, including white workers, have not been rallied to fight it—black people have never stopped fighting it. And the reason why white workers have not fought white supremacy, have in fact acquiesced in and cooperated with it, is that they enjoy their privileged status.

No Self-Interest Coalitions

Now, my point of disagreement with the approach I summarized earlier is this: I don't believe it is possible to build coalitions of black and white on the basis of the self-interest of each, if the self-interest of the whites means the maintenance of white supremacy and the white-skin privilege.

I would state, from my own experience as a worker and my travels among workers, that there are very few white workers who would object to having the Negroes "brought up to our level." Most white workers would be pleased if all the black people had a decent job and a place to live, as good as the whites' anyhow.

But if there are not enough jobs to go around, then the great majority of white workers are quite willing to invoke their privilege and say "me first," thus making them active partners in the exclusion and oppression of the black people.

Under the system of private profit, all workers compete in the sale of their labor power; yet their general tendency is to unite. However, because the competition between black and white workers is not an equal one, but is weighted by the white-skin privilege, white workers have generally preferred to unite with the boss to maintain their privileges rather than unite with the black people to destroy all privilege.

And this is the rub for our movement. History shows that, whenever masses of white poor have been radicalized and brought into struggle, the power structure has been able to hold out the crumb of the white-skin privilege, breaking any developing coalition and struggle.

Why Others Failed

The defeat of the great struggles of the labor movement, which began after the depression of 1873 and reached their climax in the railroad strike of 1877, can be traced to the failure of American labor, as a whole, to join with black labor in the South to preserve the democratic advances of the Reconstruction Era. In his great work, *Black Reconstruction*, Du Bois put forward ideas which should make us all think long and hard. He wrote:

The South, after the war, presented the greatest opportunity for a real national labor movement which the nation ever saw or is likely to see for many decades. Yet the labor movement, with but few exceptions, never realized the situation. It never had the intelligence or knowledge, as a whole, to see in black slavery and Reconstruction the kernel and meaning of the labor movement in the United States.[2]

The defeat of Populism was due to its tendency to compromise with, and ultimately capitulate to white supremacist pressure to "abandon the Negro" (see Woodward's biography of Tom Watson on this subject).

The halting of the labor movement's advances at the end of the 1930s, and its reversal and defeat in the years after World War II, was due to the same failure to challenge white supremacy. If anyone doubts this, let him consider why the Congress of Industrial Organizations (CIO), after having organized US Steel, General Motors, and General Electric by 1940, paused on the brink of the South and turned back, permitting itself to be coopted by the Roosevelt administration.

In the three great eras of struggle I have cited, probably the three greatest in post–Civil War history, in the final analysis the matter came down to this: the power structure was able to solve its problems with the white workers "within the family," by offering them privileges. By accepting these privileges, the white workers turned their back not merely on their black brothers, but on the class struggle, and renounced their right to a say in their destiny.

Of course the acceptance of privilege and the maintenance of white supremacy was not in the interest of either white or black workers! The result of the overturning of Reconstruction and the defeat of Populism is the impoverished South of today. The result of the CIO's wrong turn in 1940 is the deteriorating conditions of labor and the oleomargarine unions which dominate every industry.

The ending of white supremacy does not pose the slightest peril to the real interests of the white workers, but to their fancied interests, their counterfeit interests, their white-skin privileges.

Renouncing Privilege

Once again the signs point to an upturn in the militancy of the American workers, including the whites. And once again the white workers will be faced with a choice: unite with the black people for our common interests, including the defeat of white supremacy and the repudiation of the white-skin privilege; or unite with the boss to maintain them.

Solidarity between black and white requires more from the white than a willingness to "help the Negroes up if it doesn't lower us any." It requires a willingness to renounce our privileges, precisely to "lower ourselves" in order that we can all rise up together. If anyone says that it will be difficult to get the whites to renounce their privileges, I readily concede the difficulty—whoever said it would be easy to make a revolution? But if anyone thinks it is possible to skip this renunciation and to build coalitions between blacks and whites who want to maintain their privileges, I will point to 1877, 1904, and 1940 and say that if this task is not tackled and achieved, we will see the same thing over again: the crisis comes, conditions worsen, the working people are radicalized, and then defeat, because the white-skin privilege and its ideology were not specifically, directly, consistently, and courageously denounced and renounced, in words and in deeds.

Tactics

Now, what does all this mean for our tactics? I have some suggestions:

> 1. In all our work we should bring the question of white supremacy to the fore. Thus in opposing the Vietnam war, we should especially expose it as a racist, white supremacist war, an extension of US genocidal policies toward Indians and Afro-Americans.
> 2. We should discover, and take advantage of, every opportunity to point out to white workers the nature of the white supremacist deal and show them how it operates against them by tying them to their enemy, the bosses.
> 3. For my third suggestion, I can do no better than to quote a memo written in June 1966 by Anne Braden to the Southern Student Organizing Committee:

Now, the pendulum seems to be swinging the other way, and more and more white people are deciding they must reach the white Southerner . . . I am glad they are deciding this . . . What I disagree with is the concept that they will organize these poor white Southerners completely apart from the Negro movement—and figure that somewhere down the road, maybe several years hence, maybe they'll get together in some sort of coalition.

I don't think it can work that way . . .

Blacks Organize Whites

Again to be specific, if you are going to engage in a project (rural or urban) to organize poor white people, I can see how it might be desirable (and it may happen whether you think it is desirable or not) for Negroes to be organizing the black people in that community into an independent organization. But when you go to and organize the white people, I think you have to say to them up front, from the very word go, that if they are going to be effective and solve their problems, they are going to have to team up with those black people over there and find terms that are acceptable to the black people to do it on, and I think you should go to these white people with teams of black and white organizers working together.

White people may not be able to work in organizing Negro communities and maybe should not—for all the reasons stated recently . . . But I think black organizers are urgently needed to work in white communities.

In other words, I am saying that I think you have to confront the white Southerner you are trying to reach with this whole question of racism and what it has done to him from the very beginning.

Some may say this is impossible—it will frighten him off and you'll never get to him. I am not saying it will be easy. We will fail many times. But I think we must begin trying in the beginning because I think if you wait it will get harder as time goes on and not easier.

In fact, if you begin to organize groups of white people without tackling this issue in a very concrete way, I think the problem is much greater than that; you will just be wasting your time. I think you may be creating a Frankenstein . . .

As I understand it, Saul Alinsky had this experience in Chicago. He organized Negroes on the Southside—and he organized the Back-of-the-Yards movement which was all white and poor and very oppressed. The Back-of-the-Yards movement became very strong and effective in fighting its own oppression, but later it was the backbone of a movement to keep Negroes out of that part of Chicago . . .

What I am saying is that we must try to avoid such mistakes by beginning in the very beginning to try to convince white people that their interest lies in teaming up with Negroes—even if the Negroes want and are forming their own organizations. And if we hope to convince them, we must confront them with the issue as we start, because it will get harder as people get more organized, stronger in their own organization, more solidified, and so on.

I think Anne Braden's suggestions for Southern organizing apply with equal force throughout the country.

4. We should find and put forward slogans and issues which make concrete the repudiation of privilege and which are tied in as closely as possible with building unity and winning real benefits. For example, in a shop which is not organized, instead of trying to organize a union around the demand of straight seniority (an obvious white-skin privilege, since it was the boss who decided whom to hire first), we should try to rally the workers around a demand like the following: a contract provision that at no time in a layoff could a greater proportion of Negroes be included than their proportion in the plant. Another provision might be that workers in the most dangerous, dirtiest departments (usually Negroes) receive a special seniority bonus. I think these demands would appeal to the sense of fair play of working men and women.

Like the Draft Position of SDS

An excellent example of the practical application of my thesis is the Students for Democratic Society (SDS) position on the draft, of opposing the draft and, at the same time, denouncing the II-S student deferment as a racial (and class) privilege whose only purpose is to divide the anti-war movement, and not merely denouncing it, but calling upon all students to renounce it. I don't want to attribute the totality of my views to SDS; I merely applaud their stand as the only honest one under the circumstances.

I don't claim to have the best tactical solutions to the problem I raise. But I do say that if all of us in the movement don't find ways to win the white workers to repudiate their white-skin privileges and oppose white supremacy, then we might as well, as one of my friends says, "piss on the fire and summon the hounds," because the hunt is over. At this point the main thing, in my opinion, is to create a widespread awareness among white working people of the nature of the white supremacist deal. I am confident that the American working class, which gave birth to May Day and International Women's Day, which developed and creatively applied the tactics of the sit-in strike, roving pickets, and the slow-down, will be able to come up with plenty of ways to repudiate a deal once they have decided it is in their interest to do so.

Too Moralistic?

In discussing my thesis with movement people, I have sometimes encountered the objection that my approach is a moralistic rather than a materialistic one, that it relies on idealism rather than "self-interest." To this I answer as follows:

1. The "moralistic" John Brown made a far greater contribution to the struggle of labor than all of the sophisticated "Marxists" in the pre-Civil War labor movement (and there were some, even then) who shied away from directly opposing chattel slavery because, they felt, "the workers wouldn't go along."
2. As a worker I resent the prejudice, common among student radicals, that the workers can only be moved by narrow economic considerations while they, the students, are radicals for reasons of idealism. I point to the thousands and thousands of white workers who marched off to war for the Union singing, "As He died to make men holy, let us die to make men free." And I would predict that the next few years will show that the great acts of heroism on the part of the working people will be called forth not by demands for a nickel an hour but by

the "idealistic," "moralistic" slogans of the solidarity and humanity of
labor.

3. The repudiation of the white-skin privilege is in the interests, both
short and long range, of the white workers, and the only problem is to
help them (and some of our radicals) see it.

"Working Class" and "Poor"

Just one more point. I notice that I use the terms "working class" and
"poor" in a somewhat interchangeable manner, which might offend
some people who seem to regard them as two separate, nonoverlapping
categories. In this regard, perhaps I might be permitted to cite personal
experience. As recently as six years ago, I was running a turret lathe in a
sweatshop for $1.15 per hour. Today, I am more highly skilled and better
paid; I make $3.65 per hour. (According to the government, that is
almost enough to maintain a family of four, exactly what I have, at what
they call a "minimum adequate" standard of living.) Between the two
extremes I have had various spells of unemployment, with and without
compensation. Judging by certain developments within the economic
sphere, such as the British devaluation of the pound and the US unfavorable balance of payments, I fully expect, within the next few years, to
be glad to work again for $1.15 an hour, if I can get it. While I can clearly
see the difference between a bad job and one that's not so bad, and
between an unemployed worker and an employed one, I can't see a
difference between working class and poor, except, perhaps, that there
are other people besides workers who are poor.

7

Organizing Workers: Lessons for Radicals

Ignatiev reflects on his experiences organizing against the color line in International Harvester, where he worked at the time, and contrasts the work of trade union organizing with the imperative to challenge the color line. This essay was originally published by the Guardian *in July 1968.*

I am employed at the International Harvester Company tractor works in Chicago as a tool-and-die maker, one of the skilled trades. I would like to describe a struggle which has recently come forward sharply, my own part in it, and draw some lessons for radicals in industry.

The tractor works is the heir to some of the most militant traditions of the American working class. It was from a strike on May 1, 1886, of McCormick Reaper Works (the original plant, right across the street from the tractor works, of the Harvester chain. It is now torn down.) that the Haymarket incident grew. The May Day holiday was born out of that event.

The workers passed through some rough times in building the Congress of Industrial Organizations (CIO). In the 1941 strike Lucy Parsons, widow of the Haymarket martyr Albert Parsons, spoke to a mass meeting of strikers and declared, "Now I know my husband was not hung in vain."

The core of the local leadership (now Local 1301 of the United Auto Workers; UAW) has been with the union through its days as part of the

Farm Equipment Workers (expelled from the CIO in 1949 for "red domination") and the entry into the UAW in 1955.

Because of local militancy, [Walter] Reuther has not been able, even after fourteen years, to force on the workers the terrifying speedup that is killing the autoworkers.

At the same time, because of the accommodation which has been reached between the local and the UAW brass (Walter makes the big decisions, we make small decisions), conditions have deteriorated and interest in union affairs has declined.

Wages, especially for production workers, have not kept pace with the cost of living. In the last contract the skilled workers, 9 percent of the plant and almost all white, received a 50-cent increase for the first year while production workers, more than half black, got 17 cents. The three-year contract did nothing about automation and the cost-of-living plan was weakened.

In the last few years, as part of the general re-awakening of the rank and file, and especially as a result of the black liberation movement, there have appeared stirrings of revolt at a local level. In the recent elections for delegates to the international convention, a caucus was formed among black workers which had as one of its demands the opening of the skilled trades to non-whites. The caucus received about 35 percent of the total votes cast.

At a meeting of the local, one of the Negro workers active in the union leadership (almost all the leadership is white) introduced a resolution relating to discrimination in the skilled trades. He announced that although approximately 45 percent of the 2,500 workers in the plant are Negro and Spanish-speaking, out of 208 workers in the skilled trade departments, there are only six Negroes and no Spanish-speaking workers. He cited statistics on the number of workers trained on the job and showed that non-whites had been excluded. He proposed that the union take note of these conditions and that the grievance committee be instructed to raise it with the company for correction.

When the chairman asked for discussion from the floor, I spoke in more or less the following words:

> I want to support Brother Frank's proposal. If we really mean business, then we have to be together. When we have a plant that is almost half black and skilled trades departments that are all white, that's not

unity, that's disunity. I don't think we should allow the company to use lack of qualifications as an excuse to keep out black and Spanish-speaking workers. I never had a formal apprenticeship, and I'm working as a toolmaker. I was hired just as much for my white skin as for any skills I have. I don't know about the other skilled departments, but I think that anyone who knows how to run shop equipment and has ordinary intelligence can be a toolmaker. We should demand that the company make sure that half of the skilled trades are black. They didn't ask us how to keep black workers out, so they shouldn't ask us how to get them in, but we don't want to hear any baloney about qualifications. Speaking as a white man, I think we should all, white, Negro, and Spanish, support the proposal, so we can be together every day, because that's the only way to fight the company.

The proposal was carried unanimously; no one spoke against it. But that does not give a true picture of the reaction to my words.

Attendance at the meeting was small, but word got around the shop, and it can be said that fairly wide interest has been stirred up. Taking into account that the greatest passion is at the two poles of the dispute, that most of the workers haven't been heard from yet, and that of course there is some crossing over, the reactions can be generally summarized as follows.

The black workers responded overwhelmingly in favor. I was invited to join the caucus which until then had been totally black. A number of black workers have come over to my bench to say hello and let me know they were pleased. One young black worker came by and said that had heard that some people were giving me a rough time and that he wanted to let everybody know that a lot of people were with me.

The unskilled white workers have generally reacted with the least interest and feelings, although the more union-conscious have been stirred in a good direction. Generally, this group of workers has not been heard from. As the struggle sharpens, which way the white production workers go will be decisive.

The skilled workers in my department have reacted with hostility, more bitter and more united than I have ever seen skilled workers on any issue. The second day after the meeting I found a big sign, saying JUDAS, taped on my toolbox. The next morning there was a swastika. It is over a month now, and out of about thirty workers on the day shift, maybe eight are speaking to me. (The other skilled departments, while not agreeing with me, have not been hostile.) However, even among the skilled workers, the more union-conscious have been pushed to pay more attention to getting black workers into the skilled trades, if only to defend themselves in the controversy which has been stirred up.

The reaction of the company (always a good clue as to whether we are on the right track) was to call me in to explain some minor discrepancies on my application, which had already been cleared up. They also called up my last job, again, to get information from the foreman. Also (this may not be released) the FBI and the head of plant security were in my department talking to the foreman for a good part of one morning.

Most of the resentment generated by my remarks was due not to my "defending the Negroes" (although that played a role) but to what seemed to them my violation of the "noblest" of trade union principles: never run down a man's job. As one of them told me, "How can we go into negotiations next time for more money when one of my own men says anybody can do our work?"

(I exaggerated somewhat. When I came to work there with two toolboxes full of precision tools, the guys told me, "Take all that shit home. Around here you don't need anything but hammers and chisels." A standard crack when anyone is spending time working precisely is, "Throw it together. It's only for a tractor." On the other hand, some training is required, even beyond the knowledge of machine tools, more by way of becoming familiar with the shortcuts than with precision machining. This is part of a general phenomenon that the distinction between skilled and production workers is an artificial one fostered by the company to substitute craft pride for class consciousness. Of course, I erred in understating the amount of training required to be a toolmaker. But I insist it was a misstatement in the right direction. The proof of this assertion is that the handful of black skilled workers were not offended but regarded my statement as a blow for justice. This is not because they are black nationalists, but because they are not white, not blinded by white supremacy and afflicted with the "white blindspot," and therefore more class conscious than the white skilled workers.)

My answer to the worker was, "If building up our trade means getting more money from the company, then I'm for it. But if it means building walls between us and the black production workers and all production workers, then I'm against it, because all of us will suffer."

This contradiction becomes quite important when one comprehends the mechanism of discrimination at Harvester.

To get an apprenticeship, an applicant must achieve a certain minimum point score, a maximum of fifty from his results on his qualifying test, fifty from previous work experience, and thirty from a personal interview. If he achieves the required score, then on the basis of seniority he will be given an apprenticeship when an opening occurs. (The ratio of apprentices to journeymen is fixed by the contract.) Even if the grading and interviewing are completely objective (and inside information indicates they are), the system still operates to exclude black workers.

Obviously, any test coupled with a required high school diploma plus job experience is discriminatory. And further, the whole apprenticeship set-up is discriminatory, since a production worker transferring to an apprenticeship must swallow as much as a $1 per hour pay cut for the first year. This is a sacrifice (an investment, if you will) which is more difficult for black workers than for white.

It boils down to a choice between maintaining the high standards of the trade or bringing in black workers. It is not possible to do both.

Leaving tactics aside for the moment, the whole approach I took stands in sharp contrast to the "base-building" of some radical trade union activists, who generally advocate the traditional method of first participating in struggle around what the white workers regard as their immediate self-interest and then forging coalitions with black people based on a common interest.

The difference between the two approaches is not a tactical one between "slow" and "fast." What defines the approach I took is the recognition that the struggle against white supremacy is a definite part of the class demands of the entire working class, that it involves the choice between class struggle and class collaboration, that it is very much an immediate issue for the whole working class, and that white workers can be won to support it.

Base-building

The base-building approach generally tends to regard militant "trade-union" issues as the meat of day-to-day confrontations, confining the struggle against white supremacy to educational efforts on the part of radicals ("racism is the bosses' tool to divide the working class") that *never come to be* practical issues requiring action.

Black caucuses are springing up throughout industry. Even if they did not exist, white supremacy would be the key issue to fight on since it is the chief cause of the division of the working class. The fact that they do exist is a new reality which presents white radicals with a great opportunity. The danger is that white radicals will see the demands raised by black workers (that is, the directly anti-racist demands) not as working class demands but as "black people's issues." This will lead us into one of two bags: either liberal supportive types of relations or else attempts to build movements among white workers around nickel-and-dime issues, movements which do not incorporate the need for working class unity into their program, in a set of concrete, practical demands.

Rank-and-file caucuses, new unions, all forms which will emerge from the rebellion of labor, should be encouraged by all means. But one thing is clear from a good reading of American history: any militant movement on the part of white workers which equivocates in its opposition to white supremacy is a dead-end street.

In the Harvester situation, what is involved is a struggle against false consciousness, which can hardly be overcome by building bases on it. I appealed to class consciousness over craft and race consciousness. The fact that skilled tradesmen generally do not see the point yet is due to their having two barriers to overcome. They may well have to pass through some bitter defeats before they learn where their interests lie. The white production workers, who have only one barrier to overcome, are generally neutral and in some cases sympathetic to the question as I raised it, and that is a good sign.

The history of white labor in the United States is generally a history of struggle with the bosses over the fruits of labor—within the framework of the mutual acceptance of white supremacy, that is the monopoly of skilled jobs; the likelihood of better education, housing, and health facilities for whites than for non-whites; and so forth.

What white labor has generally failed to see is that white supremacist privileges, even though they may result in relative material advantage, are in contradiction to the struggle of labor and not a result of its victories. The failure of white labor to see the indispensable truth has led to a pattern of white "victories" and black defeats, which are really defeats of the whole working class.

Skills and Seniority

Thus, in the case of apprenticeship terms and exams: the white skilled tradesmen regard them as their protection against the foremen and superintendants bringing their brothers-in-law into the skilled trades. They regard the four-year term (longer, in some industries) as a means of limiting the number of qualified workmen in order to keep wages high. But what they do not see (generally speaking, do not care) is that these measures operate to preserve the skilled trades as a privileged sanctuary for whites only.

Take, for instance, the seniority system. Workers generally regard seniority as their protection against arbitrary firings. But seniority also acts as a guarantee (and many white workers are conscious of this) that in the event of big layoffs, the black workers, who were the last ones hired, will be the first ones laid off. (At the tractor works, where there are many black workers with high seniority, the same result is accomplished by an additional mechanism, common throughout industry: as part of plantwide seniority, workers in higher classifications can drop to lower ones, "bumping" lower classification workers with equal seniority onto the street.)

Now, how in the hell under these circumstances can radicals build bases around straight seniority and expect these bases to lead to coalitions with black workers? Isn't it clear that every step the organizers take toward strengthening straight seniority is not merely a postponement, for tactical reasons, of black–white unity but is, in fact, a step away from it?

The way out of this dilemma lies in resurrecting the concept of class interest as opposed to self-interest and making class interest the theme of our organizing.

In American history there is a current of working-class solidarity expressed in the slogan "An injury to one is an injury to all." Its most famous expression is the great song "Solidarity." We must take this tradition of class pride and use it as an organizing weapon. In the final analysis, it will be class pride, and not the desire for another nickel an hour, which will enable workers to reject white supremacy because it is the bosses' game, reject male supremacy because it is the bosses' game, reject anything which offends working class pride and acts as an obstacle to the achievement of solidarity.

Can "class pride" be translated into everyday struggles? I think so. I have heard the story of how the black and white workers at the Harvester plant in Louisville together went and tore down the walls between the segregated washrooms. When I asked the person who was telling the story what was the appeal that won the white workers over to this action, he replied, "We just asked them, 'Are you going to let the boss tell you where you can piss?'"

Why should we write long, complicated leaflets about how racism lowers white workers' wages when they can easily see that if it weren't for their privileged positions, they might be unemployed instead of the black workers? It is much truer to say that racism runs counter to their interests because it is the bosses' game—that by serving as instruments of white supremacy and accepting white-skin privileges, the white workers are lining up with the boss against the rest of the working class.

New Approach Needed

In the case of an unorganized shop: instead of trying to bring in a union with the "benefit" of straight seniority, why not try this approach:

> Listen, man, the boss has kept this place all white (or a variation: "has stuck the black workers in the dirty jobs") all these years to fool us into thinking we're getting something. We're no fools. We know we've got nothing but speedup and low wages. That's why we're talking union. Now I think if we really want to jam it up the boss, and if we really want to build something he can't break later on, then we should make it a demand that he hire fifty black workers right now. And just to make sure he can't get rid of them as soon as production drops, they should all get a five-year seniority bonus. What do you think of that—won't that make him howl?

I started this paper by referring to the Haymarket incident. Today, the great-grandchildren of the Haymarket strikers of 1886, the grandchildren of the steel strikers of 1919, and the children of the Republic steel strikers of 1937 are the people who throw rocks at civil rights marchers in Chicago.

It is time for a new generation of militant battles. Isn't it time for radicals to adopt a new approach?

8

Without a Science of Navigation, We Cannot Sail in Stormy Seas (Excerpts)

Throughout the 1960s, there were few groups as dynamic and core to the radical ferment of the period than Students for a Democratic Society; Ignatiev ended up a key figure in the organization, specifically as its members debated the future of both SDS but also the social movements that had been fighting for racial equality, an end to imperialist war, and solidarity with people fighting for self-determination. One of the leading groups of this period was the Weathermen, which this piece, published in 1969, subjects to a scathing critique. Ignatiev outlines the role of race in US class domination and demarcates it clearly from the view that white workers simply benefit from the color line. This is excerpted from a much longer piece that originally appeared in the collection "Debate within SDS. RYM II vs. Weatherman," published in 1969 by Radical Education Press.*

The significance of the SDS Convention held from June 18–22 in Chicago is that it represents the first time since the Civil War and

---

* Revolutionary Youth Movement (RYM II) was part of the Students for Democratic Society (SDS) and a rival of the Progressive Labor Party. In the late 1960s, when SDS fragmented, the RYM also split into two; RYM I became the Weathermen and RYM II (to which Ignatiev belonged) were Maoists and rejected the Weathermen's political line of armed struggle. The RYM II milieu became known as New Communist Movement, and many of its members joined the Sojourner Truth Organization in 1969.

Reconstruction period that a convention made up almost entirely of whites was held that focused on the national-colonial question as the pivot of struggle and unity. The fact that it was a convention of students rather than proletarians was an important factor in shaping its proceedings.

The convention took place against the general background of sharpening class struggles in the world, and especially the rise to preeminence of the struggles for national liberation of the oppressed peoples both outside and within the United States. It reflected the general rise in consciousness among white US radicals that the principal contradiction in the world today is that between US imperialism and the nations it oppresses.

This general rise in consciousness was expressed in the outstanding positive achievement of the convention: the expulsion of Progressive Labor Party (PLP) as a group of fiends and traitors to the worldwide struggles of the oppressed. An important role in bringing about the expulsion was played by representatives of the oppressed peoples themselves, specifically spokesmen for the Black Panther Party, the Young Lords Organization, and the Brown Berets. PLP represents a specific variant of bourgeois ideology, best characterized as social-chauvinism, that is, socialist in words and chauvinist in deeds—talk about international proletarian solidarity and a practical united front with US imperialism against the oppressed peoples.

The most pressing task for the movement in general, and SDS in particular, is the total isolation and defeat of PLP and the policies it represents. The question of the fight against PLP is not an internal one for SDS. It is a reflection of the fight against bourgeois ideology and politics, which goes on constantly among the people as the main work of proletarian revolutionaries. It would be the gravest error to make a separation between the fight against PLP within the movement and the fight against bourgeois ideology among the masses.

Either Bourgeois or Proletarian Ideology

Although PLP may temporarily be set back by advancing a more radical sounding form of bourgeois ideology, in the final analysis it can only be defeated on the basis of proletarian ideology and the practice derived from it. That is why it is necessary to examine the struggle between two lines which took place at the convention both before and after the expulsion of PLP.

In order to do this it is necessary to examine the paper "You Don't Need a Weatherman to Know Which Way the Wind Blows," published in the convention issue of *New Left Notes*. The document is especially important because it represents the thinking of the majority of the national leadership which emerged from the convention. All three national secretaries are signers of the paper; five of the eight members of the National Interim Committee (including two more signers) have been associated with its line. Therefore, every member of SDS should study it and should not allow its length to deter him from that task.

The first thing that must be noted is the title, which gave us pause when we first read it. On further reflection, it became clear that its meaning could be best brought out by counterposing it to Lenin's famous dictum: "Without a revolutionary theory, there can be no revolutionary movement." In spite of its title, however, it would be a serious underestimation to think that Weatherman does not present a political line. On the contrary, its writers are to be commended for setting forth in generally clear and consistent terms a definite political line. The question is: what class does that line serve?

While the principal contradiction of the present epoch is that between US imperialism and the nations it oppresses, the fundamental contradiction is, always has been, and always will be, as long as capitalism exists, that between socialized production and capitalistic appropriation, manifesting itself as a contradiction between the proletariat and the bourgeoisie.

The central question of political economy, to which Marx devoted his life to answering, is: how do the interests of the proletariat and the bourgeoisie stand in relation to each other? After a great deal of observation and participation, Marx summarized his findings, in *Wage-Labor and Capital*: "We see, therefore, that even if we remain within the relation of capital and wage labor, the interests of capital and the interests of wage labor are diametrically opposed."[1] From that discovery, Marx drew the conclusion: "Working men of all countries—unite!"

Now, one hundred years later, along comes Weatherman, with a "new" answer, which "improves" on Marx:

We are within the heartland of a world-wide monster, a country so rich from its world-wide plunder that even the crumbs doled out to the enslaved masses within its borders provide for material existence very much above the conditions of the masses of people of the world. The US empire, as a worldwide system, channels wealth, based upon the labor and resources of the rest of the world, into the United States. The relative affluence existing in the United States is directly dependent upon the labor and natural resources of the peoples of the Third World. All of the United Airlines Astrojets, all the Holiday Inns, all of Hertz's automobiles, your television set, car and wardrobe already belong, to a large degree, to the people of the world.[2]

In other words, the bourgeoisie and the proletariat have a joint interest in plundering the dependent nations. One could hardly ask for a more direct statement. But, argue the writers of Weatherman, capitalism has developed to a new stage since Marx's time and that new state, imperialism, has divided the world into oppressor and oppressed nations, and has in fact created a situation whereby the bourgeoisie and proletariat of the oppressor nation take part (to an unequal degree, to be sure) in the exploitation of the oppressed nations.

Yes, it is true that imperialism introduces new conditions. Lenin described these new conditions in the following manner, in *Imperialism, the Highest Stage of Capitalism*: Imperialism, which means the partition of the world, and the exploitation of other countries besides China, which means high monopoly profits for a handful of very rich countries, creates the economic possibility of corrupting the upper strata of the proletariat, and thereby fosters, gives form to, and strengthens opportunism.[3]

Or, further, from *Imperialism and the Split in Socialism*: "The bourgeoisie of a 'Great' imperialist power is economically able to bribe the upper strata of its workers, devoting one or two hundred million francs a year for this purpose, because its super-profits probably amount to a billion."[4]

Or again, from the same work: "while trusts, the financial oligarchy, high prices, etc., permit the bribing of small upper strata, they at the same time oppress, crush, ruin and torture the masses of the proletariat and the semi-proletariat more than ever."[5]

And so on. In fact, Lenin, who devoted so much attention to the connection between imperialism and the "aristocracy of labor," who showed conclusively that opportunism in the labor movement rested mainly on the corruption of the bribed upper strata, was always careful to specify that the bribe was shared by only a minority of the working class, even in the case of the English workers from 1848 to 1868, when Britain enjoyed the industrial and colonial monopoly of the whole world.

Lenin never denied that the majority of workers in a given trade or even a given country could, for a considerable time, fall under the influence of the corrupt minority. But he never conceded that they had any real stake in doing so.

> We cannot nor can anybody else calculate exactly what portion of the proletariat is following and will continue to follow the social-chauvinists and opportunists. This will be revealed by the struggle, it will be definitely decided only by the socialist revolution. But we know definitely that the "defenders of the father land" in the imperialist war represent only a minority.[6]

The writers of Weatherman themselves say that "the real interests of the masses of oppressed whites in this country lie with the Black Liberation struggle." But how do they define "real" interests?

As a whole, the long-range interests of the noncolonial sections of the working class lie with overthrowing imperialism, with supporting self-determination for the oppressed nations (including the black colony), with supporting and fighting for international socialism. However, virtually all of the white working class also has short-range privileges from imperialism, which are not false privileges but very real ones which give them an edge of vested interest and tie them to a certain extent to the imperialists, especially when the latter are in a relatively prosperous phase. When the imperialists are losing their empire, on the other hand, these short-range privileged interests are seen to be temporary (even though the privileges may be relatively greater over the faster-increasing immiseration of the oppressed peoples). The long-range interests of workers in siding with the oppressed peoples are seen more clearly in the light of imperialism's impending defeat. Within the whole working class, the balance of anti-imperialist class interests with white mother country short-term privilege varies greatly.

Thus they counterpose the short-range interests of the white workers to their long-range interests. But that is not the way Lenin put it! Lenin defined opportunism as the sacrifice of the short- and long-range interests of the entire working class to the temporary interests of a minority. There is all the difference in the world between the two formulations, as we shall see.

And this brings us to the matter of white supremacy and the white-skin privilege, of which Weatherman makes such a muddle. Now, it is true that, in regard to the upper crust of labor—foremen, some craftsmen, those who have been able to acquire enough property or stocks to be almost independent, many union officials, etc.—with regard to these sectors, white supremacy, and oppression of colonial peoples in general may serve their interests, although this is somewhat undercut by the developing crisis of imperialist policy.

How do matters stand with regard to the masses of whites? Weatherman includes them in the ranks of those whose interests are served by the white-skin privilege. And there we part company with them.

Whose Interests Are Served by White-Skin Privileges?

Are the real interests of the masses of white workers the same as or in conflict with those of black workers and other oppressed peoples? Should white workers side with the boss or with the black workers? Is the fight against white supremacy and the repudiation of the white-skin privilege in the real interests of white workers?

The answers to the above questions are decisive in determining the whole direction of strategy for white revolutionaries.

We were not the last to take note of the existence of white-skin privileges. In a paper, "The White Blindspot," which we wrote two years ago together with Ted Allen, we pointed out:

The US ruling class has made a deal with the misleaders of American labor, and through them with the masses of white workers. The terms of the deal, worked out over the three hundred year history of the development of capitalism in our country, are these: you white workers help us conquer the world and enslave the non-white majority of the earth's laboring force, and we will repay you with a monopoly of the skilled jobs, we will cushion you against the most severe shocks of the economic cycle, provide you with health and education facilities superior to those of the non-white population, grant you the freedom to spend your money and leisure time as you wish without social restrictions, enable you on occasion to promote one of your number out of the ranks of the laboring class, and in general confer on you the material and spiritual privileges befitting your white skin.[7]

The cutting edge of that pamphlet was directed at PLP, which denied and still denies the existence of any privileges accruing to whites in the United States. However, even in that context we were careful to state, and to buttress by examples, that "the ending of white supremacy does not pose the slightest peril to the real interests of the white workers; it definitely poses a peril to their fancied interests, their counterfeit interests, their white-skin privileges."

Let us look at the matter a little more closely, starting with three industries. In the auto industry, where white-skin privileges have been relatively less than perhaps any other, the workers for a fairly long period enjoyed the best conditions of any laborers in the US. However, after years of acceptance by the white workers of their own monopoly in the skilled trades, the workers face speed-up, falling real wages, plant relocations, and layoffs.

In the mining industry, where white-skin privileges took on a more hardened form—sole access to the mechanized jobs which were least susceptible to automation—the total number of workers has been cut to one-fourth of what it was, vast areas of West Virginia and Kentucky have been laid waste, medical facilities (once the pride of organized labor) are primitive, and "hillbilly heavens" have sprung up across northern cities.

In the southern textile industry, where the white-skin privilege was more highly developed to mean total exclusion of blacks from the mills, the workers live under conditions so degraded that in some areas they can only be described as barbaric.

Three industries, three degrees of white-skin privilege. The greater and more firmly established the privilege, the greater the misery. The pattern is not coincidence; in every case cited, the deterioration of the conditions of the workers, black and white, can be shown to be the result of the more or less conscious decision of the white workers to obtain, maintain, or expand their social and economic white-skin privileges, which required the renunciation of proletarian class solidarity.

And these examples are taken as separate industries, limited to "the (economic) relation of capital and wage labor." To take up the whole question of the political weakness of the US proletariat, the lack of a labor party, etc., would strengthen our argument!

In what sense, then, can white supremacy be said to be in the interests, either short or long-range, of the white workers? If the acceptance of white-skin privilege is in their interests, what would the white workers have to do to run counter to their interests?!

White supremacy is the real secret of the rule of the bourgeoisie and the hidden cause behind the failure of the labor movement in this country. White-skin privileges serve only the bourgeoisie, and precisely for that reason they will not let us escape them, but instead pursue us with them through every hour of our life, no matter where we go. They are poison bait. To suggest that the acceptance of white-skin privilege is in the interests of white workers is equivalent to suggesting that swallowing the worm with the hook in it is in the interests of the fish. To argue that repudiating these privileges is a "sacrifice" is to argue that the fish is making a sacrifice when it leaps from the water, flips its tail, shakes its head furiously in every direction, and throws the barbed offering.

Of course the class struggle involves sacrifices. Jose Marti said, "revolution is sacrifice and valor." And remember Marx's admiration for the heroic sacrifices of the Communards, who "stormed the heavens." The first group of white workers who take action against the white-skin privilege can expect to be visited by all the furies of a bourgeoisie being attacked at its most sensitive spot. These workers will be a Legion of John Browns, honored forever for the sacrifices they will surely have to make. But one thing they will not be sacrificing is their class interests, either short- or long-range. To argue otherwise is to make a mockery of proletarian morality, which is always consistent with the class interests of the proletariat.

One of two things: EITHER the struggle against white supremacy is in both the short- and long-range class interests of white workers, in which case they can be won to it; OR it is not in their short-range interests but is in their interests later on, in which case we will never get to "later on."

9

My Debt and Obligation to Ted Allen

Ignatiev reflects on the mentorship of Theodore Allen, a lifelong revolutionary and independent scholar, outlining Allen's influence on his own life and work, as well as their theoretical and methodological disagreements. This version appeared on Ignatiev's PM Press blog in 2014.

Theodore William Allen was born in 1919 to a middle-class family in Indiana. In 1929 the family moved to West Virginia, where Ted was, in his words, "proletarianized by the Great Depression." He attended college for a couple of days after high school but quit because he didn't believe college encouraged independent thought. He joined the Communist Party in the 1930s and spent three years as a coal miner in West Virginia, until he was forced to leave because of a back injury. After coming to New York in 1948, he taught classes in economics at the party's Jefferson School. He was also active in community, civil rights, trade union, and student organizing work. He worked in a factory, as a retail clerk, a mechanical design draftsman, an elevator operator, a junior high school math teacher, a mail handler, and as the "Homework Hotline" for the Brooklyn Public Library. He left the Communist Party in 1958 and joined the Provisional Organizing Committee to Reconstitute the Communist Party, but left it in 1962, breaking with "Marxism-Leninism" soon after. Ted spent much of his last forty years researching the role of white supremacy in US history, documenting and analyzing the development of the "white race" in the latter part of the seventeenth century. His research led to the two-volume *Invention of the White Race*. He died in Brooklyn in 1997.[1]

Ted was the first person to use the phrase "white-skin privilege." Unlike those in the "Undoing Racism" industry or those who have made a fetish of "privilege politics," Ted saw his studies and writing on the history and operation of the white-skin privilege system as a weapon in the class struggle. He insisted that the attachment of white workers to their race privileges was the chief cause of the failure of the working class in the United States to overturn capitalism and that the struggle against white supremacy, entailing for white workers the repudiation of the white-skin privilege, was the key to revolutionary strategy.

Ted introduced me to the notion of the white-skin privilege that has been a defining element in my political life for nearly half a century, and I owe him an immeasurable political debt. To acknowledge my debt does not require that I keep silent about our disagreements. On the contrary, it requires that I state them as forthrightly as possible.

Ted traced the origins of white supremacy to a conscious decision by the plantation bourgeoisie of the tobacco-growing regions of the Chesapeake Bay in response to the problem they faced, how to control the labor force on whom the production of surplus value depended. The role of "conscious decision" was not peripheral but central to him.[2]

At first I accepted his explanation of the origin, but the more I thought about it, the less satisfying it became. While I do not doubt that elements in the dominant classes (and not only the dominant classes) conspire, I do not believe that great historic turns can be attributed to conspiracies. I was led initially to question Ted on this point by thinking about the origins of reformism in the labor movement, particularly during the rise of the Congress of Industrial Organizations (CIO). Like the seventeenth century, the period that produced the CIO also presented revolutionary possibilities, possibilities that were contained by the form of labor organization that emerged dominant. No doubt decisions made by capitalist institutions, especially the Roosevelt administration and its left-wing auxiliaries, played a role in pushing the labor movement along a certain path and not another, and that the path taken limited the possible outcomes, but the triumph of reformism cannot be blamed on bourgeois machinations; one must look instead to its roots *within* the working-class movement. Similarly with the origins of the white-skin privilege, which certainly functioned, as Ted said it did, to suppress the revolutionary possibilities in the period in which it arose and subsequently.

The working-class movement reflects the influence of capital; but that is not to say that particular tendencies within it are the result of intervention by individual capitalists or groups of capitalists. The working-class movement contains various tendencies, each reflecting the situation of the worker in the capitalist system: some accept the permanency of capital and seek an advantage in a competitive society; others embody the possibility of a society free of the capital relation and act on the principle of universal solidarity. Which of these tendencies prevails in any situation

> arises from conflicts between many individual wills, of which each in turn has been made what it is by a host of particular conditions of life. Thus there are innumerable intersecting forces, an infinite series of parallelograms of forces which give rise to one resultant—the historical event. This may again itself be viewed as the product of a power which works as a whole *unconsciously* and without volition.[3]

Ted's tracing the origins of white supremacy to a conscious decision presents an additional problem: the complete absence of any record of such a decision. Not only is there no record of such a decision, there are no records of debates among those in authority at the time or pamphlets arguing in favor of extending privileges to European settlers in order to cement their loyalty to the colonial regime. Ted acknowledged the lack but attributed it to the destruction of the records and insisted it does not matter.[4]

Ted was moved to adopt the idea of a conscious decision by his desire to combat the view, promoted by Carl Degler, Winthrop Jordan, and others, that there was something in human nature, or at least in the English psyche, that explains the rise of white supremacy. Ted felt, correctly, that Jordan's explanation, which blames race prejudice and oppression on inherent "attitudes," absolves the ruling class of responsibility and, no less important, makes it impossible to overturn these evils. Unfortunately, his explanation is based on the same fallacy as the theory of intelligent design in biology, which holds that the suitability of a feature to its function demonstrates that it was consciously designed to fulfill that function. As Darwin discovered the law of development of organic nature (a law so simple and in such conformance with the evidence that Thomas Henry Huxley, on hearing of it, exclaimed, "How stupid of me not to have thought of that!"—in modern parlance, face-palm!), Marx discovered the law of development of human society, historical materialism, which he formulated as follows:

> In the social production of their life, men enter into definite relations that are indispensable and independent of their will, relations of production which correspond to a definite stage of development of their material productive forces. The sum total of these relations of production constitutes the economic structure of society, the real foundation, on which rises a legal and political superstructure and to which correspond definite forms of social consciousness. The mode of production of material life conditions the social, political and intellectual life process in general. It is not the consciousness of men that determines their being, but, on the contrary, their social being that determines their consciousness.[5]

Historical materialism explains the origin of white supremacy in the plantation colonies of mainland North America in the seventeenth century without resort to conspiracy theories or any other variant of "conscious decision," and also without resort to theories of the inherent character of the English soul.

Why did slavery arise in the Chesapeake Bay, the West Indies, and the northeast coast of South America? There is no mystery: under certain conditions, slavery is the cheapest, and therefore to possessors the most advantageous, method of exploitation; it has existed widely throughout human history, going back to the ancient world, without regard to color.

Why were persons from Africa enslaved? Because they could be. The structure of West African societies produced a surplus population that could not be exploited at home and who were systematically sold by a ruling elite, for whom solidarity of color had no meaning, to others who had use for their labor-power.

So far I think Ted would agree.

Why were persons from Africa the only ones who became in general the victims of lifetime hereditary slavery? Here is where it gets difficult. Barbara Jeanne Fields provides a good deal of the explanation:

Ultimately, the only check upon oppression is the strength and effectiveness of resistance to it.

Resistance does not refer only to the fight that individuals, or collections of them, put up at any given time against those trying to impose on them. It refers also to the historical outcome of the struggle that has gone before, perhaps long enough to have been hallowed by custom or formalized in law ... The freedoms of lower-class Englishmen, and the somewhat lesser freedoms of lower-class Englishwomen ... emerged from centuries of day-to-day contest, overt and covert, armed and unarmed, peaceable and forcible, over where the limits lay ... Each new increment of freedom that the lower classes regarded as their due represented the provisional outcome of the last round in a continuing boxing-match and established the fight weights of the contenders in the next round.

In the round that took place in early colonial Virginia, servants lost many of the concessions to their dignity, well-being and comfort that their counterparts had won in England. But not all. To have degraded the servants *en masse* would have driven the continuing struggle up several notches, a dangerous undertaking considering that the servants were well-armed, that they outnumbered their masters, and that the Indians could easily take advantage of the inevitably resulting warfare among the enemy. Moreover, the enslavement of already arrived immigrants, once news of it reached England, would have threatened the sources of future immigration. Even the greediest and most short-sighted profiteer could foresee disaster in any such policy ...

Some of these same considerations argued against employing African-descended slaves for life on a large scale; others did not. Needless to say, adverse publicity did not threaten the sources of forced migration as it did those of voluntary migration. Much more important: Africans and Afro-West Indians had not taken part in the long history of negotiation and contest in which the English lower classes had worked out the relationship between themselves and their superior. To put it another way: when English servants entered the ring in Virginia, they did not enter alone. Instead they entered in company with the generations who had preceded them in the struggle; and the outcome of those earlier struggles established the terms and conditions of the latest one. But Africans and Afro-West Indians did enter the ring alone. Their forebears had struggled in a different arena, which had no bearing on this one . . .

Africans and Afro-West Indians were thus available for perpetual slavery in a way that English servants were not. Indeed, Virginians could purchase them ready-enslaved and pre-seasoned.[6]

Although Fields's explanation as quoted above accounts for some things, it does not account for racial oppression (which Ted defined as "the reduction of all members of the oppressed group to one undifferentiated social status, beneath that of any member of the oppressor group"[7]). But she isn't finished:

Race as a coherent ideology did not spring into being simultaneously with slavery, but took even more time than slavery did to become systematized . . . People are more readily perceived as inferior by nature when they are already seen as oppressed. Africans and their descendants might be, to the eyes of the English, heathen in religion, outlandish in nationality, and weird in appearance. But that did not add up to an ideology of racial inferiority until a further historical ingredient got stirred into the mixture: the incorporation of Africans and their descendants into a polity in society in which they lacked rights that others not only took for granted, but claimed as a matter of natural law.[8]

Ted made much of the presence in colonial Virginia of a number of persons of African descent who owned property and exercised civil and legal rights on a par with Englishmen of their rank. It is understandable, he maintained, that slaves would have low status, and their status implied nothing racial even if they were drawn entirely from one group, so long as non-slave members of the group enjoyed a status equal to other non-slaves. Racial oppression arose, according to Ted, with the debasement of free persons of color, and could only have come about as the result of conscious decision from above to "invent" a "white race." It is true that the persons on whom Ted rested his argument existed. But they were always few in number and, more important, existed only in the early stages of the plantation system, before the great increase in the importation of laborers of African descent, which took place after 1660. As the number of Africans imported to be slaves went up, the proportion of free persons among Africans fell, the slave status came to be associated with African descent, the black skin became the badge of slavery, and the "free Negro" came to be seen as an anomaly. In 1736 Virginia Governor William Gooch wrote to the British Colonial Office, which had demanded an explanation of a Virginia law denying suffrage to free Negroes (a measure contrary to British and Virginia law and practice). Gooch wrote:

> [The] Assembly thought it necessary, not only to make the Meeting of Slaves very penal, but to fix a perpetual Brand upon free Negroes and Mulattos by excluding them from the great Privilege of a Freeman, well knowing that they always did, and ever will, adhere to and favour the Slaves.[9]

It is the only document Ted offered in support of his view of the role of conscious decision, and it does not prove what he claimed it did. Gooch justifies his decision not by the need to elevate the status of propertyless English but as a response to the sympathy shown by free persons of color to the slaves. But that sympathy would not have existed had their status been determined purely by their class position. It could only have arisen as a *consequence* of the racial oppression they *already* felt, and therefore could not have been a *cause* of it.

It will be useful to compare developments in mainland and West Indian colonies.

Initially most mainland laborers were English, serving under temporary indenture, and lines between slavery and "freedom" were indistinct and of little importance. The natural result was a great deal of interaction and solidarity among the laborers. But as the planters imported more slaves—a decision motivated purely by monetary considerations, having nothing to do with "racial" preference—and codified slavery as a distinct form, the association of the black skin with slavery came to loom large, and by reflex all those not of African descent, and therefore not slaves, came to constitute a group or, in our terms, a "race," on whose loyalty depended the stability of the social order. As for conscious decision on the part of the Chesapeake Bay planters to invent whiteness, I can do no better than to quote the French mathematician Pierre-Simon Laplace, who, when Napoleon commented that he did not see God anywhere in Laplace's work, replied "*je n'avais besoin de cet hypothese.*"[10]

The association between skin color and social status developed differently in the West Indies. There the need to control vast numbers of slaves combined with the small size of the English population compelled the planters to enroll in the militia persons of African descent and assign them a suitable social standing, thereby modifying the relation between color and status. The "mulatto" of the West Indies was the counterpart of the "poor white" of the mainland. It was in the West Indies, and not on the mainland, that conscious decision was crucial, and abundant records survive of the debates there. Discussing that process Ted wrote, "Down to the last moment, and past it, the sugar plantocracy resisted any attempt to undermine that [white] consciousness."[11]

Finally, I hope it goes without saying—but I fear it will not—that nothing I have said here is meant to detract from my appreciation for the contributions Ted made to the class struggle.

II

Black Worker/White Worker: The Sojourner Truth Organization

10

Black Worker, White Worker

Drawing on W. E. B. Du Bois's Black Reconstruction in America, *a central text in Ignatiev's political development, this classic study explores the contradictory consciousness of white workers and what it means for the development of revolutionary strategy. Ignatiev argues that white skin privilege is not in the interests of white workers and is a barrier to working-class solidarity. Ignatiev first delivered this text as a speech in Portland, Oregon in 1972, and it was first published in* Radical America *(July/August 1974).*

In one department of a giant steel mill in northwest Indiana, a foreman assigned a white worker to the job of operating a crane. The black workers in the department felt that on the basis of seniority and job experience, one of them should have been given the job, which represented a promotion from the labor gang. They spent a few hours in the morning talking among themselves and agreed that they had a legitimate beef. Then they went and talked to the white workers in the department and got their support. After lunch the other crane operators mounted their cranes and proceeded to block in the crane of the newly promoted worker—one crane on each side of his—and run at the slowest possible speed, thus stopping work in the department. By the end of the day the foreman had gotten the message. He took the white worker off the crane and replaced him with a black worker, and the cranes began to move again.

A few weeks after the above incident, several of the white workers who had joined the black operators in the slowdown took part in meetings in Glen Park, a virtually all-white section of Gary, with the aim of seceding from the city in order to escape from the administration of the black mayor, Richard Hatcher. While the secessionists demanded, in their words, "the power to make the decisions which affect their lives," it was clear that the effort was racially inspired.

At a large farm equipment manufacturing plant in Chicago, a black worker was being tried out for a repair job on an assembly line. The foreman had been harassing the man, trying to disqualify him during his three-day trial period. After two days of this, the majority of the workers on the line, black and white, walked off their jobs, demanding that the man be accepted for the job. The company backed down and work resumed.

Later on, some of the same white workers took part in racist demonstrations at a Chicago high school. The demonstrations were called against "overcrowding" in an attempt to keep out several hundred black students who had been transferred to the school as a result of redistricting.

Civil War

The foregoing anecdotes indicate some of the complexities and contradictions operating within the lives and within the minds of the white workers in this country: on the one hand, displays of democratic cooperation and fraternal relations with black workers, and, on the other hand, examples of backwardness and selfishness, which are unbecoming to members of a social class which hopes to reconstruct society in its image. What is taking place is a "civil war" in the mind of the white worker. In the community, on the job, in every sphere of life, he is being faced with a choice between two ways of looking at the world, two ways of leading his life. One way represents solidarity with the black worker and the progressive forces of society. The other way represents alliance with the forces of exploitation and repression.

I'd like to speak a bit about this "civil war" and examine some of what it means for the development of revolutionary strategy.

In order to understand the contradictory, often bewildering

behavior of people, especially white people, in this country, we must take up two questions. The first question is: on what does capitalist rule depend?

There are groups, radical groups, which seem to operate on the premise that capitalist rule depends on the monopoly of guns and tanks held by the employing class and its ability to use them whenever it pleases against the exploited majority. This view explains why some groups put such great efforts into building alliances with all sorts of liberals to preserve constitutional forms of government. They hope, through these alliances, to limit the ability of the ruling class to use force against the people.

I do not share this view of the secret of capitalist rule. I do not agree that capitalist power rests, at present, primarily on guns and tanks. It rests on the support of the majority of people. This support is usually passive, sometimes active, but nevertheless effective.

Competition among the Wage Earners

I contend that the key element in the popular acceptance of capitalist rule is the ideology and institution of white supremacy, which provides the illusion of common interests between the exploited white masses and the white ruling class.

Karl Marx wrote that wage slavery rests exclusively on competition among the wage earners. He meant that the existence of competition among the working class is responsible for the continued rule of the employing class and the inability of the working people to overthrow it and establish their rule.

Why do people compete? They compete in order to get ahead. The fact must be admitted that, from a certain point of view, it is possible to "get ahead" in this society. Years and years of unquestioning loyalty and devotion to the company will, in a certain percentage of cases, result in advancement for the employee—advancement to a position of lead man, foreman, soft job, high bonus job, etc. Working people have various uncomplimentary terms to describe this sort of behavior. Yet large numbers of them live their lives in this way, and for a certain portion of these, it "pays off."

Because of the peculiar development of America and the nature of capitalist policy in this country, there is a special element added to the general competition which exists among all workers. That special element is color, which throws the competition on a special basis, that raises color to a special place in the competition among workers.

All workers compete; that is a law of capitalism. But black and white workers compete with a special advantage on the side of the white. That is a result of the peculiar development of America and is not inherent in the objective social laws of the capitalist system.

In the same way that some individual workers gain advancement on the job by currying favor with the employer, white workers as a group have won a favored position for themselves by siding with the employing class against the non-white people. This favored status takes various forms, including the monopoly of skilled jobs and higher education, better housing at lower cost than that available to nonwhites, less police harassment, a cushion against the most severe effects of unemployment, better health conditions, and certain social advantages.

We're trying to explain why people act as they do and particularly why white workers act as they do. White working people aren't stupid. They don't act in a racist fashion simply out of blind prejudice. There are much more substantial causes—the system of white-skin privileges—which lead them to behave in a selfish, exclusionary manner.

A black steelworker told me that once, when he was working as a helper on the unloading docks, he decided to bid on an operator's job that was open. All the operators were white. He had worked with them before in his capacity as helper. They had been friends, had eaten together and chatted about all the things that workers talk about. When he bid on the operator's job, it became the task of the other operators to break him in. He was assigned to the job, sent to work with them on the equipment, and given thirty days to learn the job. It quickly became clear to him that the other workers had no intention of permitting him to get that job. They operated the equipment in such a way as to prevent him from learning how. Workers are very skilled at that sort of thing.

After two weeks, one of the white workers came to him and said, "Listen, I know what's going on here. You work with me on Monday and I'll break you in." The person who told me this story agreed—at least there was one decent white worker in the bunch. Friday afternoon came around, and the white worker approached him. With some embarrass-ment, he admitted that he had to back down from his offer. "It's bad enough when all the guys call me a n— lover, but when my own wife quits talking to me, well I just can't go through with it."

The man who told me that story never succeeded in getting that job.

What made those white workers act in the way they did? They were willing to be "friends" at the workplace, but only on the condition that the black worker stay in "his place." They didn't want him to "presume" to a position of social equality if and when they met on "the outside." And they didn't want him to presume to share in the better jobs at the workplace. Those white workers understood that keeping themselves in "their place" in the company scheme of things depended upon helping to keep the black worker in "his place."

They had observed that whenever the black people force the ruling class, in whole or in part, to make concessions to racial equality, the ruling class strikes back to make it an equality on a worse level of conditions than those enjoyed by the whites before the concessions. The white workers are thus conditioned to believe that every step toward racial equality necessarily means a worsening of their own conditions. Their bonus is cut. Production rates go up. Their insurance is harder to get and more expensive. Their garbage is collected less often. Their children's schools deteriorate.

This is how the white-skin privilege system works. If a small number of white workers do manage to see through the smoke screen and join in the fight together with the black workers, the ruling class responds with bribes, cajolery, threats, violence, and pressure multiplied a thousand-fold to drive the thinking whites back into the "club" of white suprema-cists. And the purpose of all this is to prevent the white workers from learning the black example, to prevent them from learning that if blacks can force concessions from the boss through struggle, how much more could be accomplished if the white workers would get into the struggle against the boss instead of against the black workers.

A common approach to the problem posed above is that of the white radical who goes into a shop which has a typical pattern of discrimina-tion against black workers. Instead of directly taking up that issue and attempting to build a struggle for equality, he looks for some issue, like speedup, which affects all workers to one degree or another. He aims to develop a struggle around this issue, to involve all the workers in the struggle. He hopes that in the course of the struggle the white workers, through contact with blacks, will lose their attitudes of racial superiority. This is the approach to the problem of unifying the working class, which prevails within the radical movement today.

I don't think it works. History shows it doesn't work. The result of this sort of false unity always leaves the black worker on the bottom. It always seems to be the demand for racial equality, the last one on the list, that is sacrificed in order to reach a settlement and celebrate the "great victory" of the struggle.

Present-day unions are, to a considerable extent, the end product of this sort of approach. It is black and white together on the picket line, and after the strike is over the white workers return to the skilled trades, the machining departments, and the cleaner assembly areas, and the black workers return to the labor gang and the open hearth. Every "victory" of this kind feeds the poison of racism and pushes further off the real unity of the working class, which must be established if significant progress is to be made.

There is no way to overcome the national and racial divisions within the working class except by directly confronting them. The problem of white supremacy must be fought out openly within the working class.

Hug the Chains of an Actual Wretchedness

Over eighty years ago, Tom Watson, the Georgia agrarian protest leader, wrote the following words, full of profound meaning:

> You might beseech a Southern white tenant to listen to you upon questions of finance, taxation and transportation; you might demonstrate with mathematical precision that herein lay his way out of poverty into comfort; you might have him "almost persuaded" to the truth, but if the merchant who furnished his farm supplies (at tremendous usury) or the town politician (who never spoke to him except at election times) came along and cried "Negro rule," the entire fabric of reason and common sense which you had patiently constructed would fall, and the poor tenant would joyously hug the chains of an actual wretchedness rather than do any experimenting on a question of mere sentiment . . . the argument against the independent movement in the South may be boiled down into one word—nigger.[1]

These words are as true today as when they were first written. They apply with equal force to workers as well as to farmers, and the truth of them is not limited to the South. Ted Allen has put it that white supremacy is the keystone of ruling class power, and the white-skin privilege is the mortar that holds it in place.

There are two points in what I have been saying so far that are distinctive and that I wish to emphasize.

The first point is that, for revolutionary strategists, the key problem is not the racism of the employing class, but the racism of the white worker. (After all, the boss's racism is natural to him because it serves his class interests.) It is the support by white workers for the employers' racial policies, which represents the chief obstacle to all social progress in this country, including revolution.

The second point is that this support has its basis in real conditions of life. It is not simply a matter of ignorance and prejudice, to be overcome by exhortation and appeals to reason.

The second question I wish to take up is: where does socialism come from?

To Impose Order on Chaos

In their daily activities, working people express the drive to reorganize society so that they become the masters of production instead of the servants of production—the essential meaning of socialism. I would like to cite a few examples of this striving of workers.

One of the characteristics of steel production is that it must be continuous: to stop the furnaces is a costly and time-consuming operation. (I heard a story that once in Colorado around 1912 the Industrial Workers of the World pulled a strike at a steel mill and, instead of banking the furnaces, simply walked off the job. According to the story, that furnace stands today, over sixty years later, with a solid block of iron inside of it, unusable.)

Steel is a continuous operation and has to be maintained that way. What the steel companies do is operate a system of three shifts, and a system of relief on the job: a worker can't leave the job until his relief shows up. The workers take advantage of this in various ways. There is one mill I know of in which the workers have organized a rotation system among themselves, in which they take turns calling off, allowing the person they are scheduled to relieve eight hours overtime in their place. There are a couple of dozen people involved in this, they have it organized in turns, and it would probably take a professional mathematician several weeks of studying attendance records to figure out their system. It allows each worker to get an extra day off every few weeks, and then receive, in his turn, an enlarged paycheck—without working a single hour more than normal. You see, the company posts its schedule of work, and then the workers proceed to violate it and impose their own.

Of course they don't have everything their own way. When the absenteeism gets too severe, the company cracks down and threatens reprisals, and the workers are forced to slack off for a while. Then, when the heat is off, they go back to their own schedule.

Another example. One of the characteristics of the capitalist scheme of production is the division between maintenance and production workers. This is universal under capitalism. There is one category of workers who perform the same operation minute after minute for their entire lives, and another category of workers who go around fixing machines when they break down. In the United States this division has been adapted to serve the system of white-skin privileges. White workers are generally given preference for the jobs in maintenance, which are usually easier, cleaner, more interesting, and higher paying than production jobs.

The workers respond to this division in ways that at first sight seem bewildering. When they get angry at the company, production workers will not perform the simplest and most routine maintenance task. They will stop an entire operation waiting for a maintenance worker to change a fuse.

A black worker in maintenance, one of the few, told this story. He was called to repair a piece of equipment that had failed. Unable to locate the trouble, he called his foreman to help. The foreman was also unable to find the trouble, and so he called a higher-up. They stood around for a while scratching their heads and then decided to go back to the office and study the schematic drawings of the equipment to see if they would reveal the trouble. After the foremen had left, the black maintenance worker asked the production worker, who was also black, what was wrong with the machine. He replied that he had thrown the wrong switch by mistake and blown some obscure control device. He pointed it out, after swearing the maintenance worker to secrecy, and it was fixed in three minutes. His attitude was—no one had asked him what was wrong, and if they treated him like a dope he would act like a dope.

This is one side of the workers' response to the arbitrary maintenance–production split. On the other hand, they make efforts to overcome the barriers in their way, to master the entire process of production in order to express their full human capacities. Production workers do everything they can to learn about their equipment. On some occasions they go to great lengths to make repairs themselves without calling the maintenance department.

Maintenance workers also show this striving to break down artificial barriers. Many times they voluntarily grab a shovel or perform other tasks which are outside of their job requirements. But if the foreman orders them to do it, they will curse him and refuse.

These efforts by both production and maintenance workers to break down the barriers erected between them represent the striving of working people to master the equipment which makes the things they need, to gain control over the work process so that labor itself becomes a source of satisfaction to them.

There are many other examples that indicate the efforts of workers to impose their order on the chaos of capitalist production. If we want to know what socialism in the United States will look like, we should carefully study the activities of the working people today, because the ingredients of the socialist society appear right now in embryonic, subordinated ways.

The Ultimate Exploited

Now I must tie together the two lines of argument I have been pursuing so far and pose the question—where does the black struggle fit into all this? Please note: by black struggle I mean the autonomous black movement. I do not mean any particular organization, although a number of organizations are part of it. I am referring to the tendency on the part of large numbers of black people, especially workers, to find ways of acting together independent of white control and white approval and to decide their course of action based simply on what they feel is good for black people, not what serves some so-called larger movement.

The elements of such an autonomous black movement exist. They are repressed and subordinated, just as the autonomous efforts of workers generally are repressed. The conscious and determined efforts of the white ruling class to flood the black community with drugs are one indication of the serious threat the black movement poses to official society.

In spite of all the efforts of the ruling class to suppress it, the black movement exists. How does it fit into the general movement of all the oppressed to revolutionize society? I wish to make three points.

First of all, the black workers are the ultimate exploited in this country. They have no possibility of rising as a group to oppress anyone else. In spite of what many whites think about such subjects as welfare, black people receive no favors as a group from the capitalist class.

In the second place, the daily activities of the black people, especially the black workers, are the best existing model for the aspirations of the workers generally as a distinct class of people. Other groups in society, when they act collectively on their own, usually represent partial and occasionally even reactionary interests. The activities of the black workers are the most advanced outpost of the new society we seek to establish.

The Challenge to White Workers

In the third place, the autonomous movement of black people poses a constant challenge to white workers to (in the words of C. L. R. James) "take the steps which will enable the working people to fulfill their historic destiny of building a society free of the domination of one class or one race over another."

The black movement poses a challenge, not merely to white workers in general, but to those white intellectuals, workers or not, who regard themselves as in some sense radical or revolutionary. This is a challenge which, in the past, they have generally not lived up to. This challenge is not something limited to history either; it continually comes up, in new ways as well as old ones. Let me offer a few examples.

The system of seniority was originally fought for by the unions as a defense against individual favoritism and arbitrary discipline by the boss. Through a fairly involved process, seniority has been adapted to serve the needs of white supremacy. The boss decided whom to hire first, and the seniority system placed the union label on the practice of relegating blacks to the status of "last hired, first fired." As black workers press forward with their demands for full equality in all spheres of life, they increasingly come into conflict with the seniority system and other devices which uphold white supremacy, such as certain types of tests, and so forth. The white workers often react defensively. In many cases they insist that their resistance is not due to any prejudice against black people but is merely an objection to bypassing what has become the regular procedure for advancement. On more than one occasion, black workers have forced the employer to open a new job area to them, only to run up against the rigid opposition of white workers.

White revolutionaries must understand, and help the masses of white workers to understand, that the interests of the entire working class can only be served by standing firmly with the black workers in such cases.

Or consider the dispute over jobs in the construction trades, which reached a peak several years ago in a number of cities and is still going on in some places. In Chicago it took the form of, on one side, a community coalition led by Reverend C. T. Vivian, a number of elements around Southern Christian Leadership Conference and Operation PUSH and various diverse forces from among the black community and youth, along with, apparently, some financial backing from the Ford Foundation and the Chicago Northwestern Railway.* The aim of the struggle was to gain entrance for blacks into the construction trades. The means used was to surround various ongoing construction sites with mass picketing in order to stop work on them until black workers were admitted in proportion to their numbers in the city. On the other side was a united front of the construction unions and contractors. Of course, their defense was that they do not practice racial discrimination; black workers simply had not applied for or passed the tests for admittance.

What is the position of radicals to be in a case like this? There have been arguments that the Ford Foundation and other such forces are

---

* The Southern Christian Leadership Conference was founded by Martin Luther King Jr. and other major civil rights figures following the victory of the Montgomery bus boycott. Operation PUSH (People United to Serve Humanity) was founded as an affiliate of the SCLC and advocated black self-help, civil rights, and social justice.

using the black movement to weaken the construction unions and drive down the cost of labor. That argument is not without validity; it is difficult to believe that the Ford Foundation and the Chicago Northwestern Railway are unselfishly interested in the cause of black workers.

Some radical groups, from a lofty position of supposed objectivity, took it upon themselves to advise the black coalition that instead of directing their struggle against the admittedly unfair assignment of jobs, they should recognize the fact that there was a shortage of jobs in construction and should join with the unions to expand the number of jobs, which would benefit black as well as white and avoid the danger of "dividing the working class" as the present struggle was allegedly doing. This, of course, was merely a radical-sounding version of the argument given by the construction unions and contractors themselves, who would welcome any support from any quarter which offered to expand the industry.

The response of the black masses to this argument was to press forward the struggle to open those jobs up or shut them down. Their actions showed their confidence that it was they who were using the Ford Foundation and not the other way around and that as for the problems of the construction industry, these could not be of concern to them until they became part of it.

Some listeners may sense the justice in what I have been arguing and at the same time question its practicability. Wherein lies the basis for establishing solidarity among the working class? Is it possible to expect white workers to repudiate privileges which are real in the interests of something so abstract as justice?

Poison Bait

The answer is that the system of white-skin privileges, while it is undeniably real, is not in the interests of white workers as part of a class which aims at transforming society to its roots. The acceptance of a favored status by white workers binds them to wage slavery, makes them subordinate to the capitalist class. The repudiation, that is, the active rejection, through struggle, of this favored status is the precondition for the participation by white workers in the struggle of workers as a distinct social class. A metaphor which has been used in the past, and which I still find appropriate, is that white-skin privileges are poison bait, a worm with a hook in it. To be willing to leap from the water to exert the most determined and violent efforts to throw off the hook and the worm is the only way to avoid landing on the dinner table.

Let me offer a historical parallel. Back in the 1930s when people were organizing the Congress of Industrial Organizations (CIO), one of the problems they had to face was that many workers in the plants had worked out a means of survival which consisted of gaining advancement for themselves in return for favors for the boss. Old timers still talk about how, back in the days before the union, if you wanted a promotion or even wanted to keep your job in the event of a layoff, you had to mow the boss's lawn or wash his car or give him a bottle of whiskey at Christmas. In order to bring a union into those plants, that sort of activity had to be defeated. It was undeniably true that those who washed the foreman's car were the last workers laid off. On what basis was it possible to appeal to the workers to renounce this sort of behavior which they felt was necessary to their survival? The basis of the appeal was that it was precisely that sort of behavior which bound them and subordinated them to the company, and that the interests of solidarity of the entire work force demanded the repudiation of such individual arrangements.

The appeal fell on deaf ears until it began to seem that there was a real possibility of making some basic changes in those plants. Until the CIO was present as a real force, until the momentum built up, until people began to feel that there was another way to live besides mowing the boss's lawn, they were not willing to repudiate the old way.

Today, as a result of the CIO, in vast areas of American industry, any worker who was suspected of doing the sorts of favors for the foreman that were once taken for granted would be ostracized and treated with cold contempt by his fellow workers. (Some people may argue that the previous statement is an exaggeration and that the spirit of togetherness and combativity has deteriorated over the years. To the extent that they are right, it should be noted that this deterioration is in large part due to the habit of subservience encouraged by the general acceptance by white workers of racial privileges.)

The time will come when the masses of white workers in our country will regard with disdain those among them who seek or defend racial privileges, in the same way they now have only contempt for someone who would wash the foreman's car in return for preferential treatment.

A Powerful Magnet

Today the black movement represents an alternative to the dominant mode of life in our country, in the same way the CIO represented an alternative to the old way of life in the factory. The relations which black people, especially black workers, have established among themselves, and the culture which has arisen out of their struggle, represent a model for a new society. The black movement exercises a powerful attraction on all those who come into contact with it.

Consider the matter of the position of women and relations between the sexes. Black women, as a result of their struggle for freedom as black people, have achieved a great sense of their independence, not merely from one man but from men in general. This has forced black men to accept a degree of independence for women that is rare in the rest of the population. Anyone who has observed the changes undergone by white, Latin, or Asian women once they go to work and come into contact with black women can see the extent to which the old way of women's unquestioned subservience to man has been undermined. The men may resent this process, but it is irreversible.

The rise in general working-class militancy, observed by everyone in the last few years, is directly traceable to the influence of black workers, who are generally recognized by all, including white workers, as the most militant and combative group of workers when it comes to taking on the company. The black workers are drawing on the experience they have gained in their struggle for national freedom and are beginning to transmit the lessons of that struggle to the white workers with whom they come in contact.

The same thing is true also for the insurgent movement within the military, where the GI resistance, led by black GIs, reached such proportions that it forced major changes in official government policy.

This is true also for the insurgent movement within the prisons, where the resistance and courage of black prisoners has pulled whites into the struggle for decent conditions and human dignity.

For decades, politics, to white workers, has been a dirty word. It has meant nothing more than the right to choose every four years which gang of thieves is going to loot the public treasury for the next four. Beginning in 1955 with the Montgomery bus boycott, when an entire city organized its own system of transportation as well as of public discussion and decision-making through the direct participation of thousands of people, the black movement has created a new concept of citizenship and community. Continuing through the sit-ins, freedom rides, mass marches, and urban rebellions, the black movement has given new meaning to politics and helped the American people in general to rediscover their tradition of self-organization and revolt.

Many examples of this phenomenon could be cited from the only community in this country whose members greet each other as brother and sister. But the point is made: in spite of all the obstacles placed in its way, the black movement, expressed in the patterns of life arising from struggle, represents a powerful magnetic pole to vast numbers of workers looking for a way out of the mess which is modern life.

Recall, if you will, the anecdote with which I opened this talk: the case of the white workers acting in solidarity with the black crane operators. Consider the position of the white workers in that case. They are under conflicting pressures. On the one hand, they see a group of workers preparing to strike a blow at the company and, like all workers everywhere, they want to deal themselves in, to hit back at the enemy which is oppressing them. On the other hand, to join with the black workers in such a situation means turning against habit, against tradition, against their own status as racially privileged workers.

They are faced with a choice, between their identity and interests as whites and their identity and interests as workers. What was it that made that particular group of workers in that situation decide, in the words of one activist, to be "more worker than white"?

Their actions can only be explained by the fact that, whether or not they express it in words, the black movement represented for them an alternative way of life, a way that was better and more attractive than the usual passive, subordinated life they were accustomed to. Anyone who has ever taken part in collective struggle knows that, regardless of how they may have acted afterward, the experience left a lasting impression on them.

What about the tasks of revolutionaries, and in particular white revolutionaries, in regard to this vital task of unifying the working class around its class interests?

Things have changed in the last twenty years. It is no longer possible for any group which claims to be revolutionary to openly oppose the black movement. Not if it hopes to have any following. There are one or two groups in the country that do, but nobody pays any attention to them. The point today is to define the relation between the black movement and the general class struggle. And that is where the differences come out.

Everybody in the movement is opposed to racism, everybody chants the litany that racism is the greatest barrier to class unity. Every group puts out propaganda against racism and sincerely strives to win the workers to the struggle against it.

But what about those cases where the struggle of black workers and black people against racial discrimination appears to conflict with the desire to unify the largest possible number of workers behind what are called "general class demands"? For example, as sometimes happens, when the aggressiveness of black workers in pursuing their fight for equality tends to alienate white workers who might be willing to join with them in common efforts to achieve some reform of immediate and direct benefit to both groups? Then the trouble begins. And we must admit that some left-wing groups, especially those dominated by whites, are all too willing to set aside the special demands of the black struggle.

A Bad Choice

A recent example of this might serve to clarify the difference between the two approaches. At a large electrical appliance manufacturing plant in Chicago, one of the radical groups, the Revolutionary Union, sent a few people in. The radicals began putting out a plant newsletter which raised the issues of speedup, safety, low wages—all the various grievances of the workers—and also carried on a fairly aggressive campaign against racial discrimination, against the exclusion of black workers from the better departments, etc.

The group managed to build up considerable support, most of it among black workers, which wasn't surprising since black workers made up almost half the work force and were most victimized by the oppressive conditions the group was agitating against.

After some time had passed, the strategists in the group who, it is safe to surmise, were the white radicals who had initiated it along with one or two newly radicalized workers from the plant, decided that, as a tactic, they ought to try and throw out the present union, the International

Association of Machinists, which is one of the worst unions in the Chicago area, and bring in the United Electrical Workers union (UE), the old left-led union expelled in 1949 from the CIO and still under what is called progressive leadership.

Anyhow, they took a group of workers down to the UE hall and met with the organizers there. The staff people were delighted that they were interested in bringing in the UE, but they observed that there weren't enough white workers in the committee. If they ever hoped to win the plant for the UE, they would have to involve more white workers in the organizing effort.

That was certainly a logical effort. And so, what did the group do? They went back into the plant and began campaigning for the UE, using the newsletter as their chief vehicle. But now there was a change. The main aim became to reach the white workers, and so the line of the newsletter now became: all workers unite, the boss makes no distinction between black and white, do not let race feeling divide us, bringing in the UE will benefit us all, our interests are all the same, etc. As for the exposures of racial discrimination and the campaign to abolish it in the plant, which had occupied so much of the group's attention prior to the decision to bring in the UE, that was laid aside in the interests of appealing to the broadest number of workers who could be won to the immediate goal, getting a better union.

What is there to say about a story like this? What is there to do besides shake your head? Doesn't this represent, in capsule form, the whole history of labor movement in this country—the radicalization of the workers followed by the capitulation, on the part of the leadership, to the backward prejudices of the white workers? How many times does this experience have to be repeated? Apparently an infinite number until we learn the lesson.

By the way, the upshot of the organizing campaign was that the group didn't succeed in fooling any white workers; they still considered it a black power group and kept it at arm's length. But it did succeed in cooling the enthusiasm of the black workers who were its initial base.

Was there an alternative course that could have been followed in the particular situation? I think there was.

Nothing Less Than a Total Change

The alternative would have been to encourage the group along its original lines, determined to fight consistently against white supremacy regardless of what came up or came down—to develop the group as the core of a fighting movement in the plant that carried out struggles on the shop floor around all issues of concern to its members, including the issue of racial discrimination.

It's probably true that such a group could not have been a majority movement at the beginning, or perhaps even for a considerable length of time. Most likely, as the group pushed firmly against racial discrimination it would alienate some white workers who could have been won to it otherwise. That's a choice that has to be made. The group in the plant made the wrong choice.

I think that a group such as I describe, made up perhaps in the beginning almost entirely of black workers, could have developed as a center of struggle in the plant and a center of opposition to the company and the rotten union. As time went on, it could have attracted to itself white workers who were so fed up with their situation that they were looking for radical solutions—and would even identify with a "black radical" outfit, so long as it seemed to offer a way out of the mess they were in. The very things which would make such a group repulsive to some workers would make it attractive to that increasing number of workers, black as well as white, who are coming to sense that nothing less than a total change is worth fighting for.

The course I advocate offers great difficulties—no doubt about it. It is likely that the repression directed against a radical group that relentlessly fought racial discrimination would be greater than against a more moderate group. It is possible that a group such as I describe could never have gained admittance into the UE. I freely concede all the difficulties. But then, who ever said that making a revolution was easy?

As for the alternative, the course that was actually followed, we know all too well where that leads.

11

Theses on White Supremacy: Expanded Remarks

The following essay, originally published in 1976, appears in Sojourner Truth Organization's collection, "Understanding and Fighting White Supremacy." Ignatiev is responding to a previous speech made by David Ranney at the meeting of the leadership of the New American Movement regarding the organization's positions on white supremacy and the color line.

It was raised that our position as expressed by Dave means attacking the white workers. We believe that the fight against white supremacy is in the interests of the working class, including white workers. If anyone disagrees, that person should speak up.

The principal reason the bourgeoisie upholds white supremacy is not the quest for maximum profit in an immediate and direct sense. If it were, the employers would give job preference to the cheapest labor available, black labor. No, the aim is political control, the maintenance of the white population's support.

People have characterized our position as calling on whites to "give up" hard-won gains, such as union job control. In the first place, the struggles were not waged by those who currently enjoy the benefits. In the second place, the ruling class, when forced to concede reforms, always tries to frame its concessions so as to weaken proletarian solidarity. Such is the case with the seniority system, for example, which was fought for by both black and white workers, but which now often serves to protect the superior status of whites. In a certain sense, the entire struggle of the working class is aimed at overturning past victories: bourgeois democracy, union dues check-off, compulsory education, etc.

In the third place, it is not a matter for whites of "giving up" the relative advantages they hold over blacks and other third world people. The bourgeoisie pursues white workers everywhere with tokens and reminders of superior status, and they cannot be given up, but must be cast off through militant struggle. What is the ruling class response to any serious effort by white workers to join black people in the struggle against white supremacy? Attica is one indication.

The question was raised: why do we give greater weight to the struggle against white supremacy than to other issues that hold back the working class, especially male supremacy? In doing so, we are not arguing that black people are more oppressed than women; no one can know exactly the pain felt by another. Nor are we saying that white supremacy has historically been more important in dividing the working class than male supremacy; a good case can be made to the contrary. The reasoning behind our position is this: *of all the struggles in which a popular victory would fatally weaken US capitalism, the fight against white supremacy is the one with the greatest chance of success.* This is so for several reasons, one of which is sufficient to mention here: its link with the worldwide anti-imperialist movements of the colonial and dependent peoples.

Space limitations prevent an adequate treatment of the practical implications of all this. For now, just three points:

1. We should choose to do political work in areas where there are large numbers of black and other third world people, because their presence makes it easier to raise, *among whites*, the issue of white supremacy in a way that relates to their experience, rather than as lecturing them.

2. We should give priority to those issues which have the greatest potential of immediately and directly involving a fight against white supremacy—not to the total exclusion of other issues, but as *a priority*.

3. Alan Charney listed three political groupings among black people and suggested we should work with them all. Significantly, he omitted a fourth tendency: the nationalists. Several years ago, when the

Republic of New Africa (RNA)* was peacefully pursuing its work of building the New Communities and organizing support for its projected plebiscite on the status of black people, it was attacked by officials of the State of Mississippi, which tried to assassinate a number of its citizens and, failing in that, is trying to keep them locked up for long terms. Since then there have been other repressive acts—yet how many on the white left even know of their case? Judging by the fury of its response to RNA efforts to separate from the United States, one would have to conclude that since its birth the State of Mississippi has been committed to the goal of integration. We have to seek out nationalist formations and find ways of supporting them and working with them on terms which they find acceptable.

Lastly, as to program. Everyone on the left agrees that the fight for jobs is crucial in the present period. Yet most whites ignore the fact that a major aspect of ruling class policy is to shield the white population as much as possible from the most severe effects of economic crisis by transferring the burden of inflation and unemployment onto black and other third world people inside and outside the United States. The ruling class is willing to take the risk of further angering the oppressed nationalities because the alternative, of equalizing the burden on the working class as a whole, would have harmful political consequences to continued capitalist rule. We believe that such an understanding as we have outlined above must determine our political response to the present economic situation. This means that the fight against racism is not simply another demand in a long list.

A working-class program for this period must have as its central feature the fight for equality of black, Latin, and other third world people. In terms of specific program relating to the struggle for jobs, we propose the following:

1. There are already a number of examples of black and third world groups and women resisting ruling class attempts to roll back the

---

* The RNA was founded in 1968 as a black nationalist organization and black separatist movement in the United States. It was part of a larger New Afrikan movement that supported the creation of an independent black majority in the southeastern United States and reparations to descendants of slaves.

affirmative action gains of the 1960s. In Fremont, California; Kansas City, Missouri; Fairfield, Alabama; and now in Chicago, suits have been filed against management and unions in collusion. We should take steps to bring together these various struggles in a national campaign, using both legal measures and mass action, to maintain and extend affirmative action standards. This must include a specific statement of our willingness to set aside union prerogatives wherever they conflict with equal employment rights.

2. We should develop a campaign to expose the trend toward shutting down industry in the inner-city and shifting it to the suburbs, perhaps focusing a national organizing effort on the scheme to "decentralize" the postal system.

3. We should organize to defeat the Rodino Bill and its various local versions and to stop the deportation raids on undocumented workers.*

We believe such a program is a vital necessity in order to develop among the working class as a whole the unity and will to fight effectively for useful jobs for all.

---

* Early 1970s anti-immigration bills introduced into the House by Representative Peter W. Rodino Jr., a New Jersey Congressman between 1949 and 1989.

12

No Condescending Saviors: A Study of the Experience of Revolution in the Twentieth Century (Excerpts)

As a global cycle of revolution was winding down in the second half of the 1970s, Ignatiev attempted to settle his personal accounts of his century's major revolutions, and on that basis theorize an alternative in the form of proletarian self-emancipation. This essay was published as a pamphlet by the Sojourner Truth Organization in 1976.

X. The Communist Parties in the Developed Countries

All of the cases looked at up to this point have been ones where the working class was extremely small in relation to the rest of the population and where the reactionary regime held on to power through a system of total repression. In such cases it is natural that conditions of underground existence should give rise to military conceptions of unity and discipline which, while making the party into the most effective instrument for overturning the old regime, also tend to make it suspicious of any independent initiatives from outside its own ranks, including the working class seeking to realize itself directly.

What of the situation in western Europe, North America, and Japan, where the working class is large and experienced and where for at least a generation trade union and parliamentary forms have existed to mediate the class struggle? How do the communist parties function in these countries?

At the beginning of the 1960s, when Khrushchev was at the head of the Soviet government, the communist parties in a number of western countries, with his encouragement, began to evolve theories of peaceful transition to socialism, democracy without class content, and other ideas of classical social democracy. At that time the Chinese Communist Party opposed these new tendencies in a series of polemics WHICH effectively restated the traditional principles of Marxism–Leninism and won it a great deal of support from many parties in the third world and some in the developed countries. In some countries, significant groups of "Marxist–Leninists" split away from the existing parties and began the process of building new "anti-revisionist" ones, often with Chinese encouragement and support.

Well, Khrushchev was removed from authority and in the more than a decade since, several important developments have unfolded within the Communist movement:

1. The Soviet Communist Party dropped the line of peaceful transition and so forth, and those parties that hung on to it, such as the Italian and Scandinavian parties, did so in defiance of Moscow.

2. Some parties, including some most closely aligned with the Soviet Communist Party, proved in deeds, not words, that they were quite willing to discard bourgeois democracy and become serious contenders for power, under certain circumstances. The outstanding example of this is Portugal.

3. Owing partly to the inability of the "anti-revisionist" forces to explain the above developments, they have been unable in even a single industrialized country to come together in one hegemonic organization, and moreover, have spawned a multitude of different groups, some with politics virtually indistinguishable from that of the official American Communist Party, others so sectarian that they are led to oppose every progressive movement in their own countries, with the result that the very concept of the "anti-revisionist left" is now totally without validity, except in a historical sense.

Just as in an earlier period the dramatic expropriation of private capital by the Soviet government gave rise to the view that equated socialism with expropriation, so now the drift of the communist parties toward reformism leads to the tendency to dismiss them as "class collaboration-ist" and "revisionist."

Nothing reveals the dangerous consequences of the confusion regarding the communist parties more clearly than the events in Portugal. In that country, following the April 25, 1974, overthrow of the fascist regime by a group of young officers in the Armed Forces Movement, there arose several different forces contending for power.

First were the forces grouped around the new-born Socialist Party, headed by Mario Soares; these were the elements who hoped to see Portugal evolve as a traditional, western European bourgeois demo-cratic state, based on private property in the means of production. This was the sector supported by the United States and the principal forces of European capitalism.

Second was the revolutionary proletariat seeking to establish its direct power in society and expressing its will, in a not yet clearly distinct manner, through the Workers' Commissions, Workers' Councils, and a group in the armed forces, Soldiers United for Victory. No single party was hegemonic within the proletariat. The Party of the Revolutionary Proletariat most completely identified itself with the independent revo-lutionary aspirations of the workers.

Third was the Communist Party, dominant in the trade unions, and the largest party among the workers. The Community Party represented neither of the above-mentioned forces, nor did it represent a vacillating, compromising element between them. It had its own independent policy, which it pursued throughout the stormy events of the next two years and is pursuing today. And what was that policy? Simply put, it was a policy aimed at the creation of a new Portugal, without private ownership of the means of production and with the party as the admin-istrator of the new state and manager of the state-owned property: in other words, a regime similar to that which exists in any of the eastern European states today.

In order to accomplish its strategic aim, the Communist Party must achieve two things: first, it must expropriate the property and crush the resistance of the bourgeoisie; second, it must restrict the scope of the mass working class movement and bring it under the control of the party. And it must accomplish these tasks under the special conditions prevailing in Portugal: namely, that while the bourgeoisie had been dealt a severe blow with the fall of fascism, it was stronger than the working class; and also that the party itself was a mass party and therefore necessarily responsive to various currents within the working class.

It was the need to balance various conflicting tasks and pressures that was responsible for the seemingly contradictory turns in policy. But tactics have always been subordinate to the overall goal.

When the fascists were first overthrown and Communist Party leader Cunhal returned to Portugal to assume a post in the provisional government, various analysts around the world dismissed him as a "revisionist" committed to the parliamentary road to socialism. But when he came out with statements minimizing the importance of elections and calling on the army to continue to exercise power, and then when the Communist Party twice took to the barricades to bar fascist attempts to overthrow the new regime, these same analysts were left with no explanation.

Several of the Maoist groups characterized the Communist Party as "social-fascist," meaning socialist in words, fascist in deeds. But what kind of fascist is it that takes the lead in demanding full, unconditional independence for one's own colonies, as the Communist Party did in regard to Portugal's African territories or fights for land reform, as it is doing in Portugal itself?

Both theories—the "revisionist" and the "social-fascist"—failed to explain the behavior of the Portuguese Communist Party during the postrevolutionary crisis.

On the other hand, the Communist Party was not a consistently revolutionary party. It had seized power in the trade union movement by simply moving into the offices and had used its authority to oppose strikes aimed at higher wages, on the grounds that they would jeopardize the country's economic position. And it opposed the formation of the Workers' Commissions and Workers' Councils, which were nonparty mass organizations of direct democracy, as it likewise opposed the formation of any groups within the armed forces that ran counter to the Armed Forces Movement of the rebel officers. And even while opposing one or another conservative measure of the different provisional governments, it always maintained a presence in the government.

These various maneuvers of the party can be explained in only one way: the party was, and remains, a vigorous opponent of the existing capitalist regime and a serious contender for power; but the regime it strives to establish is not the "free association" spoken of by Marx. In its efforts to attain its goal, it must utilize its influence in the government and in the mass movement to crush the traditional bourgeoisie, must use exactly the same influence to prevent the working-class movement from getting out of hand, and it must accomplish these two contradictory tasks without losing its base of popular support.

But then don't these various considerations determining Communist Party policy offer tremendous possibilities of support to the working-class movement which exists outside of party control? Of course they do, and the revolutionary movement in Portugal has taken advantage of that fact. Thus, for instance, when the Communist Party took to the barricades against the fascists, the revolutionary left joined it; when the party defended itself from the attacks of the fascists and the church, the left joined in the defense; when the Communist Party opposed the rightward drift of the sixth provisional government, the left was on the same side.

On the other hand, when the Communist Party opposed strikes or opposed the Workers' Commissions (and later tried to take them over), the left fought against it. The policy of the left toward the Communist Party in Portugal is what is meant by the working class maintaining an independent stance in the political struggle.

By contrast, those groups which claim to be followers of Mao Tse-tung Thought were blinded by their unreasonable hatred for the Communist Party, so they joined together with the CIA-backed Socialist Party against the Communist Party in the unions and joined in with the fascist mobs that were burning down party headquarters in the northern cities, on the grounds of "opposing social-fascism."

The Maoist groups are unable to analyze the role of the Communist Party and unable to arrive at a proper stance in relation to it, because they, like the Communist Party itself, are motivated by the theory that sees the rule of the vanguard party as equivalent to proletarian power. They differ from the Communist Party only in the particular foreign country to which they look as a model.

Italy is another country where the Communist Party is reaching for power and where the state capitalist theory offers the only reasonable explanation for its behavior.

The Italian Communist leaders trace their tradition back in a direct line through the anti-fascist resistance, the Civil War in Spain, the post–World War I uprisings, and the founding of the party. They are the most cynical and astute group of leaders in the western communist movement, including those in the Soviet Union, whom they undoubtedly consider "backward" and "lacking in culture."

If the Italian Communists have temporarily adopted a reformist course, it is not because they have renounced their fundamental aim of taking power in Italian society, but because they feel that such a course is best suited to their cause at the present time.

The Soviet leaders, for their own reasons, do not approve of the new line of the Italian Communist Party and exert efforts to reverse it. Paradoxically, it is the improved position of the Soviet Union in the world that makes it possible for the Italian and other western Communist Party's to stray from Moscow's strict control, by eliminating the need for the formerly weak, isolated, hounded communists to huddle together for mutual support.

For the time being, the Italian Communists are trying to gain entrance to the government by offering themselves as the only force able to bring about labor peace, that is, to halt the wave of strikes that threatens the very foundations of the Italian state.

If the Communist Party comes into the government, there is no doubt that it will have exactly the opposite effect from that intended by the bourgeoisie; namely, it will encourage the workers to be bolder in their demands.

If that happens, the pressure will be on the Communist Party either to risk its base of support among the workers by suppressing the strikes or give up its position in government.

There is a third alternative, of course—the Portuguese one. That is, to attempt to take power into the hands of the party while preventing the struggle of the working class from going too far. It should be noted, however, that Italy in the 1970s is not eastern Europe after World War II, where the Red Army was present to both suppress private capital and enforce labor discipline.

All the conceivable paths offer great difficulties to the Italian Communist Party, while holding out tremendous possibilities to the working class.

The communist parties in the advanced countries are not alien presences imposed on the working class from outside. Even if the Stalin regime had never existed in Russia, something very similar to them would have developed. Nor are they more radical versions of the old, class-collaborationist social democracy. The communist parties are products of that stage of social evolution in which the working class is not yet sufficiently mature to fulfill its historic role. They represent that element of the population which is bitterly hostile to the existing regime and is at the same time able to conceive of no alternative to it other than the substitution of a more efficient and benevolent group of rulers for the exploiting class that presently holds power. The fact that the communist parties are attempting to achieve their aim in a place and time where the working class no longer has need of their services produces terrible strains on these parties, which must eventually blow them apart.

XI. The Way Out

"Men make their own history," wrote Marx, in the famous and often-cited passage from *The Eighteenth Brumaire of Louis Bonaparte*,

> but they do not make it just as they please; they do not make it under circumstances chosen by themselves, but under circumstances directly found, given and transmitted from the past. The tradition of all the dead generations weighs like an incubus of the brain of the living.[1]

The workers' movements in Europe and the United States proved strong enough to prevent the crushing of the young Soviet Republic but not strong enough to overthrow capitalism in their own countries. The confinement of the revolution to backward Russia gave rise to a certain conception of the relation of the party to the class, a conception based on the demonstrated inability of the Russian working class to establish its direct rule. Thus, in place of the dictatorship by the proletariat, there arose the theory of the dictatorship for the proletariat, which became transformed into a dictatorship over the proletariat.

The communist parties of the various countries, strongly influenced by the Russian model, are products of that stage in development in which the working class is not yet capable of establishing its own class rule. These parties have been, on one hand, more or less effective instruments for waging the class struggle and, on the other hand, terrible weapons for the suppression of all strivings of the proletariat to express itself as a class independent of their control.

The working class in the developed countries no longer has need of these revolutionary mandarins. To take the most well-known of recent examples, in May 1968 the French working class, acting under the guidance of no leading party, showed that it is "disciplined, united, organized by the very mechanism of the process of capitalist production" and is capable of standing at the head of the nation—so much so that President de Gaulle went on a secret inspection tour of French military units in Germany, unable to rely any longer on those stationed in France itself, who had been exposed to the revolutionary virus.[2]

If the general strike and factory occupation of 1968 did not lead to the conquest of power by the proletariat, it was not because the workers were insufficiently organized, or did not possess adequate weapons, or lacked means of communication, or any of the other reasons that revolutionary attempts have failed in the past. It was because the workers themselves lacked an appreciation of their own capacity to rule.

Workers do very revolutionary things, but they think of them in old ways. The French workers, who demonstrated their ability to carry out a nationwide movement, create forms of direct democracy and regulate their relations with nonproletarian social strata—the essential tasks of any government—were unable to see that in their own actions lay the foundations of a new society. There were signs of the beginnings of such an understanding on the part of the workers, but they were stamped out by the official trade union and Communist Party leadership, which sought to interpret the events as simply a massive demonstration of the need for reform.

So long as the only models of social action articulated to the workers are either continued subordination to the bourgeoisie—the line of social democracy—or reliance on the all-knowing vanguard party to lead them to socialism in its own good time, they will be unable to arrive at the new consciousness of themselves as a potential ruling class, and thus all their movements will inevitably be contained within the framework of capitalism.

It is the view of the Sojourner Truth Organization that a Marxist–Leninist party is absolutely crucial to the process of developing among the workers the sense of themselves as part of a potential ruling class. While this is not the place for a lengthy discussion of the party question,[3] it can be stated that the process has two aspects: criticizing bourgeois consciousness as it manifests itself within the working class and linking together in a culture of struggle those elements in the working-class movement which foreshadow the socialist society. To reduce these tasks, which in our opinion constitute the essence of the party's vanguard role, to the goal of gathering all the diverse threads of the movement into the hands of the party—which is the line implicit in the "general staff" theory—can only reinforce the sense of powerlessness that workers feel.

Having offended virtually every other sector of the left, it is necessary to say a word about the Trotskyists. On this question of the role of the party in relation to the mass movement, official Trotskyism does not differ in the slightest with the position of the official communist parties. They may differ with them on certain questions of policy for the party, but when it comes to their attitude toward the independent expressions of working-class power, Trotskyism is only a subcategory of Stalinism. This has been true ever since Trotsky first hatched his plan to militarize the Soviet trade unions; it is evident today in the countless hours spent by his followers in meetings, conferences, discussion bulletins, contact commissions, and other efforts to reconstruct one or another wing of the International, the one and only International—all taking place in total isolation from the actual movement of the proletariat and in total ignorance of the fact that the working class no longer has the slightest need for them.

Marx and Engels predicted that the proletariat would first come to power in one of the developed countries and that it would sweep the rest of the world along in its train. They may turn out to have been right after all. For while it is obvious that the chain of traditional capitalism breaks first at its weakest link, the overthrow of the old bourgeoisie is not the same as the conquest of power by the working class. It is even possible that the specific country to which Marx and Engels first looked, Germany, may be the one that blazes the trail; for that is the country where the working class has the most extensive experience both with traditional bourgeois rule and with the new state capitalism of the commissars. That is just private speculation.

In any case, as Marx wrote in the preface to *The Critique of Political Economy*:

mankind always takes up only such problems as it can solve; since, looking at the matter more closely, we will always find that the problem itself arises only when the material conditions necessary for its solution already exist or are at least in the process of formation.[4]

History, through the means of state capitalism, both in the west and the east, has at last brought into existence a social formation able to take all power into the hands of the producers and establish "in place of the old bourgeois society . . . an association, in which the free development of each is the condition for the free development of all."[5]

That "association" of which Marx speaks is socialism, the only kind of socialism that will ever exist. To understand that the emancipation of the working class is the task of the workers themselves; to take that statement literally and make it the starting point for all policy is the first demand placed on any individual or grouping of individuals that wishes to contribute to the emergence of the socialist society.

13

Since When Has Working Been a Crime?

This 1977 pamphlet was written to be distributed at workplaces by members of Sojourner Truth Organization. It calls for solidarity with undocumented workers and compares the contemporary crackdowns on undocumented workers with the Fugitive Slave Act of 1850.

News from the Plant

When Frank Stewart came to work early Tuesday morning, he punched in and went up to the locker room to change clothes.

"Where were you yesterday?" asked Joe Williams, who changed at the next locker. "Don't you know we work on Mondays around here?"

"I had to go to court to fight a speeding ticket. First they kept me waiting half a day. Then I had to look at this stupid movie about how to drive."

"You missed some real excitement around here," said Joe. "The government pulled a raid."

"What do you mean, a raid?"

"Just what I said," Joe answered. "A raid. Around four guys in suits came in and started asking questions. 'Where were you born? Where are your papers?' Questions like that. As soon as some of the people in packing saw what was happening, they took off. Man, you never saw anyone disappear so fast."

"No kidding? Where did they go?"

"I don't know. Out the door. Behind the boxes in 114. In the can. Maria told me one lady in her department hid out in the garbage pail."

Frank was starting to get the picture.

"Who were these guys?"

"Bill, the union steward said they were agents from the Immigration and Naturalization Service. They were looking for people in this country without papers."

Frank was disappointed he'd missed the excitement.

"Wouldn't you know I'd pick that day to be off. How come I always miss all the fun?"

Joe looked serious.

"It wasn't much fun. I saw them hassling Julio the Puerto Rican over in assembly. They were really giving him a hard time—making him show his papers. And he's a citizen, so he hasn't got papers. They were calling him a liar. Pushing him around. They wouldn't believe he was Puerto Rican. They kept asking him if he got here by bus."

Joe clearly didn't think much of the way the agents acted.

"They were pulling every person who looked like they were Mexican off their lines and hassling them. They even stopped Steve, and he's Japanese. This one agent kept talking to him in Spanish. The place was crazy—people running all over; lines backing up; everyone getting all shook up. The only departments that weren't touched were the ones where almost everyone's white."

"Did they catch anyone?" Frank asked.

"When I saw them leaving they had Juan Lopez and Eliseo that works in packing. And they had one of the Spanish women from assembly. I think her name is Mercedes. The foreman said they were here without papers. I guess they'll all be put on a bus back to Mexico."

"Why some of those people have been here for years. Two of Juan's kids were born here. And just last week he was telling me about the plans for his son's christening."

"Maybe so," said Joe, "but the christening will have to take place in Mexico, because he's gone from here."

Frank finished changing his clothes. He didn't say much for the rest of the day, but he listened to other people talking. Some of the conversation was about the raid of the day before. People wondered if there were others without papers in the plant besides the three they caught.

That night, after Frank and his wife, Joyce, had put the children to sleep, they sat around talking. He told her about the raid.

"It doesn't seem right," she said. "Those people have been in the plant working like everyone else. Juan's wife just had a baby. How will they live with three kids and him losing his job? And both of them being sent back?"

"I don't know. Some of the guys were saying it was a good thing that they got the three of them, because it will mean more jobs for Americans. That makes sense. It's hard enough to get a job now."

"Isn't Juan the one you used to trade food with?" Joyce continued.

"That's right. He'd give me tacos from home sometimes, and I'd give him some of my lunch. He really likes your meat loaf."

Frank thought for a minute.

"The other thing some of the guys were saying is that the Mexicans who are here illegally don't pay taxes and are a drain on the economy. I read something about that in the *Tribune* last week."

"How could Juan not pay taxes?" Joyce asked, frowning. "That's ridiculous. The company deducts taxes from his check the same as they do from yours—before you even see the money."

They both sat quietly for a minute, before Joyce continued.

"You'd think that a rich country like this wouldn't have to turn away anyone looking for honest work. After all, there are plenty of things that need doing."

Workers without Papers

The incident at the plant that Frank and Joyce Stewart talked about was only one of many such incidents all over the country. It is estimated that there are 6–12 million people living in the United States without what the government calls "proper papers." They come from all over—from Canada, from Hong Kong, India and Greece, Jamaica and Haiti—but the largest number come from Mexico.

Why do they come? The answer, in most cases, is simple: a chance to work. And work they do, in agriculture, food processing and serving, clothing manufacture, transportation—wherever productive labor is carried on.

The argument is often made that the undocumented workers don't pay taxes. Exactly the opposite is true. Joyce Stewart was right when she pointed that out to Frank. Juan Lopez's employer withheld federal and state taxes from his paychecks. When Juan was returned to Mexico he was unable to recover the excess in income tax he paid during the course of the year. And taxes aren't the only losses suffered by people forced by the US Government to leave. There is the money the employer takes out for social security. If people are forced to leave, they lose it all. Even if they stay, they can't collect social security for the time they were here without papers. People also lose bank accounts, furniture, and other household goods and personal belongings—everything that can't be packed up and put on a bus with them.

There are other losses as well. Greedy lawyers charge all kinds of money to "defend" victims of immigration arrests. In the end, the people have to leave anyway, and they leave a lot poorer than before the lawyer took their money. Similarly there is the problem of notaries. In Mexico, a notary is almost like a lawyer: someone people go to for certain legal services that do not require actually going to court. In the United States, anyone with $15 can be a notary. But since the Spanish word is similar—*notaria*—and since unscrupulous notaries with neon signs outside their neighborhood offices are able to attract people with immigration problems, many notaries do a large illegal business. They steal money from people and give back false promises or simple services that are available at low cost, if the people only know where to look for them.

People without proper papers suffer other financial losses as well. There is the money that some pay to contractors for jobs and false papers. Not everyone does this, since not everyone has the money or the connections. But there are many contractors or middlemen who fix workers up with papers and jobs, in return for big sums of money. If these workers get caught by the immigration agents, they lose the money they put up for the jobs and papers, as well as everything else.

There are personal losses. Families are broken up by the immigration laws. The US Constitution says that any person born here is a citizen. This means that many undocumented workers have children who are citizens. If children are old enough to stay and work, they may choose to stay and support the family when it is sent back. Or the child may go back with the family and then return when it is old enough to work.

Also, it is very common for sisters and brothers to be separated by the immigration laws.

Discrimination in the United States

So why, with all these problems and risks, do people come? As we said before, the answer is simple: a chance to work. Because he didn't have papers, Juan Lopez was forced to take a low paying job with little union protection. Some are more fortunate and manage to get jobs in high paying industries like auto and steel. Most, however, have to settle for the $2.50 an hour jobs: in unorganized factories, in service stations, in restaurants. And the lowest paying jobs in this country are usually the hardest, the hottest, and the dirtiest.

In addition to the problems resulting from lack of official documents, Juan, like other workers of color, was a victim of the system of US white supremacy: discrimination based on skin color. Furthermore, he had to survive the discrimination against him because his first language was Spanish. Not many employers will hire people who don't speak English— even when the job has nothing to do with speaking English (or any language, for that matter). And in many jobs, if there are white people willing to do the work, other workers don't get hired. So Juan and his family faced double discrimination: color and language.

Besides discrimination at work, people like Juan live in constant fear and uncertainty. They know that if the immigration officials catch up with them, what little amount of financial security they've found will be taken away. Anything can lead to being caught: a raid, a fight with a neighbor, sending a child to school, a speeding ticket, or just walking down the street and being Mexican. Raids and other forms of harassment are still common despite the government's claim that they are no longer doing this. In and near the community of South Chicago, there have been recent raids on local restaurants and numerous workplaces such as Republic Steel, Jay's Potato Chips, Solo Cup, and two local hospitals. In the case of the hospitals, supervisors called an "employees meeting" and once the workers were assembled, the doors of the meeting room were closed and the immigration officials were brought in. Even workers with proper papers are hassled as the government is liable to stop any Mexican or person of color, trying to find "illegals." Being caught means jail, until the victim can put up $500 to $1,500 in bond or is on the bus to Mexico.

What about Mexico?

Can't they find work in their own country? Often the answer is no, and one of the reasons for that is US business. The border between Mexico and the United States, which is closed up tight to Mexican workers who want to come north, is wide open to US corporations running away to Mexico. Large corporations like to boast how their investments help underdeveloped countries grow in industrial strength. The truth is a lot different. When US corporations enter a country like Mexico, they provide jobs for just a handful of people—at the cost of distorting and retarding economic growth of the country as a whole. Thus, Mexico has been unable to develop many of the basic industries vital to any independent country because the new business enterprises are crushed by giant US agricultural, auto, pharmaceutical, and other monopolies. When US corporations invest money, large profits are sent back to the United States, to the banks and shareholders of the corporation. Thus, money is drained out of Mexico and many other countries of Asia, Africa, the Caribbean, and South America, enriching the wealthiest segments of US society. When the Lopez family came north looking for work, they were simply trying to follow the money that the Yankee exploiters have taken from their country.

Another problem that these US corporations in Mexico create for workers is the language problem. The companies often want their employees, especially those in office jobs, to speak English. And because these companies want English-speaking workers, Mexican schools want English speaking teachers. Since the arrival of US business interests in Mexico, speaking Spanish is not good enough for many jobs. So people come here to learn English while they work, in hopes of someday landing a better job back home. It is doubly aggravating to Mexican workers here to have to put up with the argument "If they live here they should speak *our* language" when even in their own country, it's getting to be important to speak *our* language.

Competing for Jobs

Many workers just stay a few years in this country before returning home. Others, like Juan, settle here and raise families. Do they compete with "American" workers for jobs? Of course they do. Under the present system, all workers compete for jobs. But we think there is something wrong with the idea that competition of workers is more important than their contribution. Workers without papers, like immigrant workers generally—be they from Africa, Europe, South America, or the East— have built the railroads, dredged the canals, and dug the mines that have given this country the mightiest industrial base on earth. With so many more tasks waiting to be performed, the country cannot afford to turn away those who come from other lands looking for work. The contribution that the immigrant workers, including those without official papers, have made in the United States is enormous: a lot greater than the contribution made by those who are seeking to deport them.

The Truth about Immigration Laws

Whenever we have high unemployment, those representing the interests of big business attempt to cover up their own responsibility for this situation by blaming working people. As the US unemployment rate rose in the last five years, new laws were introduced to the Congress which were designed to blame Mexican workers for the US economic troubles. One of these laws, the Rodino Bill, was defeated due to the united opposition of many people who understood its unjustness and the dirty trick behind it. However, a number of states have enacted similar legislation and others are attempting to do so. Furthermore, another bill, called the Eilberg Law, was sneaked through the US Congress to replace the Rodino Bill. Among other things, the Eilberg Law reduces the annual quota of Mexicans legally entering the United States from 43,000 to 20,000. It also changes the status of parents with children born in the United States by making them wait until the child is 21 before they can get the papers which would make them legal residents. This provision makes many more people liable for deportation and divides families. Such laws must be resisted and stopped. But it is even more important to resist all efforts to deport working people who are simply trying to work for the money that is being drained out of their country by US corporations.

A Page from History

Frank and Joyce Stewart didn't know it, and neither do most people, but there is a precedent in history for the kinds of reactionary deportation laws that are being enacted against workers without papers now.

In 1850, when slavery still existed throughout the US South, Congress passed the Fugitive Slave Law. This incredible law was designed to stop the steady stream of slaves escaping to the North. It provided for fines and prison terms for anyone sheltering refugees from slavery. Suspected runaway slaves could be arrested on request, or on sight, without a warrant and turned over to a claimant, on nothing more than the claimant's word that he was the owner. It was all perfectly "legal"—just like the deportation hearings are today. A person would be arrested and brought before a judge. In about one minute, the person would be charged, the owner would testify the victim was "his" slave, and the so-called trial would be over.

The appeal the slave holders made to enlist northern support for the Fugitive Slave Law was in many ways like the argument put forward today by the US Government for deporting undocumented workers. The slaveholders—the biggest and cruelest exploiters of labor of their time—painted themselves as heroes and champions of white labor. They boasted that they were protecting white people from competition for jobs by black laborers. "After all," they argued, "as long as black folks are working without wages on the plantations, they can't take away white people's jobs."

These arguments were exactly backwards. They were answered very well by Frederick Douglass, a brilliant man and a former slave himself. He showed that *it was slavery, not black people, that degraded free labor*. As long as black people were forced to work without wages on the plantations, nobody's wages—black or white—could rise very high. Unfortunately, few from the ranks of white laboring people heeded Douglass's wise words. Just like today, most white workers attached way too much importance to the benefits they received for being white. Then, they focused on the benefits of being free: as bad as things were for them, at least they weren't slaves. Today they focus on their relatively better jobs and housing; on their nicer neighborhoods and better schools. What they ignored was—and still is—the most important thing of all. As long as the corporations and the government can keep white people happy and quiet with their little privileges, they can keep the whole working class under their heel.

Resistance Grows

At the passage of the Fugitive Slave Law, fear and dread spread through the black population of the North, where it was estimated that more than 50,000 fugitives had taken refuge from slavery. Would they be caught? Would they be found, even after years of freedom? Would Congress come up with new laws making northern blacks slaves as well? Some fled to Canada.

At the same time, resistance developed. Lots of it. Opponents of slavery condemned the law, declaring that the slaveholders were attempting to turn citizens of the republic into slave catchers. They held public assemblies to marshal opposition. They formed anti-slavery societies and circulated petitions. And they made bold, heroic efforts to rescue fugitives, in open defiance of the law. Armed clashes broke out between the slave catchers and defenders—black and white—of fugitive slaves.

An outstanding example of direct resistance *to* the Fugitive Slave Law was the case of Anthony Burns.

$40,000 for a Slave

On May 24, 1854, Anthony Burns, who had learned to read and write in slavery, was arrested in Boston as a fugitive slave, put in irons, and placed under guard in the federal courthouse. The guard was a posse of special police, one-third of whom were known thugs with prison records. News of the arrest spread fast. The next day, three lawyers came to court to defend him: Charles M. Ellis, a member of the Boston Vigilance Committee, which was organized to protect the rights of black people; Richard Henry Dana Jr., author of *Two Years Before the Mast*; and Robert Morris, the city's most respected black attorney.

The next night, during a gathering nearby of citizens to protest Burns's arrest, a man cried out: "WHEN WE GO FROM THIS CRADLE OF LIBERTY, LET US GO TO THE TOMB OF LIBERTY ... THE COURTHOUSE!" And go they did. The crowd stormed the courthouse and battered down the door, attempting to rescue Burns. The attack was repulsed by armed constables and deputies, but one deputy was killed in the process.

Black people gathered around the courthouse and stood vigil around the clock. Knowing it was impossible to win Burns's freedom in court, abolitionists and black people raised $1,200, his "price" and tried to buy his freedom. The US Attorney, however, refused to allow this transaction, arguing that the Fugitive Slave Law required Burns to be returned to his owner in Virginia.

Of course, Burns did lose the legal battle. When he was to sail to Virginia a few days later, twenty-two military units were called up to make sure he didn't escape. A cannon was mounted in front of the courthouse. A crowd of 50,000 shouted "shame" as they watched the Boston police and the US Army march Burns to the docks. The town was draped in black. At one point, the crowd tried to break through a police cordon to rescue Burns, but they were forced back.

Although Anthony Burns's market value was $1,200, it had cost the government more than $40,000 to return him to his owner. Back in Virginia, the Richmond *Enquirer* printed an account: "We rejoice, but a few more such victories and the South is undone."

There were other slave rescue attempts, and some were successful. On February 15, 1851, waiter Fred Wilkins, or Shadrach, as he was known, was seized from his job and rushed to the Boston courthouse. While Shadrach was still in court, a group of fifty black people from the neighborhood pushed into the courtroom, lifted him in the air, and spirited him to a carriage. Shadrach and his rescuers moved away "like a black squall." The rescue was so fast, nobody even pursued Shadrach. His rescuers were all eventually found not guilty by a sympathetic jury.

From the beginning, black people made up the main force in the resistance to slavery. They operated on the universally recognized principle that people fighting for their freedom must themselves strike the first blow. The Civil War began with both sides fighting for slavery—the South to take it out of the Union, the North to keep it in. It was the noble efforts of the black people, free and slave, and the efforts of their white supporters, that brought about the greatest achievement of the war—the ending of the evil system of human slavery.

It Is Time to Resist Evil

If Frank and Joyce Stewart had known the history of this country—not just the part about George Washington and Abraham Lincoln they teach in school—they would have been able to answer the question a lot of people ask about deportations. What can you do?

As was described in the previous section, at the time of the Fugitive Slave Law, the widest, boldest resistance came from the direct victims of the law: slaves and free black women and men. Just as then, widest resistance now will come from Mexican residents of the United States, who bear the heaviest burden. Already, they are beginning to show the way. In Los Angeles last year, workers who are here *with* legal papers refused to show them to the immigration agents, jamming the prisons and courts with their resistance to an unjust, unfair, racist law. Also in Los Angeles, thousands of Mexican people without papers marched in defiance of the law to the Immigration Department offices. In such large numbers, and with the support of so many people, nobody was arrested.

There are many more actions that people can take to defend workers without papers. We can refuse all cooperation with the immigration agents. We can refuse to answer any questions, including where we were born. We can turn around and ask them where they were born. Or tell them to show us *their* papers, if we are stopped. All this is completely legal. And if a lot of us who are citizens or permanent residents refuse to cooperate, it will make it very difficult for the immigration police to do their dirty work.

Beyond that, we can go even further. We can begin to show our strength by acting together where we work. Workers in large plants and mills can prevent the immigration police from freely circulating around and snatching people out. There is no way that raids can be carried out at large mills like Republic Steel, the scene of a recent raid, if the people who work there decide to stop them. Furthermore, workers can respond with strike action against the deportation program. They can strike if the front office lets the immigration police in the door.

Like the slave rescues described earlier, these actions could put a fast stop to the ugly harassment and deportations of Mexican people in the United States. There is no doubt that the American working class, veteran of the eight-hour day movement, practitioner of the sit-down strike and the roving picket line, instigator of the flying wedge and the strike-on-the-job, can bring these evil deportations to a screeching halt—once they make up their minds to do it.

14

Are US Workers Paid above the Value of Their Labor Power?

This essay critically engages with the idea that US workers have been "bought off" by wages significantly higher than the value of their labor power. It was first published in Issue 10 of the Sojourner Truth Organization's journal, Urgent Tasks, *in the fall of 1980.*

The value of labor power, like that of every other commodity, is determined by the labor time necessary for its production. Since labor power resides only in the living individual, its value reduces itself to the value of those commodities which are necessary for the production and reproduction of the worker. But what is "necessary" for the production and reproduction of the worker is itself the product of historical development.

> In contradistinction therefore to the case of other commodities, there enters into the determination of the value of labour-power a historical and moral element. Nevertheless, in a given country, at a given period, the average quantity of the means of subsistence necessary for the labourer is practically known.[1]

This historical and moral element is the result of a complicated interaction between different classes in society and within the working class itself: for example, does the present standard of what constitutes a "decent" living for an American worker owe more to the struggles of the working class or to the efforts of the capitalist class to promote the "consumer society"? It reflects to a considerable extent the level of technological development attained by a society: many of the articles which today constitute virtually indispensable elements of the worker's subsistence—television, electric refrigeration, gas heat, air conditioning—have existed for only slightly over a generation.

Moreover, what Marx calls the "moral element" is significantly influenced by national and even regional tradition: for example, French workers would riot in the streets were they forced to swallow the garbage that US workers routinely shovel down their gullets in the name of nutriment, yet can easily make do with an old, small-screen, black-and-white television that even the poorest US worker would give away to the Salvation Army. This historical and moral element, once incorporated into the value of labor power, is very difficult, if not impossible, to dislodge.

Workers must be not merely fed, clothed, and housed at the level which has become customary, they must also be trained sufficiently for the tasks they will be expected to perform. The expense of this educational process makes up a portion of the value of labor power, which must be met in some fashion if labor is to reproduce itself. The curtailment of child labor in the United States and the growth of a public school system, with the consequent increase in the value of labor power entailed by the need to support nonproductive children, were related to the development of new methods of production which required more highly educated workers. (The struggle for public education is a splendid example of the negation of the negation—a working-class victory incorporated by capital to bring about a new advance in accumulation; it is the resolution of the previous contradiction becoming one pole of the current one. Truly, the working-class struggles not against its defeats but against its earlier victories!)

In spite of the above-enumerated difficulties in quantifying the value of labor power, this value in a particular time and place "is practically known." It can be observed, more or less, in that level beneath which workers do not consider it worthwhile to seek or accept employment. Anyone who has observed the workers over a period of time knows that there is a certain minimum they will accept as consistent with their dignity and the standards that have been established. Among them it is considered acceptable to turn down a job that fails to come up to that minimum, even if it means unemployment and some hardship. Obviously, this minimum acceptable wage varies with the region and especially with the times and is somewhat different among different sectors of the working class,* but it does exist, enforced by a consensual process.

The operation of the consensual process is often comical: a decade and a half ago there was common in the factories a myth of the Slavic immigrant worker—the so-called displaced person who arrived in Chicago with nothing, ate black bread and cabbage soup and lived in a cellar, and after five years bought a three-flat, and a few years later another, and eventually escaped from the factory, continuing to live in a cellar—as the janitor of his own building. The myth was based on a certain reality: there were a few cases such as I have described. But the point is, they were ridiculed by the mass of the workers. (Lest anyone suggest that the ridicule was a luxury only the highly paid workers could afford, let me point out that the story was told with greatest mirth and scorn by the lowest paid sector of the Chicago proletariat, the black, Mexican, and Puerto Rican workers, who thus showed their contempt for those who voluntarily renounced the few worldly pleasures available to a proletarian in pursuit of a dream made of ashes.) Aside from providing needed laughter, the passing around of such stories served another function: by their ridicule of such exaggerated thrift the mass of workers were enforcing discipline within the working class in order to prevent the value of labor power in Chicago from sinking to the level of the rural districts of eastern Europe.

---

* The minimum acceptable level is not so different for black and white workers as some might imagine, given similar ages, marital status, skill, and employment history. This is no small qualification, since employment discrimination generally takes the form of reserving certain jobs for whites only. This pattern reveals the flaw in the famous $30 billion figure bandied around by various left groups as representing the total of the superprofits reaped by US capital from race discrimination, a figure arrived at by multiplying the per capita income differential between black and white workers by the number of black workers. This figure would make sense only if the substance of race discrimination consisted of paying black and white workers different amounts for the same job. The real value of white supremacy to the US ruling class lies in its use as a measure of control over the entire working class, a control that underlies not "superprofits" but the entire profit system.

Social Mobility

If the value of labor power is that sum of values required to maintain and reproduce the worker, then it ought to be possible to compare it with the actual wage, or price of labor power, received by a definite group of workers. A simple statement should suffice to explain the principle: if the children of a group of workers become workers themselves at the same level as their parents, that indicates that the parents have received a wage, over time, equivalent to the value of their labor power, since they have managed to reproduce themselves as workers; if the parents are able regularly to promote their children out of the proletariat, that implies a wage above the value of labor power, exceeding it by the proportion of their children that escape; if, in the third case, the working class is unable to maintain itself but instead loses numbers owing to early death, emigration, or reduction to pauperism, then the wage of these workers is insufficient to maintain and reproduce themselves as workers, and consequently it is beneath the value of labor power.

It is evident that the numbers considered must be large enough to be statistically significant and that the concern must be with averages, not the individual case; otherwise the matter is trivialized. Moreover, a study must consider the outcome over a period of time sufficient to balance out the "seven fat years and seven lean years"; a generation should be long enough. Finally, there is one basic assumption that underlies the approach: no one stays in the working class who doesn't have to. I regard that assumption as unarguable.

Some Evidence

A number of studies have been made of social mobility in the United States. One of the more recent, briefer and more accessible of these is *Has Opportunity Declined in America?* by David L. Featherman.[2] In that monograph, the writer includes the table below.

The figures were compiled by asking a sample of men in the civilian labor force the occupation of their fathers at the time the interviewees were sixteen years old. There are certain flaws in the result: the most obvious is that women were excluded from the survey. What effect this

Mobility from Father's (or other family head's) Occupation to Current Occupation: U.S. Men in the Experienced Civilian Labour Force Aged 20 to 64 in 1973

Year and father's occupation	Son's current occupation						
	Upper white collar	Lower white collar	Upper manual	Lower manual	Farm	Total	Row percent-age
Upper white collar	52.0	16.0	13.8	17.1	1.1	100.0	18.2
Upper white collar	42.3	19.7	15.3	21.9	0.8	100.0	9.0
Upper manual	29.4	13.0	27.4	29.0	1.1	100.0	20.5
Lower manual	22.5	12.0	23.7	40.8	1.0	100.0	29.7
Farm	17.5	7.8	22.7	37.2	14.8	100.0	22.6
Total	29.9	12.7	21.7	31.5	4.1	100.0	100.0

Note: *Data are from March 1973 Current Population Survey and Occupational Changes in a Generation Survey. Occupation groups are upper white collar: professional and kindred workers and managers, officials and proprietors, except farm; lower white collar; sales, clerical and kindred workers; upper manual; craftsmen, foremen and kindred workers; lower manual; operatives and kindred workers, service workers, and laborers, except farm; farm: farmers and farm managers, farm laborers, and foremen.*

would have on the results I couldn't say. Another flaw is the imprecision of the social categories: for instance, are post office workers classified as "lower white collar" or "lower manual"? What about the effect of immigration, for which the table makes no allowance? And what about the unemployed?

Without forgetting various limitations in the data, let us examine what the table tells us. According to the figures, 31.5 percent of male workers held lower manual jobs in 1973, and 29.7 percent of all sons grew up in lower manual families—not much change between generations. Of those sons who grew up in lower manual families, only 40.8 percent were working in lower manual jobs; 23.7 percent were in upper-manual categories, 12 percent were in lower-white-collar, and 22.5 percent were classified as upper-white-collar—apparently considerable upward mobility. Whence, then, is derived the lower manual work force? From two sources—the farms (reflecting a sharp decrease in the number of farm workers over the years) and from the downward motion of those strata above lower manual: of those sons who grew up in upper-white-collar, lower-white-collar, and upper-manual families, 17.1 percent, 21.9 percent, and 29 percent respectively were at the time of the survey working in lower manual jobs. For ease of calculation, let each percentage point in the bottom row and the last column equal one million, giving us a total of 100 million in the civilian labor force (allowing the figures for men to represent the total, somewhere near the actual total). Using our trusty abacus to make the necessary cross-multiplications, we come up with the following figures, rounded off: of the 31.5 million in lower manual jobs, 12 million (40.8 percent of 29.7 million) are from lower manual families; 6 million (29 percent of 20.5 million) are from upper manual families; 2 million are from lower-white-collar families; 3 million are from upper-white-collar families; and the remainder come from the farms. Thus, the upward mobility of sons from lower-manual families is more than compensated for by downward mobility from strata above and from movement off the farms.

Now let us combine the figures for the categories which, for the purpose of this study, must represent the working class—lower white collar, upper manual, and lower manual. These categories make up 66 percent of the civilian labor force, or 66 million. Of these, 42 million come from families within the same categories. Where do the rest come from? The largest portion come off the farm: of the 22.6 million who reported themselves from farm backgrounds, 66.7 percent, or 15 million, are currently working in lower-manual, upper-manual, or lower-white-collar positions. The remainder, 9 million, have dropped down from upper-white-collar families.

How does this figure of 9 million "demoted" from upper-white-collar families into the ranks of the working class compare with the number of those promoted upward out of the ranks of the working class? Of those working today in upper-white-collar jobs, 30 million people, a majority, 16.3 million, come from the working class. (Another 4 million come from the farms, leaving only 9 million from similar upper-white-collar backgrounds, reflecting the rapid expansion of this stratum of the population.)

The working class was able to promote 16 million people out of its ranks, out of nearly 60 million of those who reported working-class backgrounds, compared to 9 million pushed down into it, leaving a net "promotion" total of 7 million, or 12 percent (disregarding movement from the farm).

Thus, according to the method I advanced earlier in this article, US workers received, on the average, a wage that exceeded the value of their labor power by approximately 12 percent—and this in a period which encompassed the thirty-year boom that ended in 1967, the longest period of continued expansion in the history of the country. Those with various theories about the "bought-off" working class are invited to make whatever use they can of that statistic. Is there something wrong with my approach or with my reading of the figures? (I am certainly not a trained statistician.) I would appreciate hearing from readers.

Finally, is it necessary to add that the research cited above bears not at all on the magnitude of the value of labor power, since that value is determined not by the quantity of use values at the workers' disposal, but by the labor time necessary to produce those values? Indeed, it is that condition which underlies the capitalist strategy of relative surplus value.

15

Introduction to the United States: An Autonomist Political History

Ignatiev compiled this political history of the United States as part of an exchange with Irish revolutionaries. The manuscript was taken to Ireland by a delegation of members of the Sojourner Truth Organization in 1978 and was meant to spark engagement and debate. Ignatiev distills many of his major arguments about the significance of the color line in US history as key for organizing in the present moment. This essay first appeared as a Sojourner Truth Organization pamphlet in 1980.

Introduction

What would the United States be like without black people? The answer to this question can be found by considering a country like Canada, which resembles the United States in many ways—a vast area of great natural resources, sparsely settled by native peoples before European colonization. Canada differs from the United States in only one significant particular—it was never given over to African slavery, nor was it ever implicated in the slave trade. And this particular is at bottom responsible for the difference between one country, which has dominated world politics throughout this entire century and today constitutes the biggest exploiter of peoples on a world scale, and another whose impact on world affairs has been far more limited. If, in the document that follows, we devote a great deal of attention to the history of the "race question" in the United States, it is not because we are humanitarians but because we recognize it as the key to the history which has made us what we are today and the key to any future transformation we hope to achieve. It is also because the matter is understood by few people, and not more widely in the United States than other places. Space limitations will prevent us from going into much detail on any subject; yet since the Civil War and Reconstruction constitute the pivot of US history, we shall spend some time on it. The portion of the document setting forth the positions of our organization on current questions is necessarily truncated. We hope that our treatment of the history will enable the reader to comprehend what we stand for and how, in general, we propose to proceed. We wish to express our gratitude to our comrades in Revolutionary Struggle who have given us this opportunity to communicate directly with their own constituency, on this occasion of our 1980 trip to Ireland.

The Shaping of America

Contrary to general belief, the first African laborers to arrive in the English colonies did not come as slaves, and the first European laborers did not come as free men and women. The labor force in the seventeenth century was composed of indentured servants imported from both Africa and the British Isles. They were bonded for a specified period, usually seven years, after which they became legally free. The rulers of colonial Virginia were faced with two problems: in addition to the labor shortage, there was the question—who would police the laborers, who were not easily reconciled to conditions of servitude in a continent where land was available for the taking?

The colonies were not rich enough to support a professional police force of sufficient size. It was essential that one part of the labor force be enlisted to police the other—while remaining laborers themselves. Could Africans fill that role? Such a solution would hardly encourage emigration from England, on which the colonies were still dependent. Therefore, the English would have to be won to perform that function.

Such a role was by no means natural to them. English and African bonded laborers lived under much the same conditions of hardship, so severe that a large portion of them failed even to survive their period of

indenture, and they reacted to their oppression as do laborers everywhere, by drawing closer together, intermarrying, plotting escape—and
by revolt.

The growing solidarity among the laborers broke out in several
bloody revolts, which threatened the security of the government of the
Virginia colony (which had two-thirds of the total population of the
English colonies as a whole). In a response which is remarkably well
documented, the colonial rulers turned, around the middle of the seventeenth century, to a policy of drawing a line between the English and
African bond laborers. Certain privileges—the first being the exemp-
tion of female European bond laborers from field work—were conferred
on the former, while special laws were passed to fix the status of the
Africans: extending the term of servitude until it became permanent
and then hereditary, imposing a pass system, denying them the right to
carry arms, etc.

The process of encoding the new status took about a half-century,
and it marks the birth of the "white race" as a social category—the emergence of a class of laborers whose community of interests with their
exploiters was legally and publicly affirmed and who functioned to
maintain social control over the entire labor force, themselves included.
By 1705, the rulers of the Virginia colony felt sufficiently confident of
the support of their European proletarians to specify that white bond
laborers finishing their period of indenture be given a musket. What a
change from barely a generation earlier, when rebel forces—European
and African—besieged, captured, and burned the colonial capitol of
Jamestown and sent the governor fleeing across the Chesapeake Bay, the
same bond laborers who, between the years 1663 and 1682 hatched no
less than ten servile revolts and revolt plots!

Left historians who are critical of the characterization of the United
States as the "Land of Liberty" commonly assert that the much-vaunted
democracy depends on the denial of rights to the African, Native
American, and other people of color. This is a good example of the
"appearance" being the reverse of the "essence"—the development of a
system of racial slavery and national oppression depended on the extension of democratic rights to the "white" population as a whole. As early
as the eighteenth century there had emerged the pattern which was to
define the distinctive course of US history: US society is not merely
bourgeois but bourgeois white supremacist; the US working-class

movement has been, in the main, not merely opportunist but white racist opportunist; the main form of opportunism in the working-class movement is not merely white racism—an idea—but the acquiescence of the white workers in the system of white skin privileges imposed by the bourgeoisie.

The country never passed through a feudal stage of development. The American War for Independence, while it had progressive features, was not a war of a rising bourgeoisie against the forces of feudal absolutism, but instead a conflict between the merchant class of New England (allied with indebted southern planters) and the colonizing power over who would reap the vast profits of the slave trade; over which would be the third corner of the famous "triangle trade" described by slaves captured in Africa, rum and tobacco produced in the West Indies, and manufactured goods from either Liverpool or Massachusetts.

The decades following the establishment of the American Republic saw the emergence of two systems of exploitation: direct slavery in the South, supporting the cultivation first of tobacco and later of cotton; and manufacture based on wage labor in New England and the Middle Atlantic states. The history of the United States for the half-century preceding the Civil War is a history of the growing encroachment of the slaveowner's power on the federal government. The Seminole Wars, which were fought in Florida from 1819 to 1821 and which were efforts to recapture slaves who had escaped to join local Indian tribes; the Missouri Compromise of 1820, which extended slavery to the western territories; the 1836 to 1848 wars to wrest from Mexico the vast area that today makes up the states of Texas, New Mexico, Arizona, California, Nevada, and Colorado; the filibustering in Central America and the efforts to annex Cuba, the Kansas-Nebraska Bill of 1854, and the Dred Scott decision of 1858, which between them struck down the last legal obstacle to the spread of slavery throughout the entire country; and the efforts to restore the slave trade which had been abolished in 1808— these events testify to the increasing subservience of the national government to 30,000 slaveholding families.

The slave system required for its survival continued expansion into new territory. Wage labor capitalism required the continued expansion of the internal market, which was impeded by slavery. The forces upholding wage capitalism organized themselves first into the Free-Soil Party, then into the Republican Party, around a program of opposing the extension of slavery into new territories. When the Republican Party won the election with a bare plurality of votes among four major candidates, the impending conflict had become irrepressible.

The Civil War began with both sides fighting for slavery—the South to take it out of the Union, the North to keep it in. The real aim of the South, however, was not to secede from the Union but, by secession and war, to reorganize it on a new basis, with the "peculiar institution," slavery, as the foundation of an empire stretching from the Great Lakes to Central America.

The aims of the northern manufacturing bourgeoisie were modest: simply to restrict slavery to those areas where it already existed. As befitted this modest aim, President Lincoln at first pursued a cautious policy, going out of his way to assure the so-called border states (those states where slavery existed but the plantation system did not) that he had no intention of abolishing slavery. The federal military policy, of avoiding decisive battle while attempting to woo the South back into the Union, reflected this stage of the conflict.

This stage did not last long. Two things brought about a change. First was the attitude of the whites enlisted in the Union cause. They opposed the spread of slavery and the breakup of the Union but were hardly enthusiastic supporters of a war that was bringing them extreme hardship while enriching their employers through government contracts. They showed their feelings early by a series of draft riots in New York, Cincinnati, and elsewhere that commonly took the form of mob attacks on free blacks.

The second factor making for a change in government policy was the role of the blacks themselves. For decades, free blacks had been the mainstay of the small organizations advocating the abolition of slavery, and the escaped slaves had been both a severe drain on the slave economy and a call to the conscience of the country. Besides running away, the slaves also had developed various means of striking and resisting their exploitation, including launching numerous revolts, the most well known led by Gabriel Prosser, Denmark Vesey, and Nat Turner. Now, as the war began, black people began to see it as part of their struggle for freedom. Free blacks in the North understood that the cause of abolition was linked to a Union victory, in spite of Lincoln's protestations that he had no anti-slavery aims. While pressuring the government at all levels to broaden the war to one against slavery, they began to enlist in the

Union armies, often against giant obstacles placed in their way by the government, which did not want them as soldiers. The famous song, "John Brown's Body," commemorating the great revolutionary abolitionist who gave his life struggling against slavery, was written and sung by the Massachusetts 54th Regiment, one of the all-black units (commanded by white officers).

At first the slaves watched and waited; it was not yet clear where their interests lay. So long as they worked the cotton, the South could place in the field of battle a disproportionate number of its white manhood. The first attempts made by the slaves to join the Union cause were repulsed; fugitive slaves, making their way to Union army camps in the South, were sent back to their owners. Gradually, under the pressure of necessity, the Union's policy began to change: fugitive slaves were reclassified as "contraband of war" and put to work building fortifications, etc. Soon they were enlisted as scouts and spies for the Union armies.

By 1863, the attempt to wage a war against a force whose strength and weakness both lay in the institution of slavery brought about a change in Lincoln's policy. This was manifest in three things: first, the adoption of a more active military policy; second, the decision to encourage the enlistment and arming of blacks; and third, the declaration of the aim of the war to be the abolition of slavery.

It should be noted that Lincoln's famed Emancipation Proclamation freed no one: it merely declared slavery abolished in those areas then in revolt, that is, those areas where it could not be enforced. But as a statement of intent, it was enough to "loose the fateful lightning"—the 600,000 black laborers who embarked on a great working-class upsurge, beginning in 1863, a mass withdrawal of labor power—a general strike—which quickly brought the South to its knees.

The American Commune

By 1865, the war was over. How to reconstruct the nation? To restore slavery was out of the question; the nearly 200,000 blacks who had fought in the Union armies and the 600,000 more who had carried out the general strike, as well as Northern public opinion, which felt a hatred toward the slaveowners, ruled out that possibility. Yet the abolition of slavery had actually increased the legislative authority of the former slaveholders, owing to an increase in the number of free men on whom representation was based. And the defeated but not yet crushed slaveowners were threatening to return to Congress to achieve there what they had failed to achieve on the battlefield: withdrawal of federal troops from the South, validation of the Confederate debt, and restoration of slavery in all but name.

Lincoln and his successor as President, Andrew Johnson, attempted to reason with the former slaveholders, offering to readmit the Southern states to the Union with the sole condition that they formally accept the abolition of slavery. When it became clear that the arrogant lords of the lash had no intention of submitting even to this mild demand, public opinion turned toward a more intransigent policy of reconstruction.

Without the secessionist states in the Union, the Republican Party— the party of northern capital, which had just carried out a war, to some extent in spite of itself, against slavery—held firm control of Congress. Within that party, the radical wing, which was made up of genuine abolitionists and friends of the freed slaves along with others who recognized the need for stern measures to be taken against the South, gained ascendancy, initiating the period known as Reconstruction, which lasted from 1868 to 1876. For a brief moment, the interests of northern capital, which sought to break the former slaveholders' resistance, and the interests of the slaves and their friends intersected. It was this intersection that made possible the emergence of the former slaves as citizens and voters, a continuation of the process that had made them soldiers.

Once again, the turn in policy was prepared by the actions of the black people themselves, who were everywhere agitating, educating, organizing, and arming themselves, in some places occupying the land of their former owners. These former slaves, taking advantage of the plight of the federal government which had forced it to rely on them, proceeded to carry the revolution forward.

The Reconstruction acts passed by the radical-dominated Congress disenfranchised former Confederate officials and stationed federal troops in the South to protect the voting rights of the former slaves. Under these conditions, Reconstruction was carried to its furthest extent in South Carolina and Mississippi, the two former pillars of the Confederacy and the only states with a black majority. Of the delegates to a convention called in South Carolina for the purpose of writing a new state convention, almost half were former slaves and another fourth were so poor that they paid no taxes. Has the world ever seen a parliament of purer proletarian composition?

The Reconstruction legislatures enacted a series of laws that brought the South the most extensive, and in some cases the only, social reform it has ever known. Child labor laws, free public education, women's property rights, credit structures to enable the poor to obtain land—these and other measures flowed out of the legislatures which the men of property, North and South, denounced as "parliaments of gorillas." And behind these legislatures stood the black masses. Their radicalism generally took the form of an agrarian radicalism but occasionally went beyond this, as for instance when the New Orleans Republican Club sent a formal message of solidarity to the Paris Commune and applied for membership in the International!

And what of the white workers—what was their attitude toward these momentous changes? To answer that question, it is necessary to go back a bit, to before the Civil War. The trade union movement was basically a Northern phenomenon, since slavery had blocked the development of wage labor in the South. The unions well understood that free labor and slavery could not co-exist. Instead of opposing slavery, however, they opposed the slave, seeing in him the cause of their own degradation. Instead of enlisting behind the banner of abolition, which they feared would throw a mass of low-wage competitors on the labor market, the unions attempted to restrict the spread of slavery and free black labor as well, by supporting the Free-Soil (for whites only) Party. On the very eve of the war, the unions took no official notice of slavery, regarding it, at best, as a subordinate part of the general labor question, less important than minor legislative reform. When the war broke out, instead of embracing the cause of the slaves as their own, white labor had to be dragged by the bourgeoisie kicking and screaming into the war, especially after the first wave of enthusiasm was spent.

They followed the same course after the war. Highly incensed at the growing might and arrogance of the industrial bourgeoisie, which dominated the government through the Republican Party, white labor turned toward efforts to build its own party, bringing it into direct conflict with Southern blacks, who had in many places transformed the Republican Party into a labor party in fact. Looking at the masses of newly freed slaves, white labor saw them not as part of their own class but as competitors and potential scabs and attempted to restrict their employment by organizing them—when they agreed to admit them to the unions at all—into separate bodies. For the legislative accomplishments of the Reconstruction governments they cared not a rap, focusing their attention on the charges of corruption and on the so-called waste of stationing federal troops in the South.

What was true of the union movement was, sadly, also true of the disciples of Marx (although it was not true of Marx himself), who were quite influential in some sections of the labor movement. So it was that New York in 1871 witnessed a march of 20,000 demonstrating solidarity with the workers of Paris—20,000 radicals who were able to look across the ocean to the Paris Commune but were unable to look five hundred miles to the South to the South Carolina commune!

When white labor turned its back on Reconstruction, the end was in sight. The northern industrial bourgeoisie had no desire to see the continuance of the southern black revolt against property once it had accomplished the aim set for it of liquidating the former slaveholders as a class. The industrialists, therefore, in control of the Republican Party on a national level, carried through a legislative maneuver in 1877 which led to the withdrawal of federal troops from the South.

The Reconstruction governments and the black masses were confronted by the Ku Klux Klan and other white supremacist terrorist formations which had been mobilizing for just such a day. White supremacist "redemption" governments were set up in South Carolina and Mississippi, parallel to the legally constituted Reconstruction governments. The counterrevolutionary violence, which had never really ceased, became more intense, and after a few months, the reactionaries succeeded in crushing the Reconstruction parliaments and gaining official recognition from the authorities in Washington. Then began several decades of white terror. Black elected officials were ousted, black voters were eliminated by force and fraud, and black power fell before the armed quasi-official counterrevolutionary mobs, given a free hand by the federal government. It was at this time that a little-known episode in history took place, the Kansas Exodus of 1879, in which 90,000 blacks attempted to emigrate from the south; all but a few were halted by terrorism along the route. Sojourner Truth, who had been a prominent abolitionist and advocate of women's rights even before the Civil War, was one of the leaders of this "walking strike."

The industrial bourgeoisie now held sway over the whole country. Though the first external manifestations of US imperialism were its seizure, in 1898, of Cuba, Puerto Rico, and the Philippines, the birth date of imperialism as a stage of capitalism can be fixed as 1877, when the southern black masses went down to historic defeat. Northern labor, mainly white, would soon feel the cost of its failure to come to the defense of southern black labor.

The Road Not Taken

The year 1877 saw the outbreak of a great strike, in which railroad workers seized the terminals from Baltimore to Chicago and in which the bourgeoisie unanimously saw the specter of revolution. It was both symbol and substance that the troops hurled against the strikers were in many cases the military units that had recently been withdrawn from the South. In St. Louis the workers, under the leadership of the Workingmen's Party, went beyond the seizure of the terminals and began to exercise power in the city through mass assemblies.

Consider for a moment what would have been the impact on US (and world) history had white labor chosen to make common cause with the great upheaval of the black toilers of the South. Will it ever be possible to know how different might the outcome have been had there existed among the thousands of professed Marxists in the country at the time even a small organized group that understood the world historic significance of Black Reconstruction and undertook to establish links between it and the militant labor movement of the North?

Because white workers did not forge these links with black labor, a continuing pattern of labor control reasserted itself. The bourgeoisie was able to redefine the white skin privilege from that of not being a slave to that of having access to the bourgeois political process. Because of the inability of white labor to see its reflection in the struggles of black people, labor militancy was transformed into fight for white labor's interests. The subsequent history of black/white labor cannot be detailed here but a few illustrations will indicate the general direction.

Within a decade of the counterrevolution of 1877, there arose once again in the South a movement which threatened the sway of capital—this time among poor white farmers, angry at extortionate interest rates and monopoly control of prices for supplies and farm products. This movement, organized in the Populist Party, for a time threatened to blow apart the "solid south" of the Democrats. The black masses extended their support to Populism and attempted to broaden its program to address the needs of sharecroppers and hired laborers as well as independent farmers. At first blacks were accepted into the movement and even defended as public speakers at its rallies. But the ruling class posed a choice to the insurgent white masses: accept the blacks into your ranks, and you will bear the full weight of state repression; break ranks with them and some of your demands will be granted. After a stormy period, the movement decided to take the latter choice. Thus, southern populism to this day continues to combine outpourings of wrath against the banks with adherence to white supremacy. Observe the curious spectacle of Tom Watson, the most prominent leader of early Populism, who was only allowed to take his seat in the US Senate after having accepted the racist compromise, making a speech in defense of the Bolsheviks on one day and another in defense of lynching on the following day.

The Socialist Party, which was born around the turn of the century and attained considerable influence over the next two decades behind the figure of its well-known and popular spokesman, Eugene V. Debs, was also fatally marred by its acceptance that the notion that politics, even radical politics, was "white men's business." There were better and worse currents within American Socialism (the best broke with it early to join the Industrial Workers of the World), but the prevalent view was that the party could gain legitimacy in the eyes of the white workers only if it distanced itself from the black masses. Thus it organized racially segregated locals in the South (when it admitted blacks at all) and failed to oppose the racist "oriental exclusion" immigration policies favored by the reformist union officials. It would be inaccurate to present a picture of unanimous adherence to the white supremacist contract within either the rank and file or the leadership of white labor. The Knights of Labor, organized in the last century, welcomed members of all colors. The anarchists grouped around Albert Parsons, hanged in Chicago in 1886 in the Haymarket affair (the origin of the May 1 holiday), were staunch defenders of proletarian solidarity. The International Workers of the World (IWW), organized at the beginning of this century as a self-conscious revolutionary movement, in many respects the best and most successful revolutionary organization the country has known since the ending of the Reconstruction, broke with the pervasive racism of the American Federation of Labor.* (Irish readers may be familiar with the IWW, since James Connolly was an active member during his sojourn in the United States.) Yet these efforts, in spite of some successes which we treasure, were never able to win the bulk of white labor away from the racist ideas and practices that tied it to capital.

It was not until the Great Depression of the 1930s that there appeared on the scene a multiracial revolutionary organization that sought to make the "Negro question" a central feature of its activities. The Communist Party, under the influence of Lenin and the October Revolution, began to challenge the notion of what constituted the labor movement and to insist on the recognition of the strivings of black people as a vital part of the general revolutionary process.

The American Communist Party, which began the decade as an organization of about 2,000 people, most of whom were foreign born and non-English speaking, had an important influence on the course of events of that time. It came to national attention through its role in several important strikes, particularly in the San Francisco general strike of 1934.

Until the Depression, the workers in the mass production industries stood largely outside of the unions. The San Francisco strike along with other battles, most notably the sit-down strike at the General Motors plant in Flint, Michigan at the beginning of 1937, showed the more farsighted sectors of the capitalist class that the old policy of confrontation with the proletariat would no longer serve their interests. These elements, represented by the Roosevelt administration, decided instead on a policy of legalizing the unions and incorporating them into the framework of bourgeois legality.

The Roosevelt administration offered concessions of considerable value: the ending of the open tyranny of the steel barons and the

---

* The International Workers of the World (IWW), also commonly referred to as the Wobblies, was founded in Chicago in 1905 with ties to syndicalist, socialist, and anarchist movements. The American Federation of Labor was the largest national federation of labor unions in the first half of the twentieth century. It was founded in Ohio in 1866 as an offshoot of the Knights of Labor and dominated by craft unions. It persists today as the largest labor federation in the United States, having merged with the Congress of Industrial Organizations (CIO) in 1955.

bringing of the Constitution into industry, as well as the passage of much-needed social welfare legislation, in which the United States was decades behind the most advanced European countries. These concessions gained significance in the context of the world march of fascism, viewed fondly by those sectors of the ruling class who were unreconciled to the Roosevelt policies.

In return, the Roosevelt administration demanded that labor, for its part, forego its political independence and in particular that it entrust its fate to the coalition represented by the Democratic Party. This course seemed reasonable enough in places like Detroit where the CIO exercised considerable influence on the Democratic Party.

The problem was that the party of the northern liberals was also the party of the southern lynchers. Any attempt to organize the southern working class would inevitably come up against the system of racial segregation. And any attempt to challenge the system of segregation would find itself quickly spilling out of the economic arena into politics, to confront the Democratic Party. As events had already shown in the campaigns to organize southern agricultural workers, the challenge would in no way limit itself to peaceful and legal forms. The idea of southern rural black toilers organized and in arms was not acceptable to any sector of the capitalist class, no matter how liberal and reformist. If the CIO and the Left chose to follow that course, they could expect not a sympathetic hearing at the White House, but machine guns and tear gas.

Faced with the alternatives, which were posed concretely over the course of several years, labor and the CIO Left, for a variety of reasons, chose to follow the line of least resistance. The left-led organizations of southern black toilers were merged into national CIO unions, where they were allowed to languish; the efforts toward a labor party were indefinitely postponed in the interests of unity behind Roosevelt; and in general the CIO Left settled into a position as the legal left wing of the liberal–labor coalition.

The acceptance on the part of the CIO Left of the race policies of the dominant sector of capital represented the "historic compromise" of that epoch. It made it possible for Ford, traditional fortress of anti-unionism, to incorporate the union into the system of industrial legality as soon as it won recognition in 1940. It enabled labor to play its role as part of the Grand Affiance that steered the country through World War II. It led to the emergence of the coalition of bourgeois liberals, the official labor movement, and Negro reformism which has dominated US politics for four decades and continues to do so, although its stability is now shaken.

Politics as serious business disappeared with the cementing of the "historic compromise" of the late 1930s. When real politics reappeared over two decades later, it was largely due to the refusal of black people to accept any longer the results of that compromise. But we shall come to that subject later.

We now turn to several topics that are among those often raised by European leftists and which reveal some of the distinctive features of the United States: the question of the labor party, the question of fascism, and the national question.

The Labor Party

Why has the United States, alone among the developed countries, failed to produce a mass labor or social-democratic party? Is American prosperity so overwhelming or are US workers so backward that they have felt no need to take any initiative that would lead them out of the two major capitalist parties? We believe the answer lies elsewhere.

What is a labor party? It is the extension of the legislative arena of the usual trade union practice of bargaining for better terms in the sale of labor power. It represents a continuation of efforts to improve the conditions of the workers within the framework of the wage system. Thus, while a struggle for a labor party can embody great mass energy and even revolutionary potential, in its realized form it represents class collaboration.

US workers, by and large, have managed to achieve within the two-party system much the same degree of influence and social reform legislation that their European counterparts have achieved through mass social-democratic and communist parties—in some areas, more. In many respects the CIO was more party than union: aside from drastically altering the face of industrial villages (e.g., Gary, Indiana, and Flint, Michigan, major steel and auto manufacturing centers respectively; in such places the police are no longer called out to break strikes, and workers are not evicted from their homes during strikes or layoffs) the CIO also managed to acquire on a national scale influence within the

Democratic Party equal to that of the unions within, say, the British Labour Party. This political influence is conditioned (as it is in England, Germany, the Scandinavian countries, France, and Italy) on the unions agreeing to confine their reform efforts to limits acceptable to capital, even if not to particular capitalists at a particular moment. As has already been explained, in the United States this means specifically avoiding a challenge to the white supremacist contract on which bourgeois hegemony rests. Thus, the unions, both in their economic functions and in their political activity, have at best striven to redress some of the most glaring "excesses" of white racism, while leaving intact the fundamental compact on which white racism rests, namely, that black, brown, yellow, and red interests shall be served only after the needs of the white workingmen have been fulfilled. An additional point: in no other developed country is there such widespread cynicism toward the electoral process as in the United States. It is taken for granted among all sectors of the working class and the entire population that all politicians steal and take bribes, that political parties are motivated purely by vulgar self-interest, and that nothing of real value can come from the parliamentary game. The proportion of eligible voters choosing to cast a ballot has steadily declined, and it is likely that the upcoming presidential elections will witness for the first time the nonvoters outnumbering the vote totals of all the candidates combined.

Given the observable cynicism of the US voter toward bourgeois politics, together with the deeply ingrained national tradition of lawlessness, it is conceivable that the working class will never go through a labor party phase, or else that it will give rise to a labor party as a side product of the emergence of revolutionary dual power forms. On the other hand, there is a possibility that the black movement may succeed in launching a mass black party; there have been signs of this development on and off in recent years. If that happened, it would represent the essential elements of a labor party, regardless of its label, and we would orient toward it wholeheartedly.

Fascism

Everything in the United States must be viewed through the prism of the white supremacist contract on which bourgeois hegemony rests. Denial of rights to, and violence against, people of color is not fascism but the ordinary operation of bourgeois legality in the United States. Indeed, this violence is premised not on the denial of bourgeois rights to the rest of the population but on the continuance of these rights. Groups like the Ku Klux Klan, resisting through the most savage violence even the slightest concession to people of color, have had as their aim not the destruction of unions, constitutional legality, etc., but their maintenance and strengthening for whites only. For example, in one fifteen-year period in the last century, there were over fifty strikes on the southern railroads with the aim of driving the black workers out of the industry and strengthening the bargaining position of the white union in relation to management. Even today, in many localities, the Klan does not oppose but leads union locals.

There do exist fascist groups, and they have some base, but if fascism is understood as a movement, with some degree of autonomy directed against "ordinary" bourgeois rule, then it must be said that, excepting for a short period in the early 1930s, fascism has never been favored by the capitalist class in its dominant sectors. (This is not to deny growing pressure toward more right-wing, repressive policies within the existing institutional framework.) Why should the bourgeoisie favor fascism? Hasn't white supremacy served to maintain its rule so far?

There is another side, however, to the question of fascism. The institutions of official society are undergoing a deep crisis, symbolized by the name, Watergate. As has already been mentioned, there is a pervasive lack of trust among the population in the conventional ways of redressing grievances. (And unlike England, the United States has no characteristic tradition of "We'll muddle through.") The bitterness and anger on the American scene, among whites no less than among people of color, can hardly be exaggerated. It is likely to increase in the coming years. If this is taken into account, and if it is borne in mind that fascism is not merely a docile tool manipulated by a conspiratorial ruling class but has a definite autonomous component, then it is not out of the question that fascism, or something like it, may come to the fore, before the bourgeoisie is "ready" for it. If this happens, it will be based not on the independent petty bourgeoisie, which no longer exists, but on the masses of white workers reacting to a declining economy and increasing political disenchantment. Some black publicists have already noted that the white worker could be transformed from the rearguard of reaction into its vanguard. Signs of this tendency have already appeared. It is questionable whether old-style liberalism, or even a new social-democratic coalition, could prove an effective barrier to this possibility; only the proletarian revolution—the dictatorship of the anti-white supremacist working class—can offer a convincing alternative to fascism to the ever-growing numbers of white workers who are hostile to official society to the very backbone of their souls.

The National Question

For many years, the ideologists of capital boasted that the United States was a "melting pot" where diverse nationalities blended together and came to lose their distinctiveness. In recent years, the line has shifted to one of touting "ethnicity," the preservation of diversity within a harmonious whole. Both of these versions of history are racist lies, denying the reality of national oppression which is the characteristic feature of US life.

The various European groups that immigrated to the United States passed through a similar experience: one generation of discrimination followed by assimilation, marked by their beginning the process of escaping from the lowest ranks of the working class they at first occupied. This pattern held true for the Germans, Scandinavians, and Irish, the groups that constituted the bulk of the immigrant population prior to the Civil War, and for the Slavic peoples, Italians, and Jews, who began to come in large numbers in the last decades of the last century; the differences in the rate of assimilation were largely due to differences in degree of urbanization prevailing in the country from which they emigrated, the proximity of their language and culture to English around which the assimilation took place, and so forth. These immigrants shared a common feature; they all came with two passports: the official paper from the government and—their white skin.

This pattern never extended to the red, brown, black, and yellow peoples who also make their home in North America. The native people, the red Indians, fell before several waves of western settlement; their land was stolen from them in a series of massacres and swindles and they were pushed off to the margins of society, left to die out. In a similar situation to that of the Indians are the other native peoples, the Eskimos of Maska and the Polynesians of Hawaii.

Between 1836 and 1850 the United States took nearly half of what then constituted the territory of Mexico, including a large population of mixed Indian, Spanish, and African stock that made up the Mexican people. In spite of treaty assurances to the Mexican government that the conquered peoples would enjoy civil rights equal to those of all other US citizens, such has never been the case. Since that time, in response to the needs of capital for more labor power—first in the building of the steel mills and the railroads, later in agriculture and diverse industry—this population was augmented by large-scale immigration from Mexico, so that now the Mexican people make up a significant element of the population in cities from Cleveland to the west coast. They are generally confined to the lowest rungs of society, are the victims of legal and, particularly in the originally territories, extralegal terror and often, in the case of immigrants, the constant fear of deportation as the demand for their labor slackens. There are over 15 million of these people within current US borders.

Puerto Rico is a nation which had achieved self-rule within the Spanish empire and was conquered and occupied by the United States in 1898. It is still maintained as a direct colony, although there is some talk of making it a state as a way of forestalling independence. Beginning after World War I, when they were made US citizens by Act of Congress, and especially following World War II, Puerto Ricans began arriving in large numbers on the mainland; today there are 2 million, concentrated in New York and other eastern cities and as far west as Chicago. This compares with 3 million on the island itself, who for many years were an important source of imperialist profits in agriculture. The islanders are now jeopardized by the growth of the petro-chemical and other capital-intensive industries and the conversion of the island into a US military fortress. These developments tend to make the island population super-fluous to the plans of US imperialism.

Among the subjugated peoples which inhabit the current borders of the United States, the largest group, and the one whose history is most intertwined with the history of the country as a whole, is that population drawn from African, native American, and European stock, known variously as black, Black, Negro, Afro-American, New African, Bilalian, and "colored." The so-called "Negro Question" has long been a thorny one for US Marxists, who have few successes and many failures to show in this area. In our view, there was nothing predetermined about the evolution of the black people of North America into a separate people. It is not at all excluded from possibility that, had the revolutionary democratic tasks of Reconstruction been fulfilled, black people could have joined their culture and blood with the other peoples who inhabited the continent to develop a single nation north of Mexico and the territories taken from it. However, the failure of the democratic revolution closed off the possibility of integration, at least for the next historic epoch, and determined that black people would embark on the path to separate nationhood. The road to nationhood and national consciousness has been a stony one for black people, because of the incredible obfuscation spread by imperialism. Through the development of a language, a culture, religion and church institutions, and other organizations of struggle, black people have moved steadily toward nationhood and the striving for self-determination. When black people are being discussed as a nation, whatever title is affixed to them (currently "Black" and "Afro American" are most widely favored) should be capitalized, a practice we should follow for the remainder of this paper.

Chinese first came to the United States in large numbers in the last quarter of the nineteenth century, drawn mainly by the demand for laborers to build the railroads. They were subjected to intense discrimination, including lynchings, and were generally regarded as competitors by the newly founded American Federation of Labor, which sought to prevent their immigration through support for the Oriental Exclusion Act. (Lenin commented on this as one of the worst examples of chauvinist unionism.)

In recent years their numbers have been augmented by immigration from Hong Kong and Taiwan. Today they are ghettoized in "Chinatowns" in most large cities, victimized by overcrowding, high rents, and extreme exploitation. (San Francisco's Chinese population is the largest of any non-Asian city.)

The case of the Japanese immigrants is instructive for understanding American reality. Coming from one of the world's most highly civilized countries, significant numbers of Japanese began to arrive on the west coast at the beginning of the century, attempting to take advantage of the plentiful land to establish themselves as independent proprietors. In contrast to the welcome given the Finns, Dutch, and other immigrants from similar background but of European stock, they were relentlessly hounded by "patriots" and subjected to extralegal and legal land theft.

The most dramatic example was the treatment meted out to the Japanese at the start of World War II, when thousands on the west coast, including many born in the United States, had their land confiscated and were rounded up and relocated in concentration camps in the midwest, on the pretext that they were "security risks." The contrasts with the almost complete lack of discrimination directed at the native German, Italian, or other groups from "enemy" countries. Largely as a result of this act, to which most of the Left offered no objection at the time, Japanese are now to be found in Chicago, Minneapolis, and other midwestern cities, as well as up and down the west coast.

As US imperialism extended its domination after World War II over new territories, numbers of people from countries suffering dislocation as a result of American economic penetration began to make their way to the metropolis. Today there are, in most major cities, communities from Asia (Koreans, Filipinos, Thais), the Middle East (Palestinians, Yemenis, Syrians, Turks), and the Caribbean (Haitians, Dominicans, Jamaicans). In addition, there are large numbers of Cubans and Vietnamese, who are a special case because of their designation as "political" refuges, but whose conditions, particularly those of the latter, come increasingly to resemble those of every other persecuted racial minority.

Thus, it can be seen that the United States, far from being a "melting pot" or a "harmonious community of diverse cultures" is in fact a seething cauldron of national oppression and strivings for freedom. And in the 1960s, that pot boiled over.

The 1960s

The decade of the 1960s has already begun to pass into the annals of legend, as a host of historical studies, novels, and films have appeared to interpret that time for those who didn't experience Jerry Rubin, Eldridge Cleaver, make-love-not-war, Black Power, and Woodstock. One feature shared by virtually all the attempts to interpret that wondrous decade is blissful omission of the fact that from the first bornings through each stage of the development, the impulse for the phenomenon known as the "sixties" came from the strivings of the oppressed peoples, and in the first place, the Black people.

The 1960s actually began in 1955 when a Black woman, Rosa Parks, refused to give up her seat to a white man on a Montgomery, Alabama bus, as the law demanded. Her arrest touched off a wave of protest and struggle, as the Black community organized itself for a boycott of the bus lines and in the process created an alternative transportation system and a communitywide system of internal communication and democracy, bringing to prominence the gifted young leader, Martin Luther King.

This single event, more than any other, broke the gravelike silence of the Cold War years and sounded the call for the youth who were suffocating under the enforced dullness and conformity of that period. It was followed by the Freedom Rides, in which Blacks and whites got on southbound buses in the north and refused to rearrange their seating when the buses crossed into the segregated south. In 1961 came the first sit-in, organized by southern Black students. In 1964 came Freedom Summer, when thousands of northern Blacks and whites went to Mississippi to assist in the voter registration campaign underway there under the auspices of the Student Nonviolent (later National) Coordinating Committee (SNCC). When two young whites and a Black were brutally murdered by white racists, the plight of southern Black people was brought to national attention for the first time in nearly a century, and the conscience of the country was for a moment stirred. Later that year, the Mississippi Freedom Democratic Party, based among Blacks in the state who were still denied the right to vote, attempted unsuccessfully to unseat the state's regular delegation to the national convention to the Democratic Party. Out of the experience of the southern freedom movement grew the northern student movement represented by the Students for a Democratic Society (SDS). There was a New Left, and virtually every radical movement now in existence can trace its origin to those days. (The most notable exceptions are the Communist Party and the Socialist Workers Party, Fourth International, which played a very small part in the events recounted above.)

In every case the leftward movement was first registered in the Black movement and then transmitted to society at large. Those features which became the hallmarks of the New Left—the recognition that racism was not an isolated flaw, the focus on direct action, the internationalization of the struggle—all these took first shape in the movement of Black people.

One of the peculiarities of the US Left, which must be thoroughly understood by anyone who hopes to make sense out of American reality, is traceable to those years. We are referring to the insistence of Black revolutionaries from about 1965 on that the problems of America lay not in the Black community but in white society and that the task of white radicals was not to colonize among Black people but to address themselves to the racism of white America; Black people must organize through their own autonomous efforts. This view, when it was first put forward by Black leaders like Stokely Carmichael and Rap Brown, caused a lot of agonizing among white radicals who had always harbored paternalistic attitudes toward Black people, but for a time it prevailed in the New Left. Even today there is a line between those leftists who recognize the autonomy of the Black movement and the movements of the other oppressed peoples, and those who attempt to speak, through "multinational" parties, in the name of the Black, Latin, Asian, and Indian movements.

By 1968, when the popular movements (with a healthy assist from the Vietnamese people) came within a hair's breadth of splitting the Democratic Party, it could accurately be said that there existed in the United States a Left that, in terms of size and impact, had nothing to be ashamed of when compared to its counterparts in Europe. The Black Panther Party brought thousands of youth, heretofore without voice, onto the center stage of politics and stimulated developments in Latin and Asian communities and among white students. The high point was reached with the founding of the League of Revolutionary Black Workers, a federation of groups from various industrial plants in the Detroit area who had organized themselves outside of the union structures and built links with the Black schools and community, as part of a conscious effort to link Marxism with the Black Revolution. This effort led many white students in SDS to look seriously to the working class as an agent for social change.

The insights of the Black movement—the fight against white supremacy, internationalism, Marxism, and an orientation toward the working class—also had their impact on the newly emerging struggles of women. Women who had worked in SNCC, SDS women, women from the broad anti-war movement, those who had been activated by the upheavals of the sixties came together and created a revolutionary current within what was to become the women's liberation movement. Many chose to organize separately from men, paralleling the development of Black organizations. Others continued to work in SDS, in women's caucuses and committees. Together they made significant contributions to extending the insights of the Black movement into white society, carrying on their battles in the streets, not the legislatures or voting booths.

What Did We Do to Deserve the 1970s?

All this motion seemed to end even more suddenly than it appeared. In the spring of 1970 when Nixon sent US troops into Cambodia, there was a mass protest on campuses across the country, which led to the fatal shooting of four students at Kent State, in Ohio. At the same time, there occurred the killing of three students at Jackson State, a Black college in Mississippi. The latter received scant attention from either the media of the white peace movement—mute testimony to the flaw that would eventually lead to its demise. Then, silence. It was as if all the participants in the stormy events of the previous decade had been gathered at the edge of a cliff and pushed off. What happened?

The Black movement had been subjected to intense repression—the jailing of prominent leaders and thousands of activists, as well as government interference through the notorious "Counter-Intelligence Program" (COINTELPRO), which sought to create dissension and battles among various organizations. This repression, together with a number of serious mistakes that were committed by the leaders, led to a loss of confidence among the masses in the future of the movement and the fragmentation of the most important Black organizations, SNCC, the Black Panther Party, and the League. The process in the white student movement was quite different: there the students had hurled themselves at the walls of power, to no apparent avail—the war was still going on. Never able to recognize the Black struggle as their own cause, unable to develop an approach to the white worker, the majority of white student radicals turned away from radicalism. The movements turned inward, toward astrology, Christianity, sterile variants of "Marxism-Leninism," individual terrorism, and private pursuits. One of the manifestations of this turn was the sudden growth of the environmental movement, deliberately fostered and given respectability by the government and the media, which began to take up efforts to save various animal and plant species from extinction—at a time when the United States was raining death on Vietnam and the Black community was being beaten, starved, and drugged into submission.

The 1970s were, in general, years of retreat; the only Left groups to show any growth were those, like the Communist Party and the Socialist Worker's Party, who played no role in the upsurge of the previous decade and those who deliberately renounced its lessons (the social democrats of the New American Movement, various "M-L" [Marxist-Leninist] groups).

There were other exceptions, more positive in character. The movements among the other oppressed peoples, which began to develop later than the Black movement and were not the victims of such early repression, continued to grow. In Puerto Rico, the armed struggle reappeared, taking the form of small-scale, clandestine attacks on the physical symbols of imperialism. On the mainland the Movimento de Libercion Nacional, which identified with the path of armed struggle, became the most important revolutionary Puerto Rican organization.

The American Indian struggle reached new heights with the successful retaking of Alcatraz, the Bureau of Indian Affairs, and Wounded Knee. Sovereignty and land rights were reasserted in seizures of stolen land by Indian nations across the country. In the last few years Indian peoples have begun to establish links with the anti-nuclear movement in order to end the "energy war" being waged largely against them. Mexicans in the southwest have also begun re-taking their land. All these movements soon began to attract their share of repression, with a number of prominent figures assassinated or jailed.

The recent period has also given indications that the Black movement has begun to rebuild. The emergence of organizations like the Afrikan People's Party, a large demonstration for human rights at the United Nations headquarters, and the recent convening of the founding conference of the National Black United Front are all signs of this rebirth. Together with the rebellions in Miami, Chattanooga, and elsewhere they offer the hope that the coming years will witness the resurgence of a movement so critical to the development of a radical climate.

The women's movement in the 1970s, entering the national consciousness to the point that the term "male chauvinist" has become part of the general vocabulary and the most popular demands of the movement are universally known, although often as caricatures. Yet the earlier radical sectors of the movement, who pioneered in the development of new ways of living and who brought the challenge to male supremacy to every sphere of life, have been largely eclipsed by a national leadership which seeks to confine the struggle to improving the position of women through legislative means. Another sector of the women's movement has turned from activism to focus on the building of "women's community"—cultural centers, services, and supportive lifestyle. More activist-oriented is the anti-violence-against-women sector of the movement. Its strength lies in women's direct action to free themselves from the danger and degradation of all types of violence. Its perhaps fatal weakness lies in its tendency to form alliances with the state, particularly the racist criminal justice system.

Encouragingly, the radical sector of the women's movement has begun to coalesce once more, mainly around the struggle for reproductive rights, including the right of abortion and an end to compulsory sterilization, which is suffered primarily by women of oppressed nationalities. This sector of the movement has emphasized and demonstrated the importance to the women's movement of linking up with the movements of the oppressed peoples within the United States and around the world.

A new political force, the gay liberation movement, was also born at the start of the 1970s. In its battle against official and unofficial harassment and repression, the gay movement has shown itself to contain a revolutionary as well as a class collaborationist wing. Since Three Mile Island the anti-nuclear movement has become a national phenomenon. Militant demonstrations and attempts at reactor site occupations, along with large marches, have taken place repeatedly, and it is obvious that many new people are being drawn into the struggle. As with every other movement, its potential depends on its ability to link its future with the struggle against white supremacy. In this respect, the anti-nuclear movement has fallen far short, and its weakness in this area plays a large part in determining its general stance. It is still largely dominated, though not without opposition, by the old leaders from the peace movement, including sectors of the Left who seek to limit it to the single question of nuclear weapons and the export of reactors, both of which touch on imperialism, and refuse to take up the "front end" of the nuclear cycle, which relates to uranium mining, most of which takes place on American Indian land. In general, the current leaders of the anti-nuclear movement are doing everything in their power to keep it from developing into an anti-racist, anti-capitalist movement.

When Congress recently reintroduced registration for the military draft, it provoked the greatest response of mass illegality in the country in a decade, as an estimated quarter of those called failed to show up. The movement is very new, but it too will undoubtedly reflect the struggle between white reformism and revolutionary internationalism that characterizes every mass appearing on US soil.

Some Current Questions

The US economy is obviously going through a crisis. The abandonment of the dollar as the dominant currency in world commerce, the high cost of energy, the runaway inflation, the recovery of Europe and Japan as competitors, the shutting down of a large portion of the physical plant of the steel industry, the near bankruptcy of Chrysler—all these occurrences point to the likelihood of hard times ahead and the consequent radicalization of the American worker.

The strong point of our organization has always been its grasp of Marxist theory and US history. Our weakness has been analysis of current trends. Recently, under the impact of events and the example of our Italian and Irish comrades, we have begun to take up questions of current analysis. For instance, what is the character of the present crisis? Is it structural, even apocalyptical, or is it another of the familiar crises of profitability and realization? Does it involve a crisis of the law of value itself? In another area, what is the relationship between the multinationalization of the capitalist ruling class and the nation-state as an instrument of rule?

The answers to these questions have practical implications. For example, it has always been the practice of US capital, in periods of economic difficulty, to shield the white workers as much as possible from the most severe burdens, by guaranteeing that the heaviest weight of unemployment falls on those sectors where the work force was predominantly Black. In the past, this has meant that Black people have gone through periods of extreme hardship, followed by their re-entrance in larger numbers than before into the basic industries. If the present crisis is of a different character than previous ones, and if the technology that emerges from it—the so-called silicon revolution—is of such a nature as to prevent the expansion of capital bringing with it the expansion of the proletariat, what impact will this have on the position of Black people and other oppressed groups? Will it be the policy of the state to push them into the status of a permanent underclass, a marginalized group with no firm and stable ties to the productive process? And what does this say about the policy of genocide as ruling class policy? What does it say about the relation of the struggle in the productive and nonproductive sectors and about the value of making such a distinction at all? Most of all, what would it mean for revolutionaries seeking to help the working class find the proper response to bourgeois policy, whatever it may be?

The above are some of the questions we have begun to consider, in a process which we expect will be protracted and which will involve our entire organization and all those close to it. We have but recently become aware of the discussions on these questions that are taking place among our comrades in the revolutionary Left in Europe. We regard it as extremely necessary that we take part in these discussions, and that end is one we hope to accomplish through the development of closer and more direct ties with our European comrades.

Strategy

The position of the working class under capitalism gives rise to two patterns of behavior, each with its characteristic consciousness. On one side are the efforts of the workers to improve their conditions of life while accepting the framework of the wage labor relation. This pattern, which manifest in ordinary trade union struggles, constitutes the basis for reformism. White supremacy, representing as it does the effort of a portion of the working class to strike a separate bargain with capital, forms part of this pattern. Alongside the above sort of activity, workers are also compelled to resist their condition as wage labor and assert themselves as producers. Such resistance takes the form of direct action, tends in the direction of proletarian solidarity, and challenges the institutional framework that ties the workers to capital. These two patterns of behavior are not imported into the working class by reformists or revolutionaries, as the case may be, but arise spontaneously out of the conditions of working-class life.

The revolutionary potential of the working class lies in its location in the production process, which compels it to act in ways that undermine the capital relation. Ordinarily, this aspect of working-class behavior is subordinated to the dominant reformist aspect; even when it arises spontaneously it is accompanied by reformist consciousness.

The task of proletarian revolutionaries is to seek out and discover those aspects of proletarian activity which foreshadow the future society, which manifest the tendency of the proletarians to constitute themselves as a ruling class, to link these sporadic activities into a coherent social bloc that exists and struggles under capitalism without accepting the permanency of capitalism, and to transform the consciousness of the participants through the criticism of bourgeois ideas as they exist within the working class.

A revolutionary strategy is, in short, a strategy of dual power. It is the treating of revolution as an act for today, as a part of the continuous struggle, instead of a dream to be indefinitely postponed in the interest of "realism."

From what we have said so far it should be evident that we regard the struggle against white supremacy as the most advanced outpost of the new society and the key ingredient in a revolutionary strategy. The waging of that struggle among whites is the main distinctive task of Sojourner Truth Organization, as befits its character as an organization made up of white people.

Reading List

The following list of books may prove helpful to those interested in doing additional reading about the United States.

W. E. B. Du Bois, *Black Reconstruction in America*, New York: Harcourt, Brace, and Howe, 1935.

Lerone Bennett, *The Shaping of Black America*, Johnson Publishing. Should be called "The Shaping of America." If you can read only one book on this list, it should be this one or the one above.

William D. Haywood, *Autobiography of Big Bill Haywood*, International. Firsthand account of the International Workers of the World by one of its greatest leaders.

Len DeCaux, *Labor Radical*, Beacon Press. Accounts of International Workers of the World and Congress of Industrial Organizations.

C. Vann Woodward, *Tom Watson: Agrarian Radical*, Oxford University Press. Good biography of an enigmatic and characteristic figure.

Robert Bruce, *1877: Year of Violence*, Quadrangle Books.

Robert and Pamela Allen, *Reluctant Reformers: Racism and Social Reform Movements in the US*, Doubleday.

Al Richmond, *A Long View from the Left*, Houghton Mifflin. An autobiography of a former Communist Party member.

Richard Boyer and Herbert Morals, *Labor's Untold Story*, United Electrical Workers. To be read with extreme caution. Revisionist, white labor apologetics.

Art Preis, *Labor's Giant Step*, Pathfinder. Trotskyist history of the Congress of Industrial Organizations. A series of lies complementary to the lies in the one immediately above.

Howard Fast, *Freedom Road*, Bantam. A novel of reconstruction.

Martin Glaberman, *Wartime Strikes*, Bewick Editions. World War II.

Harry Haywood, *Black Bolshevik: Autobiography of an Afro-American Communist*, Liberator. Autobiography of an important Communist Party leader, today a Marxist-Leninist.

Mathew Ward, *Indignant Heart: A Black Worker's Journal*, South End Press. Excellent!

Six Radicals Remember the Sixties, South End Press.

Dan Georgakas and Marvin Surkin, *Detroit: I Do Mind Dying*, St Martin's Press. Account of the League of Revolutionary Black Workers.

Hosea Hudson, *Black Worker in the Deep South*, International.

Karl Marx and Friedrich Engels, *Civil War in the US*, Citadel.

Dee Brown, *Bury My Heart at Wounded Knee*, Bantam. Popular history of American Indian struggles.

Autobiography of Malcolm X, Ballantine or Grove.

Robin Morgan, ed., *Sisterhood Is Powerful*. The major collection of writings from the women's liberation movement.

Gorda Lerner, *Black Women in White America*, Random. Redstockings, Feminist Revolution.

16

The Backward Workers

Ignatiev challenges the idea that workers are backward and in need of education or leadership, offering instead the provocative thesis that a hidden profundity animates even the seemingly backward actions of US workers. This essay first appeared in Issue 11 of the Sojourner Truth Organization journal, Urgent Tasks, *in spring 1981.*

In a medium-sized metalworking plant in the Midwest, it is time for the annual election of union stewards. In one department, the man who has been the steward for many terms and who now faces for the first time in recent memory an opposition candidate not selected by himself campaigns by telling the workers he represents, "Listen, you know we've got things pretty good over here. They let us eat in the department, they let us take breaks and wash up early, and so forth. If we elect some hothead who starts filing grievances, all that will go out the window."

He is returned to office in a close vote.

In another department a militant, reputed to be a "radical," who has served several terms as a steward, is defeated by one vote in his bid for re-election. Several of the workers—some who voted for him and some who voted against him—give the same reason for their decision: "the company doesn't like him."

Do the above examples demonstrate passivity and backwardness, as most of the left would contend? Let's look at a case where the workers chose the opposite course.

In the blast furnace division of one of the country's largest steel mills, the workers oust the committeeman who has held the post for decades and elect a young black man who has campaigned on a promise of militant struggle. The new committeeman, who is a socialist and, what is more, an honest man, takes office and begins to carry out his program— no more swapping grievances, no more hand-shake agreements, etc. Almost at once conditions in the division go to hell, as the company retaliates by abolishing early quit time, sleeping on the midnight turn, and other little arrangements the workers have managed to establish over the years. Within six months the workers are grumbling that the deterioration in working conditions is the committeeman's fault, and he is complaining bitterly of their "backwardness" and "lack of appreciation." In the next election he is turned out and a conservative is put in his place.

The three examples cited above illustrate the point that workers always have good reasons for doing what they do. This statement, which seems so obvious on first hearing, stands directly opposed to the view, widespread on the Left in one variation or another, that the problem of the workers' movement is one of leadership.

In none of the three cases cited above, which are representative of the kinds of choices ordinarily offered to workers, can it be demonstrated that the workers made the wrong decision. I wish to go further than this simple observation of fact, to the general thesis that when a significant body of workers or members of an oppressed group is offered a choice between several possibilities which they perceive as realistic, they always make the right choice.

Although I have attempted to formulate my thesis as carefully as possible, it is absolutely certain to be misinterpreted, so I shall try to clarify what I mean and what I do not mean. I do not mean that a group of workers in a struggle cannot make a mistake in picking the date of a strike, charging a police line, etc; such an assertion trivializes my argument. Nor do I mean that, apart from tactical slips, workers always act in a manner designed to advance their class interests; if that were the case, capitalism would no longer exist.

The *Communist Manifesto* says that, under capitalism, the worker is "compelled to face with sober senses, his real conditions of life, and his relations with his kind."[1] Compelled to face—it is this total attachment to reality, which is the main psychological characteristic of the exploited class, that I am exploring in my thesis.

By their actions people shape the future. Workers as a class, unlike revolutionary intellectuals (and the latter not as much as they would like to believe), do not choose between various futures based solely on what is desirable. A weighty factor in their calculations is what they consider possible.

Consider the American slaves before the Civil War. An observer travelling the US South in 1858 looking for signs of imminent rebellion would not have found them. The slaves, except for the exceptional individuals who escaped, seemed if not content at least resigned to their situation and strove to make it as tolerable as they could. Even when the Civil War broke out they did not immediately respond; as Du Bois points out, they waited and watched. Yet in 1863 they launched a general strike which broke the back of the Confederacy, bridging to an end the system of slavery.

What was the new element that transformed the Afro-American bonded population from slaves whom their masters felt safe in leaving in the care of the elderly and unarmed women while they went off to fight into militant combatants whose disregard for life itself astonished all observers at the battles of Port Hudson, Fort Wagner, Nashville, and Petersburg? It was not the exhortations of the abolitionists, since these had always been present and the slaves were always aware of them. Nor could it be the vanguard actions of a few bold individuals; upwards of three hundred documented rebellions and plots, the last major one before John Brown having taken place in 1831, had failed to spark a general uprising. The new element could only be the real war, which prevented the slaveholders from bringing the full weight of their repressive apparatus to bear on the slaves. It was the perception of this new reality by the slaves that carried their resistance to a new stage. The time they spent waiting and watching to make sure the war would not be quickly terminated through negotiations was as essential to the slaves' self-realization as were the previous years spent in mastering a new language, developing a community, gaining a knowledge of the terrain and experimenting with various forms of resistance, including strikes, sabotage, flight, and armed revolt. It should be understood that I am not denying the value of exhortation and bold action by vanguard groups; I am attempting to examine the context in which these ingredients have an effect.

It is evident that the slaves' perception of the futility of a general uprising before the Civil War and the usefulness of one after the war began was accurate. Is it always the case that the oppressed perceive with such scientific precision the possibilities of such a situation?

The spectacle of the European Jews going off peacefully to the gas chambers and organizing the delivery of their own quotas for the death camps has amazed all. What was the alternative? As a people they held no position in industry, agriculture, or territory that could have provided them with a base of power. They had no tradition in the use of arms and no access to arms had they known how to use them. Because of their place as petty traders they were despised by the masses of people in the places where they resided. It is possible that had they attempted mass violent resistance (or mass suicide as Gandhi recommended) the result would have been their extermination to the last soul. As it was, they paid a heavy price, but the Jews as a people survived.[2]

Men do not fight back out of desperation. (Nor do women: most cases of mothers' reckless courage in defense of their children can be shown to have a rational basis.) There never comes a time when people have no choice but to resist oppression. As Bernard Shaw puts it: "Man will suffer himself to be degraded until his vileness becomes so loathsome to his oppressors that they themselves are forced to reform it."[3]

Nor are people so constructed as to permit total consciousness of their oppression to exist alongside total despair at ending it. The combination leads to extinction, as happened to numerous native American peoples for whom life unfree was unthinkable.

For civilized peoples, that is, those who have come to treasure existence for its own sake and have lost all sense of the value of life, there is a connection between what is possible and what is tolerable. To survive, they invent mechanisms for blocking the reality from their consciousness. There are always consolations, if not in this world, then in the next. One can easily imagine galley slaves on a Roman ship comforting themselves with the knowledge that fresh air was one of their job benefits![4]

When a relatively rapid deterioration of conditions cracks the effectiveness of the denial mechanism at a time when no way out has yet become apparent, there follows the appearance, on a mass scale, of symptoms of mental illness. Such is the case in the United States today.[5]

Now what does all of this have to do with politics? Just this: it is an attempt to explain why the most common approach of the Left to workers doesn't work and can't work. Of all the dogma that pervades the Left, the most pervasive is the dogma of the backwardness of the working class.

The underlying assumption of most left strategies is that workers move from reform to revolution. This assumption is present regardless of the differences over what is the best reform issue, how much propaganda for revolution should be mixed in with the reform struggle, etc. The starting point is always the reform movement, the struggle for partial aims, through which workers will come to realize the need for revolutionary change. The task becomes enlisting workers in the reform movement.

Do those who operate in the way described above ever question their basic assumptions? Do they really believe that US workers are unable to see that there are demands which are unmet and that these demands are, at least in part, winnable through collective action? The problem is not that US workers don't know these things; if they appear not to know them, it is because they choose not to know them.

US workers are uneasy about the totality of their lives and their relations with their kind. They know, whether or not they ever put it in these terms, that their fundamental condition is not addressed in a program for better cost-of-living allowance, bidding procedures and dental coverage. Such things, won or lost, will not transform the reality of their lives.[6] Why should ordinary workers leave the privacy of their homes and their diversions and take the emotional risk of participating in struggle in which they have to trust other people and which is liable to raise hopes that will be disappointed—for some trivial demand that will leave them more or less as they have? Realistic people will not follow such a course, and the workers are, above all, realistic.

In a passage immediately following the one I quoted above (from *Man and Superman*) Don Juan, who is undoubtedly speaking for Shaw, goes on to speak of "the most surprising part of the whole business that you can make any of these cowards brave by simply putting an idea into his head." The character observes that "men never really overcome fear until they imagine they are fighting to further a universal purpose—fighting for an idea, as they call it."

And he sums up his argument thus:

this creature Man, who in his own selfish affairs is a coward to the backbone, will fight for an idea like a hero. He may be abject as a citizen; but he is dangerous as a fanatic. He can only be enslaved whilst he is spiritually weak enough to listen to reason. I tell you gentlemen, if you can show a man a piece of what he now calls God's work to do, and what he will later call by many new names, you can make him entirely reckless of the consequences to himself personally.[7]

Think of the greatest mass movement in our times. Does anyone really think that, when black sit-in strikers sat at a lunch counter while lit cigarettes were ground out in the back of their necks, they were doing it for a cup of coffee. Or that the southern black masses faced electric cattle prods, high pressure water hoses, and the rest in order to gain the right to vote, as if they did not know how little that right brought to their cousins in Watts, Harlem, and Chicago's South Side?

When black people marched down the dusty roads singing "Ain't gonna let nobody turn me 'round," it was a new world they sought. Their determination and willingness to sacrifice derived from the realization that the particular issue which engaged them at the moment, through the struggle itself, was an expression of their efforts to give birth to this new world. (Indeed, it was the genius of Martin Luther King, and the secret of his place in the hearts of black people, that he was able, in spite of his political weaknesses, to give voice to the mass vision, dream if you will, of a new world.)

The starting point in defining a revolutionary struggle is not the content of the specific demands put forward by the participants, but their coming to awareness, often in the course of the struggle itself, that the fact of their self-activity is more important than whether or not they win or lose on the immediate issue.

In an article published in *Urgent Tasks,* no. 9, Lee Holstein pointed out: Revolutionary consciousness cannot be taught—even by the most masterful of teachers. It can be encouraged, pointed out, distinguished from bourgeois consciousness, but it cannot be taught. It does not progress in a linear fashion, from one stage to another in higher and higher and higher levels of grasping Marxist theory. It rises to the surface in action which is a break with routine, and then submerges.[8]

We are not dealing with easy questions here. The link between the struggle and the vision is not formal but organic. It is not expressed primarily in the articulation of the socialist goal (some left groups keep permanently set in type a paragraph explaining the need for socialism, which they paste onto the end of every article they publish). Nor are we speaking of the practice of some left groups of issuing hysterical appeals for revolutionary struggle. The link is expressed in the way the struggle itself develops as a realization of the new society.

In the article cited above, Lee Holstein argues that

> every instance of working class self-activity is a break with the trade union struggle. Every break with the trade union struggle is a break with bourgeois hegemony. The workers, in these instances, jump out of the capitalist framework, rejecting its validity and legitimacy. In these instances the working class becomes autonomous of capital and acts for itself. This is revolutionary working class self-activity.[9]

The task for revolutionaries is to seek out those instances of the break with bourgeois hegemony and clarify their implications, link them together institutionally, and counterpose them to the prevailing patterns of behavior and institutions. This task has theoretical, political, and organizational aspects, and no one can claim to have achieved more than a beginning. However far the journey may take us, the first step must be the recognition that revolutionary class consciousness is not the expansion of reformist class consciousness but its negation and that while it is true that the working class only manifests its development in the struggle for partial reforms, the deeper truth is that reforms are a by-product of revolutionary struggle.

17

Influence

Ignatiev reflects frankly on the limits of his ability to engage with white workers in his time organizing on the shop floor. The essay was published in the first issue of the journal Hard Crackers: Chronicles of Everyday Life *in 2016.*

———

The summer following my first year in graduate school at the university, I took a job running a drill press in a small shop that manufactured surveying equipment. The place wasn't bad as such places go: it wasn't as dirty as some, the work wasn't physically exhausting, the foreman left you pretty much alone so long as you did your job. The main problem was boredom: take the piece out of the box, set it in the fixture, drill it, turn it over, drill the other side, tap it, take it out, blow it off with the air hose, set it in the box with the finished parts, take another piece out— every three minutes throughout the day. The noise of the machines prevented conversation except during the half-hour lunch and two ten-minute breaks. One of the drill press operators compared it to watching the same "I Love Lucy" re-run all day long. The normal workday was ten hours: the last two hours were voluntary, but most people stayed for the overtime pay.

Among the time-servers was Mike, who had been there for eight years. Less than thirty, he had already lost several of his front teeth and most of his hair. He disdained the stool the company furnished; from starting buzzer to quitting time he was on his feet doing a little two-step in front of the drill press. Shoelaces untied, shirt-tail flapping and base-ball cap turned to the side, his hands would fly over the machine levers and fixture clamps as the drill spattered oil and metal chips in every direction and the finished parts piled up in the box. In a different kind of factory he might have been seen as a menace to union standards.

As a young man I had left college to embark on a proletarian journey that would take me over the next twenty years into quite a few places like this one. Here, because I had been hired as summer help, I was identi-fied as a student. From my first day on the job Mike sought me out.

"Are you going to try and talk me into going back to school?" he asked me in our first conversation. "I've only got a GED and I was never much for school."

When I told him that I was not, he seemed satisfied, until he asked me the same question a few days later. Altogether he must have brought the subject up a half-dozen times. Nevertheless, on several occasions he remarked that in spite of my education I was "just like a regular guy. I always thought those people at the university were stuck-up, but I can talk to you."

Down the street from the shop was a creek that two centuries earlier had furnished power to the mills alongside its banks. Giant carp now flourished in the waters below its falls, finding shelter among the tires, beer cans, and shopping carts people had discarded there. Often Mike and I would go down to the creek side at lunch and drop a line in. Eating the fish was out of the question, but they were fun to catch.

The main topic of conversation at these sessions was schemes for getting out of the shop. Mike pursued the subject with passionate inten-sity. I, of course, having already in part effected my escape, could not bring a full commitment to the exercise, but I did my best to hold up my end. No proposal was too fantastic for consideration, no idea was rejected without careful examination. Legality entered not at all into our calculations: only fear of getting caught led us to decide against most of the plans put forward. We rejected carrying a gun on a "job" because it increased the likelihood of our getting hurt and the penalties in case of capture. I don't remember that the danger of hurting someone else ever came up.

"I got a kid," began Mike, as he explained to me one idea that stood out for being perfectly legal. "I figure that if I start him in his fourth birthday, with three hours a day practice the kid ought to be able to learn to kick field goals and extra points every time. Do you know how much money those guys get for a couple hours work a few Sundays a year? They never get tackled, they don't get dirty, they hardly work up a sweat. It's not even like the kid has to be some great athlete or anything, just be good at kicking the ball between the goal posts. Anybody can learn that if you start him young enough. I sure wish my old man did that for me— then I wouldn't have to be in a place like this." He paused and shrugged his shoulder. "Probably," he concluded, "if I did bring up the kid to be a placekicker, by the time he got old enough for the pros, they'd pass a new rule outlawing platooning."

Most of our dreams for getting out fell back on the common fantasies: inheriting money from an unknown relative, striking oil in the back-yard, winning the lottery. The lottery had a special appeal: virtually everyone in the shop played, most relying on number combinations they believed to possess mystical properties. Although all were aware that the odds were against them, there was a logic to their regular purchase of the tickets: everyone who had been playing for a while had either won or knew others who had won small prizes—a hundred dollars or so. The few dollars lost each week didn't seriously alter the financial status of someone already accustomed to doing without, but the rare hundred-dollar windfall was the occasion for a spree, a personal treat the winner could relive over and over again while inserting pieces into the drill press. It was a form of saving for a sunny day. And there was always a chance for the big kill. In that shop, not religion but the lottery was the sigh of the oppressed, the spirit of a spiritless condition. (The substitution of the lottery for heaven was a sign of progress, since the odds against making a big score in the lottery were only a million to one.)

On one occasion Mike tried to explain his rapid pace of work, for which he took a lot of ribbing from others in the shop. "The reason I work so hard is that this is the only thing in my life I've ever succeeded at. I was never any good in school. I was rejected by the navy. I screwed up my marriage because I drank too much. But in here, as long as I put out the work, I'm OK. It's something I'm good at. Can you understand that?"

One noon toward the end of summer, Mike and I were standing on the shipping dock, watching the members of the congregation drift back from the watering holes where they had drunk their lunches. I was mulling over an incident that had occurred the day before. I had left after eight hours instead of the customary ten. The foreman had assigned another man to my machine for the last two hours and asked me to show him the job. I had run through the operation, taking care to warn the man, a recent immigrant from Poland, that if he fed the drill down too quickly it would grab the soft aluminum, spin it out of his hands, break the drill, and maybe hurt him. The next morning when I came in, I went over to ask him how he had done. In reply he showed me two bandaged fingers and proudly pointed to a box full of finished parts. A quick count revealed that he had turned out almost as many parts in two hours as I was accustomed to turning out in a day.

As I was going over in my mind plans for getting the guy to slow down before he killed the rate on the job (including breaking his other eight fingers if necessary), one of the assemblers, a black man, turned the corner to head into the shop. Mike muttered something.

My mind elsewhere, I didn't hear him clearly. "What did you say?" I asked.

"Are you from out of state or something?" said Mike. "I called him a nigger. Don't they use that word where you come from?"

"Well, I don't," I said.

"Oh, I forgot, you're at the university. They're all liberals there," he said with a laugh.

Before I could reply, the buzzer sounded, calling us to our devotions.

Now Mike, although brought up in a neighborhood world-famous for its resistance to school integration, lived on a street where the majority of residents were black. In response to questions from whites on the job, he simply explained that he liked living with black people. He got along well with most of the black workers. I wanted to learn more about how he thought. But first, I would have to straighten something out: no one was going to get away with calling me a university liberal. When mid-afternoon break came around, I walked over to Mike's work station and said, "I want to ask you a question and I want you to think before you answer. I've spent twenty years in places like this. Do you really think that a couple of years of college makes that much difference in what I am?"

Without a moment's hesitation, Mike replied, "Oh, I was just kidding. You know I think you're OK." He slapped me on the shoulder. "Hey, there's a lot of smart people at the university," he added, citing a member of the law faculty who had recently been in the news for winning a major court decision on behalf of a local pornographer.

It was no use. The more he praised me as one of the boys and spoke of his admiration for the university, the clearer it became that between us there was a great gulf fixed and that a summer together in the shop and a few storytelling sessions would not erase his accumulated suspicion of the academic world and all of its representatives.

After that he always greeted me either as "Einstein" or by the name of the university. We never had our talk about racial attitudes; there didn't seem to be any point. He no longer used the word "nigger" in my presence (once or twice visibly checking himself as he was about to do so). And I never did figure out how to get that Polack to slow down on the job.

III

Abolish the White Race: The *Race Traitor* Project

18
Abolish the White Race—by Any Means Necessary

This was the first editorial statement of the journal Race Traitor, *cowritten with John Garvey and published in the journal's first issue, Winter 1993. It outlines the mission of the journal: to examine the historical, political, and social forces that hold together the white race, and what it would take to abolish it. In the tradition of John Brown, the authors encourage race treason and loyalty to humankind.*

The white race is a historically constructed social formation—*historically* constructed because (like royalty) it is a product of some people's responses to historical circumstances; a *social* formation because it is a fact of society corresponding to no classification recognized by natural science.

The white race cuts across ethnic and class lines. It is not coextensive with that portion of the population of European descent, since many of those classified as "colored" can trace some of their ancestry to Europe, while African, Asian, or American Indian blood flows through the veins of many considered white. Nor does membership in the white race imply wealth, since there are plenty of poor whites, as well as some people of wealth and comfort who are not white.

The white race consists of those who partake of the privileges of the white skin in this society. Its most wretched members share, in certain respects, a status higher than that of the most exalted persons excluded from it, in return for which they give their support to the system that degrades them.

The key to solving the social problems of our age is to abolish the white race. Until that task is accomplished, even partial reform will prove elusive, because white influence permeates every issue in US society, whether domestic or foreign.

Advocating the abolition of the white race is distinct from what is called "anti-racism." The term "racism" has come to be applied to a variety of attitudes, some of which are mutually incompatible, and has been devalued to mean little more than a tendency to dislike some people for the color of their skin. Moreover, anti-racism admits the natural existence of "races" even while opposing social distinctions among them. The abolitionists maintain, on the contrary, that people were not favored socially because they were white; rather, they were defined as "white" because they were favored. Race itself is a product of social discrimination; so long as the white race exists, all movements against racism are doomed to fail.

The existence of the white race depends on the willingness of those assigned to it to place their racial interests above class, gender, or any other interests they hold. The defection of enough of its members to make it unreliable as a determinant of behavior will set off tremors that will lead to its collapse.

Race Traitor aims to serve as an intellectual center for those seeking to abolish the white race. It will encourage dissent from the conformity that maintains it and popularize examples of defection from its ranks, analyze the forces that hold it together and those which promise to tear it apart. Part of its task will be to promote debate among abolitionists. When possible, it will support practical measures, guided by the principle, *Treason to whiteness is loyalty to humanity.*

Dissolve the Club

The white race is a club, which enrolls certain people at birth, without their consent, and brings them up according to its rules. For the most part the members go through life accepting the benefits of membership, without thinking about the costs. When individuals question the rules, the officers are quick to remind them of all they owe to the club and warn them of the dangers they will face if they leave it.

Race Traitor aims to dissolve the club, to break it apart, to explode it. Some people who sympathize with our aim have asked us how we intend to win over the majority of so-called whites to anti-racism. Others, usually less friendly, have asked if we plan to physically exterminate millions, perhaps hundreds of millions of people. Neither of these plans are what we have in mind. The weak point of the club is its need for unanimity. Just as the South, on launching the Civil War, declared that it needed its entire territory and would have it, the white race must have the support of all those it has designated as its constituency, or it ceases to exist.

Elsewhere in this number, readers will find an account of John Brown's raid on Harpers Ferry and some of the events it set in motion. Before the Civil War, the leading spokesmen for the slaveholders acknowledged that the majority of white northerners, swayed above all by the presence of the fugitive slave, considered slavery unjust. The Southerners also understood that the opposition was ineffective; however much the white people of the north disapproved of the slave system, the majority went along with it rather than risk the ordinary comforts of their lives, meager as they were in many cases.

When John Brown attacked Harpers Ferry, Southern pro-slavery leaders reacted with fury: they imposed a boycott on northern manufactures, demanded new concessions from the government in Washington, and began to prepare for war. When they sought to portray John Brown as a representative of northern opinion, Southern leaders were wrong; he represented only a small and isolated minority. But they were also right, for he expressed the hopes that still persisted in the northern population despite decades of cringing before the slaveholders. Virginia did not fear John Brown and his small band of followers, but his soul that would go marching on, though his body lay a-mould'rin' in the grave.

When the South, in retaliation for Harpers Ferry, sought to further bully northern opinion, it did so not out of paranoia but out of the realistic assessment that only a renewal of the national proslavery vows could save a system whose proud facade concealed a fragile foundation. By the arrogance of their demands, the Southern leaders compelled the people of the north to resist. Not ideas but events were in command. Each step led inexorably to the next: Southern land-greed, Lincoln's victory, secession, war, blacks as laborers, soldiers, citizens, voters. And so the war that began with not one person in a hundred foreseeing the end of slavery was transformed within two years into an anti-slavery war.

It is our faith—and with those who do not share it we shall not argue—that the majority of so-called whites in this country are neither deeply nor consciously committed to white supremacy; like most human beings in most times and places, they would do the right thing if it were convenient. As did their counterparts before the Civil War, most go along with a system that disturbs them, because the consequences of challenging it are terrifying. They close their eyes to what is happening around them, because it is easier not to know.

At rare moments their nervous peace is shattered, their certainty is shaken, and they are compelled to question the common sense by which they normally live. One such moment was in the days immediately following the Rodney King verdict, when a majority of white Americans were willing to admit to polltakers that black people had good reasons to rebel, and some joined them. Ordinarily the moments are brief, as the guns and reform programs are moved up to restore order and, more important, the confidence that matters are in good hands and they can go back to sleep. Both the guns and the reform programs are aimed at whites as well as blacks—the guns as a warning and the reform programs as a salve to their consciences.

Recently, one of our editors, unfamiliar with New York City traffic laws, made an illegal right turn there on a red light. He was stopped by two cops in a patrol car. After examining his license, they released him with a courteous admonition. Had he been black, they probably would have ticketed him and might even have taken him down to the station. A lot of history was embodied in that small exchange: the cops treated the miscreant leniently at least in part because they assumed, looking at him, that he was white and therefore loyal. Their courtesy was a habit meant both to reward good conduct and induce future cooperation.

Had the driver cursed them, or displayed a bumper sticker that said, "Avenge Rodney King," the cops might have reacted differently. We admit that neither gesture on the part of a single individual would in all likelihood be of much consequence. But if enough of those who looked white broke the rules of the club to make the cops doubt their ability to recognize a white person merely by looking at him or her, how would it affect the cops' behavior? And if the police, the courts, and the authorities in general were to start reading around indiscriminately the treatment they normally reserve for people of color, how would the rest of the so-called whites react?

How many dissident so-called whites would it take to unsettle the nerves of the white executive board? It is impossible to know. One John Brown—against a background of slave resistance—was enough for Virginia. Yet it was not the abolitionists, not even the transcendent John Brown, who brought about the mass shifts in consciousness of the Civil War period. At most, their heroic deeds were part of a chain of events that involved mutual actions and reactions on a scale beyond anything they could have anticipated—until a war that began with both sides fighting for slavery (the South to take it out of the Union, the north to keep it in) ended with a great army marching through the land singing, "As He died to make men holy, let us fight to make men free."

The moments when the routine assumptions of race break down are the seismic promise that somewhere in the tectonic flow a new fault is building up pressure, a new Harpers Ferry is being prepared. Its nature and timing cannot be predicted, but of its coming we have no doubt. When it comes, it will set off a series of tremors that will lead to the disintegration of the white race. We want to be ready, walking in Jerusalem just like John.

What Kind of Journal Is This?

Race Traitor exists, not to make converts, but to reach out to those who are dissatisfied with the terms of membership in the white club. Its primary intended audience will be those people commonly called whites who, in one way or another, understand whiteness to be a problem that perpetuates injustice and prevents even the well-disposed among them from joining unequivocally in the struggle for human freedom. By engaging these dissidents in a journey of discovery into whiteness and its discontents, we hope to take part, together with others, in the process of defining a new human community.

Really, there are two questions—who are our readers and who are our writers? We imagine that both will be quite diverse. We expect to be read by educators, by clergy, by scholars, by parents, by teenagers—in short, by many people for whom the willingness to question their membership in the white club might be the only thing they hold in common. We anticipate that if we are successful, those individuals will come to have a great deal more in common.

About our writers: several months ago, we sent out a letter and brochure, mostly to people we knew, either personally or by reputation, and asked them to consider submitting articles for the premier issue of *Race Traitor*. We were delighted at the response and we hope that you share our enthusiasm. In addition to the articles included here, we have already received some that we will be publishing in our next issue.

At the time of the initial request, we provided some clues about the type of articles we hoped to receive but made it clear that we were willing to consider all submissions. We remain willing to do so and encourage all our readers to submit material.

You may wonder what kind of articles we want. We want to chronicle and analyze the making, remaking, and unmaking of whiteness. We wish neither to minimize the complicity of even the most downtrodden of whites with the system of white supremacy nor to exaggerate the significance of momentary departures from white rules. We want to get it right. With this, our first issue, we think we have barely made a beginning. Here are some topics we would like to have investigated and written about:

Movies—reviews of films such as *The Commitments*, *Q & A*, the newly released *Zebrahead*, and *Malcolm X*.

Sports—articles examining the ways in which the participation and interest in organized sports affects notions of excellence and ability.

Schools—a look at the California social studies textbook controversy and the issue of multiculturalism.

Political Representation—an article on the recent redistricting of the New York City Council, which drew race lines all across the city in order to promote the goal of group representativeness among local legislators.

Unions—an article on the contrast between the public posture of most of the trade unions, which stresses their support for civil rights and equality, and their everyday practices which continue to provide preferential treatment for whites, usually men.

Young People—articles not only about, but by, young people—about their schools, their neighborhoods, their friends, their conflicts (and their alliances) with their parents.

Political Philosophy—an article exploring the issue of responsibility.

Who is responsible for things going on the way they do? How important is intent?

Literature—both original fiction and poetry and interpretive essays, especially on American writers.

Graphics—photographs and artwork. To do so, we need artistic and technical assistance from our readers.

Debate—criticism and discussion through letters.

Music—of course.

These are only ideas. We are sure that our readers will have many more of their own—stories to tell, questions to ask. Please do not be shy. If you are not sure, write us and tell us about your ideas and we will respond.

We should say that there are some articles we are not interested in publishing. Since we are not seeking converts, we probably will not publish articles which lecture various organizations about their racial opportunism. Also we probably will not publish articles promoting interracial harmony, because that approach too often leaves intact differential treatment of whites and blacks and provides subtle confirmation of the idea that different races exist independently of social distinctions.

Finally, a note about tone and style: we want well-written articles and are willing to work with contributors on revisions we think necessary. We want the journal to be accessible to a wide audience. We welcome scholarly articles, but we may ask the authors to include more background explanation than they would for a professional journal.

In the original film version of *Robin Hood* (starring Errol Flynn), the Sheriff of Nottingham says to Robin, "You speak treason." Robin replies, "Fluently." We hope to do the same.

19

The American Intifada

This essay was written in the fall of 1991, six months before the Los Angeles uprising, for a New Politics *symposium on the question "Is There Life after the AFL-CIO?" In it, Ignatiev considers how white supremacy has shaped American social democracy and fragmented the revolutionary potential of the American working class. The editors of* New Politics, *who solicited the piece, chose not to publish it. This version appeared in the first issue of* Race Traitor.

Just about the time the Democratic Reform Progressive Concerned Rank-and-File Fightback Caucus ousts the last remaining clique of right-wing bureaucrats from local union office, unions as we know them will cease to exist, and the radicals of various stripes who placed their hopes on union reform will be left in undisputed possession of a dead horse.

The strength of unionism was a component of a social democratic compact, the American Historic Compromise. Since white supremacy was the cement that held it together, it is fitting that the black workers led in toppling the deal; but they were not alone. The working class used the gains of a period of accumulation to launch a struggle that went beyond unionism. New forms emerged, based upon shop floor organization, direct action, and community solidarity. The struggle was against the capital relation itself and it invaded all spheres. If Dodge Main and Lordstown were the high points of the conflict at the point of production, they cannot be understood apart from Watts, Columbia, and Attica.

Because the unions could no longer discipline the workers in the mass production industries, the employers withdrew their support for the collective bargaining system and began a new round of union-busting, computerization, and relocation; the amount of functioning plant and equipment they were willing to scuttle in the search for a more malleable labor force is the exact index of their fear of the working class.

In America, the comic futility of the Democratic Party, and in Europe, the course of French Socialism as well as the defeat of the Party of Austerity, Swedish Section of the Second International, herald the bright future of social democracy, which is brought closer by the integration into the world market of the low-wage areas formerly (or still) ruled by communist parties. (This does not rule out the possibility of the Democrats returning to office and repeating the whole dreary cycle, until they are dispersed by a Nazi corporal and nine soldiers or something else.) "For the rest," wrote Hegel,

> it is not difficult to see that our epoch is a birth-time, and a period of transition. The spirit of the time, growing slowly and quietly ripe for the new form it is to assume, disintegrates one fragment after another of the structure of its previous world.[1]

The old is dying and the new has not yet been born. The paradox of the moment is that, while social democracy can no longer call forth the energies of the revolutionary class, the forms of activity that anticipate the new society do not yet constitute a visible alternative. Where to look for them?

For most of the four centuries of its existence, capitalism has meant one or another form of bound labor: slavery, indentured servitude, apprenticeship, prison labor, peonage, and so on. The formally free, waged proletarian prevailed only in some branches of production in a few countries for a certain period. The political forms associated with "free" labor—the electoral franchise and collective bargaining—have been exceptions in history. Now as capital dissolves the large concentrations of workers in the mass production industries, "once again, the physiognomy of the world proletariat i.e., that of the pauper, the vagabond, the criminal, the panhandler, the street peddler, the refugee sweatshop worker, the mercenary, the rioter" and the prison rebellion, squatting, and the food riot become the characteristic forms of proletarian resistance.[2] The intifada is the mass strike of our day.

Are there any hints of an approaching American intifada? I cite three.

1. A few years ago, in some cities, jobs in the fast-food industry that traditionally paid the minimum wage were going begging despite a wage rate in some cases as high as $5.50 per hour. The increase in the minimum wage, which the unions had sought without success, the black youth who normally filled those jobs accomplished by direct action. Those young people are the sector of American society least touched by official institutions. No one knows how they communicated and enforced agreement among themselves as to what constitutes an acceptable wage, whether they boycotted the jobs entirely or worked them only long enough to buy a new pair of hundred-dollar sneakers or sunglasses, but their ability to act cohesively means that the forces of the intifada are gathering.

2. Numerous observers have identified as a product of oppression the high proportion of children of black mothers born out of wedlock. It is more than that. The large numbers of young women who are having children despite the absence of a husband with a dependable wage are doing so with full knowledge of the consequences; they are aware, from observation, that raising a child on welfare closes off their chances of escaping the poverty that surrounds them. To give birth under those circumstances must be viewed, therefore, as a choice—to link their future and that of their child with the community they belong to, above all with the women in it, rather than to pursue the limited opportunities for upward mobility that exist. It is a decision not to rise out of the working class but with it—a display of the kind of solidarity essential to an oppressed class preparing to assert itself.

3. Years ago I knew a Chicago steelworker whose son liked to throw rocks at the buses that carried black workers to the mill. "I asked the kid," he recounted, "what do you want to bother the niggers for? They're just going to work." What led that young man, just out of high school, to elevate the white supremacy his father took for granted into a program

for militant action? It was the knowledge that he would never get the sort of decently paying, fairly steady job his father held—or the fear that he would. Many like him, for whom traditional union white supremacy with a human face can no longer deliver the goods, are turning toward national socialism.

I am aware of the pathological elements present in each of the examples I have cited. As currently manifest they are, at best, negations. Each, however, represents a departure from the conventional wisdom of reform, and each expresses a deeply felt sentiment that a total change is necessary.

As I write these lines, two items come to my attention. The first is a reference, in the *New Yorker*, of September 23, 1991, to black youth as "Brooklyn's intifada." The second is a fundraising letter from a civil rights group which recently won a $12,500,000 lawsuit against Tom Metzger, head of the fascist organization, White Aryan Resistance (WAR). Since Metzger's personal fortune consists of a modest home, the legal strategists expected the suit to put him out of business. WAR, however, responded to the court decision with a declaration of war against the white liberal judges who uphold the system. This in turn led to the appeal for funds.

What clearer confession of futility than an appeal for donations immediately following a successful multimillion-dollar lawsuit?

Only the vision of a new world can bring the angry proletarians who make up the WAR constituency together with the Brooklyn intifada. The black proletariat forms the historical antipode to capital. When the workers of the world learn to say, as did The Commitments, "I'm black and I'm proud"—the modern rendition of "Workers of all countries, unite!"—then the new world will be at hand. Will they learn it? No one can say; but one thing is certain: no regenerated social democracy, no bigger and better welfare state, can compete with WAR for the allegiance of the alienated, dispossessed white youth .

The alternatives are the society of freely associated labor or barbarism. There is no longer a difference between reform and revolution. Put another way, no serious reform is possible without the overthrow of capital. The question is not how to defend the interest of the workers against the multinational corporations, but how to maximize the revolutionary potential of the working class. Today the proletariat is subordinated to capital, and the expressions of its potential class rule are sporadic, fragmented, and imbricated in retrograde tendencies. Under these circumstances it is not surprising that we see through a glass darkly. Nonetheless, the rough beast slouches toward Bethlehem to be born.

20

Immigrants and Whites

Ignatiev explores the relationship between whiteness and the American identity. He argues that whiteness is not a self-evident natural category, but the product of a set of choices European immigrants actively embraced. In doing so, he says, they forfeited the ability to be truly American, an experience best embodied by the descendants of enslaved Africans. This article, written in the spring of 1987, appeared in Konch Volume 1, Issue 1, *in a slightly different form, under the title "'Whiteness' and the American Character." This version appeared in* Race Traitor Issue 2 *in the summer of 1993.*

At the turn of the century, an investigator into conditions in the steel industry, seeking employment on a blast furnace, I was informed that "only Hunkies work on those jobs, they're too damn dirty and too damn hot for a 'white' man." Around the same time, a West Coast construction boss was asked, "You don't call an Italian a white man?" "No, sir," came the reply, "an Italian is a dago." Odd though this usage may seem today, it was at one time fairly common. According to one historian, "in all sections native-born and northern European laborers called themselves 'white men' to distinguish themselves from the southern Europeans they worked beside."[1] I have even heard of a time when it was said in the Pacific Northwest logging industry that no whites worked in these woods, *just a bunch of Swedes.*

Eventually, as we know, Europeans of all national origins were accepted as "whites"; only rarely and in certain parts of the country is it any longer possible to hear the Jew or the Italian referred to as not white. The outcome is usually hailed as a mighty accomplishment of democratic assimilation. In this essay, I shall argue two points: first, that the racial status of the immigrants, far from being the natural outcome of a spontaneous process, grew out of choices made by the immigrants themselves and those receiving them; second, that it was in fact deeply tragic, because to the extent the immigrants became "white" they abandoned the possibility of becoming fully American. Finally, I shall speculate a bit on the future.

The general practice in the social sciences is to view race as a natural category. A representative example of this approach is the book by Richard Sennett and Jonathan Cobb, *The Hidden Injuries of Class*.[2] The authors declare the subject of their study to be the "white working class." As well-trained sociologists, they are careful to specify what they mean by "working class," but they do not find it necessary to define "white." *Of course everybody knows* what is "white." However, for some, including this writer, the inquiry becomes most necessary just at the point Sennett and Cobb take for granted.

It is beyond the scope of this essay to review the work showing the origins in the seventeenth century of "white" as a social category. The term came into common usage only in the latter part of the century, that is, after people from Africa and people from Europe had been living together for seven decades on the North American mainland.[3]

In an April 1984 essay in *Essence*, "On Being 'White' . . . and Other Lies," James Baldwin wrote that "No one was white before he/she came to America." Once here, Europeans became white "by deciding they were white . . . White men from Norway, for example, where they were *Norwegians*—became white: by slaughtering the cattle, poisoning the wells, torching the houses, massacring Native Americans, raping Black women."[4]

Now it is some time since settlers from Norway have slaughtered any cattle, poisoned any wells, or massacred any Indians, and few Americans of any ethnic background take a direct hand in the denial of equality to people of color; yet the white race still exists as a social category. If it is not an inherited curse, whiteness must be reproduced in each generation. Although Sennett and Cobb treat it as a natural classification, they recount a story that reveals some of how it is recreated. One of the characters in their book is a man they call Ricca Kartides, who came to America from Greece, worked as a building janitor and, after a few years, "bought property *in a nearby suburb of Boston*" (emphasis added).

What social forces, what history framed the fearful symmetry of Mr. Kartides's choice of location? Was that the turning point in his metamorphosis from a Greek immigrant into a white man? What alternative paths were open to him? How would his life, and his children's lives, have been different had he pursued them? There is a great deal of history subsumed (and lost) in the casual use of the term "white." Even in the narrowest terms, "white" is not a self-evident category. Barbara J. Fields recounts the apocryphal story of an American journalist who once asked Papa Doc Duvalier what portion of the Haitian people was white. Duvalier answered unhesitatingly, "Ninety-eight percent." The puzzled reporter asked Duvalier how he defined white. "How do you define black in your country?" asked Duvalier in turn. When the answer came back that in the United States anyone with any discernible African ancestry was considered black, Duvalier replied, "Well, that's the way we define white in my country."[5] Along the same lines, every character in Mark Twain's novel, *Pudd'nhead Wilson*, black and white, is of predominantly European descent.

If whiteness is a historical product, then it must be transmitted. Like all knowledge, white consciousness does not come easily. In one case in a small town in Louisiana at the beginning of the century, five Sicilian storekeepers were lynched for violating the white man's code: they had dealt mainly with black people and associated with them on equal terms.[6] In her short story, "The Displaced Person," Flannery O'Connor describes how the immigrant is taught to be white. The story takes place shortly after World War II. A Polish immigrant comes to labor on a small southern farm. Among the other laborers are two black men. After he has been on the farm for a while, the Pole arranges to pay a fee to one of the black men to marry his cousin, who is in a displaced persons camp in Europe, in order for her to gain residence in the United States. When the farm owner, a traditional southern white lady, learns of the deal, she is horrified and undertakes to explain to the Pole the facts of life in America.

"Mr. Guizac," she said, beginning slowly and then speaking faster until she ended breathless in the middle of a word, "that nigger cannot have a white wife from Europe. You can't talk to a nigger that way. You'll excite him and besides it can't be done. Maybe it can be done in Poland but it can't be done here . . ."

"She no care black," he said. "She in camp three year."

Mrs. Mcintyre felt a peculiar weakness behind her knees.

"Mr. Guizac," she said, "I don't want to have to speak to you about this again. If I do, you'll have to find another place yourself. Do you understand?"

The story ends tragically as a consequence of the Pole's failure to learn what is expected of him in America.

In what relation, then, does whiteness stand to Americanism? If adoption by the immigrant of prevailing racial attitudes is the key to adjusting successfully to the new country, does it then follow that to become white is to become American? The opposite is closer to the truth: for immigrants from Europe (and elsewhere, to the extent they have a choice), the adoption of a white identity is the most serious barrier to becoming fully American. *

Like Cuba, like Brazil, like other places in the New World in which slavery was important historically, the United States is an Afro-American country. In the first place, persons of African descent constituted a large portion of the population throughout the formative period (how large no one can say, but probably around one-fifth for most of the first two centuries). Second, people from Africa have been here longer than most of the immigrant groups—longer in fact than all groups except for the Indians, the "Spanish" of the Southwest (themselves a mixture of Spaniards, Africans, and Indians), and the descendants of early English settlers (who by now also include an African strain). Above all, the experience of people from Africa in the New World represents the distillation of the American experience, and this concentration of history finds its expression in the psychology, culture, and national character of the American people.

What is the distinctive element of the American experience? It is the shock of being torn from a familiar place and hurled into a new

---

* From a *political* standpoint, the degree of cultural assimilation is largely irrelevant. The two least culturally assimilated groups in the country are the Amish of Lancaster County—the so-called Pennsylvania Dutch—and the Hasidic Jews; yet both enjoy all the rights of whites.

environment, compelled to develop a way of life and culture from the materials at hand. And who more embodies that experience, is more the essential product of that experience, than the descendants of the people from Africa who visited these shores together with the first European explorers (and perhaps earlier, as recent researchers have suggested), and whose first settlers were landed here a year before the Mayflower?

In *The Omni-Americans,* Albert Murray discusses the American national character.[7] He draws upon Constance Rourke, who saw the American as a composite, part Yankee, part backwoodsman (himself an adaptation of the Indian), and part Negro. "Something in the nature of each," wrote Rourke,

> induced an irresistible response. Each had been a wanderer over the lands, the Negro a forced and unwilling wanderer. Each in a fashion of his own had broken bonds, the Yankee in the initial revolt against the parent civilization, the backwoods man in revolt against all civilization, the Negro in a revolt which was cryptic and submerged but which nonetheless made a perceptible outline.[8]

"It is all too true," writes Murray,

> that Negroes unlike the Yankee and the backwoodsman were slaves . . . But it is also true—and as things have turned out even more significant—that they were slaves *who were living in the presence of more human freedom and individual opportunity than they or anybody else had ever seen before.*[9]

Later he writes:

> The slaves who absconded to fight for the British during the Revolutionary War were no less inspired by American ideas than those who fought for the colonies: the liberation that the white people wanted from the British the black people wanted from white people. As for the tactics of the fugitive slaves, the Underground Railroad was not only an innovation, it was also an *extension* of the American quest for democracy brought to its highest level of epic heroism.[10]

American culture, he argues, is *"incontestably mulatto."*

After all, such is the process by which Americans are made that immigrants, for instance, need trace their roots no further back in either time or space than Ellis Island. *By the very act of arrival,* they emerge from the bottomless depths and enter the same stream of American tradition as those who landed at Plymouth. In the very act of making their way through customs, they begin the process of becoming, as Constance Rourke would put it, part Yankee, part backwoodsman and Indian—and part Negro![11]

It is very generous of Murray, as a descendant of old American stock, to welcome the newcomers so unreservedly. But what if their discovery, as he puts it, of the "social, political, and economic value in white skin" leads them to "become color-poisoned bigots?"[12]

Their development into Americans is arrested. Like certain insects which, under unfavorable conditions, do not complete their metamorphosis and remain indefinitely at the larval stage, they halt their growth at whiteness.

John Langston Gwaltney wrote:

The notion that black culture is some kind of backwater or tributary of an American "mainstream" is well established in much popular as well as standard social science literature. To the prudent black American masses, however, core black culture *is* the mainstream.[13]

At issue is not, as many would have it, the degree to which black people have or have not been assimilated into the mainstream of American culture. Black people have never shown any reluctance to borrow from others when they thought it to their advantage. They adopted the English language—and transformed it. They adopted the Christian religion—and transformed it. They adopted the twelve-tone musical scale and did things with it that Bach never dreamed of. In recent years they have adopted the game of basketball and placed their own distinctive stamp on the style of play. And they have adopted spaghetti, okra, refried beans, noodle pudding, liver dumplings, and corned beef, and modified them and made them a part of ordinary "drylongso" cuisine.

It is not black people who have been prevented from drawing upon the full variety of experience that has gone into making up America. Rather, it is those who, in maddened pursuit of the white whale, have cut themselves off from human society, on sea and on land, and locked themselves in a "masoned walled-town of exclusiveness."

All this is not to deny that whites in America have borrowed from black people. But they have done so shamefacedly, unwilling to acknowledge the sources of their appropriations, and the result has generally been inferior. The outstanding example of this process was Elvis Presley, who was anticipated by Sam Phillips's remark, "If I can find a white man who sings like a Negro, I'll make a million dollars." Other examples are Colonel Sanders's chicken and Bo Derek's curls. There are exceptions: Peggy Lee comes immediately to mind.

Can the stone be rolled back? If race, like class, is "something which in fact happens (and can be shown to have happened) in human relationships" (to borrow the words of E. P. Thompson), then can it be made to unhappen? Can the white race be dissolved? Can "white" people cease to be?

I cite here two details which point to the possibility of the sort of mass shifts in popular consciousness that would be necessary to dissolve the white race. The first is the sudden and near-unanimous shift by Afro-Americans in the 1960s from the self-designation "Negro" to "black" or "Black." (Among prominent holdouts are Ralph Ellison and the Negro Ensemble Company.) The shift involved more than a preference for one term over another; although its precise implications were and still are unclear, and although much of its substance has disappeared or been reduced to mere symbol, there seems little doubt that the initial impulse for the change was a new view among black people of their relation to official society. "Black" stood in opposition to "white."

The second detail I cite was an apparently trivial incident I happened to witness. At Inland Steel Company's Indiana Harbor Works in East Chicago, there used to be a shuttle-bus system that operated at shift-change time, picking up workers at the main gate and delivering them to the various mills within the plant, which may be as much as a mile away. One morning, as the bus began to pull away from the gate, I saw, from my passenger's seat, a man running to catch it. He was in his early twenties, apparently white, and was dressed in the regulation steelworker's garb: steel-toed shoes, fire resistant green jacket and pants, and hard hat, underneath which could be seen shoulder-length hair, in the fashion of the time, the early 1970s. The driver pulled away and, as he did so, said over his shoulder, "I would have stopped for him if he'd had short hair."

That small incident brought home to me with great force some of the meaning of the revolution in style that swept so-called white youth in those years. At the time, many young people were breaking with the values that had guided their parents. In areas as seemingly unrelated as clothing and hair styles, musical tastes, attitudes toward a war, norms of sexual conduct, use of drugs, and feelings about racial prejudice, young people were creating a special community, which became known as the counterculture. In particular, long hair for males became the visible token of their identification with it. It was a badge of membership in a brotherhood cast out from official society—*exactly the function of color for Afro-Americans*. As that incident with the bus driver reveals, and as anyone who lived through those years can testify, it was perceived that way by participants and onlookers alike.

Granted that only a minority of eligible youth ever identified fully with the counterculture, that the commitment of most participants to it was not very deep, that few in it were aware of all its implications, that the whole movement did not last very long, and that its symbols were quickly taken up and marketed by official society—nevertheless, it contained the elements of a mass break with the conformity that preserves the white race.

Normally the discussion of immigrant assimilation is framed by efforts to estimate how much of the immigrants' traditional culture they lose in becoming American. Far more significant, however, than the choices between the old and the new is the choice between two identities which are both new to them: white and American.

21

The White Worker and the Labor Movement in Nineteenth-Century America

This essay was originally a talk given at the History Department Seminar at Queens University in Kingston, Ontario, on March 16, 1992. It was republished in Issue 3 of Race Traitor *in the spring of 1994. Ignatiev challenges historians to examine black resistance as an essential expression of class struggle and an integral part of US labor history.*

Ask a panel of labor historians, old or new, to name the most important worker uprisings in America's past, and chances are they will list the Flint Sit-Down, the 1919 Steel Strike, Pullman, 1877, perhaps one or two others. No matter how long the list, it will never include the New York City insurrection of July 1863.

It began at the hour of work, as a strike at the city's railroads, machine shops, shipyards, foundries, and building sites. Employing a familiar tactic, strikers formed a procession and marched through the industrial district, closing down shops and calling upon workers to join in. The strike quickly turned into a full-scale insurrection, as workers fought with the police, erected barricades, and attacked symbols and representatives of the government in Washington. Within hours of the outbreak, the insurrectionists managed to acquire weapons, post sentinels and set up internal communications, and form committees to clear the tenements of enemy agents. They developed mechanisms to identify supporters and opponents among the commercial strata and imposed a rigid moral conformity in their neighborhoods. When the possibility came up of the authorities summoning troops from Albany, the crowd dispatched contingents to cut telegraph lines, tear up railroad tracks, and destroy ferry slips. As in every popular uprising, women and children played a vital part. In short, the insurrectionists created the rudiments of dual power—without a single newspaper, labor union, political club, or public figure coming forth to identify with the insurrectionists and speak openly in their name (and, we may add, without any vanguard party to instruct them in the art of insurrection).

The insurrectionists committed horrible atrocities against the city's black population—estimates of the number of black victims go as high as 1,000, many with their bodies mutilated. They burned homes and even a colored orphanage.

The uprising took place during a bitter war, at a time when enemy forces were a hundred-odd miles away. Quite mindful of the circumstances, the insurrectionists raised the enemy flag and cheered the name of its president. (Had Lee managed to avoid engagement at Gettysburg and instead marched his troops into New York City, the Civil War might have had a different outcome.) On the whole, the five days of July 1863 in New York City call out for comparison with the Communards of Paris who stormed the heavens eight years later.

The events I recount are, of course, familiar under the name of the New York City Draft Riots. Historians normally chronicle them in the annals of race relations, in accounts of social disorder and the emergence of the modern state, or as an episode of the Civil War—anywhere but as part of labor history. Yet everyone knows that they were sparked by class inequities in the military draft and grew out of an effort of laborers and industrial workers to enforce a white monopoly of certain occupations.[1]

The Draft Riots were thoroughly consistent with prewar attitudes of the labor movement toward slavery and the Afro-American. For example, in an 1840 article, "The Laboring Classes," Orestes Brownson compared the systems of slave and free labor. "Of the two," he wrote,

the first is, in our judgement, except so far as the feelings are concerned, decidedly the least oppressive. If the slave has never been a free man, we think, as a general rule, his sufferings are less than those of the free laborer at wages. As to actual freedom one has just about as much as the other. The laborer at wages has all the disadvantages of freedom and none of its blessings, while the slave, if denied the blessings, is freed from the disadvantages.[2]

The comparison between free and slave labor in favor of the latter was more than a rhetorical flourish; it was a guide to action for the early movement of the free laborers. This was explicitly stated by George Evans, follower of Robert Owen and Fanny Wright, activist in the New York Working Men's party after 1829, and editor of the *Working Man's Advocate*. Evans attained his greatest prominence as a proponent of free land in the West (a program which found white supremacist form in the Free-Soil and Republican Parties). In a letter to the anti-slavery leader, Gerrit Smith, Evans wrote:

I was formerly, like yourself, sir, a very warm advocate of the abolition of slavery. This was before I saw that there was white slavery. Since I saw this, I have materially changed my views as to the means of abolishing negro slavery. I now see, clearly, I think, that to give the landless black the privilege of changing masters now possessed by the landless white, would hardly be a benefit to him.

In response to the argument that he justified slavery by saying it was not as bad as the situation of the free laborer, Evans insisted that he opposed slavery, but added, "there is more real suffering among the landless whites of the north, than among the blacks of the south" and that the abolitionists "err[ed] in wishing to transfer the black from the one form of slavery to the other and worse one."[3]

Evans was giving voice to the commonly held views of white labor radicalism on those occasions when it was forced to express itself on the slavery question. He was not alone. The American Fourierists criticized the abolitionists for thinking slavery was the only social evil to be extirpated and warned of the dangerous consequences of their view. "Negro slavery in the South," they explained,

was one only of many forms of slavery that existed on the earth . . . Consequently [the Associationists] did not contemplate the removal of this one evil alone and direct their exertions wholly against it; they wished to abolish all evil and all forms of slavery.

The abolitionists had a ready reply to these arguments:

> Before we can settle the relations of man to society, we must know who and what is man . . . Anti-slavery then underlies all other reforms, for it asserts the natural equality of all men, without regard to colour or condition. Until this principle is recognized as practically true, there can be no universal reform. There can be even no partial reform . . . for the evils of Slavery . . . permeate the relations of every individual in the land.[4]

Involved in this exchange were fundamental issues of direction for free labor radicalism. The story of one activist, Seth Luther, shows the consequences of the choices that were made. Luther was born in Rhode Island in 1795, the son of a Revolutionary War veteran. He grew up in poverty and had only a few years of common-school education, but did manage to learn carpentry. As a young man he took off on a tour of the west and south. Returning to New England, he did a stint in the cotton mills, which he left for a career as an itinerant agitator. A circular he wrote for a strike of Boston carpenters sparked the 1835 Philadelphia general strike. In 1832 he made his Address to the Working Men of New England, which he delivered on numerous occasions and which was printed the following year in a New York edition on George Evans's presses and went through several editions afterwards. In that address, Luther angrily denounced the factory system at length for its cruelties. He repeatedly compared its victims to Southern slaves, usually to the disadvantage of the free laborer. For example, he pointed out that children of six years old worked longer hours in the mills than slaves in the West Indies, whose workday was limited to nine hours. He noted that "the wives and daughters of the rich manufacturers would no more associate with a 'factory girl' than they would with a negro slave." He pointed out that the women who labored their life away in the mills "have not even the assurance of the most wretched cornfield negro in Virginia, who, when his stiffened limbs can no longer bend to the lash, must be supported by his owner." And he noted that "the slaves in the South enjoy privileges which are not enjoyed in some of our cotton mills. At Dover, N. H., we understand, no operative is allowed to keep a pig or a cow . . ."

What are we to make of this rhetoric? In the first place, Luther was not exaggerating the evils of the factory system (although he was omitting from the comparison with chattel slavery the degradation of being property, which no wage laborer suffered). In the second place, Luther was personally sympathetic to the plight of the slave; in another address he told of his travels in the South and his conversations with slaves, which taught him to respect their intelligence and pity their condition. But he could not see slavery as part of the labor problem.[5] Not only slavery but race discrimination, South and North, was absent from his calculations, as we shall see.

In the state of Rhode Island, a high property qualification for suffrage kept about two-thirds of the state's white male adults from voting. As part of the popular upsurge of the period, a movement developed aimed at striking down the restrictions. It gained quite a bit of support, particularly among working men, and Luther became involved; he delivered "Address on the Right of Free Suffrage" in 1833 in Providence. In 1840 Providence mechanics and working men formed the Rhode Island Suffrage Association, which renewed agitation for the franchise. The leader of the movement, Thomas Dorr, was a descendant of an old Yankee family, graduate of Phillips Exeter and Harvard; in the past he had supported abolitionist causes.

What to do when the group legally empowered to broaden the franchise refuses to do so? The Suffrage Association decided to go ahead and call a People's Convention to draft a new constitution for the state.

At first black people took part in suffrage meetings and voted in association elections. The issue of their role came up explicitly in September 1841 when a black Providence barber, Alfred Niger, was proposed as treasurer of the local suffrage association. His nomination was defeated, and conflicting resolutions on the subject were brought to the People's Convention, which met in October. Some of the leading New England abolitionists, including Abby Kelley and Frederick Douglass, visited Rhode Island, agitating to strike the word "white" from the proposed constitution. The convention, after debate, refused. Thus, the misnamed People's Convention answered the question, what is a man? At the convention Dorr argued in favor of black suffrage. Once his plea was rejected, however, he chose to remain with the Suffragists, even at the cost of breaking his ties with abolition. Garrison expressed abolitionist sentiment when he wrote, "It is not for me to espouse the cause of any politician, especially one like Thos. W. Dorr."[6]

The convention, naming Dorr as its candidate for governor, resolved to hold elections in April of the following year, based on universal white manhood suffrage. In the fall of 1841, the Law and Order Party was on the defensive as the suffragists campaigned to mobilize people to vote in the spring. The only active opposition came from the abolitionists, who denounced the attempt by "pseudo friends of political reform, to make the rights of a man dependent on the hue of his skin." Mobs of suffragists broke up their meetings, made proslavery speeches, and denounced the Law and Order Party as the "nigger party." Dorr was present on one occasion while a mob broke up an abolition meeting and watched silently.[7]

The suffrage association went ahead with its election in April 1842. Announcing that it represented a majority of voters, it declared Dorr governor. Rhode Island was now presented with a classic situation of dual power—two administrations, each claiming to be the legal government of the state. It was an unstable situation, and everyone knew it.

Each side rallied its forces; in a clever maneuver, the Law and Order Party offered to grant the vote to black men on the same terms as to whites (on the basis of a somewhat broadened electorate), in return for their support against the Dorrites, and recruited black men into militia units. On the night of May 18, the Dorrites attempted to capture the arsenal. The attempt failed. Black militia units guarded vital points in Providence and played a key role in defeating the Dorrite assault. Following the failure of the arsenal attempt, black volunteers helped suppressed Dorrite resistance throughout the state.[8]

I submit that those black people who fought on the side of the Law and Order Party were acting as much in the interests of the working class as those whites who fought for the Suffrage Association. They were declaring their intention to enter the movement as full equals or not at all. In doing so they were carrying out what C. L. R. James called the essence of principled politics:

> to let the class of which you are a member and the country in which you live go down to defeat before an alien class and an alien nation

rather than allow it to demoralize and destroy itself by adopting means in irreconcilable conflict with the ends for which it stands.[9]

Their deal with the Law and Order Party gave the black people of Rhode Island equal voting rights with whites. Rhode Island was the only state where black people, having lost the right to vote, regained it prior to the Civil War. They were able to make use of it over the next two decades, particularly in Providence, where they sometimes constituted the balance of power in closely contested elections.

What of Seth Luther? He fought valiantly in the assault on the arsenal and served as organizational secretary in the Dorrite encampment, but was captured and imprisoned. Held after other prisoners were released (perhaps because he refused to renounce the suffrage cause, instead denouncing cowards and turncoats), he was put on trial for treason. Convicted and sentenced to jail, he attempted to escape, failed, was discharged from prison, immediately rearrested, and was finally released in March 1843. He at once embarked on a tour of the West, where he sought to enlist support for Dorr. From Illinois he wrote, "Thousands are ready, able and willing to march on Rhode Island equipped and provisioned to the rescue of Governor Dorr . . ." One of his initiatives was an effort to strike a deal with Senator John C. Calhoun, the leader of the proslavery party in the Senate. Calhoun refused, on the grounds that if he came out in support of suffrage for propertyless whites in Rhode Island, some anti-slavery congressman would be sure to introduce a resolution supporting the right of the slaves to form a constitution; but the overture was significant. Luther returned to the east, and then (in what some have called a striking departure and attributed to a mental breakdown but which was more consistent than at first appears) he volunteered to serve in the army for the Mexican War. Nothing came of his offer (he was forty-seven years old), and the next heard of him was an unsuccessful attempt to rob a bank in Cambridge, Massachusetts. He was committed to a lunatic asylum, shifted around among institutions, and died in an asylum in Brattleboro, Vermont on April 29, 1863—barely two months before the outbreak of the New York City Draft Riots, the roots of which can be seen in his personal trajectory.

The tragedy of Seth Luther was not his defeat (revolutionaries had been defeated before); it was that his devotion and sacrifice went toward

building a movement not of labor but of white labor. To find a movement representative of the interests of all members of the working class,
it is necessary to look away from white labor radicalism to the slaves and
free persons of color.

The task is to look at a bird and see a snake. The historian faces the
problem that while black resistance before the Civil War has been
extensively studied, only rarely have the categories of the labor movement been applied to it. As an example of this problem, I cite a conversation I recently had with a scholar of what is called Black Studies: I
was looking for statistics of fugitive slaves by year, on the chance that
they might show a correlation with the fluctuations of the northern
economy. The person of whom I was inquiring informed me that the
figures did not exist (he is probably right) and that moreover they
would show no correlation to the economic cycle, as slaves could not
have been aware of economic conditions at their destination. Now I
do not know if the figures would reveal any significant fluctuations,
but I do know that anyone who thinks slaves could not have been
influenced by the availability of jobs in New York City, as Irish and
German immigrants were, is revealing his own blindness to the slave
as a worker.[10]

Nat Turner's Rebellion of 1831 began a new phase in the struggle
against slavery. Since the repression following it made open revolt difficult, the slaves turned toward developing a culture of resistance, which
found expression in religion, music, folklore, family ties, sabotage, and
flight.[11] The repression also led large numbers of free black people to
migrate from the South to the north, where they began to develop new
institutions, including the black church, schools, fraternal organizations, newspapers, and especially the Underground Railroad—the most
important of all the railroads credited with making an American nation.
They also made up the base of abolitionism.

The solidarity of the free Afro-American with the slave was not as
obvious as it might seem; it did not, for instance, exist in eighteenth-
century Saint Domingue, or in Jamaica before Emancipation, where
persons who in the United States would have been classified as black
made up part of the force that maintained slavery. It was a product of the
peculiar American race line, which enlisted the poor whites in policing
the slaves and explained the white supremacy of a plebeian radical like
Seth Luther. This solidarity leads me to assert, as provocatively as

possible, that the black church has historically been more of a proletarian organization than the white labor union.

John Brown's assault on Harper's Ferry on October 16, 1859, opened a new cycle of working-class struggle. The Civil War began with both sides, in the words of Frederick Douglass, fighting for slavery—the South to take it out of the Union, the north to keep it in. At the start of the war, the slaves watched and waited. As the northern armies advanced into the South, they began to leave the plantation, gathering at the Union encampments. At first, they were sent back to their owners. But deny it though the North tried, the war was being fought over slavery, and the slaves knew it better than anyone. The trickle of fugitives became a flood; before it was over, 500,000 workers had fled the plantation. (How much work was being done by those remaining behind is hard to say.) Those who made their way to the northern armies were put to work, their labor now at the service of the invader. Thousands of poor whites, forced by the withdrawal of plantation labor to bear a greater war burden, deserted the Confederate army to return to their fields, or followed the black fugitives into the Union camps. It was a general strike of black and white labor. Barely a year after it began, the Confederacy disintegrated.[12]

From the beginning, abolitionists and northern free black people lobbied the government in Washington to abandon the border-state policy and turn the war into a crusade against slavery. The change came about partly in response to the growing refusal of northern white labor to fight the war, of which the Draft Riots were the most dramatic demonstration, and partly in response to the movement of the slaves. If white labor would no longer fight, Lincoln would turn to those who would. Three measures indicated the shift in northern policy: the Emancipation Proclamation, the enlistment of black troops, and the replacement of McClellan by Grant (who, at the battle of Vicksburg, invented modern warfare). To all of these measures the activity of the Negroes proved decisive: as laborers and soldiers they provided the margin of northern victory.[13]

If we began with one worker uprising that is omitted from the history books, we conclude with another: the general strike of plantation labor that went on from 1863 to 1865. Two points, then, will summarize what I have been saying: first, it was not the North that freed the slaves, but the slaves and free Negroes who freed the United States from the domination of the southern system; second, in the period before the Civil War, the class movement of American workers was not expressed in the trade unions, working men's parties, and suffrage and land reform efforts of white labor, but in the striving of the black slave and free person.

22

When Does an Unreasonable Act Make Sense?

This essay was cowritten with John Garvey as an editorial statement for Issue 3 of Race Traitor, *published in the spring of 1994. The editorial encourages its readers to take up any action to abolish the white race, including "unreasonable acts" that defy the racial order and what it means to "act" or "be white."*

Two points define the position of *Race Traitor*: first, that the "white race" is not a natural but a historical category; second, that what was historically constructed can be undone. The first of these points is now widely accepted; scientists have concluded that there are no biological standards for distinguishing one "race" from another, and social scientists have begun to examine how race was constructed and how it is reproduced. However, few scholars or activists have taken the next step: indeed, one might say that up to now the philosophers have merely interpreted the white race; the point, however, is to abolish it. How can this be done?

The white race is like a private club, which grants privileges to certain people in return for obedience to its rules. It is based on one huge assumption: that all those who look white are, whatever their complaints or reservations, fundamentally loyal to it.

What happened to Rodney King was not exceptional. All over the world, cops beat poor people; that is their job. What is unusual is that they do not routinely beat some people for whom every mark save one—their color—would indicate a beating. For those in power, the privileges granted to whites are a small price to pay for the stability of an unjust social system.

What if the white skin lost its usefulness as a badge of loyalty? What if the cop, the judge, the social worker, the schoolteacher, and the other representatives of official society could no longer recognize a loyal person merely by looking; how would it affect their behavior? And if color no longer served as a handy guide to the dispensing of favors, so that ordinary whites began experiencing the sort of treatment to which they are normally immune, how would this affect their outlook?

Elsewhere in this issue it is pointed out that the rules of the white club do not require that all members be strong advocates of white supremacy, merely that they defer to the prejudices of others. The need to maintain racial solidarity imposes a stifling conformity on whites, on any subject touching even remotely on race.

The way to abolish the white race is to disrupt that conformity. If enough people who look white violate the rules of whiteness, so flagrantly that they jeopardize their white standing, their existence cannot be ignored. If it becomes impossible for the upholders of white rules to speak in the name of all who look white, the white race will cease to exist.

We recognize that this advice flies in the face of what is usually regarded as sound, practical sense. Even (we might say especially) in the ranks of the reformers the conventional wisdom teaches that the way to achieve social change is to strive to express the desires of an existing constituency. That is perhaps why most social reform is so useless.

We are calling for the opposite: a minority willing to undertake outrageous acts of provocation, aware that they will incur the opposition of many who might agree with them if they adopted a more moderate approach.

How many will it take? No one can say for sure. It is a bit like the problem of currency: how much counterfeit money has to circulate in order to destroy the value of the official currency? The answer is, nowhere near a majority—just enough to undermine public confidence in the official stuff. When it comes to abolishing the white race, the task is not to win over more whites to oppose "racism"; there are "anti-racists" enough already to do the job.

In a previous issue we wrote:

In a certain sense, the entire project of *Race Traitor* is to examine, from every possible angle, the moment when Huck Finn, and all the modern Huck Finns, decide to break with what Huck calls "sivilization" and that will lead to Jim's, and their own, freedom.

Since we are talking about acts which are, by definition, unreasonable (because they fly in the face of all contemporary reasonable opinion), we could reformulate as follows the central problem *Race Traitor* seeks to address: When does the unreasonable act make sense?

In our pages we have published accounts from the past and present, where so-called whites have committed acts which defy reason but which turn out to have been socially effective. There are others we know of but have not written about, and still others we do not know of but want to report. We believe that to popularize such examples will contribute to altering current notions of what constitutes reason and will encourage others to be still bolder.

Finally, we know how devilishly difficult it is for individuals to escape whiteness. The white race does not voluntarily surrender a single member, so that even those who step outside of it in one situation find it virtually impossible not to step back in later, if for no other reason than the assumptions of others. But we also know that when there comes into being a critical mass of people who, though they look white, have ceased to act white, the white race will explode, and former whites will be able to take part, together with others, in building a new human community.

23

Antifascism, Anti-Racism, and Abolition

Cowritten with John Garvey as an editorial statement for Issue 3 of Race Traitor, *published in the spring of 1994, this essay critiques the modern anti-racist and antifascist movements for focusing on liberal individualism instead of the state institutions and societal structures that reinforce the racial order.*

There now exist in this country and around the world a number of organizing projects, research centers, and publications that call themselves "anti-racist." Among those that have come to our attention are the *Monitor,* published by the Center for Democratic Renewal (P.O. Box 50469, Atlanta, GA 30302-0469); *The Racemixer*, published by Communities Against Hate (485 Blair Boulevard, Eugene, OR 97402); and *Turning the Tide,* published by People Against Racist Terror (P.O. Box 1990, Burbank, CA 91507). These publications all provide useful coverage, and we recommend them to our readers.

The three publications cited above are obviously produced by people who understand that the denial of equality to people of color is but one among a number of things wrong with this society and that others include the oppression of women, the persecution of those who enjoy sex with people of their own sex, hatred of Jews and the foreign-born, neglect of the aged and the infirm, poverty and homelessness, disdain for the natural environment, and so forth. The "anti-racist" movement by and large is sympathetic to all efforts to correct these wrongs, and one of the publications we named, *Turning the Tide,* states repeatedly its commitment to transforming the entire society.

Yet almost all the attention of the "anti-racist" movement is focused on groups like the Nazis and the Klan that explicitly avow their racism, and on various movements like anti-abortion and anti-gay rights that are largely led by people on the far right of the political spectrum, and its programmatic initiatives are directed almost exclusively at combating these forces.

We think this is a mistake. Just as the capitalist system is not a capitalist plot, *race is not the work of racists.* On the contrary, it is reproduced by the principal institutions of society, among which are the schools (which define "excellence"), the labor market (which defines "employment"), the law (which defines "crime"), the welfare system (which defines "poverty"), and the family (which defines "kinship")—and it is reinforced by various reform programs which address many of the social problems traditionally of concern to the "left."

Racist and far-right groups in the main represent caricatures of reality in this race-defined society; at most they are efforts by a few to push the race line farther than what is currently considered proper. If that is the case, the "anti-racist" movement is seriously misreading the roots of the race problem and pursuing an erroneous strategy for addressing it.

Race Traitor believes that the main target of those who seek to eradicate the color line should be the institutions and behaviors that maintain it: the schools, the criminal justice and welfare systems, the employers and unions, and the family. In this we stand with the original abolitionists, who never tired of pointing out that the problem was not the slaveholders of Carolina but the loyal citizens of Massachusetts.

The December issue of the anarchist paper *Love and Rage* carries several comments on a recent attempt to stop a group of self-proclaimed Nazis from holding a "gay-bashing" fest in New Hope, Pennsylvania. The entire story is too long to recount here (we advise readers to obtain a copy of this excellent publication by sending $1 to P.O. Box 853, Stuyvesant Station, New York, NY 10009), but, briefly, what happened is this: on learning that the Nazis planned to march and rally, a group of their opponents called a counter-rally. The Nazis, fearful for their safety, called off their march but proceeded with the rally, which took place as scheduled behind a wall of police, who protected them from the hostile crowd. The report states:

Residents of New Hope and anti-fascist organizers alike claimed the cancellation of the march as a victory for anti-fascist organizers. By creating the possibility of hundreds or thousands of counter-protestors willing to physically confront the Nazis, we made it impossible for them to march. This strategy, of organizing for the possibility of physical confrontation, and bringing hundreds of people willing to carry it out, is clearly a successful one and needs to be pursued in the future.

We are not so sure. That the cancellation of the march was a defeat for the Nazis we have no doubt; but it seems to us that it was more of a victory for the state than for the anti-fascist organizers, because the state was able to emerge as the defender of both free speech and law-and-order, marginalizing the "extremists" on both sides—those who want to build death camps and those who want to prevent their construction. We are inclined to agree with another commentator who called the counterdemonstration "ineffective."

We favor beating Nazis off the streets wherever they appear and confronting "racists" or other reactionaries of the right (or the left). But we ask, what is the purpose of this "strategy"? If it is to do material damage to the fascists, then it takes no genius to point out that such damage can be done more effectively on virtually any day of the year other than when they appear in public surrounded by an army of cops and television cameras. If it is to win people out of the Nazi ranks, we have no way of knowing how effective such actions are. If the aim is to expose the state as the defender of Nazis, that is only a very partial truth; the state is the defender of public order and has shown itself quite willing to repress Nazis and other white supremacist groups who threaten that order. And if the purpose is to win people to a vision of a world without race barriers, then we must say that any action which aims to crush the Nazis physically and fails to do so because of state intervention has the effect of reinforcing the authority of the state, which, as we said, is the most important agency maintaining race barriers.

24

Aux Armes! Formez Vos Bataillons!

This essay was cowritten with John Garvey and Beth Henson as an editorial statement for Issue 5 of Race Traitor, *published in 1996. The editors argue that the anti-establishment ethos of American libertarianism must be embraced by leftist revolutionaries, instead of the latter making common cause with the state against the far-right.*

Time was one might have expected opponents of official society to welcome a grassroots movement arming to defend individual liberties against federal encroachment. Contrary to such expectations, many who are pleased to locate themselves on the "left" have raised a cry of alarm at the militia movement surpassing even that from government circles.

A flyer published by an Oregon group calling itself "Communities Against Hate" seeks to warn the public about the militia movement. "Blood will be spilled in the streets of America," it quotes one militia leader saying.

People join militias for various reasons, explains the flyer:

They see the violence at Waco, Texas or the incident between white supremacist Randy Weaver and federal officials and believe they too will be attacked; others see the ban on assault weapons in 1994 as a sure sign that the Federal Government is out to subvert the Constitution.

"The Government did make mistakes at Waco and with Randy Weaver," admits the flyer. So the incineration of eighty people and the assassination of a woman and child by federal officials are "mistakes," when they happen to people these opponents of "hate" disagree with.

But the militias are paranoid, we are told.

> They believe that there will be an armed confrontation with the Federal Government sooner or later. Militias say that our [our?] government and the United Nations are going to create the New World Order, where Americans will be slaves to international bankers and if you resist, militia leaders claim, you'll be hauled away to a concentration camp.

If the authors of the flyer expect these views to turn us against the militias, they will be disappointed. So far, we have agreed with the opinions cited above.

But the militia movement was initiated by militant white supremacists, insists the flyer. We do not doubt it; certainly, white supremacist groups exercise considerable influence within it. Why should anyone be surprised? White supremacy is rampant in this society, and militant white supremacists seek to establish their hegemony within popular movements. But we note that Michigan, home of reputedly the strongest militia in the country, was the scene of one of Jesse Jackson's greatest electoral triumphs, and we bet that many militia members voted for him in 1988. Wherever they stand now, they could not have been motivated principally by white supremacy. One thing for sure: the law-and-order stance of the so-called anti-racists can only reinforce white supremacist influence.

The flyer advises us, "The key to protecting the rights and civil liberties of all Americans does not lie in forming armed paramilitary groups who want to take the law into their own hands."

We can think of no better way.

The conventional "left," however, seeks protection elsewhere. Consider a recent fundraising letter from the Southern Poverty Law Center (SPLC), which claims to have "the most extensive computerized files on militias and hate groups in existence," including over 11,000 photographs, reports on 14,000 individuals, and intelligence on over 3,200 groups. The SPLC boasts of having written to Attorney General

Janet Reno in October 1994, before the Oklahoma City bombing, warning her of impending illegal, violent activity by white supremacist groups. It publishes the *Intelligence Report,* which goes out regularly to over 6,000 law enforcement agencies.

Does this snooping and snitching foreshadow the brave new world they seek to build?

The SPLC says it has no interest in stopping groups with unpopular views or interfering with "legitimate" shooting clubs. It merely seeks to stop "unauthorized" militias. But if "unauthorized" militias are repressed, the only armed groups remaining will be the "authorized" ones.

We think it was Dwight Macdonald who said that what gave him hope for the future of this country was the deeply ingrained tradition of lawlessness. Like the Los Angeles Rebellion and the "wigger" phenomenon, the militia movement is a rebellion against the massive, faceless, soul-destroying system that is sucking the life out of ordinary people in this country and around the world. Of course, it carries with it danger as well as promise. Insofar as it has a vision of the future, it is not ours. We do not underestimate the importance of this difference. But it has done more to shatter the image of government invulnerability than any other development of recent times. That the "left" fails to see the potentials it reveals and does less than nothing to develop its own challenge to power is an index of its irrelevance.

From its first issue, *Race Traitor* has insisted that only the vision of a new world can compete with the fascists for the loyalty of those angry whites who think that nothing less than a total change is worth fighting for. Abolitionists must draw a line between themselves and the "loyal opposition." If they fail to do so, they will not be heard.

25

How the Irish Became White

In the introduction to his classic 1995 book, Ignatiev introduces his argument that the Irish—a previously oppressed racial group—became white in the United States through forswearing solidarity with black workers.

No biologist has ever been able to provide a satisfactory definition of "race"—that is, a definition that includes all members of a given race and excludes all others. Attempts to give the term a biological foundation lead to absurdities: parents and children of different races, or the well-known phenomenon that a white woman can give birth to a black child, but a black woman can never give birth to a white child.[1] The only logical conclusion is that people are members of different races because they have been assigned to them.

Outside these labels and the racial oppression that accompanies them, the only race is the human. I'll be examining connections between concepts of race and acts of oppression.

By considering the notion of "racial oppression" in terms of the substantive, the operative element, namely "oppression," it is possible to avoid the contradictions and howling absurdities that result from attempts to splice genetics and sociology. By examining racial oppression as a particular system of oppression—like gender oppression or class oppression or national oppression—we find further footing for analyzing ... the peculiar function of the "white race" ... The hallmark of racial oppression [is the reduction of] all members of the oppressed group to one undifferentiated social status, a status beneath that of any member of any social class [within the dominant group].[2]

It follows, therefore, that the white race consists of those who partake of the privileges of the white skin in this society. Its most wretched members share a status higher, in certain respects, than that of the most exalted persons excluded from it.

This book looks at how one group of people became white. Put another way, it asks how the Catholic Irish, an oppressed race in Ireland, became part of an oppressing race in America. It is an attempt to reassess immigrant assimilation and the formation (or nonformation) of an American working class.

The Irish who emigrated to America in the eighteenth and nineteenth centuries were fleeing caste oppression and a system of landlordism that made the material conditions of the Irish peasant comparable to those of an American slave. They came to a society in which color was important in determining social position. It was not a pattern they were familiar with and they bore no responsibility for it; nevertheless, they adapted to it in short order.

When they first began arriving here in large numbers they were, in the words of Mr. Dooley, given a shovel and told to start digging up the place as if they owned it. On the rail beds and canals, they labored for low wages under dangerous conditions; in the South they were occasionally employed where it did not make sense to risk the life of a slave. As they came to the cities, they were crowded into districts that became centers of crime, vice, and disease.

There they commonly found themselves thrown together with free Negroes. Irish and Afro-Americans fought each other and the police, socialized and occasionally intermarried, and developed a common culture of the lowly. They also both suffered the scorn of those better situated. Along with Jim Crow and Jim Dandy, the drunken, belligerent, and foolish Pat and Bridget were stock characters on the early stage. In antebellum America it was speculated that if racial amalgamation was ever to take place, it would begin between those two groups.

As we know, things turned out otherwise. The outcome was not the inevitable consequence of blind historic forces, still less of biology, but the result of choices made, by the Irish and others, from among available alternatives. To enter the white race was a strategy to secure an advantage in a competitive society.

What did it mean to the Irish to become white in America? It did not mean that they all became rich, or even "middle-class" (however that is defined); to this day there are plenty of poor Irish. Nor did it mean that they all became the social equals of the Saltonstalls and van Rensselaers; even the marriage of Grace Kelly to the Prince of Monaco and the election of John F. Kennedy as president did not eliminate all barriers to Irish entry into certain exclusive circles. To Irish laborers, to become white meant at first that they could sell themselves piecemeal instead of being sold for life and later that they could compete for jobs in all spheres instead of being confined to certain work; to Irish entrepreneurs, it meant that they could function outside of a segregated market. To both of these groups, it meant that they were citizens of a democratic republic, with the right to elect and be elected, to be tried by a jury of their peers, to live wherever they could afford, and to spend, without racially imposed restrictions, whatever money they managed to acquire. In becoming white the Irish ceased to be Green.

To view entry into the white race as something the Irish did "on" (though not by) themselves is to make them the actors in their own history.

On one occasion many years ago, I was sitting on my front step when my neighbor came out of the house next door carrying her small child, whom she placed in her automobile. She turned away from him for a moment, and as she started to close the car door, I saw that the child had put his hand where it would be crushed when the door was closed. I shouted to the woman to stop. She halted in mid-motion, and when she realized what she had almost done, an amazing thing happened: she began laughing, then broke into tears and began hitting the child. It was the most intense and dramatic display of conflicting emotions I have ever beheld. My attitude toward the subjects of this study accommodates stresses similar to those I witnessed in that mother.

26

"The Point Is Not to Interpret Whiteness but to Abolish It"

This essay was initially given as a talk at an academic conference, the Making and Unmaking of Whiteness, held at the University of California, Berkeley in 1997. Critiquing the growing academic industry around studying so-called whiteness, Ignatiev makes the case for abolition as a political project distinct from liberal anti-racism. He reexamines the strategies of nineteenth-century abolitionism and their relevance for contemporary movements against white supremacy.

Now that White Studies has become an academic industry, with its own dissertation mill, conference, publications, and no doubt soon its junior faculty, it is time for the abolitionists to declare where they stand in relation to it. Abolitionism is first of all a political project: the abolitionists study whiteness in order to abolish it.

Various commentators have stated that their aim is to identify and preserve a positive white identity. Abolitionists deny the existence of a positive white identity. We at *Race Traitor*, the journal with which I am associated, have asked some of those who think whiteness contains positive elements to indicate what they are. We are still waiting for an answer. Until we get one, we will take our stand with David Roediger, who has insisted that whiteness is not merely oppressive and false, it is nothing but oppressive and false. As James Baldwin said, "So long as you think you are white, there is no hope for you."

Whiteness is not a culture. There is Irish culture and Italian culture and American culture—the latter, as Albert Murray pointed out, a mixture of the Yankee, the Indian, and the Negro (with a pinch of ethnic salt); there is youth culture and drug culture and queer culture; but there is no such thing as white culture. Whiteness has nothing to do with culture and everything to do with social position. It is nothing but a reflection of privilege and exists for no reason other than to defend it. Without the privileges attached to it, the white race would not exist, and the white skin would have no more social significance than big feet.

Before the advocates of positive whiteness remind us of the oppression of the white poor, let me say that we have never denied it. The United States, like every capitalist society, is composed of masters and slaves. The problem is that many of the slaves think they are part of the master class because they partake of the privileges of the white skin. We cannot say it too often: whiteness does not exempt people from exploitation, it reconciles them to it. It is for those who have nothing else.

However exploited the poor whites of this country, they are not direct victims of racial oppression, and "white trash" is not a term of racial degradation analogous to the various epithets commonly applied to black people; in fact, the poor whites are the objects of race privilege, which ties them to their masters more firmly than did the arrows of Vulcan bind Prometheus to the rock. Not long ago there was an incident in Boston in which a well-dressed black man hailed a taxi and directed the driver to take him to Roxbury, a black district. The white cab driver refused, and when the man insisted she take him or call someone who would, as the law provided, she called her boyfriend, also a cabdriver, on the car radio, who showed up, dragged the black man out of the cab and called him a "nigger." The black man turned out to be a city councilman. The case was unusual only in that it made the papers. Either America is a very democratic country, where cab drivers beat up city councilmen with impunity, or the privileges of whiteness reach far down into the ranks of the laboring class.

We are anti-white, but we are not in general against the people who are called white. Those for whom the distinction is too subtle are advised to read the speeches of Malcolm X. No one ever spoke more harshly and critically to black people, and no one ever loved them more. It is no part of love to flatter and withhold from people what they need to know. President Samora Machel of Mozambique pointed out that his people had to die as tribes in order to be born as a nation. Similar things were said at the time Afro-Americans in mass rejected the term "Negro" in favor of "black." We seek to draw upon that tradition, as well as—we do not deny it—an even older tradition, which declares that a person must die so that he or she can be born again. We hold that so-called whites must cease to exist as whites in order to realize themselves as something else; to put it another way: white people must commit suicide as whites in order to come alive as workers, or youth, or women, or whatever other identity can induce them to change from the miserable, petulant, subordinated creatures they now are into freely associated, fully developed human subjects.

The white race is neither a biological nor a cultural formation; it is a strategy for securing to some an advantage in a competitive society. It has held down more whites than blacks. Abolitionism is also a strategy: its aim is not racial harmony but class war. By attacking whiteness, the abolitionists seek to undermine the main pillar of capitalist rule in this country.

If abolitionism is distinct from White Studies, it is also distinct from what is called "anti-racism." There now exist a number of publications, organizing programs, and research centers that focus their energies on identifying and opposing individuals and groups they call "racist." Sometimes they share information and collaborate with official state agencies. We stand apart from that tendency. In our view, any "anti-racist" work that does not entail opposition to the state reinforces the authority of the state, which is the most important agency in maintaining racial oppression.

Just as the capitalist system is not a capitalist plot, so racial oppression is not the work of "racists." It is maintained by the principal institutions of society, including the schools (which define "excellence"), the labor market (which defines "employment"), the legal system (which defines "crime"), the welfare system (which defines "poverty"), the medical industry (which defines "health"), and the family (which defines "kinship"). Many of these institutions are administered by people who would be offended if accused of complicity with racial oppression. It is reinforced by reform programs that address problems traditionally of concern to the "left"—for example, federal housing loan guarantees. The simple fact is that the public schools and the welfare departments are doing more harm to black children than all the "racist" groups combined.

The abolitionists seek to abolish the white race. How can this be done? We must admit that we do not know exactly, but a look at history will be instructive.

When William Lloyd Garrison and the original abolitionists began their work, slavery was the law of the land, and behind the law stood the entire machinery of government, including the courts, the army, and even the post office, which banned anti-slavery literature from Southern mail. The slave states controlled the Senate and Presidency, and Congress refused even to accept petitions relating to slavery. Most northerners considered slavery unjust, but their opposition to it was purely nominal. However much they disapproved of it, the majority "went along," as majorities normally do, rather than risk the ordinary comforts of their lives, meager as they were.

The weak point of the slave system was that it required the collaboration of the entire country, for without the support of the "loyal citizens" of Massachusetts, the slaveholders of South Carolina could not keep their laborers in bondage (just as today without the support of the law-abiding, race discrimination could not be enforced). The abolitionists set to work to break up the national consensus. Wendell Phillips declared that if he could establish Massachusetts as a sanctuary for the fugitive, he could bring down slavery. They sought to nullify the fugitive slave law, which enlisted the northern population directly in enforcing slavery. They encouraged and took part in attempts to rescue fugitives—not, it must be pointed out, from the slaveholders, but from the Law. In all of this activity, the black population took the lead. The concentrated expression of the abolitionist strategy was the slogan, "No Union with Slaveholders," which was not, as has often been charged, an attempt to maintain their moral purity but an effort to break up the Union in order to establish a liberated zone adjacent to the slave states. It was a strategy that would later come to be known as dual power, and neither Garrison's pacifism nor his failure to develop a general critique of the capitalist system should blind us to its revolutionary character.

John Brown's attack on Harpers Ferry was not an aberration but the logical application of the abolitionist strategy. The slaveholders retaliated for it by demanding new guarantees of loyalty from the federal government, including a stronger fugitive slave law, reopening of the slave trade, and especially the expansion of slavery into the territories.

As Phillips said, Brown "startled the South into madness," precipitating a situation where people were forced to choose between abolition and the domination of the country as a whole by the slaveholders. It was not the abolitionists but the slaveholders who, by the arrogance of their demands, compelled the north to resist. From Harpers' Ferry, each step led inexorably to the next: Southern bullying, Lincoln's election, secession, war, blacks as laborers, soldiers, citizens, voters. The war that began with not one person in a hundred foreseeing the end of slavery was transformed within two years into an anti-slavery war, and a great army marched through the land singing, "As He died to make men holy, let us fight to make men free."

The course of events can never be predicted in other than the broadest outline, but in the essentials, history followed the path charted by the abolitionists. As they foresaw, it was necessary to break up the Union in order to reconstitute it without slavery. When South Carolina announced its secession, Wendell Phillips was forced into hiding to escape the Boston mob that blamed him; two years later he was invited to address Congress on how to win the war. He recommended two measures, both of which were soon implemented: (1) declare the war an anti-slavery war; (2) enlist black soldiers. Has ever a revolutionary been more thoroughly vindicated by history?

The hostility of white laborers toward abolitionism, and their failure to develop a labor abolitionism, was not, as some have claimed, an expression of working-class resentment of bourgeois philanthropists but the reflection of their refusal to view themselves as part of a class with the slaves—just as a century later white labor opposition to school integration showed that the laborers viewed themselves more as whites than as proletarians.

The white race is a club. Certain people are enrolled in it at birth, without their consent, and brought up according to its rules. For the most part they go through life accepting the privileges of membership, without reflecting on the costs. Others, usually new arrivals in the country, pass through a probationary period before "earning" membership; they are necessarily more conscious of their racial standing.

The white club does not require that all members be strong advocates of white supremacy, merely that they defer to the prejudices of others. It is based on one huge assumption: that all those who look white are, whatever their reservations, fundamentally loyal to it.

For an example of how the club works, take the cops. The natural attitude of the police toward the exploited is hostility. All over the world cops beat up poor people; that is their job, and it has nothing to do with color. What is unusual and has to be accounted for is not why they beat up black people but why they don't normally beat up propertyless whites. It works this way: the cops look at a person and then decide on the basis of color whether that person is loyal to the system they are sworn to serve and protect. They don't stop to think if the black person whose head they are whipping is an enemy; they assume it. It does not matter if the victim goes to work every day, pays his taxes, and crosses only on the green. Occasionally they bust an outstanding and prominent black person, and the poor whites cheer the event, because it confirms them in their conviction that they are superior to any black person who walks the earth.

On the other hand, the cops don't know for sure if the white person to whom they give a break is loyal to them; they assume it. The nonbeating of poor whites is time off for good behavior and an assurance of future cooperation. Their color exempts them to some degree from the criminal class—which is how the entire working class was defined before the invention of race and is still treated in those parts of the world where race, or some functional equivalent, does not exist as a social category. It is a cheap way of buying some people's loyalty to a social system that exploits them.

What if the police couldn't tell a loyal person just by color? What if there were enough people around who looked white but were really enemies of official society so that the cops couldn't tell whom to beat and whom to let off? What would they do then? They would begin to "enforce the law impartially," as the liberals say, beating only those who "deserve" it. But, as Anatole France noted, the law, in its majestic equality, forbids both rich and poor to sleep under bridges, to beg in the streets, and to steal bread. The standard that normally governs police behavior is wealth and its external manifestations—dress, speech, etc. At the present time, the class bias of the law is partially repressed by racial considerations; the removal of those considerations would give it free rein. Whites who are poor would find themselves on the receiving end of police justice as black people now do.

The effect on their consciousness and behavior is predictable. That is not to say that everyone now regarded as "white" would suddenly become a progressive, any more than everyone now "black" is. But with color no longer serving as a handy guide for the distribution of penalties and rewards, European-Americans of the downtrodden class would at last be compelled to face with sober senses their real condition of life and their relations with humankind. It would be the end of race.

When it comes to abolishing the white race, the task is not to win over more whites to oppose "racism"; there are "anti-racists" enough already to do the job. The task is to gather together a minority deter- mined to make it impossible for anyone to be white. It is a strategy of creative provocation, like Wendell Phillips advocated and John Brown carried out.

What would the determined minority have to do? They would have to break the laws of whiteness so flagrantly as to destroy the myth of white unanimity. What would it mean to break the rules of whiteness? It would mean responding to every manifestation of white supremacy as if it were directed against them. On the individual level, it would mean, for instance, responding to an anti-black remark by asking, What makes you think I'm white? On the collective level, it would mean confronting the institutions that reproduce race.

The abolitionists oppose all forms of segregation in the schools, including tracking by "merit," they oppose all mechanisms that favor whites in the job market, including labor unions when necessary, and they oppose the police and courts, which define black people as a crimi- nal class. They not merely oppose these things but seek to disrupt their functioning. They reject in advance no means of attaining their goal; even when combating "racist" groups, they act in ways that are offensive to official institutions. The willingness to go beyond socially acceptable "anti-racism" is the dividing line between "good whites" and traitors to the white race.

A traitor to the white race is someone who is nominally classified as white but who defies white rules so strenuously as to jeopardize his or her ability to draw upon the privileges of whiteness. The abolitionists recognize that no "white" can individually escape from the privileges of whiteness. The white club does not like to surrender a single member, so that even those who step out of it in one situation can hardly avoid step- ping back in later, if for no other reason than the assumptions of others— unless, like John Brown, they have the good fortune to be hanged before that can happen. But they also understand that when there comes into

being a critical mass of people who look white but do not act white—
people who might be called "reverse oreos"—the white race will undergo
fission, and former whites, born again, will be able to take part, together
with others, in building a new human community.

27

Abolitionism and the White Studies Racket

Ignatiev explores the key pitfalls of so-called whiteness studies, including the promotion of whiteness as a legitimate identity to be embraced in a framework of pluralistic and multiracial democracy. He reaffirms the abolitionist perspective, arguing that political revolution and the practical abolition of whiteness are the only way out of the present racial order. This essay first appeared in Issue 10 of Race Traitor, *published in winter 1999.*

Over the past few years, "white studies" has become an academic industry. Scarcely a week goes by that does not see a new book on "the construction of whiteness." There are at least five college Readers on the subject. At least three universities have sponsored conferences on whiteness, and more are planned. The dissertation mill is operating around the clock, and "white studies" may soon boast its own junior faculty. The mainstream press has caught on to the excitement, reporting (often with a snicker) the latest discovery by the academy, that white people have race, too. "White studies" may not survive the first frost; nevertheless, among those studying whiteness there have appeared differing tendencies. From a political standpoint, the two camps are the preservationists and the abolitionists.

At the present time, those whom I have chosen to call preservationists seek to identify and preserve a white identity apart from white supremacy and racial oppression. The Center for the Study of White

American Culture, based in New Jersey, conducts an internet discussion group and has sponsored three conferences on whiteness. Its founder and moving spirit, Jeff Hitchcock, says, "We need people who are conscious of being white, and we need to give them room to be white."[1]

Among the preservationists are Matt Wray and Annalee Newitz, editors of the book *White Trash*, who declare "it is time we use our imaginations to invent alternative forms of white identity which ... understand the disasters which constitute all forms of racial domination." Seeking "an acceptable, multicultural form of white racial identity," they naturally turn their attention toward elements of popular culture that might plausibly be described as "white."[2] Among the elements they look at are the Elvis cult, ice hockey, and gun shows.

There are obvious problems with all of these. From the standpoint of culture, it is ridiculous to describe Elvis as "white." As for ice hockey, I remember before they let black players into the National Basketball Association, when people said that basketball was a white sport. And gun shows—surely no one would claim that love of guns is a white monopoly. If those in attendance at gun shows are overwhelmingly white, it is because those shows are organized strongholds of the Ku Klux Klan and other white-power types. Like everything else about whiteness, it has nothing to do with culture. It has to do with exclusion.

Recently at an academic conference, I denied the existence of a valid white culture. What, I asked, did it consist of? What would anyone put in a White Museum? One of the other panelists answered, "Well, people are doing research on that." Her answer was an admission of defeat. If I had asked for examples of German culture, or French, or Italian, no one would have had to say that people were conducting research to discover them.

Nor will it help to call what they are looking for "Euro American" rather than "white," as some people in the academy, as well as some in the white power movement, are doing. American culture is, as Albert Murray said, incontestably mulatto, and its mulatto character can be heard, seen, and felt in the music, dance, dress, language, rhythms of speech, varieties of religious expression, and other things that together make up American culture. And by the way, the culture of Europe was not solely a European product.

Newitz accuses the abolitionists of "hopelessness, brutality, and

nihilism," of "demonizing" white people, and even of promoting "preju-
dicial destruction."[3] We may be guilty of many sins, but we do not
patronize white working-class people, or treat them as specimens, the
way some of our accusers make careers out of doing. On the faculty at a
Chicago art school is a person who sports a cowboy hat, tattoos, and
tank top, bills herself as "White Trash Girl," and employs academic
jargon to celebrate vulgarity: "I'm adhering to this white trash aesthetic
now . . . It's part of my identity . . . I think it's also a socioeconomic situation . . . I am busty, and I am loud, and I love bad taste. I am bad taste."[4]
The interview with her was published in the book edited by Wray and
Newitz.

   In their eagerness to preserve a white identity, the preservationists
sometimes slip back into biological rationales for it. Newitz says whiteness is "an identity which can be negotiated on an individual level. It is
also a diversity of cultures, histories, and finally, an inescapable physical
marker."[5] Contrary to her claim, whiteness is not about nature or culture,
but rather status. Without the privileges attached to the white skin, the
white race would not exist, and skin color would have no more significance than foot size or ear shape.

   To promote whiteness as a legitimate identity is to play a dangerous
game. A few years back, a prominent American fascist said that what
gave him the greatest encouragement was the development of a white
ethnicity and white pride. He was right. But if whiteness is a valid
culture, as both he and many in the white studies industry claim, then
what is wrong with "white pride"? I predict that before long the white-
power camp will latch onto "white studies" and use it to advance their
own goals. If I now appear alarmist, wait and see: in fact, last year at a
conference in Boston sponsored by the Center for the Study of White
American Culture, the organizers were confronted with a white-power
advocate who demanded he be allowed to attend, insisting that he was
motivated only by the desire to foster white pride. The organizers
debated it amongst themselves for weeks, because although they did not
want him there, they had no principled basis on which to exclude him.
We abolitionists have no such problem, since we are proudly anti-white.
A corollary of the defense of white identity is that it leads its practition-
ers to pander to the *white* side of the poor whites. Newitz carries this
tendency to the extreme, declaring that conscientious support for
affirmative action is "self-shaming rituals" and complaining that "images

of violent police culture . . . grow out of already-existing stereotypes of a brutal, ignorant white working class."[6] Oh, the poor cops, victims of unjust stereotyping.

A second danger of white studies is that it encourages "racial sensitivity" workshops and "diversity training" instead of political struggle. A recent newspaper piece cited a white woman who had gone through "anti-racism" training and as a result learned that she was a "racist" and that it was her job to go out and educate other whites that they were "racists." No, that is not her job. That is not what the struggle for justice is about. A young white man wrote me complaining that the abolitionists were too confrontational. He preferred gatherings from which people came away feeling good about themselves—as if the purpose of the struggle against white supremacy was to make white people feel good about themselves. It has been said that people must feel good about who they are, because if they do not, they cannot be "organized." There is a grain of truth in that, but it is not an argument for white identity. For myself, on those occasions when I am silent in the face of white supremacy or otherwise complicit with it, I feel bad, and on those occasions when I resist it, I feel good.

We abolitionists favor personal growth and transformation, but we believe they take place best in a context of struggle against oppressive institutions, and when self-examination is put forward as a substitute for institutional struggle, then it is a barrier to progress. One example of the sort of thing I am railing against is the film *The Color of Fear*. In it a few men, white, black, Asian, and Latino, get together and talk about their feelings. Among them is one white guy who insists that he has no race problem. The dynamic of the situation then requires that the others present spend their time arguing with him, which rules out their talking about other things. Finally, it gets to him that the rest consider him the problem. He has an epiphany and starts to weep. Then of course they all have to gather around and reassure him and welcome the reformed sinner into their fraternity—except that there is no indication that anything will be different. He will still go back to his white neighborhood, etc. And this film is grossing big money. It is being sold for hundreds of dollars a pop. The "diversity" industry does not depend on small groups of well-intentioned people meeting in church basements, but on lucrative contracts with corporations to conduct seminars for executives on how to manage their labor force. Some of the people in the "diversity" industry remind me of doctors who secretly love the disease they are supposed to be fighting. It is fortunate that in the nineteenth century they had abolitionists instead of diversity consultants; if not, slavery would still exist, and representatives of slaves and slaveholders would be meeting together—to promote mutual understanding and good feeling.

The knowledge that whiteness is socially constructed leads some to conclude that it is too deeply implanted in the society to be overturned. Howard Winant writes:

> Like any other complex of beliefs and practices, "whiteness" is imbedded in a highly articulated social structure and system of significations; rather than trying to repudiate it, we shall have to rearticulate it. That sounds like a daunting task, and of course it is, but it is not nearly as impossible as erasing whiteness altogether, as the new abolitionist project seeks to do.[7]

The best we can say of this tendency is that it represents a failure of political nerve. To its proponents we reply: you may, if you wish, try to "rearticulate" rape or child abuse, but do not ask us to rearticulate whiteness. We agree with the words of James Baldwin, "So long as you think you are white, there is no hope for you."

Whiteness is one pole of an unequal relationship, which can no more exist without oppression than slavery could exist without slaves. The abolitionists study whiteness in order to abolish it—not to "reframe," or "redeem," or "deconstruct" it, but to abolish it.

28
Reality and the Future

This short essay was cowritten with John Garvey and Beth Henson as an editorial statement for Issue 12 of Race Traitor, *published in the spring of 2001. The authors examine persistent attempts to suppress the black vote, and struggles against them, through a historical lens.*

Not once upon a time, but once again, an assault on the rights of Afro-Americans is the story. The widespread denial of voting rights to the black citizens of Florida in the 2000 presidential election should remind all of two previous presidential elections—those of 1876 and 1964.

The 1876 election, pitting the Democrat Samuel Tilden against the Republican Rutherford B. Hayes, eventually resulted in a deal to withdraw federal troops from the states still under reconstruction after the Civil War. That withdrawal opened the door for the night riders of the Ku Klux Klan and other groups to mount a campaign of terror against the freed slaves and their children and for the plantation owners to install and enforce a system of sharecropping that differed but little from the slave system that the war had been fought to end. It took this country more than seventy-five years to recover from the Hayes-Tilden Compromise.

It required the civil rights revolution of the post–World War II era to recover federal protections for Afro-American rights. But as should be well known, that revolution faced stubborn opposition from the defenders of Jim Crow and segregation. Although by 1964 the Democratic

Party had emerged as the one of the two parties more formally committed to equal rights, the party remained dominated by the Dixiecrats—
the Democrats in the South committed to preserving segregation. In
1964, the Mississippi Freedom Democratic Party (MFDP) held free and
open nominating conventions across the state to elect delegates to the
Democratic National Convention who would be pledged to end unequal
treatment within the party. When the delegates of the MFDP arrived at
the convention in Atlantic City, they were met not only by opposition
from the segregationists but by their supposed supporters in the party's
liberal wing. None other than the liberal hero, Hubert Humphrey (later
to be the losing Democratic candidate in 1968), was sent out to inform
the freedom fighters that there would be no room for them at the
convention.

Two lessons from the past—the first from a time when the Democratic
Party supported taking rights away from black people and the second
from a time when it was supposed to be in favor of restoring them.

And what can we learn from 2000? It seems clear that the one thing
that Al Gore and the architects of his postelection campaign to win
Florida refused to do was to make the widespread disenfranchisement
of black citizens the centerpiece of his argument. Someday, perhaps,
we'll read in his memoirs of his sleepless nights as he reluctantly decided
to turn his back on the outraged voices of the people of Florida. In the
meantime, it would be wise to recognize that the Democrats of 2001
remain prepared to do whatever they think necessary to preserve the
larger stability of the country that they rule over with the Republicans.

At the same time, it is of course black folks who voted for Al Gore or
who wanted to vote for Al Gore who are raising the demand that justice
be done. Is there a way to reconcile a conviction that the Democrats are
part of the problem with an unqualified support for the demands of
those who supported those same Democrats? In 1958, in *Facing Reality*,
C. L. R. James and colleagues urged those who wanted to promote radical change to have "an attitude of respect for the Negro people and their
ideas." They went on to say:

> Great changes in recent American society, the greatest of which has
> been the organization of the C.I.O., have been the motive force creat-
> ing new attitudes to race relations among Negroes and whites. But it
> is the Negroes who have broken all precedents in the way they have

used the opportunities thus created. In the course of the last twenty years they have formed the March on Washington Committee which extorted Executive Order 8802 from the Roosevelt Government. This was the order which gave the Negroes an invaluable weapon in the struggle to establish their right to a position in the plants. Negro soldiers, in every area of war, and sometimes on the battlefield itself, fought bloody engagements against white fellow soldiers, officers, generals, and all, to establish their rights as equal American citizens.

The Negroes in the North and West, by their ceaseless agitation and their votes, are now a wedge jammed in between the Northern Democrats and the Southern. At any moment this wedge can split that party into two and compel the total reorganization of American politics.[1]

We still live in the political era established by the split that James and his co-authors anticipated in 1958. All those who yearn to fight for a new world should remember their advice to be respectful and resist the easy temptation to tell people what they need to know. As James also pointed out in 1958,

> If Negroes outside of the South vote, now for the Democratic Party and now for the Republican, they have excellent reasons for doing so, and their general activity shows that large numbers of them see voting and the struggle for Supreme Court decisions merely as one aspect of a totality. They have no illusions.[2]

The world of 2001 is not the same as the one of 1958. But in the same way that the world was remade and new possibilities created by the civil rights movement that was under way in 1958, we may yet find that the turmoil in Florida allows us once again to face reality and dream of the future.

29

Abolitionism and the Free Society

This essay was cowritten with John Garvey, Beth Henson, Chris Niles, and Joel Olson, for Issue 12 of Race Traitor, *published in the spring of 2001. The authors evaluate the political project of new abolitionism, assessing the project, its shortcomings, and its accomplishments. The discussions around this text helped lead to the formation of Bring the Ruckus, a revolutionary organization, which Ignatiev was close to but never joined.*

The primary creative force will be the collective actions of the mass seeking to solve the great social problems which face them in their daily lives. Intellect will play a high role, higher than ever, but it will be the intellectual activities of millions of men, dealing with realities. Intellectuals will be of use to the extent that they recognize the new forces but as a class they will recognize it only when they see and feel the new force. The role that they played between 1200 and today will be over, because the condition of that role, the passive subordinate mass, will be undergoing liquidation in the very action of the mass which will be creating a totally new society, an active integrated humanism. The ideas demanded and the will to achieve them unfold one from the other, and with the consciousness of power, ideas, hopes, wishes, long-suppressed, because thought unattainable, but now come into the open—that is the process . . . But the great masses become abolitionist now; themselves to wipe away the conditions of their own slavery. These cannot be abolished by anyone else.

C. L. R. James

It seems to me the idea of our civilization, underlying all American life, is that men do not need any guardian. Not only the inevitable, but the best power this side of the ocean, is the unfettered average common sense of the masses. Institutions, as we are accustomed to calling them, are but pasteboard, and intended to be, against the thought of the street.

Wendell Phillips

The time has come to reconsider the original premises of what has come to be known as the new abolitionist project. Thus far, that project (not yet ten years old) has attracted a good deal of media and academic attention, has influenced a number of national discussions on race, has sharpened debates in at least some quarters, and has earned a sympathetic hearing among relatively large groups of anti-white supremacist audiences. At the same time, since the initiators of the project had always intended to be guided by the axiom that "the point was to change it," the project thus far must be considered only a very partial success. Frankly, we had hoped that, by this time, supporters of our project would have been able to establish functioning new abolitionist chapters across the country and that those chapters would have been able to develop effective public projects embodying abolitionist politics. This has not happened.

We have some questions for ourselves and for those we imagine to be more or less critical supporters. Is abolitionism sufficient for the development of a new insurgency—an insurgency that might resume where the insurgency of the 1960s left off? Is it capable of making a decisive contribution to the return of dreams of unqualified human freedom to the popular political imagination?

Race Traitor, characterized by its founding editors as the "journal of the new abolitionism," was launched in the fall of 1992. What follows reconstructs the political history of the project, evaluates its contribution and potential, and invites others to respond and to join in what might become a new project.

Since the initial publication of the journal, the editors and a relatively small number of associates have attempted to articulate an abolitionist vision for an American revolution. They did so in the context of an observation that almost all on the left who had imagined the necessity or desirability of social revolution in the 1960s and early 1970s had abandoned that goal and they hoped that a new articulation, in a distinctively American idiom, might contribute to a rebirth of radical activism.

The following are essential elements of the vision:

- race was an historical and social construction and had no biological reality;
- the white "race" was composed of individuals who partook of the advantages of the white skin;
- the advantages of the white skin were universal and substantial and led even the most downtrodden whites to ally themselves with their rulers;
- the white race needed to be abolished if we hoped to make progress in the country's social life;
- abolitionism was not anti-racism since anti-racism implicitly admitted the existence of races; in addition, anti-racism tended to reduce the necessary struggle to a struggle over the content of the ideas in people's heads rather than over the circumstances that gave rise to those ideas; furthermore, anti-racism often focused on groups like the Nazis and the Klan or conservative politicians as the perpetrators of racism; instead, we argued that race was reproduced by the principal institutions of society—the schools, the labor market, the law, the family *and* was reinforced by reform programs;
- the existence of the white race required the all but unanimous support of its members;
- the defection of enough "whites" would lead to the collapse of the white race and, by extension, would lead to a profound challenge to the entirety of the established social order;
- most white folks were not deeply nor consciously committed to white supremacy, nor were they primarily motivated by prejudice.

In addition, we have:

- reasserted the new abolitionist project's connection to nineteenth-century abolitionism and to the politics of John Brown;

- expressed an appreciation for the essential contributions made to the American freedom struggle by Afro-Americans;
- associated ourselves with the conviction that the ordinary people of the nation were prepared to rule the society;
- acknowledged the potential and the limitations of cultural "cross-overs"—whites who embraced and/or became participants in traditional and contemporary black cultural practices;
- asserted that "a new world, and nothing less, is worth fighting for." At the same time we never detailed what this new world might be like. This refusal in part reflected our reluctance to be associated with those who saw the new society as a series of ever more ambitious five-year plans, in part our realization that many poets and revolutionaries in the past had suggested ways of imagining the future more beautifully than we might, and in part our conviction that the new world would be made by the people who created it and could not be predicted;
- developed a critique of whiteness studies (embodying critiques of postmodernism and multiculturalism as political positions that reflected despair over the possibility of radical change);
- argued that whiteness was primarily made and remade by those who wanted to be white and was not foisted upon them by clever rulers;
- argued that various "new" immigrants were in the process of being incorporated as whites, and opposed analyses informed by a view of the United States as a "multiracial" society;
- suggested that whiteness was analogous to European social democracy in the sense that it represented an accommodation by some of the exploited to their continuing exploitation at the expense of still others of the exploited;
- recognized that the privileges of whiteness had been eroded during the last twenty-five years and that the erosion had occurred simultaneously with the erosion of social democracy;
- qualified our estimate of the erosion of whiteness with an appreciation of the significance of what might be considered "sedimented" social relations—insofar as they, for example, contributed to continuing inequalities in wealth between white and black while income differentials tended to decline;
- recognized that the turns to the right that had occurred in both the United States and Europe were, in part, the result of these erosions

of privileges but, unlike some others, we insisted on the importance of distinctions between what might be considered the conservatives and the fascist revolutionaries;

- reaffirmed a conviction that the appeal of the fascists would not likely be countered by a defense of the institutions and, to the chagrin of some, argued that relying on the state to defeat the fascists would only strengthen the state and, ultimately, the fascists themselves;
- welcomed and published the views of those who argued that "white" rebels had perhaps shed some of their whiteness in the course of their rebellion.

A Balance Sheet

Looking back upon this record, we believe that much of what we have said appears sound. Nonetheless, there are some shortcomings:

- We failed to take account of the full significance of what might be considered a world-historical break in 1973—a break that initiated real development in what had until then appeared to be a permanently undeveloped third world, the de-industrialization of a substantial part of what had previously been the industrial bases of the capitalist world system, the rebuilding of central American cities (concomitant with gentrification) and the incorporation of Afro-Americans into the ruling strata of the United States.
- We too infrequently acknowledged the ways in which we saw ourselves as the inheritors of what might be considered the Johnsonite tradition in American politics. That tradition was begun by C. L. R. James (using the pseudonym of J. R. Johnson) and other colleagues in the late 1940s and early 1950s. Its distinguishing elements can be summarized as follows: (1) a challenge to the existing order will develop as a result of the self-activity of the workers by which they will overcome internal barriers to their development as a potential ruling class (and not as the result of the work of political vanguards); (2) a deep appreciation of America as the country where the development of the

productive forces (including both the means of production and the workers) was most advanced; (3) an appreciation of the centrality of the black struggle to the self-realization of the proletariat.

- Although we have said that our aim was not racial harmony but class war, we have not managed to project effectively our view that whiteness was the key "internal barrier" to be overcome in the process of proletarian self-development and that our abolitionism was directly connected to our revolutionary vision. As a result, we have attracted support from individuals who would be upset if they understood the implications of our undertaking. Those individuals include some people who retain deeply held convictions about the unfulfilled promise of the American system and others who oppose all forms of discriminatory thought and behavior (for example, those who oppose "classism" as much as they oppose "racism").

- We were unprepared for the emergence of the new anti-globalization movement and have found ourselves to be relatively insignificant external commentators on its strengths and weaknesses. We would not want to underestimate this failure. While people in the hundreds, if not thousands, were prepared to confront directly the organized power of the state, we had no role to play. Those activists may be unaware of important political matters but they were the ones taking the risks and there were precious few abolitionists or revolutionaries from other traditions alongside them.

- We were also unprepared for the extent of the erosion of white privilege and the concomitant appearance of blacks in positions of authority within traditionally white-dominated institutions.

- We have not yet fully understood the significance of the erosion of whiteness being done to the working class and not by it. We also did not reconsider whether our "all or nothing" characterization of the white race had stood the test of time. Put it this way: what did it mean if some were no longer white, but the white race had not collapsed?

- We have developed only the most tentative of programmatic demands that might serve as the basis for the development of more or less sustained popular campaigns.

Abolitionism and the New Society

We need to reconsider abolitionism one more time. We hope it is clear that we fully understand that the great mass of the abolitionists consisted of the slaves, the runaways, and the free blacks who worked tirelessly in more or less open fashion to destroy slavery. Abolitionism was the first great moment of black liberation in this country. Then, as later, it served to inspire others not oppressed as blacks to join together with the oppressed in a common struggle for freedom and, more or less simultaneously, to embrace dreams of a new world—a world without fixed gender identities, a world characterized by new understandings of the relationship between the individual and the society, a world infused with a new understanding of the spiritual, and so forth. Consistent with the Johnsonite tradition, we believe this was no accident. In spite of the fact the Afro-Americans were branded as no other Americans were, they nonetheless became the most fully American and, when they engaged in popular struggle, gave expression to the deepest desires of the larger American population:

> The great unsatisfied desire of the American population is for social organization, free association, for common social ends. It is the only means whereby the powerful and self-destroying individualism can find fulfillment. The Americans are the most highly self-organized people on earth. Every city, every suburb, every hamlet has organizations of some sort, Elks, Shriners, Rotarians, clubs for everything under the sun. But the Negroes are the most highly organized of Americans. Government statistics show that of some 14 million Negroes in the United States, over 10 million are listed as belonging to some organization. Whatever the variety of these organizations every one has openly or implicitly as part of its program the emancipation of the Negro people.[1]

On the one hand, the blacks are those who express the desire of all for all and, on the other, they are the people who are often denied everything that is given to everyone else. The contradiction is an excruciating one:

> Thus, on all the basic economic and political problems of the day, the Negro, segregated as he is, is an integral part of American life. And it

is this contradiction between this fundamental need for complete and total integration demanded by the whole modern development in conflict with the powerful interests which demand and perpetuate segregation that lies the sharpness and the intolerable strains of the whole Negro question.[2]

So long as the issue is not confronted directly and completely, things endlessly appear to become better and worse at the same time:

> ... the fact above all which so demoralizes the modern world, that the greater the efforts made, the more terrible are the new forms in which the old social problems reappear.[3]

So, What to Do?

From the beginning we have drawn support from many who, whether they call themselves communists, anarchists, surrealists, or something else, consider themselves revolutionaries. If abolitionism without a vision of a new society is incomplete, the new society without abolitionism is impossible. It follows that we unequivocally welcome the erosion of whiteness no matter what quarter it comes from, and oppose any attempts to respond to the relative weakening of the white position by rearticulating a new whiteness.

We would like to invite those who read this reconsideration and believe that it represents, however imperfectly and incompletely, a useful starting point to get in touch with us, to write in response, to come together in more or less formal meetings to discuss what we have written and to think seriously about the possibility of developing a new political project that preserves and transcends the new abolitionist one. We are especially interested in hearing from those who were active on the streets of Seattle, Washington, Philadelphia and Los Angeles.

30

The American Blindspot: Reconstruction according to Eric Foner and W. E. B. Du Bois

Ignatiev examines how Eric Foner and W. E. B. Du Bois differ in their interpretation of the Reconstruction period of American history: whereas Foner placed Reconstruction within the framework of bourgeois revolution, Du Bois foregrounded class struggle and the revolutionary efforts of black workers to establish a dictatorship of the proletariat. Ignatiev focuses on Du Bois's notion of "abolition democracy" to explore how the question of slavery pushed radicals from the program of bourgeois revolution to proletarian power. The essay was first published in Volume 31 of the journal Labour/Travail *in 1993.*

In the teaching of US history, Reconstruction occupies a position analogous to the Revolution in France or the Khyber Pass in military affairs: whoever controls it controls the terrain below. Among the changes brought about by the civil rights movement was the emergence of a school of historians who, breaking with the redemptionist Burgess-Dunning school, viewed the Reconstruction regimes with sympathy. Eric Foner's book, *Reconstruction: America's Unfinished Revolution*, is the synthesis of three decades of revisionist scholarship. As such it is the closest thing that exists to a standard work; Foner, more than any historian of his generation, owns the period.

In his preface to *Reconstruction*, Eric Foner calls *Black Reconstruction in America* by W. E. B. Du Bois "a monumental study." Du Bois, according to Foner, "in many ways anticipated the findings of modern scholarship."[1] Since he nowhere in the book refers to any disagreements with Du Bois, the reader may conclude that the differences between them result largely from the advances of scholarship in the fifty years since *Black Reconstruction* was published.

That would be a false conclusion; Du Bois's interpretation of the period stands apart from Foner's. In this essay I shall attempt to demonstrate the truth of this assertion and to suggest some additional issues raised by the discussion.

Du Bois described the slaveholders not merely as a wealthy elite, but as owners of capital. The world market "set prices for Southern cotton, tobacco and sugar which left a narrow margin of profit for the planter" (p. 37). If the slaveholders were capitalists, it followed that the laborers were proletarians. He expressed this notion throughout the book, beginning with the title of the first chapter, which he called not "The Black Slave" but "The Black Worker."

Foner identifies capitalism with the wage form. His references to the slaveholders as a "reactionary and aristocratic ruling class" (p. 46) and as "Bourbons" (p. 130) imply a model based on the French *ancien regime*. He carefully avoids using the terms "worker" or "proletarian" to describe the slaves. To him they were—slaves.[2]

Because Du Bois identified the slaves as proletarians, he applied the categories of the labor movement to them. The fourth chapter of his study focuses on the mass withdrawal of labor power from the plantation that led to the downfall of the slaveocracy. The title of the chapter is "The General Strike." Foner makes no mention of the general strike. Slaves, apparently, could rebel, but only the worker could strike.

Was there a general strike? Du Bois reported that some 500,000 black workers transferred their labor from the Confederate planter to the northern invader. Behind them stood 3.5 million more still on the plantation; how much work they were doing after 1863 is hard to say. Hegel wrote:

> The truth is the whole. The whole, however, is merely the essential nature reaching its completeness through the process of its own development. Of the Absolute it must be said that it is essentially a result, that only at the end is it what it is in very truth . . .[3]

To determine whether there was a general strike, it is necessary to take the story further. The war ended; had the slaves (now freedmen) receded into passivity, or become merely supporting actors in the drama, one could deny that the strike ever happened. As both Du Bois and Foner document, they did neither of these things. In whose interests did they act? Here the differences sharpen.

Foner places Reconstruction squarely with the bourgeois revolution. In the South, it produced "a new class structure . . . the consolidation . . . of a rural proletariat class . . . and of a new owning class . . . subordinate to Northern financiers and industrialists" (p. 170). In the north it led to the "consolidation of the capitalist economy" under "an increasingly powerful class of industrialists and railroad entrepreneurs" (p. 460). Du Bois saw not one, but two Reconstructions.

> By singular coincidence and for a moment, for the few years of an eternal second in a cycle of a thousand years, the orbits of two widely and utterly dissimilar economic systems coincided and the result was a revolution so vast and portentous that few minds ever fully conceived it [p. 308].

The first was the effort of "a little knot of masterful men [to] so organize capitalism as to bring under their control the natural resources, wealth and industry of a vast and rich country and through that, of the world." Alongside it was the effort of black labour "to establish a dictatorship of the proletariat ending in industrial democracy" (p. 346). It is this latter effort he had in mind when he called Reconstruction "a revolution comparable to the upheavals in France in the past, and in Russia, Spain, India and China today" (p. 708).

From the two writers' conflicting views of class relations follow differing estimates of the Radicals. Foner says they were "a self-conscious political generation" whose social and economic program "derived from the free labor ideology," men hoping "to reshape Southern society in the image of small-scale competitive capitalism of the North," for whom "class relations [were] beyond the purview" (pp. 228, 234–7).

The Radical Republicans, Du Bois acknowledged, shared the American assumption "that any average worker can by thrift become a capitalist." He called Phillips, Sumner, and Stevens representatives of the "abolition-democracy, the liberal movement among both laborers and small capitalists, who . . . saw the danger of slavery to both capital and labor." So far the two descriptions sound similar. But, Du Bois added, under the pressure of southern intransigence, "abolition-democracy was pushed towards the conception of a dictatorship of labor" (pp. 183–5). By this formulation, he shifted the most extreme of the Radicals out of the framework of the bourgeois revolution into the camp of the proletariat.

At issue, more than an assessment of the Radicals, is the algebra of revolution. The desires of a social class can change from one epoch to the next. While the French bourgeoisie showed after 1789 that it could live with the peasants' seizure of the feudal estates, in the specific circumstances of the post–Civil War South, land redistribution, advocated by Stevens, Julian, and Phillips, carried implications too subversive for any sector of capital. Again, while capital generally tends to reduce all distinctions between one individual and another to impersonal relations of the marketplace, in America, where consensus depended heavily on the existence of a color line, Stevens may have threatened the social order more by his decision to be buried in a "colored" graveyard than by the way he manhandled the Constitution. The notion of abolition-democracy stands astride two phases of a single revolutionary process. By introducing it, Du Bois revealed a revolution without fixed limits, in which one phase could pass over imperceptibly to the next. Phillips personified the historical movement: beginning as a Garrisonian, by the time he was finished he was speaking out in defense of the Commune and may have joined the International.[4]

In what was perhaps the boldest assertion in the book, Du Bois called black political power in the South "one of the most extraordinary experiments of Marxism that the world, before the Russian revolution, had seen . . . a dictatorship of labor" (p. 358). In a revealing footnote to Chapter 10, he commented, "I first called this chapter 'The Dictatorship of the Black Proletariat in South Carolina,' but it has since been brought to my attention that this would not be correct . . ." He finally settled for a more restrained title but continued to insist that South Carolina "showed tendencies toward a dictatorship of the proletariat" (p. 391).

Engels called the Paris Commune an example of the Dictatorship of the Proletariat (upper case). The most drastic economic reform introduced by the Commune was the abolition of night work for bakers. Compared to the moderation of the Commune, the accomplishments of Reconstruction in South Carolina seem like the wildest radicalism:

abolishing property qualifications for holding office, apportioning representation based on population not property, abolishing imprisonment for debt, founding the public school, extending rights for women, building asylums for the insane and the handicapped, modifying the tax structure, and other reforms. A program of this sort, carried out against a background of mass movement, may not yet be communism, but it is no longer capitalism.

Just as the great social measure of the Commune was its own working existence, the real story of Reconstruction was the actors: of 124 members of the South Carolina Constitutional Convention, 76 were black. Of these, 57 had been slaves. The total taxes paid by all the delegates was $878, of which one white conservative paid $508. Fifty-nine of the black and twenty-three of the white delegates owned so little property that they paid no taxes whatever (*Black Reconstruction in America*, p. 390). Was either the Paris Commune or the Petrograd Soviet of purer proletarian composition than the South Carolina Convention of 1867?

A speech made in Tallapoosa County, Alabama by a man named Alfred Gray showed the character of the movement. Gray was speaking at a meeting on the eve of elections for the state constitution, which were to take place on February 4, 1868:

> The Constitution, I came here to talk for it. If get killed will talk for it . . . I afraid to fight the white man for my rights? No! I may go to hell, my home is hell, but the white man shall go there with me . . .
>
> My father, god damn his soul to hell, had 300 niggers, and his son sold me for $1,000. Was this right? No! I feel the damned spirit of damnation in me and will fight for our rights until every rascal who chased niggers with hounds is in hell . . .
>
> Remember the 4th of February. And every one come in and bring your guns and stand up for your rights! Let them talk of social equality, mixed schools, and a war of races. We'll fight until we die, and go to hell together, or we'll carry this constitution.

A speech like that, made by a legislator serving in a militia of the propertyless class, is a sign that we are no longer talking about a bourgeois parliament.[5]

Foner knows all about the activity of the freedmen. Indeed, he lists

"the centrality of the black experience" as one of the broad themes unifying his narrative and offers a great deal of information about "the political mobilization of the black community" (pp. xxiv–xxv). Because he
ascribes no distinctive class character to that mobilization, he in effect
makes it an auxiliary, albeit a radical auxiliary, of a modernization
project led by northern industry.[6]

That is the difference, reduced to its essentials: Du Bois wrote "an
essay toward a history of the part which black folk played in the attempt
to reconstruct democracy in America, 1860–1880" (subtitle). It is the
story of the striving of a group of laborers, taking advantage of conflicts
among the propertied classes, to advance their own interests. Foner tells
how the industrialists manipulated the freedmen to overcome the resistance of the former slaveholders and reconstruct the South along capitalist lines. The two books are not about the same revolution, that is all.

Nowhere do the differences between the two writers emerge so clearly
as when we compare what they have to say about the labor movement.
Du Bois, as we have seen, considered the black worker, during and after
slavery, the vanguard of the working class. Foner is willing to recognize
the existence of a southern black proletariat after Emancipation, including timber workers, longshoremen, and others, but he limits it to those
who worked for wages. He says that the great rail strike of 1877 "ushered
in two decades of labor conflict the most violent the country had ever
known" (p. 585)—this a few pages after he recounts the Hamburg
Massacre, the Colfax Massacre, the battle of Vicksburg, the insurrection
at New Orleans, and other incidents which antedated the rail strike and
were part of a wave of terror in which thousands of black laborers died.
Because his category "labor conflict" coincides with the contours of
trade unionism, it cannot encompass the struggle over black worker
power in Reconstruction. (At one point he describes the 1869 [colored]
National Labor Union Convention as "composed mostly of politicians,
religious leaders, and professionals, rather than sons of toil" [p. 480].
Would he describe the 1917 Russian Congress of Soviets, dominated by
Lenin, Trotsky, and other editors and publicists, in the same terms?)

Foner attributes the defeat of Reconstruction to several causes. He
recounts how the increasing demands of the northern poor "helped
propel the urban bourgeoisie to the right," leading to "the growth of
bourgeois class consciousness." And then he writes, "The erosion of the
free labor ideology made possible a resurgence of overt racism that

undermined support for Reconstruction" (pp. 517–18, 525). That is a curious statement and merits closer examination.

"Free labor" was the ideology of the producers at a time when that group included both laborers and manufacturers. As the ideology of free labor gave way among the industrialists and railroad entrepreneurs to the gospel of wealth and monopoly, they lost their sympathy for the laborer, black or white. So far, so good. But to attribute the defeat of Reconstruction to changes in ruling-class attitudes is a tautology, like blaming the French bourgeoisie for the defeat of the Commune. The capitalists opposed labor's rule because it was in their class interests to do so; any "resurgence of overt racism" among them explains nothing, since they opposed Reconstruction for reasons having nothing to do with race.

On the working-class side, the erosion of the free labor ideology accompanied an increase in militant labor struggles. Foner says these struggles were marked by "Unprecedented cooperation between . . . black and white" (p. 585). We shall take up this claim below, but there is an evident contradiction in attributing a rise in both cooperation and race hatred to the erosion of the free labor ideology. Any cooperation that did not entail support for Reconstruction could be at most ephemeral. The waning of such support among white laborers suggests that the "resurgence of overt racism" was not confined to the employers.

Foner writes, "The failure to develop an effective long-term appeal to white voters made it increasingly difficult for Republicans to combat the racial politics of the Redeemers" (p. 603). If the subject and predicate are reversed the statement will be true: the attachment of white voters to racial politics made it difficult to win their support for Reconstruction. The problem was not that the Radicals failed to develop an appeal to whites, but that the emancipation of the labouring class in half the nation never came to constitute such an appeal.

Before the war, white labor "refused, in the main, to envisage black labour as part of its problem" (*Black Reconstruction in America*, p. 29). The first Congress of the (white) National Labor Union (NLU), meeting in 1866, addressed the issue of black labor. Unable to agree on a position, the union called for the organization of trade unions and eight-hour leagues among blacks, to prevent the employers from using them against white labor. "Here was a first halting note," commented Du Bois. "Negroes were welcomed to the labor movement, not because they were laborers but because they might be competitors." Three years later, at its

Philadelphia Congress, the NLU urged black workers to organize separately. "Through this separate union, Negro labor would be restrained
from competition and yet kept out of the white race unions where power
and discussion lay" (pp. 354, 356).

The differences between the NLU and black labor came to a head over
the issue of the labor party. At its 1870 meeting in Cincinnati, the privilege of the floor (which had earlier been extended to a white former
Democratic) was denied to a black Republican congressman. The
Congress then voted a labor party resolution, over the objections of
some black delegates that in the South the Republican Party was the
party of labor.

White labor, notwithstanding its increasing awareness of its distinct
interests, was unable to sever its ties with capital; whereas black labor, in
pursuit of the American dream of every man his own master, steered a
course which led it into collision with all sectors of wealth. Here is the
solution to the famous problem, why no socialism in America?

The labor radicals of that time, like their counterparts in later generations, were unable to recognize labor's struggle when it appeared in a
dark face. As Du Bois noted, "The main activity of the International was
in the North; they seemed to have no dream that the place for its most
successful rooting was in the new political power of the Southern
worker." (p. 360) An example of how what Du Bois called the American
Blindspot (p. 367) afflicted radicals was the eight-hour day parade in
New York City on September 13, 1871. At least 8,000 marched behind
the red flag bearing the slogan, "Workingmen of All Countries, Unite!"
A company of Frenchmen carried a banner inscribed "Comite
International" and were greeted with cries of "*Vive la Commune!*" A
mass meeting following the march voted unanimously to throw off all
allegiance to the Democratic Party in the fall elections—but there was
no mention of black grassroots political power in the South. The *Herald*
called the demonstration "a fraternization of the laboring classes of this
city with the great Internationale of Europe." Apparently, American
Internationalists were able to look across the ocean to the Paris
Commune, but could not cast their eyes southward to the South Carolina
Commune.[7]

Foner makes much of the St. Louis general strike of 1877, which he
claims "brought together 'white and colored men . . . in one supreme
contest for the common rights of workingmen'" (p. 584). In that strike

the white leadership of the Workingmen's Party turned away 500 black workers who sought to join it, did their best "to dissuade any white men from going with the niggers," and called off public activities rather than open them to black participation.[8] Du Bois summarized the shortsightedness of white labor:

> The South, after the war, presented the greatest opportunity for a real national labor movement which the nation ever saw or is likely to see for many decades. Yet the labor movement, with but few exceptions, never realized the situation. It never had the intelligence or knowledge, as a whole, to see in black slavery and Reconstruction, the kernel and meaning of the labor movement in the United States [p. 353].

The point is not to excoriate people dead for a century, but to observe that they were not the last to suffer from what Du Bois called "the blindspot in the eyes of America and its historians" (p. 577).

Du Bois took for granted the "Counter-Revolution of Property" (title of Chapter 14); to him it was simply a matter of time until the owners of industry and the owners of land patched up their differences: "Northern and Southern employers agreed that profit was most important and the method of getting it second." But he looked elsewhere for the condition that made the counterrevolution possible: "When white laborers were convinced that the degradation of Negro Labor was more fundamental than the uplift of white labor, the end was in sight" (p. 347). Let that stand as Reconstruction's epitaph.

Just as northern capital sought to attach the freedmen to its own reconstruction project, so Foner enfolds *Black Reconstruction* into his "coherent, comprehensive modern account of Reconstruction" (p. xxiv). It will not wash. Far from "anticipating the findings of modern scholarship," Du Bois's book occupies a unique interpretative space. As he wrote, "The unending tragedy of Reconstruction is the utter inability of the American mind to grasp its real significance, its national and worldwide implications" (p. 708).

Foner was not the first to view Reconstruction as America's bourgeois revolution. In 1927 Charles and Mary Beard, in a chapter called "The Second American Revolution," had drawn the parallels between the triumph of "northern capitalists and free farmers" over the "planting aristocracy" and the Puritan and French Revolutions.[9] In 1937 James S.

Allen restated the thesis in Marxian terms, calling the conflict begun by the Civil War "basically a revolution of a bourgeois democratic charac- ter, in which the bourgeoisie was fighting for power against the landed aristocracy." Appropriately he placed greater emphasis than the Beards on the activity of the former slaves.[10] Foner includes Allen's book in his bibliography, without discussing it. A comparison of the two works shows their consistency.

Allen's book was less important as a historical study than as a political statement. He was a member of the Communist Party and one of its theoreticians on the "Negro question." At the time he wrote it, the Burgess-Dunning School dominated Reconstruction historiography. If his aim was to oppose that view, he must have known that Du Bois's book was a powerful polemic; indeed he called it "a spirited defense of the Reconstruction governments" (p. 91). Allen's book must be seen, therefore, not as the Communists' answer to "Birth of a Nation," but as their reply to Du Bois. To underscore this point, the editor's foreword criticized "Du Bois' failure to grasp the fundamental bourgeois charac- ter of the revolution," which had led him "into the error of characteriz- ing the Reconstruction governments of the epoch as dictatorships of labor (that is, the proletariat) despite the fact that at the time such a dictatorship was out of the question."[11]

Why did the party feel called upon to reply to Du Bois on a historical issue in which both held minority positions? The explanation is to be found in the political alignments of the time the books appeared. Although Du Bois later developed friendly relations with the Communist Party and even applied for membership (on the eve of his permanent departure for Africa), relations between them were not cordial in those years. A resolution drafted for the party's 1934 Convention linked Du Bois with Walter White and William Pickens as "the chief social supports of imperialist reaction."[12] That was during the days of the "Negro Soviet Republic" slogan.

In 1935 the Party changed to the policy of the Popular Front, which entailed, in place of the old "class against class" approach, an alliance with liberal capitalists. As part of the new line, it discovered the liberal tradition in America, stretching back to Paine, Jefferson, and Lincoln (and up to Roosevelt). Reconstruction became the task of the bourgeoi- sie, which it had unfortunately failed to complete.

Allen concluded in his book that the failure of Reconstruction had "chalked up on the scoreboard of history [a good example of popular front language] a whole series of obligations which only the new revolutionary and progressive forces of our epoch can fulfill" (p. 215). In the context of the party's actual maneuvering with Congress of Industrial Organizations leaders and the liberal wing of the Democratic Party, his conclusion could only be taken as a call for an alliance reaching from Browder to Roosevelt.

Du Bois was having none of it. Relentlessly he insisted that "the rebuilding, whether it comes now or a century later, will and must go back to the basic principles of Reconstruction in the United States during 1867–1876—Land, Light and Leading for slaves black, brown, yellow and white, under a dictatorship of the proletariat" (p. 635). Du Bois's book was not then, nor is it now, a historical justification for the Popular Front.

31
Whiteness and Class Struggle

In this 2003 review published in the journal Historical Materialism, *Ignatiev discusses Alexander Saxton, David Roediger, and Theodore Allen's books on whiteness—respectively,* The Rise and Fall of the White Republic, Wages of Whiteness, *and* The Invention of the White Race. *Ignatiev evaluates their individual and collective contributions and asserts that their starting point of class struggle sets their work apart from most academic studies on whiteness. He concludes by arguing that even as racial boundaries continue to change and transform, the color line remains the most important obstacle to working-class solidarity.*

A recent electronic search yielded fifty-one books with the word "whiteness" in their titles, almost all published in the last decade and most within the last five years, and 373 articles published since 1985 with "whiteness" in their titles, citations, or abstracts.[1] Admittedly the list is imperfect, since it contains works relating to physical science and omits some that do not contain the word in their titles, and the count has increased since the tally was made; nevertheless, it reflects an explosion of awareness in the academy of the social and historical dimension of whiteness. Some of this work is postmodern silliness, verging on self-parody. Nevertheless, the effort to analyze race, and the white race in particular, as a social category offers a great deal to those interested in working-class politics.

Among scholars, it was W. E. B. Du Bois who first called attention to the problem of the white worker. In a 1932 essay, he recounted an incident where white American trade unionists, helped by the Labor Party acting in the name of labor solidarity, drove black workers from jobs building a new British Embassy in Washington. "Black brothers," he asked, "how would you welcome a dictatorship of this proletariat?"[2] In *Black Reconstruction in America*, he wrote of "the subordination of colored labor to white profits the world over . . . by the insistence of white labor."[3]

> By the insistence of white labour . . . Not acquiescence, but insistence. And why did the white labourers act as they did? Not because they were backward or misled, but because they were rewarded with what he called "a public and psychological wage."[4]

As a matter of survival, the direct victims of white privilege have always studied it. Black Americans, in particular, have long understood that the white race is not a biological but a social formation, whose existence depends on its members' willingness to reproduce it through their actions.[5] The 1960s brought a new generation of radicals who, influenced by worldwide movements for national liberation and the high tide of black struggle in the United States, sought to address the white problem. After 1967, the idea gained currency within Students for a Democratic Society, for better and for worse, that white supremacy constituted the principal internal barrier to revolution in the United States and that the struggle against it was the key to revolutionary strategy. But it lost much of its hold in the 1970s, and, moreover, was detached from its class moorings, leaving only a semantic residue among diversity consultants and other debris left on the beach after the revolutionary tide receded. And then, in 1990, Alexander Saxton published *The Rise and Fall of the White Republic,* and, a year later, David Roediger published *The Wages of Whiteness,* which reawakened interest in the white problem. Roediger, in asking why some people wanted to be white, and attempting to identify the historical moment when they became so, captured the imagination of readers. Saxton's and Roediger's studies were followed by one by Theodore Allen, on which he had been working on for many years, and by my own *How the Irish Became White.*[6]

What these works have in common, and what distinguishes them from some other studies of whiteness, is that they take the class struggle as their starting point and seek to explain why some members of the working class act in the interests of a group rather than the interests of a *class,* that is, as *whites* instead of as proletarians. One might expect labor historians in particular to welcome inquiry along these lines, but such has not proven universally to be the case. Eric Arnesen dismisses the new scholarship on whiteness, citing as evidence studies showing that "self-interest" has sometimes "prompted organized labor to encourage collaboration across the racial divide."[7] He misses the point: the issue is not the willingness of white workers to take joint action with others to raise their own wages when they think it is to their advantage to do so; the issue is their clinging to a notion of themselves as a group with distinct interests. The following passage captures Arnesen's worldview:

> Only if one accepts . . . the "theory of laboring class unity" . . . does the failure of white workers to recognize their common interests with blacks, their creation of a labor movement that excludes people of color, and their own embrace of white racial privileges require explanation . . . The whiteness project becomes a variant on the question that will not die, the old "why no socialism in America" [yes!—NI] or at least the "why no working-class unity" question . . . What *is* problematic is the very notion of unitary "common working-class interests," a notion that most labor historians, excluding whiteness scholars, have themselves jettisoned . . . The problem is that at least some of Du Bois's assumptions remain alive and well in the form of a persistent "Marxism lite"—the expectation that common oppression or common enemies should promote unity, that all workers more or less share class interests regardless of race, and that the working class play the role of agent assigned to it by radical theory.[8]

Arnesen may reject the notion that the working class is the gravedigger of capitalism, but to label what he is rejecting "Marxism lite" is to do violence to Marx. "The working class is revolutionary or it is nothing." To Arnesen, it is nothing, a view that supremely equips him to conduct labor history classes for functionaries of US unions.

If Arnesen's white-labor apologetics can be easily disposed of from a revolutionary perspective, there remain serious questions among those who seek to examine the effect of whiteness on the class struggle.

As I write, I have just received the new edition of Saxton's *Rise and Fall* with a foreword by Roediger in which, with characteristic modesty, he describes it as the best study of whiteness since *Black Reconstruction*.[9] *Rise and Fall* recounts how white supremacy was adapted to serve the interests of successive ruling coalitions in the nineteenth century. To Saxton, white supremacy is ideology, a system of beliefs that rationalizes experience so as to enable a particular group to present its interests as those of the entire society. He sees little difficulty in understanding how a belief in white superiority arose out of the need to justify a class that grew rich by enslaving Africans, expropriating Indians, and later on plundering Mexico and China. But why did non-property-holding whites acquiesce in racial ideology? The closest he offers by way of explanation is a remark that they did so because they "shared willingly, if not equally, in the profits of racial exploitation." That assertion has been made before, but, to my knowledge, no one has ever explained how the profit-sharing takes place. To stand at the head of the employment line and the rear of the layoff line and to hold a monopoly of the best jobs and mostly stay out of prison are certainly privileges, but they do not entail sharing in the profits (surplus value) drawn from racial exploitation. In context, Saxton's gliding over this issue is unimportant, because his argument does not depend on it. But it touches on political questions of importance to revolutionaries.

Wages of Whiteness errs in the opposite direction from *Rise and Fall*. Not wishing to suggest that white workers constitute an exploiting group in the literal sense, Roediger offers psychological and cultural explanations for their unproletarian behavior. But there is a problem here, too, one which is the flipside of Saxton's. Without an attendant material advantage, what would be the psychological value of the white skin? Again: to stand at the head of the employment line and the rear of the layoff line and to hold a monopoly of the best jobs and mostly stay out of prison may not grant the white worker a share of the profits, but the pay is more than psychological. Roediger may be reacting against the third-worldist, anti-working-class currents that emerged in the last days of the New Left—here, I only speculate, as we have never discussed this. I do not know enough about psychoanalysis to venture a judgment on how much it can explain by itself. In his foreword to the new edition of *Rise and Fall*, Roediger refers to the "cruder monetary payoffs of white supremacy." It may be—again, I only speculate—that he regarded these payoffs as so obvious they scarcely needed comment, but I wish he had talked about them in *Wages*, because his stress on psychology and culture independent of market forces rendered him vulnerable to some of the shafts Arnesen aims at him.[10]

While I would not choose to dispute the point, in my opinion, Allen's is the best recent study of whiteness. First, Allen has provided a careful definition of racial oppression as a particular form of oppression in which a portion of the exploited class is enlisted in maintaining the rule of the dominant class through a system of privileges that elevate the most degraded member of the privileged group above *any* member of the oppressed group. Second, he has compiled a mass of evidence show-ing the origins of racial oppression—and hence the white race—in the colonial period. Third, he has provided a materialist explanation for the emergence of racial oppression, thoroughly refuting those who ascribe it to prior prejudice. Fourth, he has indicted the white-skin privilege system as the chief cause of the failure of the working class in the United States to overturn capitalism. And he has accomplished all these things in two volumes that are exhaustively researched, rigorously argued, scrupulously fair to opponents, and unashamedly partisan. These are no small accomplishments, and I am sure there are others I have failed to mention.

Allen explains racial oppression as the result of conscious decisions made by the plantation bourgeoisie of the tobacco-growing regions of the Chesapeake in response to specific problems of labor control. One problem is the lack of documentary evidence: Here is an "invention" more valuable to capital than the steam engine, the police force, and the two-party system—and the inventor is unknown. Allen acknowledges the lack but asserts that it does not matter.[11]

Is there a simpler explanation for the American color line that does not attribute it to something in the English soul? In both mainland and West Indian colonies, people from Africa made up the slave-labor force, with the result that the black skin became the badge of slavery. The asso-ciation between skin-color and social status developed more slowly on the mainland than in the islands, because, initially, most mainland laborers were English, serving under temporary indenture, and lines between slavery and "freedom" were indistinct and of little importance. The natural result was a great deal of interaction and solidarity among the laborers. But as the planters imported more slaves—a decision motivated by purely monetary consideration, having nothing to do with "racial" preference—and codified slavery as a distinct form, the association of the black skin with slavery came to loom large, and, by reflex, all those not of African descent, and therefore not slaves, came to constitute a group—or, in our terms, a race—on whose loyalty depended the stability of the social order.[12] As for conscious decisions on the part of the Chesapeake planters to invent whiteness, *je n'ai besoin de cette hypothèse.*

In the West Indies, the need to control vast numbers of slaves compelled the planters to enlist in the militia persons of African descent, thereby complicating the relation between color and freedom. It was in the West Indies, and not on the mainland, that conscious decision was crucial, and records survive of the debates there. Allen writes, "Down to the last moment, and past it, the sugar plantocracy resisted any attempt to undermine that [white] consciousness."[13]

A crucial challenge facing those who look critically at race is to make sense of the "new immigrants." (The quotation marks are there because many of those in question are neither new nor immigrants.) There are numerous signs that people from Asia and elsewhere may now be undergoing the whitening process that immigrants from Europe underwent in the past. Old-fashioned American color prejudice is far from dead, but it is by no means obvious that Chinese, Mexicans, and even Ethiopians are subject to greater hostility from official society and the mass of American stupidos than were Irish and Italians in the past.

US political stability has traditionally depended on a majority held together by racial definition. Whiteness has served as a sort of disaster insurance for the ruling class. Some groups occupy intermediate positions, sociologically: everyone knows that European-American ethnic groups vary in wealth and status; what makes them all white is their access to things from which others are excluded *by racial definition.* The United States may be multi*ethnic,* but the traditional mode of class rule demands two *races* and no more, the racially oppressed and the racially privileged. The day California or some other state develops a racially oppressed majority is the day the Rodney King rebellion becomes permanent. The pitfalls of the multiracial model are exemplified by a recent book that hailed South Asian New York City cabdrivers as the "vanguard" in the struggle against racism—just a few months before they were revealed to be a main force denying taxi service to black men.[14] One might as well have hailed the 1863 New York City Irish as fighters against white supremacy for their determined opposition to nativist bigotry.

As in the nineteenth century, the white race is being recomposed and, as at that time, boundaries are not always clear. A great deal of the quarrel about "people of color" and "intermediate" races has to do with determining which groups will be socially white in the twenty-first century. It has already been suggested that all that is missing for the reconfiguration of the dominant race is the appearance and general acceptance of a new term for everyone other than born-in-the-USA-black folk.[15] Of course, the evidence can be read in several ways, and the outcome is not settled; what is needed is for people to look at the issue without assuming the conclusion as a premise.

Finally, the future of race itself is in doubt. In order for the white race to function effectively as a means of social control, the most degraded white man must feel himself socially superior to any person of color who walks the earth—a feeling undermined by the existence of a desegregated "multiracial" propertied class. In this regard, too, the country is changing. There are now thousands of black millionaires. Evidently, a million dollars is not what it used to be, and there have always existed Afro-Americans of exceptional wealth; what is new is that many of them now operate outside the segregated Afro-American community. Black Americans now hold or have recently held positions on the Supreme Court, in the Cabinet, in Congress, as mayors of large cities, at the head of influential private foundations, and at the highest levels of the military. In 1996, a black man was widely touted as a candidate for President, and polls reported that, if he ran, he would be elected, by more white votes than black. These people exercise authority not merely over black people but over institutions that have been traditionally regarded as white. Not long ago, and not far away, the only time a black man or woman was seen in a public space was with a mop; today, black people stride through airports and corporate headquarters carrying briefcases and talking on cellular telephones. Perhaps the most visible and important sign of change is the black police officer. In 1940, there was not a single black policeman in any Deep South state and only a handful in Northern cities; now, there are black cops in major cities all over the country, and black police chiefs as well. They are even authorized to arrest white people. This is beyond tokenism.

Meanwhile, the New Deal compact with the labor unions, which institutionalized the protected status of white labor, has collapsed. As a result, many whites find themselves living under conditions scarcely different from those of the black poor (as depicted in the recent film *8 Mile*). There are signs that the United States is becoming something like Brazil, where color, instead of being an absolute marker of caste, is one element on a gradient, so that dark skins are to be found disproportionately at the bottom and fair skins at the top, and money whitens.

If white supremacy is the American counterpart of European social democracy, a compact between the ruling class and a portion of the working class—indeed, the United States' "historic compromise"—its collapse is to be welcomed no matter the source. As John Garvey has quipped, maybe we should declare victory and go home. But the blurring of the color line appears alongside growing immiseration and even marginalization of a sector of the black population. Not only are Afro-Americans largely absent from growing areas of the economy, one hundred black men are in prison for everyone who graduates from college—an ominous statistic. The decline of traditional forms of racial oppression, like any popular victory, gives rise to new problems; the question of working-class autonomy becomes even more crucial than in the past.

32

12 Million Black Voices

This essay appeared as the foreword to the 2002 edition of Richard Wright's book 12 Million Black Voices. *Ignatiev explores the changes in the political, social, and economic life of black workers since the book was first published in 1941 and evaluates its importance for understanding the enduring problem of the color line today.*

Until World War II, three-quarters of black Americans lived in the South, a "nation within a nation." There, a system of color caste resting ultimately on legal and extralegal terror maintained millions of Negroes (as the people of mixed African, European, and Amerindian descent were then politely referred to) in semi-serfdom directly subject to the Lords of the Land, kept millions more working long hours for low wages in domestic service and extractive industries, and distorted the growth of a professional-entrepreneur class among them. The shadow of the plantation fell even over the North, where a color line operating largely apart from (although not usually against) the law restricted black people to the worst jobs, schools, and neighborhoods, beneath even the millions of poor whites ground under the heels of the Bosses of the Buildings. ("Lords of the Land" and "Bosses of the Buildings" were terms employed by Richard Wright in the text that follows.)

This in brief was the reality when *12 Million Black Voices* came out, and, taking words and pictures together, never has a work of comparable length more powerfully and accurately depicted that reality. A great deal has changed since 1941, however, and it will be necessary to review some of the changes in order to assess the importance of the work to the modern reader.

The cotton fields of Mississippi have given way to the synthetic fiber plants of Indonesia, the black peasant has gone the way of the mule, and the Lords of the Land now speculate in shopping malls and tennis resorts. The black laborer has been replaced by the digitally controlled, computer-operated robot in mine and mill, hearth and dock, killing floor and assembly line, and in an eerie, symbolic echo of the custom of Nation of Islam members, the United States Steel Corporation, once master of hundreds of thousands of black and white industrial proletarians in the North and South and mighty among the Bosses of the Buildings, has renounced its "slave name" and become USX, operator of restaurant and hotel chains employing mainly immigrants. Sixty percent of black women employed outside their homes were domestic servants in 1940; today very few are, a majority holding white-collar jobs.

There are now thousands of Afro-American millionaires. Of course a million dollars is not what it used to be, and there have always existed Afro-Americans of exceptional wealth; what is new is that many of them now operate outside the segregated Afro-American community. A recent magazine story profiled twenty black women who are senior executives in big corporations, including Xerox, Owens Corning, Kraft Foods, American Express, IBM, Blue Cross, Coca-Cola, and Johnson Publishing. Of the corporations, only the last-named is especially linked to black America. The women wield authority over budgets and revenues totaling more than $36 billion and receive yearly compensations that range from $250,000 to more than $1 million. The only comparable figure in 1941 was Madam C. J. Walker, founder of the cosmetics empire, who made a fortune catering to a segregated market.

Black Americans now hold or have recently held positions on the Supreme Court, in the Cabinet, in Congress, as mayors of large cities, at the head of influential private foundations, and at the highest levels of the military. In 1996 a black man was widely touted as a candidate for President, and polls reported that if he ran he would be elected, by more white votes than black. These people exercise authority not merely over black people but over institutions that have been traditionally regarded as white.

Boston magazine touched off a flap by running a profile of Henry Louis Gates, Jr. under the headline "Head Negro in Charge." Amidst all the controversy around the headline (which originally meant the slave who bossed the other slaves), hardly anyone pointed out that Gates is *not* a figurehead appointed by massa' to rule over the other slaves, but an academic superstar, chairman of a department and research institute at Harvard boasting more floor space than any other, member of important university committees, one of Harvard Corporation's most successful fundraisers, a frequent commentator in the press and over the airwaves about life in America. Certainly whites hired him, but he now makes decisions that affect the lives of black *and* white people.

Not so long ago, the only time a black man or woman was seen in a public space was with a mop; today black people stride through airports and corporate headquarters carrying briefcases and talking on cellular telephones. Black women and even black men, decked out in bright-colored nylon, jog along the Charles or the Hudson—a far cry from the days when any black man running outside of darktown would be set upon by local guardians of the peace.

Perhaps the most visible and important sign of change is the black police officer. In 1940 there was not a single black policeman in any Deep South state and only a handful in northern cities; now there are black cops in major cities all over the country, and black police chiefs as well.

Racial oppression exists where color or some other arbitrary marker confers a status *apart from* that which grows out of occupation, wealth, language, age, sex, education, kinship, or other traits that have in most parts of the world determined an individual's social position. Racial oppression tends to level all those within the subordinate group (and elevate all those within the dominant group). Malcolm X captured its essence with his question, *What does a white bigot call a black PhD?* Answer: *nigger.*

By that standard, it must be admitted that race as a category has been eroded in the United States. The black skin is no longer the badge of total degradation it once was. Before joining the celebrant chorus, people should remember that conditions have not improved for Afro-Americans in general.

Back in the days when the black "bourgeoisie" consisted of undertakers, makers and sellers of ointments for straightening hair, numbers bankers, and professionals serving a segregated market, they lived in the black community and exerted pressure on white authorities to maintain a certain minimum level of services to it. Now that they have moved out, the situation of those left behind is in many ways bleaker than before—neighborhoods of burned-out buildings and no stores, grown men standing on corners in the middle of the day, schools that are little more than warehouses, and torn-up streets that resemble nothing so much as Warsaw 1944. The number of black women and men in prison has grown faster than the number holding professional and managerial positions in predominantly white firms and agencies.

And notwithstanding Oprah Winfrey, Skip Gates, Michael Jordan, Colin Powell, and Bill Cosby, a black man still cannot get a taxicab in New York City. Some may dismiss the complaint as trivial—after all, many whites cannot afford to take taxicabs—but it has a special meaning because it is a reminder of the days when skin-color trumped money in the quest for status.

Could that day return? Probably not—history never runs backward. But as Faulkner said, the past is never dead; it's not even past. Much of the human population today consists of people who are useless for the production of wealth and an absolute drain on accumulation. Those people are different from the reserve army of labor of the past, useful for holding down wages and expanding production in times of economic growth. To capital—the impersonal personified that dominates the planet—they make up a permanent surplus population. The capitalist system organizes the production of death as it does the production of coal, computer chips, and cocaine. Nazism was not merely death but planned, systematic, organized death; it was the logical result of capitalist development, though its racial form was the product of the history and tradition of the place where it arose.

It is not difficult to imagine a US equivalent. For the first time since they came to America, people of African descent are no longer as a group central to the production of wealth. *12 Million Black Voices* contains a photograph of a lynching. The passions that used to motivate thousands of whites to travel miles to gather festively at such events are still there, repressed only temporarily by speech codes and other expressions of multicultural orthodoxy. It is certain that a major economic depression or comparable crisis would produce a movement to rid the country once and for all of the burden of race. Genocide is as American

as cherry pie, and cries of genocide can no longer be dismissed as hyper-
bole, as evidenced most recently by the general failure across the political spectrum to register the absolute fall in the average life expectancy of
black men.

Could a racially motivated genocidal movement gain power, or even
exist as a contender (as it does in various European countries), without
affecting not merely the so-called underclass of black society but respectable sectors as well, those who many think have reached escape velocity?
In that case, the work that follows would be of prophetic as well as
historical value. *De te fabula narratur!**

---

* Marx wrote *Capital* in England, which was undergoing rapid industrialization.
However, the book was written in German, and in the preface he explained the relevance
of the English experience for Germany, which was by that point largely agrarian, with
the Latin phrase "De te fabula narrator," which roughly translates as "Of you the tale is
told." Marx meant that the future of Germany's industrialization was visible across the
water in England.

33
Palestine: A Race Traitor Analysis

Ignatiev makes the case that Israel is a racial state that resembles South Africa under apartheid. He explores how accusations of anti-Semitism are effectively used by Zionists to pacify political dissent. This essay was originally published as the introduction to the final issue of Race Traitor *in 2005.*

The aim of *Race Traitor* is to abolish the white race, which is neither a biological nor a cultural formation but a social construct, existing only because of the privileges its members enjoy within the state and the legacy of those privileges. Given our stand it is logical that we would be led to the struggle against Zionism, which defines "Jew" not by language or religion but by descent (or ascribed descent)—the essence of race.

I am a history professor. On September 11, 2001, I was delivering a lecture in my first-year survey class in US history. Since it was near the beginning of the semester I had only got up to the seventeenth century and the wars between the Puritan settlers of New England and various indigenous peoples, wars that led to the elimination of the indigenous peoples from that region. A colleague poked her head in the door and informed me that someone had just flown an airplane into the World Trade Center. Uh huh, I said, and continued with my lecture. A few minutes later, someone came around and told me that the school was being closed. I ignored her: What better use could I make of my time, I asked myself, than to provide students with some history that might explain why someone would want to attack the World Trade Center? However, a few minutes later one of the senior administrators entered my classroom and ordered me to leave immediately. I bowed to superior force and dismissed the class.

Recalling that incident highlights something a friend has recently pointed out to me, that the United States of America was the world's first Zionist state: that is, it is the first place settled by people who arrived with the certainty that God had promised them the land and authorized them to dispossess the indigenous population. It is the similarity in origin of the two states as much as anything that leads Americans to see their image in Israel and support it notwithstanding the opinion of most of the rest of the world.

From the beginning of the Zionist project, it was evident that the establishment of the Jewish state demanded the expulsion of the indigenous Palestinians. As was stated by one of the most authoritative figures in the Zionist state:

> Among ourselves it must be clear that there is no place in our country for both peoples together . . . The only solution is Eretz Israel, or at least the western half of Eretz Israel, without Arabs, and there is no other way but to transfer the Arabs from here to the neighboring countries, transfer all of them, not one village or tribe should remain.[1]

Moshe Dayan, former defense minister, stated in a famous speech before students at the Israeli Institute of Technology in Haifa in 1969:

> Jewish villages were built in the place of Arab villages. You do not even know the names of these Arab villages, and I do not blame you because geography books no longer exist. Not only do the books not exist, the Arab villages are not there either. Nahalal arose in the place of Mahlul; Kibbutz Gvat in the place of Jibta; Kibbutz Sarid in the place of Huneifis; and Kefar Yehushua in the place of Tal al-Shuman. There is not a single place built in this country that did not have a former Arab population.[2]

It is a mistake to draw a moral line between Israel and the occupied territories. It is all occupied territory. The 1967 war, as a result of which Israel conquered and occupied East Jerusalem, the West Bank of the

Jordan River, the Syrian Golan Heights, and the Sinai Peninsula, was a continuation of the process that began in 1948. It will be drearily familiar to any who know the history of the displacement of the Indians from the lands they occupied in North America. As we have argued before in our pages, complicity in murder need not entail pulling the trigger. Standing by when the shot is fired is crime enough. The Jews in Israel who consider themselves Zionists (for or against "peace," for or against settlements) are witnesses to murders they could have and should have prevented. Their supporters in the United States are as guilty as they.

Unlike many countries, including the United States since the Civil Rights Acts, the Israeli state does not belong, even in theory, to those who reside within its borders, but is defined as the state of the Jewish people, wherever they may be. That peculiar definition is one reason why the state has to this day failed to produce a written constitution, define its borders, or even declare the existence of an Israeli nationality. Moreover, in the "outpost of democracy," no party that opposes the existence of the Jewish state is permitted to take part in elections. It is as if the United States were to declare itself a Christian state, define "Christian" not by religious belief but by descent, and then pass a "gag law" prohibiting public discussion of the issue.

If one part of the Zionist project is the expulsion of the indigenous population, the other part is expanding the so-called Jewish population. But here arises the problem, which has tormented Israeli legal officials for fifty years: what is a Jew? (For 150 years, US courts faced similar problems determining who is white.) The Zionists set forth two criteria for determining who is a Jew. The first is "race," which is a myth generally and is particularly a myth in the case of the Jews. The "Jewish" population of Israel includes people from fifty countries, of different physical types, speaking different languages, and practicing different religions (or no religion at all), defined as a single people based on the fiction that they, and only they, are descended from the biblical Abraham. It is so patently false that only Zionists and Nazis even pretend to take it seriously. In fact, given Jewish intermingling with others for 2,000 years, it is likely that the Palestinians—themselves the product of the mixture of the various peoples of Canaan plus later waves of Greeks and Arabs— are more directly descended from the ancient inhabitants of the Holy Land than the Europeans displacing them. The claim that Jews have a special right to Palestine has no more validity than would an Irish claim of a divine right to establish a Celtic state all across Germany, France, and Spain on the basis that Celtic tribes once lived there. Nevertheless, on the basis of ascribed descent, the Zionist officials assign those they have selected a privileged place within the state.

Zionist ideology has led to widespread bigotry that would inspire outrage in respectable circles in the United States. Israeli law forbids the marriage of a Jew with a non-Jew. An Israeli company has required thousands of Chinese workers to sign a contract promising not to have sex with Israelis.[3] According to the Israeli Institute for Democracy,

> As of 2003, more than half (53 per cent) of the Jews in Israel state out loud that they are against full equality for the Arabs; 77 per cent say there should be a Jewish majority on crucial political decisions; less than a third (31 per cent) support having Arab political parties in the government; and the majority (57 per cent) think that the Arabs should be encouraged to emigrate.[4]

Consider the following:

> If a European cabinet minister were to declare, "I don't want these long-nosed Jews to serve me in restaurants," all of Europe would be up in arms and this would be the minister's last comment as a minister. Three years ago, our former labor and social affairs minister, Shlomo Benizri, from Shas, stated: "I can't understand why slanty-eyed types should be the ones to serve me in restaurants." Nothing happened . . . And if a European government were to announce that Jews are not permitted to attend Christian schools? . . . But when our Education Ministry announces that it will not permit Arabs to attend Jewish schools in Haifa, it's not considered racism.
>
> What would happen if a certain country were to enact legislation forbidding members of a particular nation to become citizens there, no matter what the circumstances, including mixed couples who married and raised families? No country anywhere enacts laws like these nowadays. Apart from Israel. If the cabinet extends the validity of the new Citizenship Law today, Palestinians will not be able to undergo naturalization here, even if they are married to Israelis . . . And if the illegal Israeli immigrants in the United States were hunted down like animals in the dark of night, the way the Immigration

Police do here, would we have a better understanding of the injustice we are doing to a community that wants nothing other than to work here?

What would we say if the parents of Israeli emigrants were separated from their children and deported, without having available any avenue of naturalization, no matter what the circumstances? . . . What would happen if anti-Semites in France were to poison the drinking water of a Jewish neighborhood? Last week settlers poisoned a well at Atawana, in the southern Mount Hebron region . . .

And we still haven't said anything about a country that would imprison another nation, or about a regime that would prevent access to medical treatment for some of its subjects, according to [their] national identity, about roads that would be open only to the members of one nation or about an airport that would be closed to the other nation.[5]

The Zionists are so desperate to increase the loyal population of the state that they are willing to admit hundreds of thousands of people who do not meet the official definition of a Jew because they have only a male grandparent or are merely married to a Jew. Since there is no such thing as Israeli nationality in Israel (there being only Jewish nationality and "undetermined"), these people who do not qualify as Jews (mainly from the former Soviet Union) are therefore registered as "under consideration." Again, the parallel with the United States is evident: the first US naturalization law was passed in 1790, followed by the militia law of 1792. The standards for eligibility were the same in both: "white" (in the case of the militia, there was the added qualification "male"). Thus, "citizen" meant "white," and "white" meant someone who could be relied on to suppress Indian wars and slave rebellions. So in Israel, "Jew" means anyone who can be relied on to repress the indigenous Palestinians.

Those whom the gods would destroy they first make mad. Recently the Israeli press reported on a group of Indians from Peru who had converted to Judaism and moved to Israel, where they were relocated on what was once Palestinian land. Nachson Ben-Haim (formerly Pedro Mendosa) said he had no problem with that. "You cannot conquer what has in any case belonged to you since the time of the patriarch, Abraham." Ben-Haim said he was looking forward to joining the Israeli army to defend the country. Ben-Haim and his coreligionists had moved to

Israel with the agreement of the Jewish community in Peru, which did not want them because of the Indians' low socioeconomic status.[6]

The Peruvian case points to the second criterion for being recognized as Jewish: conversion by an approved religious official, which means Orthodox rabbis only. In Israel today, Conservative and Reform rabbis are prohibited from leading their congregations, there is no civil marriage for Jews, and—in a measure reminiscent of medieval Spain— all residents support the established church, in this case the Orthodox rabbinate. The stranglehold of organized religion in a state where the majority of the Jewish population is secular and even atheistic is the price paid to maintain the biblical justification for Zionist occupation. "God does not exist," runs the popular quip, "and he gave us this land."

Israel is a racial state, where rights are assigned on the basis of ascribed descent or the approval of the superior race. In this respect it resembles the American South prior to the passage of the Civil Rights and Voting Rights acts, Ireland under the Protestant Ascendancy, and, yes, Hitlerite Germany. But in its basic structures it most closely resembles the old South Africa. It is therefore not surprising that Israel should have developed a close alliance with South Africa when that country was still under apartheid. After the first talks held in 1970 between Shimon Peres and South Africa's defense minister, Botha, cultural, commercial, and military cooperation between the two racial regimes developed. These relations were publicly celebrated during the visit of South African prime minister Vorster to Israel in 1976—the same Vorster who held the rank of general in the pro-Nazi organization Ossewabrandwag during World War II.[7]

Israel's greatest support comes from the United States, $3 to $5 billion a year, more than what the United States gives to any other country and exceeding the total of US grants to the whole of Africa south of the Sahara. Every shell fired into a Palestinian village, every tank used to bulldoze a home, every helicopter gunship is paid for by US dollars.

Not only does Zionism shape US policy, it stifles discussion of alternatives. To cite a few personal examples: In 2011 a PBS reporter interviewed me on the eve of the UN-sponsored conference on racism about to be held in South Africa. I made some remarks about Israel, and afterward I asked her if she would use what I said. "Of course not," she replied. "I agree with you, and so do all the journalists I know, but we can't run any criticism of Israel without following it by at least ten refutations."

The greatest ideological weapon in the Zionist arsenal is the charge of anti-Semitism. Students and faculty members at Harvard begin a campaign to make the university sell off its stock in companies that sell weapons to Israel (modeled on past campaigns seeking divestment from South Africa), and the president of Harvard denounces the organizers of the campaign as "anti-Semitic in effect, if not in intent." A faculty committee at the Massachusetts College of Art invites eminent poet Amiri Baraka to deliver a lecture, and members of the Critical Studies faculty circulate a petition calling upon the college president to denounce Baraka as an anti-Semite, citing as its main evidence a poem he wrote about the historic oppression of black people in which he refers to alleged acts by the Israeli government prior to the World Trade Center attack.[8]

Cynthia McKinney, Afro-American congresswoman from Atlanta, was the most outspoken critic in Congress of US Middle East policy, including unconditional support for Israel. As a result, Jewish groups around the country targeted her and, by channeling money to her opponent, succeeded in defeating her bid for reelection in 2002. Were they within their legal rights to do so? Yes, they were; there is no law barring people in one district from contributing to a campaign in another. But do they think their intervention went unnoticed by black voters in Atlanta and around the country? People will reap what they sow. If American Jews insist on identifying themselves with Israel, should they be surprised if others make the same mistake?

Nobel Peace Prize winner Bishop Desmond Tutu of South Africa said, "The Israel government is placed on a pedestal [in the United States]. People are scared in this country to say wrong is wrong because the Jewish lobby is powerful—very powerful."[9] If US ruling circles ever decide to distance themselves from Israel state, they will suddenly "discover" that it is the number one outlaw state in the Middle East, has defied scores of United Nations resolutions, been condemned by the UN more than any other member or non-member, and is the only state in the Middle East that possesses actual weapons of mass destruction. And they will find a tremendous response, more than anyone anticipates, from many ordinary people who go along with US support of Israel in the same absent-minded way they go along with all of America's imperial adventures but among whom there is a growing resentment of Israel's defenders for constructing a picture of the past that makes discussion impossible and cheapens the lives of all those, Jews and non-Jews, who suffered at the hands of the Nazis. We need to pose a challenge to the "anti-Semitism" discourse of the Zionists. We simply do not believe that the non-Jewish peoples of this earth are motivated by a primordial hatred of Jews. To the extent that superstition exists, we confess our inability to overcome it by argument. But superstition is being defeated by modern life. Those who insist that Jews have always been and will always be hated must be confronted.

But Jews by themselves could not determine US Middle East policy, any more than the Florida Cubans by themselves could determine US Caribbean policy. By no means does all the organized support for Israel in the US come from Jews. Aside from imperialist interests—and it is not clear whether Israel is an asset or a liability in this regard—Israel has gained support from a surprising quarter:

At first sight, the scene is very familiar: one that happens in Washington DC and other major American cities all the time. On the platform, an Israeli student is telling thousands of supporters how the horrors of the year have only reinforced his people's determination. "Despite the terror attacks, they'll never drive us away out of our God-given land," he says.

This is greeted with whoops and hollers and the waving of Israeli flags and the blowing of the shofar, the Jewish ceremonial ram's horn. Then comes the mayor of Jerusalem, Ehud Olmert, who is received even more rapturously. "God is with us. You are with us." And there are more whoops and hollers and flag-waves and shofar-blows.

But something very strange is going on here. There are thousands of people cheering for Israel in the huge Washington Convention Centre. But not one of them appears to be Jewish, at least not in the conventional sense. For this is the annual gathering of a very non-Jewish Organization indeed: the Christian Coalition of America.

... [T]here is little doubt that, last spring, when President Bush dithered and dallied over his Middle East policy before finally coming down on Israel's side, he was influenced not by the overrated Jewish vote, but by the opinion of Christian "religious conservatives"—the self-description of between 15 and 18% of the electorate. When the president demanded that Israel withdraw its tanks from the West Bank in April, the White House allegedly received 100,000 angry emails from Christian conservatives.

What's changed? Not the Book of Genesis . . .

What has really changed is the emergence of the doctrine known as "dispensationalism" . . .

Central to the theory . . . is the Rapture, the second coming of Christ, which will presage the end of the world. A happy ending depends on the conversion of the Jews. And that, to cut a long story very short, can only happen if the Jews are in possession of all the lands given to them by God. In other words, these Christians are supporting the Jews in order to abolish them.

Oh yes, agreed Madon Pollard, a charming lady from Dallas who was selling hand-painted Jerusalem crystal in the exhibition hall at the conference. "God is the sovereign. He'll do what he pleases. But based on the scripture, those are the guidelines." She calls herself a fervent supporter of Israel . . .

This conference began with a videotaped benediction straight from the Oval office. Some of the most influential Republicans in Congress addressed the gathering including—not once, but twice—Tom DeLay [majority leader of the House of Representatives, arguably the most powerful man on Capitol Hill].

"Are you tired of all this, are you?" he yelled to the audience.

"Nooooooo!" they roared back. "Not when you're standing up for Jews and Jesus, that's for sure," he replied.

. . . Ariel Sharon, the Israeli prime minister, [was] reportedly greeted "like a rock star" by Christian evangelicals in Jerusalem last month.

. . . DeLay was followed by Pat Robertson, the coalition's founder, sometime presidential candidate and the very personification of the successful American TV evangelist. Robertson . . . cites the stories of Joshua and David to prove Israel's ownership of Jerusalem "long before anyone had heard of Mohammed."[10]

Osama Bin Laden was speaking no more than the truth when he said that the Islamic world is facing an alliance of Crusaders and Zionists. It may have been the strength of that alliance that reportedly led Sharon to brag that he had Arafat under house arrest in Ramallah and Bush under house arrest in Washington.

Less extreme supporters of Israel advocate the partition of Palestine into two states. But history has shown, in Ireland, India, Cyprus, and everyplace else it has been tried, that partition of a territory along lines of descent—whether called "racial" or "religious"—is a guarantee of permanent war. In the view of the editors, there is only one solution: a single state in historic Palestine (the area between the Mediterranean Sea and the Jordan River), in which every person is recognized as a citizen and has one vote. The special advantages given to "Jews," including the "right of return," must be terminated, and the Palestinians who were forced into exile after 1948, and their descendants, must be granted the right to live there, with the state undertaking practical measures to make it possible for them to do so. Both Hebrew and Arabic (at least) must be declared official state languages, residents must be granted the right to publish newspapers and maintain cultural institutions in any language they choose, and the special position of Orthodox Judaism must be ended.

As I write these words, July 14, the anniversary of the French Revolution, the idea of one-person, one-vote—the democratic secular state—is seen to be so subversive that it can scarcely gain a hearing even among critics of Israeli policy. To those who hold that after all the blood that has been shed and the bitterness that has accumulated it will not be possible for "Israelis" and "Palestinians" to live together, we have three responses: the first is the experience of South Africa, a place whose history of bitterness is no less than Palestine's; the establishment of majority rule there, while it by no means solved all the problems, did not cause the earth to open and swallow the people. Our second response comes from Sherlock Holmes: after you have eliminated all the impossible solutions, Watson, the one remaining, no matter how improbable, must be the right one. Our third response is to cite recent indications that the idea of the single democratic secular state is again coming to seem plausible to an increasing number of Palestinians. Its reemergence is in part a response to Israel's gobbling up so much territory that nothing is left for a Palestinian state. The new reality is acknowledged by no less than columnist Thomas L. Friedman, who quotes a prominent Israeli Arab:

> If Palestinians lose their dream to have an independent state, then the only thing that might guarantee for them a dignified life will be asking to live in one state with the Israelis. When this struggle starts, it will find allies among the one million Palestinian Arabs inside Israel . . .

We will say, "Don't evacuate even a single West Bank settlement. Just give us the vote and let us be part of one community."

Friedman reports a poll showing that 25 to 30 percent of Palestinians now support the idea of one state—"a stunning figure, considering it's never been proposed by any Palestinian or Israeli party." (This is not quite true: it was for many years the official goal of the PLO* and was abandoned under US pressure.) He calls it "the law of unintended consequences."[11]

If Israel appears to the outsider to be in convulsion, neither is all well in the First Zionist State. The flavor of life in the United States has been well captured in a recent novel by an immigrant who has lived there for many years and is consequently able to look at the country with the eyes of an outsider:

I drove toward the bleeding strip of neon, the solitary cars here and there, seeing the small drive-in windows, glass tombs encasing high-school dropouts, mostly young girls, some male misfits, the dim of mind, all banished to the night shift for minimum wage. It was this new destiny of strip malls and eateries that scared the shit out of me, that made me wince and understand why people kill each other . . . Along these strips of neon were the killing fields of our post-industrialism, these glasshouse eateries of disaffection where people get big eating bleeding burgers, clogging up their arteries and going about dying slowly over black tar coffee. Out here at this hour you bore witness to the attenuated deaths, the casualties that go uncounted. And when the sun rises, the radio whispers of the night that passed, it gives the grim statistics of pulverising rapes, robberies where clerks were pistol-whipped and tied up in freezers, or shot in the face and left to bleed to death, a young woman with two children missing from a seven-eleven [convenience store], a solitary sentry, working alone of course—margins of profit dictate there can't be two clerks on duty. And it passes itself off, this violence, this madness, as nothing to do with politics. Somehow we are an apolitical nation. There are no collective actions of warfare. Everything can be dismantled to the

---

* The Palestinian Liberation Organization was founded in 1964 with the stated goal of freeing Palestine through armed struggle.

level of the individual. Each act of violence is isolated; it forms no mood; it feeds into no general rebellion. It's maybe the greatest secret we possess as a nation: our sense of alienation from everyone else around us, our ability to have no sympathy, no empathy for others' suffering, a decentralised philosophy of individual will, a culpability that always lands back on each of us. "You can be whatever you want to be" . . . It was the mantra of our society.[12]

Anyone who understands human psychology knows that the time must come when the perpetual, generalized, undirected violence described here so well, this constant road-rage where millions of people turn into crazed killers whenever they get behind the wheel of an automobile, must sooner or later explode. The form of the explosion cannot be predicted. But there can be no doubt that it will open up possibilities of striking for freedom for many, including the indigenous people of Palestine, now held down by the power of the United States. That same explosion will also open up possibilities for tyrannies beyond even those of the last century. The outcome in Palestine will play a large part in determining which of the two possible futures comes to pass.

History offers occasional examples of small groups to whom it is given to play a greater role in world events than their numbers would normally indicate. The indigenous people of Palestine are such a group. When the present nightmare is ended, the human race, and North Americans in particular, will record a great debt to the Palestinian people, whose refusal to submit to overwhelming power has set a shining example, and may even succeed in humanizing the mighty United States of America, whose residents need all the help they can get.

34

Zionism, Anti-Semitism, and the People of Palestine

Ignatiev examines the historical context and ideology that shaped Zionism as a political project. He surveys the contemporary struggles for Palestinian self-determination and proposes a one-state solution within historic Palestine. This essay was originally published in Counterpunch *in 2004.*

———

Zionism as a political movement developed in the late nineteenth century. Its founder, Theodor Herzl, was influenced by two phenomena: the extent of French anti-Semitism revealed by the Dreyfus Trial and nationalist ideals then popular in Europe. Herzl held that Jews cannot be assimilated by the nations in which they live and that the only solution to the "Jewish question" was the formation of a "Jewish state" in which all the Jews would come together. The early Zionists contemplated as the site of the future state Argentina or Uganda, among other locales. Herzl favored Palestine, because, although an agnostic, he wanted to make use of the custom, widespread among Jewish mystics, of going on pilgrimages to the "holy land" and establishing religious communities there.

In 1868, there were 13,000 Jews in Palestine, out of an estimated population of 400,000. The majority were religious pilgrims supported by charity from overseas. They encountered no opposition from the Muslims, and their presence led to no clashes with the Arab population, whether Muslim or Christian.

In 1882, Baron Rothschild, combining philanthropy and

investment, began to bring Jewish settlers from Eastern Europe to build a plantation system along the model the French used in Algeria. They spoke Yiddish, Arabic, Persian, and Georgian. Significantly, Hebrew was not among the languages spoken. The outcome of Rothschild's experiment was predictable: Jews managed the land, while Arabs worked it. This was not the result the Zionists had in mind; a Jewish society could not be based on Arab labor. Consequently, they began to encourage the immigration of Jews to work in agriculture, industry, and transport.

In 1917 British foreign minister Lord Balfour, seeking support for Britain's efforts in World War I, issued his famous declaration expressing sympathy with efforts to establish a Jewish homeland in Palestine. The Zionists immediately seized upon this statement, which they interpreted to mean support for a Jewish state. At the time of Balfour's declaration, Jews comprised less than 10 percent of the population and owned 2.5 percent of the land of Palestine.

The problem of building a Jewish society among an overwhelming Arab majority came to be known as the "conquest of land and labor." Land, once acquired, had to remain in Jewish hands. The other half of this project, known as Labor Zionism, called for the exclusive use of Jewish labor on the land acquired by the Jews in Palestine. The Labor Zionists maintained this dual exclusionism (or apartheid, as we would now call it) in order to build up purely Jewish institutions.

To achieve the conquest of the land, the Zionists set up an arrangement whereby land was acquired not by individuals, but by a corporation known as the Jewish National Fund (JNF). The JNF acquired land and leased it only to Jews, who were not allowed to sublet it. Thus, land was acquired in the name of "the Jewish people," held for their use, and not subject to market conditions. The idea was for the JNF to gradually acquire as much land as possible as the basis for the expected Jewish state.

Naturally, in order for the land to serve this function, Arab labor had to be excluded. Leases from the JNF specifically prohibited the use of non-Jewish labor on JNF plots. One way to achieve this goal was to lease land only to those Jews who intended to work it themselves. In some cases, when land was bought from Arab absentee landlords, the peasants who resided on and worked the land were expelled. Jewish landholders who refused to exclude Arab labor could lose their leases or be faced with a boycott.

The conquest of labor pertained not only to agriculture but also to industry. The Labor Zionists formed an institution to organize Jewish labor and exclude Arabs: the Histadrut. The Histadrut was (and largely is) an all-Jewish combination trade union and cooperative society providing its members with a number of services. From the beginning it was a means of segregating Arab and Jewish labor and bringing into existence a strictly Jewish economic sector. Even when Arab and Jewish laborers performed precisely the same job, Jewish workers were paid significantly higher salaries. These policies were the death knell for any attempt to organize labor on a nonracial basis. The "laborism" of Labor Zionism killed and continues to kill efforts at building a unified labor movement.

Despite these policies and even with the encouragement of the British government, in the thirty years following the Balfour Declaration, the Zionists were able to increase the Jewish-owned portion of the land of Palestine to only 7 percent. Moreover, the majority of the world's Jews showed no interest in settling there. In the years between 1920 and 1932, only 118,000 Jews moved to Palestine, less than 1 percent of world Jewry. Even after the rise of Hitler, Jews in Europe did not choose Israel: out of 2.5 million Jewish victims of Nazism who fled abroad between 1935 and 1943, scarcely 8.5 percent went to Palestine; 182,000 went to the United States, 67,000 to Britain, and almost 2 million to the Soviet Union. After the war, the United States began to encourage Jewish settlement in Palestine. Aneurin Bevin, postwar British foreign minister, publicly blurted out that American policy mainly arose from the fact that "they did not want too many of them in New York." The Pakistani delegate to the UN was to make the same point sarcastically:

> Australia, an overpopulated small country with congested areas, says no, no, no; Canada, equally congested and overpopulated, says no; the United States, a great humanitarian country, a small area, with small resources, says no. This is their contribution to the humanitarian principle. But they state, let them go into Palestine, where there are vast areas, a large economy and no trouble; they can easily be taken in there.[1]

The US limitation on the number of Jews allowed into the country coincided with Zionist policy, as enunciated by David Ben-Gurion, first prime minister of Israel:

If I knew that it would be possible to save all the children in Germany by bringing them over to England, and only half of them by transporting them to Eretz Yisrael, then I would opt for the second alternative. For we must weigh not only the life of these children, but also the history of the People of Israel.[2]

This policy of attaching more importance to the establishment of Israel than to the survival of the Jews led the Zionists to collaborate with Nazism and even be decorated by Hitler's government. The best-known case was that of Rudolf Kastner, who negotiated the emigration to Palestine of some of Hungary's most prominent Jews in return for his help in arranging the orderly deportation of the remainder of Hungary's Jews to the camps. For his efforts, Kastner was praised as an "idealist" by no less an authority than Adolf Eichmann. (The best study of Zionist–Nazi relations is Lenni Brenner, *Zionism in the Age of the Dictators*.[3])

The Zionists knew they had to rid themselves of the Arab majority in order to have a specifically Jewish state. Although 75,000 Jews moved to Israel between 1945 and 1948, Jews still constituted a minority in Palestine. The 1948 war afforded the Zionists an excellent opportunity to rectify this; as a result of the war, more than three-quarters of a million Arabs fled their homes. The case of Deir Yasin, in which Israeli paramilitary forces, under the command of future prime minister Menachem Begin, massacred over 250 civilians, sending a message to Palestinians that they should depart, is the most well-known example of how this flight was brought about. In his book, *The Revolt*, Begin boasted that without Deir Yasin there would have been no Israel, and adds, "The Arabs began fleeing in panic, shouting, 'Deir Yasin.'"[4] Recent writings by Israeli revisionist historians have refuted the longtime insistence of Israeli officials that the departures were voluntary. Some of the refugees went to neighboring Arab countries; others became refugees in their own country. Those 750,000 expelled from their homes and their descendants, who together total 2.2 million people, make up the so-called refugee problem. Although the United Nations has repeatedly demanded they be allowed to return, the Israeli government has refused to agree. The war ended with the Zionists in control of 80 percent of Palestine. In the next year, nearly 400 Arab villages were completely destroyed. This was no accident but the result of deliberate policy, as

shown in the following statement by one of the most authoritative officials of the Zionist state:

> Among ourselves it must be clear that there is no place in our country
> for both peoples together. The only solution is Eretz Israel, or at least
> the western half of Eretz Israel, without Arabs, and there is no other
> way but to transfer the Arabs from here to the neighboring countries,
> transfer all of them, not one village or tribe should remain.[5]

Moshe Dayan, former defense minister, stated in a famous speech before
students at the Israeli Institute of Technology in Haifa in 1969:

> Jewish villages were built in the place of Arab villages. You do not
> even know the names of these Arab villages, and I do not blame you
> because geography books no longer exist. Not only do the books not
> exist, the Arab villages are not there either. Nahial arose in the place
> of Mahlul; Kibbutz Gvat in the place of Jibta; Kibbutz Sarid in the
> place of Huneifis; and Kefar Yehushua in the place of Tal al-Shuman.
> There is not a single place built in this country that did not have a
> former Arab population.[6]

It is a mistake to draw a moral line between Israel and the occupied
territories; it is all occupied territory. The 1967 war, as a result of which
Israel conquered and occupied East Jerusalem, the West Bank of the
Jordan River, and the Sinai Peninsula, was a continuation of the process
that began in 1948. It will be drearily familiar to any who know the
history of the displacement of the Indians from the lands they occupied
in North America. Today it would be called "ethnic cleansing."

The first census of the state of Israel, conducted in 1949, counted a
total of 650,000 Jews and 150,000 Arabs. The legal foundation for the
racial state was laid down in two laws passed in 1950. The first, the Law
of Return, permitted any Jew, anywhere in the world, the right to "return"
to Israel. This right did not apply to non-Jews, including the Palestinian
Arabs who had recently become refugees. In addition, the Absentee
Property Law confiscated the property of Arab "absentees," and turned
it over to the Custodian of Absentee Property. Arab refugees within
their own country were termed "present absentees" (what a phrase!) and
not allowed to return to their property. A number of refugees who

attempted to do so were termed "infiltrators," and some were shot in the attempt. Confiscated property accounted for the vast majority of new settlements. These confiscated lands, in accordance with the procedures that were established in the Mandate period by the Jewish National Fund, have become Israel Lands, with their own administration. This administration, controlling 92.6 percent of all of the lands in Israel, only leases these lands to Jews.

Unlike many countries, including the United States, the Israeli state does not belong, even in principle, to those who reside within its borders, but is defined as the state of the Jewish people, wherever they may be. That peculiar definition is one reason why the state has to this day failed to produce a written constitution, define its borders, or even declare the existence of an Israeli nationality. Moreover, in this "outpost of democracy," no party that opposes the existence of the Jewish state is permitted to take part in elections. It is as if the United States were to declare itself a Christian state, define "Christian" not by religious belief but by descent, and then pass a "gag law" prohibiting public discussion of the issue.

If one part of the Zionist project is the expulsion of the indigenous population, the other part is expanding the so-called Jewish population. But here arises the problem, which has tormented Israeli legal officials for fifty years: what is a Jew? (For 150 years, US courts faced similar problems determining who is white.) The Zionists set forth two criteria for determining who is a Jew. The first is race, which is a myth generally and is particularly a myth in the case of the Jews. The "Jewish" population of Israel includes people from fifty countries, of different physical types, speaking different languages and practicing different religions (or no religion at all), defined as a single people based on the fiction that they, and only they, are descended from the biblical Abraham. It is so patently false that only Zionists and Nazis even pretend to take it seriously. In fact, given Jewish intermingling with others for two thousand years, it is likely that the Palestinians—themselves the result of the mixture of the various peoples of Canaan plus later waves of Greeks and Arabs—are more directly descended from the ancient inhabitants of the Holy Land than the Europeans displacing them. The claim that the Jews have a special right to Palestine has no more validity than would an Irish claim of a divine right to establish a Celtic state all across Germany, France, and Spain on the basis that Celtic tribes once lived there. Nevertheless, on the basis of ascribed descent, the Zionist officials assign those they have selected a privileged place within the state. If that is not racism, then the term has no meaning.

The Zionist commitment to racial purity has led to expressions of bigotry at the highest levels of Israeli society that would inspire outrage in respectable circles in the United States. An Israeli company has required thousands of Chinese workers to sign a contract promising not to have sex with Israelis. A company spokesman said there was nothing illegal about the requirement. Israeli law forbids the marriage of a Jew with a non-Jew.[7]

Prejudice breeds arrogance: this past January the Israeli ambassador to Sweden destroyed an art installation in a Stockholm museum which he found offensive. The work commemorated a young Palestinian woman who killed herself and nineteen others in an attack in Haifa. (It does not become Americans, who learn as schoolchildren to recite the last words of Nathan Hale, "My only regret is that I have but one life to give for my country," to denounce Palestinian patriots as "suicide bombers.") The museum director pointed out that if the Ambassador did not like the exhibit, he was free to leave.[8]

The Zionists are so desperate to increase the loyal population of the state that they are willing to admit hundreds of thousands of people, mainly from the former Soviet Union, who do not meet the official definition of a Jew because they have only a male grandparent or are merely married to a Jew. Since there is no such thing as Israeli nationality in Israel (there being only Jewish nationality and "undetermined"), these people, who do not qualify as Jews, are therefore registered as "under consideration."

Those whom the gods would destroy they first make mad. Recently the Israeli press reported on a group of Indians from Peru who had converted to Judaism and moved to Israel, where they were relocated on what was once Palestinian land. Nachson Ben-Haim (formerly Pedro Mendosa) said he had no problem with that. "You cannot conquer what has in any case belonged to you since the time of the patriarch, Abraham." Ben-Haim said he was looking forward to joining the Israeli army to defend the country. Ben-Haim and his coreligionists had moved to Israel with the agreement of the Jewish community in Peru, which did not want them because of the Indians' low socioeconomic status."[9]

The Peruvian case points to the second criterion for being recognized as Jewish: conversion by an approved religious official, which means

Orthodox rabbis only. In Israel today, Conservative and Reform rabbis are prohibited from leading their congregations, there is no civil marriage for Jews, and—in a measure reminiscent of medieval Spain—all residents support the established church, in this case the Orthodox rabbinate. The stranglehold of organized religion in a state where the majority of the Jewish population is secular and even atheistic is the price paid to maintain the biblical justification for Zionist occupation. "God does not exist," runs the popular quip, "and he gave us this land."

Israel is a racial state, where rights are assigned on the basis of ascribed descent or the approval of the superior race. In this respect it resembles the American South prior to the passage of the Civil Rights and Voting Rights Acts, Ireland under the Protestant Ascendancy, and, yes, Hitlerite Germany. But in its basic structures it most closely resembles the old South Africa. It is therefore not surprising that Israel should have developed a close alliance with South Africa when that country was still under apartheid. After the first talks held in 1970 between Shimon Peres and South Africa's defense minister, Botha, cultural, commercial, and military cooperation between the two racial regimes developed. These relations were publicly celebrated during the visit of South African prime minister Vorster to Israel in 1976—the same Vorster who held the rank of general in the pro-Nazi organization Ossewabrandwag during World War II.

Israel's greatest support comes from the United States, $3 to $5 billion a year, more than what the United States gives to any other country and exceeding the total of US grants to the whole of Africa south of the Sahara. Every shell fired into a Palestinian village, every tank used to bulldoze a home, every helicopter gunship is paid for by US dollars.

Is one permitted to say above the level of a whisper that US policy toward Israel has something to do with Jewish influence in the United States? Perhaps Nobel Peace Prize winner Bishop Desmond Tutu of South Africa can get away with it: "The Israel government," he observed, "is placed on a pedestal [in the US]. People are scared in this country to say wrong is wrong because the Jewish lobby is powerful—very powerful."[10]

Not only does Zionism shape US policy, it stifles discussion of alternatives. To cite a personal example: Two years ago a PBS reporter interviewed me on the eve of the UN-sponsored conference on racism about to be held in South Africa. I made some remarks about Israel, and afterward I asked her if she would use what I said. "Of course not," she replied. "I agree with you, and so do all the journalists I know, but we can't run any criticism of Israel without following it by at least ten refutations." Harvard professor Daniel Pipes and Martin Kramer of the Middle East Forum have begun a website, Campus Watch, to denounce academics deemed to have shown "hatred of Israel." Students are to inform on professors.

The greatest ideological weapon in the Zionist arsenal is the charge of anti-Semitism. Students and faculty members at Harvard begin a campaign to make the university sell off its stock in companies that sell weapons to Israel (modeled on past campaigns seeking divestment from South Africa), and the president of Harvard denounces the organizers of the campaign as "anti-Semitic in effect, if not in intent." A faculty committee at the Massachusetts College of Art invites eminent poet Amiri Baraka to deliver a lecture, and members of the Critical Studies faculty circulate a petition calling upon the college president to denounce Baraka as an anti-Semite, citing as its main evidence a poem he wrote about the historic oppression of black people in which he refers to reported actions by the Israeli government prior to the World Trade Center attack. As the Israeli commentator Ran HaCohen points out:

> When Palestinians attack soldiers of Israel's occupation army in their own village, it's anti-Semitism. When the UN general assembly votes 133 to 4 to condemn Israel's decision to murder the elected Palestinian leader, it means that every country on the planet except the US, Micronesia, and the Marshall Islands is antisemitic.

This is ironic, he says, given present reality:

> With one revealing exception (Israel, where non-orthodox religious Jews are discriminated against), Jews enjoy full religious freedom wherever they are. They have full citizenship wherever they live, with full political, civic, and human rights like every other citizen.

Nowadays, an Orthodox Jew can run for the most powerful office on earth, the president of the United States. A Jew can be mayor of Amsterdam in "anti-Semitic" Holland, a minister in "anti-Semitic" Britain, a leading intellectual in "anti-Semitic" France, a president of

Abolish the White Race

"anti-Semitic" Switzerland, editor-in-chief of a major daily in "anti-Semitic" Denmark, or an industrial tycoon in "anti-Semitic" Russia. [A]nti-semitic Germany gives Israel three military submarines, anti-Semitic France has proliferated to Israel the nuclear technology for its weapons of mass destruction, and anti-Semitic Europe welcomes Israel as the single non-European country to everything from football and basketball leagues to the Eurovision Song Contest and has granted Israeli universities a special status for scientific fundraising.

"The use of alleged anti-Semitism is morally despicable," says HaCohen.

> People abusing this taboo in order to support Israel's racist and geno-cidal policy towards the Palestinians do nothing less than desecrate the memory of those Jewish victims, whose death is meaningful only inasmuch as it serves as an eternal warning to the human kind against all kinds of discrimination, racism, and genocide.[11]

If I accomplish nothing else in this talk, I hope to create space for some who are repelled by Israeli actions but are held back from condemning Zionism by a desire not to be anti-Semitic.

Does what I have just said mean that I dismiss the possibility of a revival of anti-Semitism? No, it does not. History shows that anti-Semitism ebbs and flows and that it may return. Time prevents me from exploring that history in any depth; let me instead recommend two books: *The Jewish Question* by Abram Leon and *The Origins of Totalitarianism* by Hannah Arendt (in particular the first part, "anti-Semitism"). For now I will say only that anti-Semitism (or more accurately, anti-Jewish sentiment) is rooted neither in human nature or Christian theology; it is the product of social relations, including the historic concentration of Jews as representatives of commerce in noncommercial societies. The peculiar occupational distribution of European Jews led members of the dispossessed classes among the non-Jewish population to direct their animosity toward the Jews as the visible agents of oppression. "Anti-Semitism," as the nineteenth-century German Socialist August Bebel put it, "is the socialism of fools." It is not beyond historical explanation (as is implied by a term like "The Holocaust," which takes anti-Semitism out of history and relocates it in the realm of natural phenomena).

But of course the Jews by themselves could not determine US Middle East policy, any more than the Florida Cubans by themselves could determine US Caribbean policy. By no means does all the organized support for Israel inside of US politics come from Jews. Aside from imperialist interests—and it is not clear whether Israel is an asset or a liability in this regard—Israel has gained support from a surprising quarter. From the *Guardian*, February 28, 2002:

> At first sight, the scene is very familiar: one that happens in Washington, DC, and other major American cities all the time. On the platform, an Israeli student is telling thousands of supporters how the horrors of the year have only reinforced his people's determination. "Despite the terror attacks, they'll never drive us away out of our God-given land," he says.
>
> This is greeted with whoops and hollers and the waving of Israeli flags and the blowing of the shofar, the Jewish ceremonial ram's horn. Then comes the mayor of Jerusalem, Ehud Olmert, who is received even more rapturously. "God is with us. You are with us." And there are more whoops and hollers and flag-waves and shofar-blows . . . But something very strange is going on here. There are thousands of people cheering for Israel in the huge Washington Convention Centre. But not one of them appears to be Jewish, at least not in the conventional sense. For this is the annual gathering of a very non-Jewish Organization indeed: the Christian Coalition of America . . .
>
> [T]here is little doubt that, last spring, when President Bush dithered and dallied over his Middle East policy before finally coming down on Israel's side, he was influenced not by the overrated Jewish vote, but by the opinion of Christian "religious conservatives"—the self-description of between 15 and 18% of the electorate. When the president demanded that Israel withdraw its tanks from the West Bank in April, the White House allegedly received 100,000 angry emails from Christian conservatives.[12]

What's changed? Not the Book of Genesis.

What has really changed is the emergence of the doctrine known as "dispensationalism," popularized in the novels of the Reverend Tim LaHaye and Jerry Jenkins.

Central to the theory is the Rapture, the second coming of Christ, which will presage the end of the world. A happy ending depends on the conversion of the Jews. And that, to cut a long story very short, can only happen if the Jews are in possession of all the lands given to them by God. In other words, these Christians are supporting the Jews in order to abolish them.

Oh yes, agreed Madon Pollard, a charming lady from Dallas who was selling hand-painted Jerusalem crystal in the exhibition hall at the conference. "God is the sovereign. He'll do what he pleases. But based on the scripture, those are the guidelines." She calls herself a fervent supporter of Israel.

This conference began with a videotaped benediction straight from the Oval Office. Some of the most influential Republicans in Congress addressed the gathering including—not once, but twice—Tom DeLay [majority leader of the House of Representatives, arguably the most powerful man on Capitol Hill].

"Are you tired of all this, are you?" he yelled to the audience.

"Nooooooo!" they roared back. "Not when you're standing up for Jews and Jesus, that's for sure," he replied.

Ariel Sharon, the Israeli prime minister, [was] reportedly greeted "like a rock star" by Christian evangelicals in Jerusalem last month.

DeLay was followed by Pat Robertson, the coalition's founder, sometime presidential candidate and the very personification of the successful American TV evangelist. Robertson cites the stories of Joshua and David to prove Israel's ownership of Jerusalem "long before anyone had heard of Mohammed."

These are the people my grandfather warned me about—the people who want to ban Darwin from the schools, who want to send to camps people who have sex with members of their own sex—and antisemeets (as he used to say), Jew-haters to the backbone of their souls.

Osama Bin Laden was telling no more than the truth when he said that the Muslim world is facing an alliance of Zionists and Crusaders.

Before I get around to proposing solutions, I want to address the present state of the Israeli peace movement. As everyone knows, there are forces inside of Israel who oppose the government now in office. Some of these people, particularly the soldiers who refuse service in what they call the occupied territories or who refuse to carry out atrocities such as bombing civilians, and those who encourage them, are people of exemplary courage. Yet all of them, with one notable exception (to which

I shall return), are handicapped and in the long run rendered ineffective by their acceptance of the fundamental premise of Zionism, the legitimacy of the Jewish state. "Land for peace" implies the permanent partition of Palestine. It was under the leadership of the Labor Party, with which much of the opposition is affiliated, that the initial dispossession and exclusion of the Palestinian people from their homeland took place and the expansion into the West Bank, the Gaza Strip, and the Golan Heights was carried out.

History has shown, in Ireland, India, and everyplace else it has been tried, that partition of a territory along lines of descent whether called "racial" or "religious" is a guarantee of permanent war. It is understandable that some Palestinians, having been subjected to torture for over two generations, have reluctantly agreed to accept as a substitute for justice a Palestinian State built on less than a fourth of their original land. But they are making a mistake. Such a state, if it is ever established, will be a Bantustan, a reservation where the only attributes of a free nation will be a flag and a national anthem. I am no more a Palestinian Zionist than I am a Jewish Zionist.

What solution, therefore, do I propose? A simple and moderate one: within historic Palestine, the area between the Mediterranean Sea and the Jordan River, live 10 million people. I propose that there be established there a single state, in which every person who declares his intention to live there and adopt citizenship be recognized as a citizen and have one vote. I propose further that the special advantages given to Jews be terminated, that the Palestinians who were forced into exile after 1948, and their descendants, be granted the right to live there, and that the state undertake practical measures to make it possible for them to do so by building housing and extending to them to right to rent or buy, if necessary providing funds to help them. I propose further that both Hebrew and Arabic be declared official state languages to be taught in the schools, that all residents be granted the right to publish newspapers and maintain cultural institutions in any language they choose, that the special position of Orthodox Judaism be ended, and that the state declare freedom of worship and make no law respecting an establishment of religion or prohibiting the free exercise thereof.

It is a simple and, I repeat, a moderate program. It does not entail driving anybody into the sea, and it recognizes the elementary right of people to live where they choose.

Some might object that such a thing is impossible, that after all the blood that has been shed and the bitterness that has accumulated, it will not be possible for Jews and Arabs to live peacefully together. To that argument I have three responses: the first is the experience of South Africa, a place whose history of bitterness is no less than Palestine's; there the establishment of majority rule did not cause the gods to weep or the earth to open and swallow the people. My second response comes from Sherlock Holmes: after you have eliminated all the impossible solutions, Watson, the one remaining, no matter how improbable, must be the right one. My third response is to cite recent indications that the idea of the single democratic secular state—once the official goal of the PLO and then abandoned under US pressure—is once again emerging as a pole of discussion. Its reemergence is in part a response to Israel's gobbling up so much territory that nothing is left for a Palestinian state. The new reality is acknowledged by no less than columnist Thomas L. Friedman, who quotes a prominent Israeli Arab:

> If Palestinians lose their dream to have an independent state, then the only thing that might guarantee for them a dignified life will be asking to live in one state with the Israelis. When this struggle starts, it will find allies among the one million Palestinian Arabs inside Israel. We will say, "Don't evacuate even a single West Bank settlement. Just give us the vote and let us be part of one community."

Friedman reports a poll showing that 25 to 30 percent of Palestinians now support the idea of one state—"a stunning figure, considering it's never been proposed by any Palestinian or Israeli party." He calls it "the law of unintended consequences."[13]

The one exception to my earlier generalization about the Israeli opposition is a fraction of Orthodox Jews in Israel, who reject the State of Israel on religious grounds; according to them, the exile from the holy land was divinely ordained, and therefore the Jews are to live among the nations in every corner of the earth and not attempt to establish a State before the coming of the Messiah. Allow me to read from a statement by one of them, Rabbi Mordechi Weberman:

> It is precisely because we are Jews that we march with the Palestinians and raise their flag! It is precisely because we are Jews that we demand

that the Palestinian peoples be returned to their homes and properties! Yes, in our Torah we are commanded to be fair.

We are called upon to pursue justice. And, what could be more
unjust then the century-old attempt of the Zionist movement to
invade another people's land, to drive them out and steal their
property?

We have no doubt that would Jewish refugees have come to
Palestine not with the intention of dominating, not with the intention
of making a Jewish state, not with the intention of dispossessing, not
with the intention of depriving the Palestinians of their basic rights,
that they would have been welcomed by the Palestinians, with the
same hospitality that Islamic peoples have shown Jews throughout
history. And we would have lived together as Jews and Muslims lived
before in Palestine in peace and harmony.

To our Islamic and Palestinian friends around the world, please
hear our message. There are Jews around the world who support your
cause. And when we support your cause we do not mean some partition scheme proposed in 1947 by a UN that had no right to offer it.

When we say support your cause we do not mean the cut-off and
cut-up pieces of the West Bank offered by Barak at Camp David
together with justice for less than 10 percent of the refugees.

We do not mean anything other than returning the entire land,
including Jerusalem, to Palestinian sovereignty!

At that point justice demands that the Palestinian people should
decide if and how many Jews should remain in the Land.

We have attended hundreds of pro-Palestinian rallies over the
years and everywhere we go the leaders and audience greet us with
the warmth of Middle Eastern hospitality. What a lie it is to say that
Palestinians in particular or Muslims in general hate Jews. You hate
injustice. Not Jews.

Fear not my friends. Evil cannot long triumph. The Zionist nightmare is at its end. It is exhausted. Its latest brutalities are the death
rattle of the terminally ill.

We will yet both live to see the day when Jew and Palestinian will
embrace in peace under the Palestinian flag in Jerusalem. And ultimately when mankind's Redeemer will come the sufferings of the
present will long be forgotten in the blessings of the future.[14]

I am not a believer, but I find Rabbi Weberman's words moving.

One last point: I spoke earlier about the possibility of a resurgence of anti-Semitism in the United States. In 1991 George H. W. Bush, the father of the man who sits in the White House and the only member of his family ever to have been elected president, demanded that the Israelis stop building new settlements in Palestinian territory. Unlike previous presidents, Bush sounded serious, threatening to block billions in loan guarantees if Israel disobeyed. As might have been predicted, the dominant voices among American Jews were outraged, and Bush responded by complaining at a press conference that "Jews work insidiously behind the scenes." On another occasion he reminded critics that the United States gives "Israel the equivalent of $1,000 for every Israeli citizen," a remark that detractors took as anti-Semitic. Later on Bush's Secretary of State James Baker made his famous "fuck the Jews" remark in private conversation, noting that Jews "didn't vote for us anyway." And it was true: when he lost to Bill Clinton in 1992, Bush got the smallest percentage of the Jewish vote of any Republican since 1964.

The present occupant of the White House seems for the time being to have recouped much of his party's loss of favor among Jews, in part due to his appointment of so many to positions of power and influence in his administration. But I will go out on a limb and make a prediction (something I rarely do because I hate to be wrong): one-sided support for Israel, while it may win votes among American Jews and some fundamentalist Christians, is not necessarily wise from the standpoint of US oil interests and may even cost votes among that increasing number of Americans who can pick up the newspaper almost any day and see another story about Israeli tanks surrounding the residence of the Palestinian president, or massacring children, or assassinating a crippled half-blind cleric. I predict that if Dubya manages to extend his control of the White House in 2004, he will present the bill to whoever is in power in Israel, and that bill will include withdrawal from some of the territories occupied after 1967. If the Israelis respond negatively to this demand, which there is every reason to believe they will, and are supported by American Jews, which there is every reason to believe they will be, the younger Bush, already born-again, will be reborn yet one more time and will start making remarks about special minorities with divided loyalties and so forth. In other words, he will stoke up anti-Semitism, carefully of course, as befits the leader of the free world. And he will find a tremendous response, more than anyone anticipates, from many ordinary people who are tired of picking up the tab for the number one outlaw state in the Middle East, the state that has defied scores of United Nations resolutions, been condemned by the UN more than any other member or non-member, the only state in the Middle East that possesses actual weapons of mass destruction.

Cynthia McKinney, Afro-American congresswoman from Atlanta, was the most outspoken critic in Congress of US Middle East policy, including unconditional support for Israel. As a result, Jewish groups around the country targeted her and, by channeling money to her opponent, succeeded in defeating her bid for reelection in 2002. Were they within their legal rights to do so? Of course they were; there is no law barring people in one district from contributing to a campaign in another. But do they think their intervention went unnoticed by black voters in Atlanta and around the country?

If American Jews insist on identifying themselves with Israel, equating anti-Zionism with anti-Semitism, should they be surprised if others make the same mistake?

35

Beyond the Spectacle: New Abolitionists Speak Out

Cowritten with John Garvey for Counterpunch in 2015, this essay revisits Race Traitor's perspective on new abolitionism and highlights its importance for understanding how race and whiteness are being redefined in the twenty-first century.

Our initial reaction to the Rachel Dolezal story was: what's the big deal? America has always been a land of shape shifters, and if she isn't stopped for "driving while black" or followed while shopping, and if her sons are not targeted by cops, then how is she different from the politician who is Italian on Columbus Day and Irish on Saint Patrick's Day?

However, the more we saw the wolves circling around, the more we came to sympathize with her. By way of example, Matt Lauer on The Today Show kept badgering her with the question, "Are you Caucasian?"— ignoring her insistence that it was more complicated than that. We're inclined to think that judgments about her actions and explanations are mostly a matter for discussion among her immediate family members (specifically, her son and her adopted brother), her friends, perhaps her students at Eastern Washington University, and her political associates. This is, as Craig Wilder observed, a "local" story. We're not going to say much more about our views about Ms. Dolezal but we do want to examine the surrounding social and political contexts. Like others, we have been struck by the extent to which the whole discussion has been reduced to a spectacle and how little of it has been informed by perspectives grounded in history or coherent thinking. It has become commonplace to describe race as socially constructed (although clearly people like Matt Lauer have not yet heard the news). The corollary, usually forgotten, to the claim that race is socially constructed is that it can be socially dissolved.

We're going to approach the issues from the perspective we developed as the cofounders of *Race Traitor: Journal of the New Abolitionism*, which was published from 1993 to 2005. Our aim was to abolish the white race, by disrupting the institutions and practices that reproduce it (for example, the criminal justice system, the educational system, the labor market, and the healthcare system). To do that, we sought to enlist people nominally classified as white who defied white rules so strenuously that they jeopardized their ability to draw upon the privileges of whiteness—people who might be called race traitors—thereby contributing to the birth of a new community.

We were aware that even those who step out of being white in one situation can hardly avoid stepping back in later, if for no reason other than the assumptions of others (unless, like John Brown, they have the good fortune to be hung before that can happen). Many of the people commonly called whites who feel that the definition does not fit them have been told all their lives that they are crazy; some of them have been made crazy. One of our goals in publishing *Race Traitor* was to reach out to these dissidents, to let them know they were not alone. We confess that had Rachel Dolezal submitted an account of her life, we probably would have published it—not without reservations. But that's what politics is about—provisional arguments, not repetitions of the same old ones.

More fundamentally, we were interested in breaking up the white race to establish the basis for working-class solidarity. Many years later, we continue to argue that the time-honored "Unite and Fight" approach will lead nowhere. Instead, when it comes to slogans, we prefer "An injury to one is an injury to all" or the same thing in a different idiom: "Remember them that are in bonds as bound with them." Solidarity premised on the reproduction of inequalities within the working class, with the elimination of those inequalities to come later in "the sweet by and by," is no solidarity at all.

In retrospect, we believe that *Race Traitor* provided a coherent framework for examining and discussing race. As we acknowledged in an essay published in issue no. 12, we could have and should have approached some things differently—perhaps especially about the relationship we saw between the abolition of whiteness and the possibility of an anti-capitalist revolution. But we believe that much of what we wrote remains valuable today.

We emphasized the cross-class character of the white race formation and repeatedly acknowledged that being in the white race did not exempt its working-class members from poverty or misery of all sorts. At the time, we pointed out that the privileges of membership were enough for almost all whites to want to remain members. More than twenty years on, whiteness is not what it used to be, but it ain't nothing.

We never used, endorsed, or promoted identity politics; we railed against multiculturalism and diversity; we were scornful of those who wanted to preserve the "good aspects" of "white culture" or to rearticulate whiteness. We wanted nothing to do with the growing academic field of "whiteness studies." We insisted that abolition was the goal of our words and our modest deeds.

Although we were often accused of bashing white people, we actually think that we had more confidence in them than many of those who rush to diminish white workers' responsibility for the perpetuation of racial oppression. We were partisans of the notion that new forms of consciousness can emerge from the working out of internal contradictions. While we agreed with David Roediger "that whiteness was not merely empty and false, it is nothing but empty and false," we never thought that thinking of one's self as white was an all-consuming affair (other than for white supremacists and "white nationalists"). We knew perfectly well from our own experiences in families, schools, workplaces, and political organizations and movements that whites also identified themselves in many other ways.

We never imagined that white and black were hermetically sealed realities or categories, and we published more than a few articles that explored, and took quite different views on, various kinds of crossover phenomena. In that context, we articulated an appreciation for many elements of traditional African American culture (which we do not regret to this day). An aspect of that traditional culture was the willingness of black communities to welcome white defectors. In spite of the wall between white and black, there have always been so-called whites, thousands of them (usually female), who married black partners, had children with them, and lived in the black community (the only place they could live at the time)—without agonizing over their "identity."

At the same time, we did not want to overestimate the potential of white appreciations of aspects of black culture. We kept in mind Ralph Ellison's 1977 observation:

> What, by the way, is one to make of a white youngster who, with a transistor radio, screaming a Stevie Wonder tune, glued to his ear, shouts racial epithets at black youngsters trying to swim at a public beach—and this in the name of the ethnic sanctity of what has been declared a neighborhood turf?[1]

We urged our readers and followers to study and learn from central moments of US history: (a) the abolition of slavery and post–Civil War Reconstruction and (b) the modern civil rights movement of the 1950s and 1960s. In this regard, we took our lead from C. L. R. James's argument in 1948:

> We say, number one, that the Negro struggle, the independent Negro struggle, has a vitality and a validity of its own; that it has deep historic roots in the past of America and in present struggles; it has an organic political perspective, along which it is travelling, to one degree or another, and everything shows that at the present time it is travelling with great speed and vigor.
>
> We say, number two, that this independent Negro movement is able to intervene with terrific force upon the general social and political life of the nation, despite the fact that it is waged under the banner of democratic rights and is not led necessarily either by the organized labor movement or the Marxist party.
>
> We say, number three, and this is the most important, that it is able to exercise a powerful influence upon the revolutionary proletariat, that it has got a great contribution to make to the development of the proletariat in the United States, and that it is in itself a constituent part of the struggle for socialism.[2]

We did share some vocabulary with individuals and organizations that were travelling on different roads to different places. The most significant instance of this was the word "privilege." In light of the political travesties that have developed under the term since, we wish we could have found some better way of differentiating ourselves from those who wanted to make careers (in journalism, social work, organizational development, education, and the arts) by insisting that the psychic battle against privilege must be never-ending. The last thing in the world they wanted was for the white race to be abolished; if it were, they might have to make an honest living.

Our voice was never dominant. "Privilege politics" became a way of avoiding serious thought or political debate and a way of avoiding direct confrontations with the institutions that reproduce race and with the individuals responsible for the functioning of those institutions. The focus shifted to an emphasis on scrutinizing every interpersonal encounter between black people and whites to unearth underlying racist attitudes and to guide people in "unlearning" them. This has developed into a tendency to strictly enforce the boundaries between the races—not only (as in the past) by white supremacists but by proponents of what might be considered black advancement.

Unlike some who see privileges as prerogatives worth defending or rights that some workers have won through struggle and that other excluded workers should be provided, we insisted then and now that privileges are not rights. We assume that our views on that matter will be no more persuasive today to the unthinking troops of the sectarian left than they were twenty years ago.

At the present time, we acknowledge that the privileges have been eroded and that the protections once afforded to white people, and more specifically white workers, have become less significant than they were in the past. In that context, a constant hectoring of people about their privileges (which was never our approach) becomes an annoyance rather than a challenge. On the other hand, we would insist that something like race still matters a great deal—as is perhaps self-evident during a period of time characterized by a spate of police murders of black men and the murderous assault in the Charleston church. We would, however, urge people to look beneath the deeds that provoke immediate outrage from all sectors of society and appreciate the ways in which the everyday operations of institutions remain profoundly destructive of the well-being of African Americans.

And still further, we would argue that it not be imagined that those institutions work without human beings doing things. We especially need to be alert to the ways in which struggles presenting themselves as being for the benefit of all, such as the 2015 Chicago Teachers' Union strike, obscure the damage that is inflicted by teachers and others in the schools, in pursuit of their desire to address legitimate grievances regarding wages and benefits, on the black children enrolled in the nation's public schools.

Perhaps we should address a perennial objection to our views—that we reduce many different forms of oppression to a binary of black and white. Let us repeat—our project was never designed to minimize the extent of misery experienced by anyone. For example, we were and are quite aware of the dire circumstances of immigrants from Asia and Latin America (especially in the past). But the exploitation and oppression of those individuals do not take place outside of the larger circumstances of the American economy and society. The black/white binary preexists, and it is the framework within which all other "new-to-America" groups are situated. As Nell Painter has argued in *The History of White People*, "the fundamental black/white binary endures even though the category of whiteness—or we might say more precisely, a category of non-blackness—effectively expands."[3]

Although some may think we are living and dreaming in a different world than the real one, we want to note that we know that Barack Obama was elected as the first black president and that the ranks of the rich and powerful, and even the "middle class," now include a significant number of black people in positions previously reserved for whites. While such individuals are still subject to slights and insults from many quarters, and Charleston shows that even prominent black clergymen and state senators can be the victims of attack by white supremacist terrorists, their lives are not defined by official repression in the way they were in the past or the way the lives of people in the poor districts on the south side of Chicago, West Baltimore, Brooklyn's East New York/Brownsville, or many other places are today.

It may be that race is again being redefined and that the degraded race will no longer be all those who share the characteristic of the visible black skin but only those who are poor and workers. Whatever its characteristics, the task of challenging those who enforce it will remain an essential one.

IV

Dual Power Is the Key to Revolutionary Strategy

36

The Lesson of the Hour: Wendell Phillips on Abolition and Strategy

This is the introduction to Ignatiev's edited volume of selected speeches by Wendell Phillips, published by Charles H. Kerr in 2001. Ignatiev challenges mainstream views of abolitionism as white and committed to non-violence, arguing instead that black resistance was at the heart of abolitionism. He also explores the revolutionary strategies of abolitionists, and how they were shaped in response to the gradualism of the moderate wing of the anti-slavery movement.

During the winter of 1860–61, as South Carolina and other states responded to Lincoln's election by announcing their intention to secede, the great abolitionist Wendell Phillips walked the streets of Boston under the threat of attack from mobs that blamed the abolitionists for the breakup of the Union. Barely one year later, when Phillips traveled to Washington, the vice president of the United States welcomed him to the Senate chamber, the Speaker of the House invited him to dinner, and the President received him as a guest at the White House. What brought about the change in Phillips's standing, from a member of a hated and isolated sect to an honored tribute?

Although slaves and others had opposed slavery from its inception, the Abolitionist Movement entered a new phase on January 1, 1831, when William Lloyd Garrison began publishing the *Liberator* with the now-famous declaration:

I am aware that many object to the severity of my language; but is there not cause for severity? *I will be* as harsh as truth, and as uncompromising as justice. On this subject I do not wish to think, or speak, or write, with moderation. No! No! Tell a man whose house is on fire to give a moderate alarm; tell him to moderately rescue his wife from the hands of the ravisher; tell the mother to gradually extricate her babe from the fire into which it has fallen; but urge me not to use moderation in a cause like the present! I am in earnest. I will not equivocate—I will not excuse—I will not retreat a single inch—AND I WILL BE HEARD.[1]

The *Liberator* began at a low point of the anti-slavery movement. The anti-slavery sentiment of the Revolutionary Period had been stifled by the country's growing dependence on cotton and the general unwillingness of its citizens to imagine it with a large free black population. The Constitution placed slavery in the states beyond the reach of federal legislation; slaveholders controlled the executive and judicial branches and half the Senate. Free Negroes lost what political and civil rights they had, were driven out of trades they once held, and became the target of mobs seeking to reduce all those of African descent to the status of slaves.

If respectable anti-slavery sentiment had lessened, there were developments among slaves and free Negroes that would later be seen as pointing to a turn. In 1829 David Walker, a North Carolina–born free Negro living in Boston, published his *Appeal to the Colored Citizens of the World*, which called openly for slave insurrection. It quickly went through three editions and was thought so seditious that possession of it became a crime in several slave states. The unrest reached its peak in 1831 with the rebellion in Virginia led by Nat Turner.

Turner's rebellion was suppressed and was followed by a wave of repression in the slave states, directed against both the slaves and the free black population. The period of uprisings came to an end, as slaves concluded that they could not succeed and turned their attention inward, toward developing a culture of survival and resistance.

The receding of the hope of revolt also led many slaves to flee the plantation, and intensified repression led many free Negroes to leave the South. As more black people came north, they began to develop new institutions, including churches, schools, fraternal organizations, newspapers, conventions, and especially the underground railroad (the most important of all the railroads to which the nation owes its existence). This black population became the base of abolitionism. Negroes made up three hundred of the first 400 subscribers to the *Liberator* and were a majority of its readers throughout the life of the paper. As C. L. R. James wrote:

> The revolting slave, the persecuted free Negro, and the New England intellectual had got together and forced the nation to face the slavery question. When Garrison wrote, "I will be heard," he was not being rhetorical. That was the first problem: to be heard. After Turner's revolt that problem was solved for Garrison.[2]

The same issue of the *Liberator* that carried Garrison's prediction that he would be heard also carried his apology to the slaves for having previously supported the "pernicious" doctrine of gradual emancipation. Here he was expressing the central tenet of Abolitionism—immediate, unconditional, uncompensated emancipation. By taking an absolute position, the abolitionists were making their stand on the grounds of morality rather than expediency. It was not, as some have charged, that they ruled out the possibility of partial measures or compromise but that they thought it necessary to establish the movement on a firm foundation: slavery was evil and must be destroyed.

The abolitionists also stood for full equal rights for the Negro. It must be remembered that American slavery was *racial* slavery, a point not as obvious as it might appear. Unlike the situation in the West Indies, for instance, where people who in the United States would have been considered "black" were enlisted in policing the slaves, in the US slavery rested solely on the support of those called "white," giving rise to a system of color caste in which the lowliest of "whites" enjoyed a status superior to that of the most exalted of "blacks." In response, free persons of color by and large identified their own cause with that of the slave, an alignment quite different from that which prevailed in, say, Saint-Domingue or Jamaica. Another consequence was that the mass of "whites," with nothing but their color to distinguish them from the slaves, were infected with racial hatred beyond any known elsewhere. By and large Americans were uneasy with slavery. But most found it easier to tolerate slavery than to imagine themselves living alongside large numbers of free Negroes. (That, of course, was Jefferson's dilemma.) Equal rights for all, therefore, was not merely an ideal statement but the answer to the main argument against abolition, the supposed unassimilability of the Negro. For the abolitionists the two demands were inseparable. As Paul Goodman notes in his study of abolitionist racial attitudes, in linking the fight against slavery with the struggle for civil, legal, and social equality between black and white, the abolitionists were following the lead of David Walker and other early black leaders who had set out, in defiance of the American assumption that race prejudice was natural and insurmountable, to win over "a small but prophetic vanguard of white men and women." The abolitionists' unqualified commitment to emancipation defined them as revolutionary and led them to various positions that placed them in conflict with all those who sought to make the movement respectable.

The first expression of the abolitionists' revolutionary approach was Garrison's campaign against the American Colonization Society (ACS), which promoted manumission for slaves with compensation to their owners and their deportation to Liberia. Founded fifteen years earlier, the ACS was supported by many who disliked slavery and who thought to solve thereby what they called the problem of the free Negro in their midst. Its underlying premise was the inability of "whites" and free Negroes to live together, either because of the ineradicable prejudices of the former or the inherent inferiority of the latter. Having been educated by free black people, who insisted on their right to share in the country they had helped build, Garrison exposed colonization as a way of postponing emancipation forever and moreover as a scheme of the slaveholders to rid the country of their most dangerous opponents, the free Negroes. Within two years he succeeded in discrediting it as a legitimate current in anti-slavery ranks.

The first group to organize on Garrisonian principles was the New England Anti-Slavery Society, founded in 1832. A year later there were enough abolitionists in New England to permit the formation of state societies. In December 1833, delegates from nine states met in Philadelphia and founded the American Anti-Slavery Society (AASS), with a Declaration of Sentiments written by Garrison. The first annual convention of the AASS took place in New York in May 1834. Along with local and regional societies, there were organizations for women, youth, and college students. By 1838, there were 1,350 societies in the national organization, with a membership of about 250,000. The greatest strength was in New York, Massachusetts, Pennsylvania, and Ohio.

The work of the societies revolved around the efforts to petition Congress for the abolition of slavery. The aim was to force the issue onto the national agenda and in the process "abolitionize" public opinion. In 1837 they collected over 400,000 signatures. The societies fielded agents, who traveled throughout the free states, speaking publicly, selling literature, and helping to form new societies. In 1833 the AASS hired eleven agents. They were supported by dues and contributions from members and sympathizers and money raised at fairs, where crafts of various sorts, mostly made by female members, were sold. Garrison and other well-known spokesmen typically spoke to crowds of 2,000 or more, and Abolitionist literature, including the *Liberator* and other newspapers and pamphlets, sold widely.

The House of Representatives responded to Abolitionist agitation by refusing to receive petitions relating to slavery, and the postal service responded by banning anti-slavery newspapers and pamphlets from Southern mail. The unofficial response was, if anything, even more hostile. In New York, Philadelphia, and almost every other city in the "free" states, mobs broke up Abolitionist meeting and attacked their halls. Sometimes the violence spilled over into attacks against free Negroes; sometimes it went the other way, with attacks beginning against the black community leading to attacks on the homes of well-known abolitionists. The first time Phillips saw Garrison, in 1835, the editor was being dragged by a rope through the streets of Boston by a mob determined to lynch him. In 1837 Elijah Lovejoy was killed in Alton, Illinois, while defending his press from a mob that had destroyed it twice before. In 1838 a mob burned Pennsylvania Hall in Philadelphia, which the abolitionists had just built by subscription.

The mobs united native-born and immigrants, brought laborers and apprentices together with merchants and bankers. The gentry were motivated by direct ties to the slave system; the proletarians feared that the ending of slavery would place them on the same level as the Negroes.

It is important to note that most people in the North—probably not less than 70 percent—opposed slavery. If some way could have been found to guarantee the merchants their profits and to guarantee the laborers that the freed slaves would all remain in the cotton fields, it is likely that their natural human sympathies would have come into play. But they knew better, and so did the abolitionists, who insisted on linking the struggle for an end to slavery with the demand for equal rights for the Negro everywhere.

Not only did they link the demands programmatically, they sought to embody them in practice. It has been charged—often by persons seeking to discredit the movement—that white abolitionists were no different from other white Americans in their feelings of superiority and condescension toward black folk. If so, they surely fooled their opponents at the time, who held it as one of their greatest crimes that they refused to observe the color line.

By 1838 some people in the movement and outside of it were beginning to question its direction. If the movement were to succeed, they reasoned, it would have to win a majority, and to do that it would have to shed its extremist image. Differences developed over political action and over how abolitionism should present itself to the public.

The abolitionists had always been political. They regularly interrogated candidates for public office as to their views on the internal slave trade and slavery in the District of Columbia and called upon their supporters to vote accordingly. They sought to repeal the fugitive slave laws and to pass personal liberty laws. The question now came up, should they launch a new political party? Garrison opposed it, first, because he opposed all government in principle; second, because candidates would be required to swear an oath of loyalty to the Constitution, which he believed upheld slavery; third, because the need to gather votes would require the abolitionists to dilute their program; and fourth, because he thought it would be ineffective. If, he argued, the new party limited itself to the slavery question, it would not meet the needs of voters who had other concerns; if it adopted positions on a broad range of issues, it would antagonize some portion of voters who agreed with it on slavery. Far better, he reasoned, for those who believed in voting to demand of all candidates that they use their offices to oppose slavery.

The political action controversy took the form of a dispute over whether the Constitution was a proslavery document; not merely a dispute over the meaning of a text, the debate reflected the difference between the revolutionary and the reformer. Those most aware of the inherent limitations of the electoral system sided with Garrison, but the lines between the two sides were not always the same: many who did not share his principled opposition to government nevertheless opposed forming a new party.

Differences also broke out over the proper attitude toward religion and the churches. Garrison was an anti-Sabbatarian and a believer in human perfectibility (and hence rejected the doctrine of original sin). He also denied the divine authority of the scriptures. A number of clergymen in the movement objected to these views, but more important they found embarrassing his and some of his associates' regular denunciations of the sects as complicit with slavery. Garrison replied that his views were his own, that he did not attribute them to the movement, but that he was determined to expose and break up all the institutions that upheld the slave system.

The controversy came to a head over what was then called the "woman question." In the 1830s, two sisters from South Carolina, Sarah and Angelina Grimke, former slaveholders revolted by the degradation of female slaves, began speaking in the North against slavery, at first to women only, and then to "mixed" audiences. Soon a number of women began to assume responsibility in abolitionist circles, both as behind-the-scenes organizers and as public speakers. Women speaking in public to "promiscuous" audiences and exercising leadership in "mixed" groups provoked widespread hostility. Garrison, as might be expected, was an advocate of full equality for women: political, civil, social, and sexual. As might also be expected, some within the movement noted the disfavor it brought and demanded that AASS repudiate his views and adopt traditional restrictions on women's public role. In a replay of the dispute over religion, Garrison insisted that his views were his own, and he did not attribute them to the movement as a whole. On one point, however, he would not budge: the right of women to speak at abolitionist meetings and take part in the movement as full equals. At the 1840 World Anti-Slavery Congress in London, female delegates from the United States were denied their seats. In protest, Garrison sat with them in the balcony. At the next annual convention of the AASS, after failing to capture the society, a minority walked out, forming another group, the "American and Foreign Anti-Slavery Society" (A&F). The minority included a number of prominent clergymen and several of the society's biggest financial supporters. The A&F lasted only about a year, but the membership in the AASS shrunk to 60,000.

At bottom, the dispute turned over whether abolitionism was

revolutionary and whether the movement should try to make itself respectable. By and large, those who believed that slavery was a symptom of a fundamentally sick society took one side, while those who considered it an aberration in an otherwise healthy organism the other. The "woman question" served as the test of commitment to the goal (in much the same way anti-communism did in the 1950s). When, shortly after the Convention, a correspondent asked about the recent "split" among the abolitionists, Garrison replied that there was no split, merely some former abolitionists who have gone off in another direction. The abolitionists, he said, remained united.

By no means all of those who remained in the AASS agreed with Garrison on all questions, but they agreed that the society itself would determine its own positions and not pressure from outsiders. Nor did they limit themselves to work within the AASS; many took part in other activities, including challenges to segregation, setting up schools for black children, and working with the Underground Railroad and the vigilance committees that aided fugitive slaves. The fugitive slave issue was crucial to the development of anti-slavery feeling, because it embodied in a tangible way the complicity of the North with slavery. In the work with fugitive slaves, free Negroes took the lead.

Shortly after the 1840 convention the AASS, denouncing the Constitution as a "covenant with death," began a campaign to get the North to secede from the Union. This was not a quixotic effort to remain uncontaminated by association with slavery, but the expression of a conscious strategy. The abolitionists took seriously their assertion that the North, through its military backing, was the true upholder of slavery. By taking it out of the Union, they hoped to free it from the need to enforce the Fugitive Slave Law. "All the slave asks of us," declared Phillips, "is to stand out of his way, withdraw our pledge to keep the peace on the plantation; withdraw our pledge to return him ... and he will right himself." The slogan "No Union with Slaveholders" translated itself at every abolitionist rally into a pledge never to send back the fugitive slave who set foot on free territory. The abolitionists did not limit themselves to agitation; whenever possible they tried to rescue fugitives from the law. Phillips wrote in 1851:

The long evening sessions—debates about secret escapes—plans to evade where we can't resist—the door watched that no spy may enter—the whispering consultations of the morning—some putting property out of their hands, planning to incur penalties, and planning also that, in case of connection, the Government may get nothing from them—the doing, and answering no questions—intimates forbearing to ask the knowledge which it may be dangerous to have— all remind me of those foreign scenes which have been hitherto known to us, transatlantic republicans, only in books.[3]

When Garrison stood up at a public meeting on July 4, 1854, and burned the Constitution, he was making more than a symbolic gesture. He was seeking to resist official authority, not merely oppose it, and to thwart its operation. In the twentieth century it would become known as a strategy of dual power.

The abolitionists have often been described as pacifists, and formally many were, but the term conceals more than it reveals. As C. L. R. James noted, "They took part in the rescue of fugitive slaves, not only by underground methods but in open defiance of all authority," and "the violence of the polemic, the attack without bounds upon everything that stood in the way, the unceasing denunciations of slave property, the government, the constitution, the laws, the church was in itself a repudiation of pacifism."

In 1849, Frederick Douglass made a speech calling for slave insurrection; the *Liberator* published it in full. When anti-slavery forces sent arms to free-state settlers in Kansas, Garrison asked:

If such men are deserving of generous sympathy, and ought to be supplied with arms, are not the crushed and bleeding slaves at the South a million times more deserving of pity and succor? Why not, first of all, take measures to furnish them with Sharp's rifles?[4]

At a meeting after the death of John Brown, Garrison declared himself still a nonresistant and asked how many others were in the audience of 3,000. Only one hand went up. Garrison then replied, "as a peace man— an 'ultra' peace man—I am prepared to say: 'Success to every slave insurrection at the South, and in every slave country.'" Those were strange words for a pacifist. Above all, the abolitionists were revolutionaries. Again quoting James, they were willing to tear up by the roots the foundation of the Southern economy and society, wreck Northern commerce, and disrupt the Union irretrievably . . . They renounced all traditional politics . . . They openly hoped for the defeat of their own country in the Mexican War . . . They preached and practiced Negro equality. They endorsed and fought for the equality of women.[5]

Like their Puritan ancestors—like all revolutionaries—they were intolerant. As James said, "They hated and mercilessly excoriated all who had the slightest touch with slavery . . . They argued over every comma of their doctrine with the utmost pertinacity and unyieldingness." "Sincerity," said Phillips, "is no shield for any man from the criticism of his fellow-laborers." They sought no rewards, counting their wages in beatings, stonings, and mobbings. On one occasion when the mayor of Boston begged a meeting of abolitionist women to disband because he was unable to protect them from a mob, Maria Weston Chapman, probably the person most responsible for directing the day-to-day work of the movement, replied, "If this is the last bulwark of freedom, we may as well die here as elsewhere." On another occasion Phillips, ignoring a barrage of hurled missiles, leaned forward and began speaking softly to the journalists in the first rows, thus quieting the howling mob that had drowned out his voice. James summed them up as a "clearly recognizable replica of the early Christians, the Puritans, and later the early Bolsheviks."

Abolitionism, it has been shown, took shape not in direct opposition to slaveholders and overt proslavery ideas but to moderate elements within the anti-slavery camp.

As for those whom Garrison called "former Abolitionists," they mostly went into electoral politics, forming the Liberty Party in time for the 1840 elections. When that party drew fewer votes than the number of members of the A&F, they found themselves under pressure to discard various planks from its platform. Having freed themselves from the taint of association with women's rights, most had little difficulty abandoning the commitment to racial equality (a vote-loser if ever there was). Next to go was the demand for complete abolition, since that could not be accomplished constitutionally. They also rejected as incendiary any public support for the efforts of slaves to run away or rebel. That left the internal slave trade and slavery in the District of Columbia, and on these issues the party took its stand. Salmon Chase, Liberty Party leader in Ohio, and later Secretary of the Treasury and Justice of the Supreme Court, distinguished between abolition, which "seeks to abolish slavery everywhere," and anti-slavery, which aims at reducing the slaveholders' power over the federal government. He called upon the party to reject the abolitionist label on the grounds that "while abolition is not properly speaking a political object, anti-slavery is." To their credit, some of the so-called political abolitionists resisted the pressures in that direction, and some of them performed creditable work privately, including providing arms to those willing to use them. But of those public men— and of course they had to be men—who deserted the AASS, their names, with one exception, have been forgotten by all but specialists; the exception is Frederick Douglass, and sadly it must be admitted that he, too, wavered after he ceased to identify himself as a Garrisonian.

For several years the contest between pro- and anti-slavery forces stood still, until in the mid-1840s President Polk began beating the drums for war with Mexico. Americans were divided: most welcomed the opportunity to expand the country; many, however, saw the war as a scheme to gain new territory for slavery, and even the young Illinois congressman, Abraham Lincoln, serving his first and only term, opposed it. In August 1846, only three months after the start of the war, Representative David Wilmot, Democrat from Pennsylvania, introduced an amendment to the Texas annexation bill, banning slavery from any territory that might be acquired from Mexico. Wilmot's Proviso marked the birth of the Free-Soil Party.

Free-Soil was the name given to the movement to exclude slavery from the territories. It was not "soft" abolitionism: it was the enemy of abolitionism. The young Free-Soil journalist Walt Whitman expressed its meaning clearly: "The whole matter of slavery," he wrote, "will be a conflict between the totality of White Labor, on the one side, and on the other, the interference and competition of Black Labor, or of bringing in colored persons on *any* terms."[6] Free-Soilers hated slavery because they hated and feared the black worker. At the same time the demand for Free-Soil disrupted the coalition that had governed the country since its birth. It ranged against the slaveholders' powerful forces, including manufacturers, farmers, and craftsmen. For the first time there were elements in the country, apart from the abolitionists, who contested the slaveholders' dominance of the Union.

From 1846 on, slavery was the central issue in American politics.

There were three main factions: the slaveholders; the abolitionists; and those whom we shall call anti-slavery, who opposed the extension of slavery into the territories. The shifting relations among them shaped the course of events through the Civil War and Reconstruction; of the three, the abolitionists were the weakest—at first.

The election of 1848 revealed divisions between pro- and anti-slaveholder factions within both major parties, Whigs and Democrats, and saw the appearance of a new party standing for "Free Soil, Free Speech, Free Labor, and Free Men" (whites only). In 1850, congressional leaders worked out a compromise, which they hoped would bury the slavery issue. It had four provisions: (a) it outlawed the slave trade in the District of Columbia; (b) it admitted California to the Union as a free state; (c) it left slavery in the remainder of the territories taken from Mexico to the decision of the territorial legislatures; and (d) it enacted a new fugitive slave law, which eliminated jury trials and placed the burden of proof on the suspected fugitive.

The Compromise of 1850 succeeded for a while in removing slavery from the national agenda, but the fugitive slave wrecked it, by making it impossible for northerners to deny their complicity with slavery. Who could forget Eliza on the ice? In 1854, Anthony Burns, a former slave living in Boston, was ordered returned to slavery. A crowd stormed the courthouse in a failed attempt to rescue him, and on the day of his delivery to the ship that was to take him back, US infantry and artillery units guarded the courthouse and cleared the streets, while a large body of police, an entire brigade of the state militia, and a special armed guard of 200 men accompanied him to the dock as a crowd of 20,000 hissed and groaned. Stores were closed and buildings were draped in black. "An awful lot of folks turned out just to watch a colored man walk up the street," said Burns, and one observer said, "We went to bed one night old-fashioned, conservative, Compromise Union Whigs, and waked up stark mad Abolitionists." The proslavery Richmond *Enquirer* admitted, "One more victory like that and the South is lost."

On the heels of the Burns case, Congress passed an Act opening Kansas to slavery, which had previously been banned there. The Act authorized the territorial legislature to decide whether Kansas would enter the Union as a free or slave state. Proslavery forces poured in to influence the elections, while land-hungry farmers from the free states also migrated there. The result was a dress rehearsal for the Civil War.

Free-staters in Kansas were opposed to the plantation system because it brought them into competition with slave labor, but they had no desire to work alongside free Negroes. They rejected Douglass's suggestion to settle in Kansas 1,000 free black families, who would constitute a "wall of fire" against slavery there. But the necessities of war compelled them to make common cause with the abolitionists, and it was in Kansas that for the first time John Brown's name became known.

John Brown was a Connecticut-born, Ohio-raised, "pitch-pine Yankee," descendant of Mayflower stock (some today might call him a "WASP") who, after long association with black people, decided at the age of fifty to devote the remainder of his life to the abolition of slavery. When conflict broke out in Kansas, he went there with his sons to take part. Near Pottawatomie Creek he killed five proslavery settlers in retaliation for massacres that had been carried out earlier against free-staters, thus beginning a guerrilla war that lasted for two years and resulted in a victory for free-state forces. While free-staters had welcomed Brown's intervention in the Kansas War, they were also glad to see him go, and the first constitution of the state barred free Negroes from emigrating there. Before retiring from Kansas, Brown crossed with his men into Missouri, where he attacked two plantations, liberating eleven slaves whom he then accompanied on a 1,000-mile exodus to Canada, with the US Army in pursuit.

The Kansas conflict gave rise to the Republican Party. Like its Free Soil predecessor, the Republican Party sought to take federal power out of the hands of the slaveholders and prevent the expansion of slavery into the territories. It did not, however, oppose slavery, still less did it advocate rights for free Negroes; in fact, it billed itself as the defender of white labor and denounced the Democrats as the "nigger party," since the Democrats stood for the unrestricted expansion of slavery.

The country was moving toward Civil War. In 1856 a Southern congressman assaulted Republican Senator Charles Sumner with a heavy metal cane on the senate floor, nearly killing him. In 1857 the Supreme Court ruled in the Dred Scott case that Congress had no power to prohibit slavery anywhere, by implication declaring unconstitutional the main plank in the Republican platform. The slaveholders began agitating to legalize the slave trade, and the government in Washington declared its interest in annexing Cuba, where slavery still existed. The Republican Party grew as more and more people in the North began to resent the encroachments of the slaveholders.

And then on October 16, 1859, John Brown and a small band of followers, black and white, attacked the federal arsenal at Harpers Ferry, Virginia. What was his aim? Many at the time and since have thought that the raid was to be the signal for a general slave uprising, but Brown denied it. W. E. B. Du Bois suggests that his aim was to seize arms and withdraw into the surrounding hills, from which he would conduct guerrilla warfare against the slave system, gradually attracting slaves and others to his ranks and establishing a liberated zone, much like the maroon republics that were widespread in the West Indies and Brazil. The attack on Harpers Ferry was not an aberration but the logical implementation of the abolitionist strategy.

Brown and his men captured the arsenal, but instead of withdrawing in a timely fashion, they allowed the government time to bring in additional troops, and most, including Brown himself, were taken. If it failed to accomplish its military objective, the raid succeeded beyond expectations in other ways. For the six weeks between the raid and his hanging on December 2, Brown was the focus of national attention. Millions, including many who thought his act ill-advised, cheered his courage and acknowledged sympathy for his goal. A popular writer, Lydia Maria Child, offered to go to Virginia to nurse him. The wife of a senator from Virginia undertook to engage Child in a debate on the merits of the northern and southern systems. Attempting to show the ties of affection between slaves and masters, she referred to the custom among plantation mistresses of nursing their slaves through childbirth and illness. Child replied that in New England as well the more privileged women customarily assisted the less privileged; the difference was that "after we have helped the mothers, *we do not sell the babies.*" The exchange was reprinted in papers across the country.

The defenders of slavery were routed; Thoreau declared Brown the reincarnation of a seventeenth-century Puritan hero; Emerson said his hanging would make the gallows as glorious as the cross. As usual, Wendell Phillips saw farthest. In a speech at Brown's graveside on December 8, he said Brown had

> abolished slavery in Virginia. You may say this is too much . . . History will date Virginia Emancipation from Harper's Ferry. True, the slave is still there. So, when the tempest uproots a pine on your hills, it looks green for months—a year or two. Still, it is timber, not a tree.[7]

Brown, said Phillips, "startled the South into madness." The slaveholders reacted with fury to the raid: they imposed a boycott on northern manufacturers, demanded new concessions from the government in Washington, and began preparing for war.

When they sought to portray Brown as a representative of northern opinion, southern leaders were wrong; he represented only a small and isolated minority. But they were also right, for he expressed the hopes that still persisted in the populace despite decades of cringing before the slaveholders. The South did not fear John Brown and his small band of followers, but rather his soul that would go marching on, though his body lay a mould'rin' in the grave. When the South sought to bully northern opinion, it did so not out of paranoia but out of the realistic assessment that only a renewal of the national proslavery vows could save their fragile system. By the arrogance of their demands, the slaveholders *compelled* the people of the North to resist.

"If the telegraph speaks truth," declared Phillips in 1860, "for the first time in our history the slave has chosen a President of the United States . . . John Brown was behind the curtain." But for the national discussion touched off by Harpers Ferry, it is unlikely Lincoln would have been elected. But for Lincoln's election, the Civil War would not have broken out when it did.

The slave system bred rebellion, which provoked repression, which led black people to leave the South, which gave rise to a black community in the north, which was the basis of Abolitionism, which engendered John Brown, who provoked Southern retaliation, which compelled northern resistance.

But there is more.

Why did the slaveholders launch the Civil War? The reason could not have been fear of having their property taken away, because the Republican platform pledged not to touch slavery where it existed. What had the slaveholders lost? Domination of the Union, which they had held throughout the century. While the Republican Party was not an abolitionist party, its electoral victory marked the passing of the presidency into the hands of a party determined to end the slaveholders' control of the federal government. Aided by the weapon of federal patronage, that party would grow stronger, inevitably linking with the southern white opposition to the slaveholders. (Hinton Helper's *The Impending Crisis of the South* was the bible of that opposition, hitherto suppressed but never extinguished.)

The war aim of the South could not have been simply secession, the formation of a separate country, as has usually been said. The war aim of the South was to reconstitute the Union on the old basis, with the protection and expansion of slavery as the avowed national purpose, with the ultimate goal being the formation of a slave republic, modeled on ancient Rome, extending from Canada to Brazil and including as its auxiliaries the agriculture, commerce, and manufacture of the North. Southern leaders made their purpose clear, as when the Confederate Secretary of War predicted that before the war ended, the Stars and Bars would fly over Faneuil Hall in Boston.

Phillips hailed the outbreak of war. "All my grown-up years," he said, "have been devoted to creating just such a crisis as that which is now upon us." Phillips went from being an advocate of disunion to a supporter of war. There are those who interpret this shift as marking a repudiation of his former stance. They miss the point. For Phillips the issue of Union or no Union had always been contingent, a mere detail. His concern was the slave. The cornerstone of his policy had always been to take the North, or as much of it as he could manage, out of the control of the slave power, and thus bring down slavery. The outbreak of war accomplished his aim, and it made little difference to him if the separation resulted from northern secession or southern. He was ready, because he had always striven to break up a Union devoted to the defense of slavery.

> Many times this winter, here and elsewhere, I have counseled peace—urged, as well as I knew how, the expediency of acknowledging a Southern Confederacy, and the peaceful separation of these thirty-four states. One of the journals announces to you that I come here this morning to retract those opinions. No, not one of them! I need them all—every word I have spoken this winter—every act of twenty-five years of my life, to make the welcome I give this war hearty and hot.[8]

The task was to transform the war for the Union into a war against slavery. The first problem was the Republican moderates. Lincoln had been elected on a platform promising to ban slavery from the territories. He took office doing everything he could to avoid war, reiterating his pledge not to touch slavery where it existed. Among his first acts was to issue an order for strict enforcement of the Fugitive Slave Law. His efforts, however, had not been not enough to reassure the South, and the war began, in the words of Frederick Douglass, with both sides fighting for slavery—the South to take it out of the Union, the North to keep it in.

Over the winter of 1861–62, 5 million people read Phillips's speeches or heard him call for emancipation, the enlistment of black soldiers, and the adoption of an active military strategy. In the face of loss after loss, Lincoln defended his policy of conciliating the slaveholders. To declare abolition the aim of the war, he reasoned, would cost him the support of loyal Southerners: he would have liked to have Mr. Phillips, but he *must* have Kentucky. Secondly, he asked how Phillips knew that the black soldiers would fight. Two things led him to change his mind. The first was the growing northern war-weariness. The second was the actions of the slaves, who demonstrated their willingness to help the enemy of their enemy by leaving the plantations and making their way to Union lines.

And so Lincoln's policy shifted, as Marx said, from constitutional to revolutionary. The shift was embodied in three measures: the Emancipation Proclamation, the enlistment of black soldiers, and the appointment of Grant as head of the Union Armies.

The Emancipation Proclamation actually freed no one, since it applied only to those areas of the country then in rebellion, that is, to those areas of the country where it could not be enforced. But it was important as a statement of purpose. The trickle of slaves leaving the plantation turned into a flood. Before it was over, more than 500,000 slaves had withdrawn their labor power from the Confederacy, and not too much work was being done by those who stayed behind. Thousands of poor whites, forced by the withdrawal of black labor to bear a greater burden, deserted the Confederate Army and returned to their fields. Du Bois called it a general strike of black and white labor.

The enlistment of black soldiers marked the turning point. At Fort Wagner and elsewhere they laid to rest forever any doubts about their willingness to fight for their freedom. By the end of the War, over 200,000 had served in the Union forces; Lincoln declared that they meant the difference between victory and defeat. Years later, Douglass recorded the conversation he had with Lincoln shortly after the Emancipation Proclamation.

> I agreed to undertake the organizing of a band of scouts, composed of colored men, whose business should be somewhat after the original plan of John Brown, to go into the rebel states, beyond the lines of our

armies, and carry the news of emancipation, and urge the slaves to come within our boundaries.[9]

And that is of course is what happened, as Grant, the inventor of modern warfare, advanced on the South "somewhat after the original plan of John Brown," the slaves rallied to his banner, and the Confederacy collapsed.

It was not the North that freed the slaves, but rather the slaves and free Negroes who freed the country from the domination of the slave system. Each step led inexorably to the next: southern land-greed, Lincoln's victory, secession, war—and the overthrow of slavery.

The course of events can never be predicted in other than the broadest outline, but in the essentials history followed the path charted by the abolitionists. As they foresaw, it was necessary to break up the Union in order to reconstitute it without slavery. More than that: if by 1863 millions were marching through the land singing (to the tune of "John Brown's Body") "As He died to make men holy let us fight to make men free," and if (as Du Bois said) for a shining moment after the War the majority of Americans believed in the humanity of the Negro, it was not because the abolitionists won them over (though they surely tried, and may even have thought that that was what they were doing). It was because their actions brought about a new situation, which led millions to act and think in new ways.

Have ever revolutionaries been more thoroughly vindicated by events? Have ever revolutionaries had a greater impact on events?

History has not been kind to the abolitionists. Even those who profess to admire them for their dedication to the cause of freedom most often dismiss them as romantics who had little or no effect. (The IWW gets the same treatment.) Yet how could anyone in possession of the facts deny the abolitionists their place as shapers of history? To appropriate Du Bois's phrase used in another context, "It is only the blindspot in the eyes of America and its historians."

The more I study the Civil War and Reconstruction, the more I am confirmed in the belief (derived from Du Bois) that, taken together, they represent a revolutionary upheaval as great as any. Slavery was not abolished through constitutional process but through war and revolution, and the 13th, 14th, and 15th Amendments merely ratified what had already been achieved on the battlefield. Not the English Revolution of the seventeenth century nor the French of the eighteenth involved such great masses of people nor such tremendous armies as did the American Civil War; neither the Russian nor the Spanish Revolution of the twentieth took people from such a low state and hurled them so close to power as did the revolution that took 4 million people who had been *property* and turned them overnight into soldiers, citizens, voters, and officeholders. Only the Haitian Revolution of the eighteenth century and the Chinese Revolution of the twentieth compare with the American experience in breadth and depth, and in neither case did the downtrodden classes come as close to power for so long as did American slaves after the Civil War.

Phillips was born in Boston in 1811, "the child of six generations of Puritans." He attended Harvard College and Harvard Law School. He was a thorough Yankee; like that other New Englander, W. E. B. Du Bois, he did not equate "Yankee" and "white":

> Some men say they would view this war as white men. I condescend to no such narrowness. I view it as an American citizen, proud to be the citizen of an empire that knows neither black nor white, neither Saxon nor Indian, but holds an equal scepter over all.[10]

His 1850 speech welcoming British abolitionist George Thompson to America could serve as a self-description:

> Whether his voice cheered the starving Hindoo crushed beneath British selfishness, or Hungary battling against treason and the Czar; whether he pleaded at home for bread and the ballot, or held up with his sympathy the ever-hopeful enthusiasm of Ireland—every true word spoken for suffering man, is so much done for the Negro bending beneath the weight of American bondage.

Although Garrison is the most widely known of the abolitionists and is rightly regarded as the founder, within ten years of Phillips's joining he was the real leader of the movement. It is doubtful whether he ever shared Garrison's absolute commitment to nonresistance. Yet all his life he referred to himself as a "Garrisonian." His modesty in this regard reminds me of no one more than Malcolm X, who until the last year of his life was content to describe himself as a devoted follower of the Honorable Elijah Muhammad.

   While continuing after the Civil War to fight for the rights of freed people and women, he expanded his activities to include the cause of the wage laborer. As a Labor Reform candidate for governor in 1870 (the only time he allowed his name to be put up for political office), he resisted the anti-Chinese campaign that had gained the support of many self-proclaimed friends of labor. He joined the dreaded "International" and spoke out in defense of the Paris Commune. Summarizing his career, he said he had "worked 40 years, served in 20 movements and been kicked out of all of them." He died in 1884. His death was announced on the floor of the Senate with the words, "Wendell Phillips of America is dead in Boston."

37

The World View of C. L. R. James

C. L. R. James was a revolutionary who deeply impacted Ignatiev's political life. The following essay is the introduction Ignatiev wrote for two seminal James essays published by PM Press under the title A New Notion: Two Works by C. L. R James *in 2010. Ignatiev provides a political biography of James, including his dialectical approach to working-class struggles, James's revolutionary optimism, and his political activity. Ignatiev argues James's insistence that the working class is capable of building a better world remains his most important contribution to future generations of revolutionaries.*

———

Cyril Lionel Robert James was born in Trinidad in 1901 to a middle-class black family. He grew up playing cricket (which he credited with bringing him into contact with the common folk of the island). He also reported on cricket, and wrote a novel, several short stories, and a biography of Captain Cipriani, a Trinidadian labor leader and advocate of self-government. In 1932, James moved to England, where he covered cricket for the Manchester *Guardian* and became heavily involved in Marxist politics.

He wrote a history of the San Domingo revolution and a play based on that history, in which he and Paul Robeson appeared on the London stage. He wrote a history of the Communist International, *The History of Negro Revolt*, and translated into English Boris Souvarine's biography of Stalin. Together with his childhood friend, George Padmore, James founded the International African Service Bureau, which became a center for the struggle for the independence of Africa, helping to develop Jomo Kenyatta, Kwame Nkrumah, and others. He also spent time with coal miners in Wales (among whom he reported he felt no consciousness of race).

In 1938, James came to the United States on a speaking tour, ending up staying for fifteen years. He had discussions with Trotsky in Mexico and took part in the Trotskyist movement in the United States. While in the US, James wrote a study of Hegel and the application of the dialectic in the modern world, a study of Herman Melville, a 300-page outline for a study of American life (later published as *American Civilization*), and a number of shorter works (including the first of the two in this volume). During World War II he lived among and organized sharecroppers in southeastern Missouri. In 1952 James was arrested and interned on Ellis Island; the following year he was deported from the United States. (His deportation was perhaps one of the greatest triumphs of McCarthyism: how might history have been different had he been in the country during Malcolm X's rise?)

For most of the next few years, C. L. R. James lived in the United Kingdom, returning to Trinidad briefly to edit *The Nation* (the paper of the People's National Movement) and serve as secretary of the Federal West Indian Labour Party (which advocated a West Indian federation). He left in 1961 after a falling out with Eric Williams, prime minister of Trinidad and a former student of James's, over Williams's turn toward supporting US imperialism. Before leaving, he delivered a series of lectures aimed at providing the citizens of the new nation with a perspective on Western history and culture; these lectures, which for years were kept locked in a warehouse in Trinidad, have been published under the title *Modern Politics*.[1]

In 1968, taking advantage of the rising mood of revolution on the campuses, a group of black American students at Northwestern University brought James to the United States. There he held university teaching posts and lectured widely until 1980. For the last years of his life, he lived in south London and lectured on politics, Shakespeare, and other topics. He died there in 1989.

In the West Indies, James is honored as one of the fathers of independence and in Britain as a historic pioneer of the black movement; he is regarded generally as one of the major figures in Pan-Africanism. And he led in developing a current within Marxism that was democratic, revolutionary, and internationalist.

Obviously, this is a great variety of activities for a single individual to undertake. If the word "genius" has any meaning, then it must be applied to C. L. R. James. Most important, however, is not his individual qualities, but the worldview that enabled him to bring light to so many different spheres of activity. James says in *Notes on Organization* that when you develop a new notion, it is as if you have lifted yourself to a plateau from which you can look at familiar things from a new angle. What was James's notion, and how did it enable him to make unique contributions in so many areas?

For James, the starting point was that the working class is revolutionary. He did not mean that it is potentially revolutionary, or that it is revolutionary when imbued with correct ideas, or when led by the proper vanguard party. He said the working class is revolutionary and that its daily activities constitute the revolutionary process in modern society.

This was not a new idea. Karl Marx had said, first, that capitalism revolutionizes the forces of production and, second, that foremost among the forces of production is the working class. James, in rediscovering the idea and scraping off the rust that had accumulated over nearly a century, brought it into a modern context and developed it.

James's project was to discover, document, and elaborate the aspects of working-class activity that constitute the revolution in today's world. This project enabled James and his cothinkers to look in a new way at the struggles of labor, black people, women, youth, and the colonial peoples and to produce a body of literature far ahead of its time, works that still constitute indispensable guides for those fighting for a new world.

James and his cothinkers focused their attention on the point of production, the scene of the most intense conflicts between capital and the working class. In two trailblazing works, "An American Worker" (1947) and "Punching Out" (1952), members of the Johnson-Forest Tendency led by James documented the emergence on the shop floor of social relations counter to those imposed by management and the union, relations that prefigured the new society.

Not every example James cited was from production. In "Negroes and American Democracy" (1956) he wrote:

the defense of their full citizenship rights by Negroes is creating a new concept of citizenship and community. When, for months, 50,000 Negroes in Montgomery, Alabama do not ride buses and overnight organize their own system of transportation, welfare, and political discussion and decision, that is the end of representative democracy. The community as the center of full and free association and as the bulwark of the people against the bureaucratic state, the right of women to choose their associates as freely as men, the ability of any man to do any job if given the opportunity, freedom of movement and of association as the expansion rather than the limitation of human personality, the American as a citizen not just of one country but of the world—all this is the New World into which the Negro struggle is giving everybody a glimpse.[2]

That is the new society and there is no other: ordinary people, organized around work and activities related to it, taking steps in opposition to capital to expand their freedom and their capacities as fully developed individuals. It is a leap of imagination, but it is the key to his method. The new society does not triumph without an uprising; but it exists. It may be stifled temporarily; capital, after all, can shut down the plant, or even a whole industry, and can starve out an entire community. But the new society springs up elsewhere. If you want to know what the new society looks like, said James, study the daily activities of the working class.

James insisted that the struggles of the working class are the chief motor in transforming society. Even before it overthrows capital, the working class compels it to new stages in its development. Looking back at US history, the resistance of the craftsmen compelled capital to develop methods of mass production; the workers responded to mass production by organizing the Congress of Industrial Organizations (CIO), an attempt to impose their control on the rhythms of production; capital retaliated by incorporating the union into its administrative apparatus; the workers answered with the wildcat strike and a whole set of shop-floor relations outside of the union; capital responded to this autonomous activity by moving the industries out of the country in search of a more pliant working class and introducing computerized production to eliminate workers altogether. The working class has responded to the threat of permanent separation from the means of obtaining life with squatting, rebellion, and food riots; this is a continuous process, and it moves the society forward—ending, as Marx said, in the revolutionary reconstitution of society at large or in the common ruin of the contending classes.

James observed the triumph of the counterrevolution in Russia, the crushing of the workers' movement in Europe by fascism, and the role of the Communist parties, and he concluded that these developments indicated that capitalism had reached a new stage. This new stage, like every development of capitalist society, was a product of workers' activity. The labor bureaucracy, that alien force ruling over the working class, grows out of the accomplishments of the workers' movement. In a modern society like the United States, the working-class struggles not against past defeats but against past victories—against the institutions that the workers themselves have created and which have become forms of domination over them. The social role of the labor bureaucracy is to absorb, and if necessary repress, the autonomous movement of the working class, and it scarcely matters whether it is Communist in France, Labour in Britain, or the American Federation of Labor AFL-CIO in this country.

"The Stalinist bureaucracy is the American bureaucracy carried to its ultimate and logical conclusion; both of them products of capitalist production in the epoch of state-capitalism," wrote James in *State Capitalism and World Revolution*.[3] In that work he called the new stage state capitalism, a system in which the state assumes the functions of capital and the workers remain exploited proletarians. He said that Russia was this type of society. Others before him had come to similar conclusions. James's theory was distinctive: it was a theory not of Russia but of the world. It applied to Germany, England, and the United States as much as to Russia. He wrote:

> What the American workers are revolting against since 1936 and holding at bay, this, and nothing else but this, has overwhelmed the Russian proletariat. The rulers of Russia perform the same functions as are performed by Ford, General Motors, the coal operators and their huge bureaucratic staffs.[4]

This understanding of the "organic similarity of the American labour bureaucracy and the Stalinists" prepared James and his colleagues to see the Hungarian Revolution of 1956, the French General Strike of 1968, and the emergence of the US wildcat strikes of the 1950s and the League of Revolutionary Black Workers in Detroit in 1967 as expressions of a global revolt against the domination of capital.

In an industrial country, it is not the guns and tanks of the government that hold the workers down. When the working class moves, the state is powerless against it. This was true in Hungary in 1956, it was true in France in 1968, and it was true in Poland in 1980. It is not guns and tanks but the relations of capital within the working class, the deals that different sectors of it make with capital, that hold the workers back. According to James, the working class develops through the overcoming of internal antagonisms, not external foes. He saw a civil war within the ranks of the working class and within the mind of each individual worker: two ways of looking at the world, not necessarily fully articulated, manifest in different sorts of behavior. Consistent with this notion, he saw the autonomous activities of groups within the working class as a crucial part of its self-development. As a Marxist, James believed that the working class, "united, disciplined, and organized by the very mechanism of capitalist production," had a special role to play in carrying the revolution through to the end. But he also believed that the struggles of other groups had their own validity and that they represented challenges to the working people as a whole to build a society free of the domination of one class over another. In "The Revolutionary Answer to the Negro Problem in the USA," he opposed "any attempt to subordinate or push to the rear the social and political significance of the independent Negro struggle for democratic rights."[5] In that same work, written long before the Black Power movement, James spoke of the need for a mass movement responsible only to the black people, outside of the control of any of the Left parties.

He and his colleagues adopted a similar attitude toward the struggles of women and youth. "A Woman's Place" (1950), produced by members of the tendency led by James, examined the daily life of working-class women in the home, the neighborhood, and the factory, and took an unequivocal stand on the side of women's autonomy. They brought the same insights to the struggle of youth.

James also paid close attention to the struggle against colonialism. In 1938, he wrote *The Black Jacobins: Toussaint L'Ouverture and the San Domingo Revolution*.[6] In it he spoke of the tremendous creative force of the colonized peoples of Africa and the West Indies and established the link between the masses of San Domingo and the masses of Paris. His appreciation of the struggles of black people, of women, of youth, and of the colonial peoples expressed his dialectical thinking. Here you have this revolutionary working class, said James, and at the same time you have the domination of capital, which also expresses itself within the working class. One of the places this conflict appeared was in culture.

The dominant tradition among Marxists held that popular culture is just brainwashing, a distraction from the class struggle. To James and his cothinkers, the point was: how do the outlines of the new world manifest themselves in culture? In *Mariners, Renegades and Castaways: The Story of Herman Melville and the World We Live In*, James demonstrated that the struggle for the new society was a struggle between different philosophies as they are lived.[7] (It is my personal favorite among his works; among other virtues, it offers the most exciting explanation I have ever read of the process of literary creation.) His autobiographical book on cricket, *Beyond a Boundary*, was not merely a sports book.[8] It was about the people he knew intimately in the West Indies and how their actions on the playing field showed the kind of people they were. There is a need for a similar study of basketball and the Afro-American people. Anybody can write about how black athletes are exploited by the colleges and later on by professional basketball and the TV and the shoe manufacturers—and all that is true. But for James the question was, How have the black people placed their stamp on the game and used it to express their vision of a new world?

Consider the figure of Michael Jordan in this light. Here is a person who has achieved self-powered flight. Every time he goes up with the ball, he is saying in your face to the society of exploitation and repression. His achievements are not his alone, but the product of an entire community with a history of struggle and resistance. The contrast between the general position of the Afro-American people, pinned to the ground, and the flight they have achieved on the basketball court is an example of the new society within the shell of the old. (I wrote this paragraph in 1992; since then, a book has appeared that does for basketball what James did for cricket: *Hoop Roots* by John Edgar Wideman.[9] Wideman has said he wrote it with a copy of *Beyond a Boundary* on his desk.)

The task of freeing that new society from what inhibits it led James to a certain concept of organization. It has been asserted that James opposed organization—more particularly, that he opposed any form of organization that assigned distinctive tasks to those who sought to dedicate their lives to making revolution. The general charge is easily refuted: James spent his whole life building organizations of one kind or another, from the International African Service Bureau in Britain to a sharecroppers' union in Missouri to the Workers and Farmers Party in Trinidad. The function of these organizations was not to "lead the working class" but to accomplish this or that specific task. The more particular charge requires closer examination.

James argued that, in industrial societies, in which the very mechanism of capitalist production unites, disciplines, and organizes the working class, in which people take for granted modern communications and mass movements, the idea that any self-perpetuating group of people can set itself up to lead the working class is reactionary and bankrupt. In other words, he was a determined opponent of the vanguard party idea. But he did more than curse the Stalinists (and Trotskyites, whom he called "the comedians of the vanguard party"): in *Notes on Dialectics: Hegel, Marx, Lenin*, he analyzed the organizational history of the workers' movement and showed that the vanguard party reflected a certain stage of its development.[10]

In that same work, James anticipated the new mass movements (France, Poland) that would erase the distinction between party and class. (He did not oppose the vanguard party for peasant countries, where he thought something like it might be necessary to mobilize and direct the mass movement—but even there he searched for ways to expand the area of autonomous activity. *Nkrumah and the Ghana Revolution*, a collection of articles and letters he wrote between 1958 and 1970, shows James grappling with the problem of leadership in a country where the forces of production are undeveloped.[11] It is the least satisfying of his works.)

In modern society, whoever leads the working class keeps it subordinated to capital. A revolutionary crisis is defined precisely by the breakdown of the traditional institutions and leadership of the working class. James argued that it was among the sectors of society least touched by official institutions that relations characteristic of the new society would first appear. It is not the job of the conscious revolutionaries to "organize" the mass movements; that is the job of union functionaries and other bureaucrats. James's rejection of the vanguard party, however, did not lead him to reject Marxist organization. For proof, one need only recall the great attention and energy he dedicated to building Facing Reality, an avowedly Marxist organization headquartered in Detroit with branches around the United States. (These efforts are recounted and documented in *Marxism for Our Times: C. L. R. James on Revolutionary Organization*, edited by Martin Glaberman.[12]) But what would the Marxist organization do? This is where it gets difficult. I once asked him that question and got from him the reply, "Its job is not to lead the workers." Very well, I said, but what was it to do? For an answer, I got the same: It was not to act like a vanguard party. It was obvious that James was not going to elaborate with me, a person who might for all he knew carry with him the vanguardist prejudices of the "left" he had been fighting for decades. I would have to extrapolate the answer from his works. To these, then, I turned.

In *Facing Reality*, coauthored by James, Grace Boggs, and Cornelius Castoriadis, in the section "What To Do and How to Do It," it says, "Its task is to recognize and record."[13] That is a start. Over the next few pages, *Facing Reality* lays out a plan for a popular paper that will document the new society as it emerges within the shell of the old. As should surprise no one, it is most concrete when discussing what was then called "The Negro Question in the United States":

> For the purpose of illustrating the lines along which the paper of the Marxist organization has to face its tasks (that is all we can do), we select two important issues, confined to relations among white and Negro workers, the largest sections of the population affected.
>
> 1) Many white workers who collaborate in the most democratic fashion in the plants continue to show strong prejudice against association with Negroes outside the plant.
>
> 2) Many Negroes make race relations a test of all other relations . . .
>
> What, then, is the paper of the Marxist organization to do? . . .
>
> Inside such a paper Negro aggressiveness takes its proper place as one of the forces helping to create the new society. If a white worker . . . finds that articles or letters expressing Negro aggressiveness on racial questions makes the whole paper offensive to him, that means it is he who is putting his prejudices on the race question before the interests

of the class as a whole. He must be reasoned with, argued with, and if necessary fought to a finish.

How is he to be reasoned with, argued with, and if necessary fought to a finish? First by making it clear that his ideas, his reasons, his fears, his prejudices also have every right in the paper . . .

The paper should actively campaign for Negroes in the South to struggle for their right to vote and actually to vote . . . If Negroes outside of the South vote, now for the Democratic Party and now for the Republican, they have excellent reasons for doing so, and their general activity shows that large numbers of them see voting and the struggle for Supreme Court decisions merely as one aspect of a totality. They have no illusions. The Marxist organization retains and expresses its own view. But it understands that it is far more important, within the context of its own political principles, of which the paper is an expression, within the context of its own publications, meetings, and other activities in its own name, within the context of its translations and publications of the great revolutionary classics and other literature, that the Negroes make public their own attitudes and reasons for their vote. [Published 1958; given the massive disenfranchisement of black people in 2000, 2004, and 2008, which no major or minor candidate has chosen to make an issue, it might not be a bad thing if revolutionaries, without abandoning their view of the electoral system, were to join in a campaign on behalf of prisoners' right to vote.—NI]

Such in general is the function of the paper of a Marxist organization in the United States on the Negro question. It will educate, and it will educate above all white workers in their understanding of the Negro question and into a realization of their own responsibility in ridding American society of the cancer of racial discrimination and racial consciousness. The Marxist organization will have to fight for its own position, but its position will not be the wearisome repetition of "Black and White, Unite and Fight." It will be a resolute determination to bring all aspects of the question into the open, within the context of the recognition that the new society exists and that it carries within itself much of the sores and diseases of the old.[14]

While the above passage focuses on the role of a paper, it provides a guide for other aspects of work. James's approach was in the best tradition of Lenin (whom James much admired). Lenin, it must be remembered, did not invent the soviets (councils). What he did, that no one else at the time was able to do, not even the workers who invented them, was to recognize in the soviets the political form of the new society. The slogan he propagated, "All Power to the Soviets," represented the intervention of the Marxist intellectual in the revolutionary process. In basing his policy on the soviets, those "spontaneous" creations of the Russian workers, he was far removed from what has come to be understood as vanguardism.

I recall once in the factory, a group of workers walking out in response to a plant temperature of 100 degrees-plus with no fans. Our little group, schooled in the teachings of James and Lenin, understanding that the walkout represented a way of dealing with grievances outside of the whole management–union contract system, agitated for a meeting to discuss how to make that walkout the starting point of a new shop-floor organization based on direct action.

That was not vanguardism but critical intervention.

Another example from personal experience: I once worked a midnight shift in a metalworking plant. There were two other workers in the department on that shift, Jimmy and Maurice. Maurice had been having money troubles, which caused him to drink more than he should, which led to missed days and more trouble on the job, which led to troubles at home, etc. I came to work one night after missing the previous night, and Jimmy told me that Maurice had brought a pistol to the plant the night before, planning to shoot the general foreman if he reprimanded him in the morning about his attendance. "Did you try to stop him?" I asked. "No, what for?" queried Jimmy. "What happened?" I responded. "When the foreman came in," explained Jimmy, "instead of stopping to hassle Maurice, he just said hello and kept going to his office. He doesn't know how close he came to dying."

I, of course, did not want Maurice to shoot the general foreman because I did not want him to spend the rest of his life in prison for blowing away an individual who was no worse than the generality of his type. Jimmy looked at matters differently: for him, Maurice's life was already a prison that could be salvaged by one dramatic NO, regardless of the consequences. Who was right? Well, I had read all the books and knew that ninety-nine times out of a hundred nothing would come of Maurice's action: the plant guards or the cops would take him away or kill him on the spot. But on the hundredth time, something different might happen: the workers would block the plant guards, fight the cops, and the next thing you knew you had the mutiny on the Potemkin. The new society is the product of those two kinds of knowledge, Jimmy's and mine, and neither could substitute for the other. As a person who had decided to devote his life to revolution, my job was to Recognize and Record the new society as it made its appearance.

In 1969, a black worker at a Los Angeles aircraft plant, Isaac ("Ike") Jernigan, who had been harassed by management and the union and then fired for organizing black workers, brought a gun to work and killed a foreman; then he went to the union hall and killed two union officials. Our Chicago group published a flyer calling for workers to rally to his defense. Not much came of it until the League of Revolutionary Black Workers in Detroit reprinted our flyer in their paper. A Chrysler worker, James Johnson, responding to a history of unfair treatment including a suspension for refusing speedup, killed two foremen and a job setter and was escorted from the plant saying "Long Live Ike Jernigan."

The League waged a mass campaign on Johnson's behalf, including rallies on the courthouse steps, while carrying out a legal defense based on a plea of temporary insanity. The high point of the trial came when the jury was led on a tour through Chrysler; it found for the defense, concluding that working at Chrysler was indeed enough to drive a person insane. (This was Detroit, and many people already knew that to be true.) Johnson was acquitted and sent to a mental hospital instead of to prison; as an added insult, Chrysler was ordered to pay him workmen's compensation. Such was the political power contained in the simple words, Recognize and Record.

The task of revolutionaries is not to organize the workers but to organize themselves—to discover those patterns of activity and forms of organization that have sprung up out of the struggle and that embody the new society, and to help them grow stronger, more confident, and more conscious of their direction. It is an essential contribution to the society of disciplined spontaneity, which for James was the definition of the new world.

The two works that follow illustrate James's worldview. *The Invading Socialist Society* was published in 1947 under the authorship of James, F. Forest (Raya Dunayevskaya), and Ria Stone (Grace Lee Boggs) as part of a discussion within the Trotskyist Fourth International.[15] Inevitably it bears the marks of its birth, and some readers will be put off by the unfamiliar names and context. That would be unfortunate. As James wrote in his preface to the 1962 edition, "The reader can safely ignore or not bother himself about the details of these polemics, because *The Invading Socialist Society* is one of the key documents, in fact, in my opinion it is the fundamental document" of his political tendency. I shall not attempt to list its main points, but merely urge readers to note the astonishing degree to which it anticipated subsequent events, including the French General Strike of 1968 and the Polish Solidarity of 1980, which together marked the transcendence of the old vanguard party by the politicized nation, and the collapse of the Soviet Union and its satellites, and with it the collapse of the illusion that there ever existed more than one world system.

The second document, "Every Cook Can Govern," published in 1956 and written for a general audience, was equally prophetic.[16] It is short enough, and rather than attempt to list its main points, I urge readers to read it bearing in mind the counterposing of representative and direct democracy that became so important to Student Non-Violent Coordinating Committee and other components of the New Left of the 1960s (best described in Chapter 14 of *Ready for Revolution: The Life and Struggles of Stokely Carmichael* by Stokely Carmichael and Ekwueme Michael Thelwell).[17]

Together, these two works represent the principal themes that run through James's life: implacable hostility toward all "condescending saviors" of the working class, and undying faith in the power of ordinary people to build a new world.

38

Modern Politics

_____

This introduction was written for PM Press's 2013 republication of C. L. R. James's Modern Politics, *a collection of six lectures James delivered in 1960 in his native Trinidad. It was based on a speech Ignatiev gave at the Joel Olson's Memorial Conference at Northern Arizona University in 2013.*

———

Modern Politics consists of a series of lectures C. L. R. James delivered in 1960 at the Adult Education Center in Port-of-Spain, Trinidad.[1] During his twenty-five-year absence from his native land, James had become known to a few in the radical movement as the founder and leader of a distinctive current of Marxism and more widely as a writer on sports, history, philosophy, and culture, and he had been recognized as one of the pioneers of West Indian independence.[2] The lectures are a survey of Western civilization. Why did James, a black man who knew the crimes of the West firsthand, speaking to a mostly black audience of colonials, choose to lecture on Western civilization?

James is seeking to explain the meaning of socialism. For him, socialism is complete democracy. Therefore, he begins the first lecture with democracy in the ancient Greek city-state. He tells us why: "because I could not do without it." The Greeks invented direct democracy.[3]

From Greece he goes to Rome and the Revelations of St. John. He says he chose John because he was a colonial subject of Rome. John had a sense of historic sweep, and in his vision of God's Kingdom he was addressing the questions that occupied the Greeks, above all the relation of the individual and the collective.

From the ancient world James moves to the city-states of the Middle Ages and to the class struggles that tore them apart. He talks about the English Civil War and the birth of a new form of government, representative democracy,[4] citing Shakespeare, "the great dramatist of individual character," as an example of the emerging spirit. (James referred to Shakespeare frequently in his works; a series of lectures on Shakespeare he delivered on the BBC has been lost.) He takes up philosophy, the Age of Reason, and Rousseau's repudiation of that way of thinking and of representative government. After touching on the American and French revolutions, he ends the lecture by defining the problem he will be addressing:

> Much of our study of modern politics is going to be concerned with this tremendous battle to find a form of government which reproduces, on a more highly developed economic level, the relationship between the individual and the community that was established so wonderfully in the Greek City-State.[5]

The classics of the West have shaped the modern world. The European Renaissance was a moment of world-historic significance, and the great works of antiquity were sources of it. It is impossible to deny these facts. However, to accept a genealogy in which "ancient Greece begat Rome, Rome begat Christian Europe, Christian Europe begat the Renaissance, the Renaissance the Enlightenment, the Enlightenment political democracy and the industrial revolution" and so forth is misleading.[6]

The ancient Greeks traced their culture back to Egypt.[7] Egypt drew upon the Upper Nile (modern Sudan). The Book of Genesis came from Mesopotamia; according to the biblical account, Abraham was an Iraqi shepherd. During the Hellenistic age, Greece faced east, not west; Alexander the Great conquered Persia, and Persia conquered Alexander. Christian doctrine drew heavily on notions that were circulating widely in the Eastern Mediterranean, including matings between gods and humans, virgin birth, the Messiah, resurrection, and afterlife.[8]

Following the "fall" of Rome, Byzantium and the Islamic world preserved the works of the Greeks and Romans and kept alive the classical traditions of humanism and scientific inquiry. Islam was influenced by East and West.

Cultures are not products of separate regions isolated from each other.

Settled agriculture, urban life, patriarchal religion, and the state were born in the Tigris-Euphrates Valley around 7000 BCE. The first literary object to emerge from Britain that anyone from anywhere else would take any interest in was Beowulf, c. 1000 CE. In other words, about 8,000 years elapsed between the birth of what is called civilization and anything of literary value from Britain, 3,000 miles away. Yet that vast gap in time and space did not prevent the inhabitants of Britain from going on to lead the world in producing works from Chaucer to Jane Austen and beyond that illuminated the human condition everywhere. Nor has it stopped them from asserting their ownership of literary works they had no direct hand in producing.

And that is as it should be. Everything created by human beings anywhere is and ought to be the property of all human beings everywhere. I used to know a poet who called Milton black. On being asked why, she replied, "Well, I'm black and I like him." C. L. R. James would have agreed with her. (He refers to *Paradise Lost* in these lectures, comparing it to the Revelations of St. John.)

———

Class struggle is a constant theme in the lectures. Whether talking about fifteenth-century Flemish city-states or twentieth-century Detroit, James stresses the class struggle as the force that drives history. When I met James, he asked me what I did for a living. I told him I worked in a factory. He said he regretted that he had never had the opportunity to do that. I naturally replied that his writings had helped me make sense of my own experience. Yes, he said, people have told me that, but I still wish I had experienced it directly. In order to illustrate James's worldview and as partial repayment for what he taught me, I shall here recount some things I saw in twenty-three years as a worker in industry.

I once had a job operating a horizontal boring mill in a plant that manufactured punch presses, machine tools, and die sets. My job was to bore holes and mill contours on large—often 6′ × 8′—steel slabs to be made into die sets to customers' specifications. The mill was an old-fashioned, manually controlled machine, well built and originally quite expensive, capable of turning out high-quality work.

The plant operated on an incentive-pay system: each job was time-rated for the machine on which it was to be performed, and the operator received a bonus for all he or she managed to produce above the eight-hour norm. Jobs varied, but the bonus could account for as much as half the total wage for one worker.

In order to be fair to the employees on the bonus system—and the company was nothing if not fair—it was necessary to make allowances for the time spent outside of direct production, sharpening tools, loading parts on the machine (including waiting for the overhead crane when it was occupied elsewhere), filling the coolant tank, and so forth. The allowances were recorded through red computer-coded cards punched in a clock.

When I started on the job, one of the veteran operators called me aside and explained the system. "You see those red cards?" he asked, pointing at the rack where they were stacked. "If the company won't give you a raise, you take those red cards and give yourself a raise. That's what they're for."

I took his advice and studied hard and soon became sufficiently adept with the red cards to assure myself several hours' bonus most days. I remember one of the operators asking me what I considered the most valuable tool in my box. I held up a pencil.

To lower costs the company installed a new tape-controlled mill, able to do more or less the same work as the one I was on in about half the time. They then reset the standards, reducing the time allotted for all jobs, even those still being sent to the old machine. Our bonuses evaporated.

There were three of us on the horizontal mill, one on each shift. We petitioned for a return to the old rates. The company denied our petition. With the new rates, the most we could turn out, even with intense effort and trouble-free operation, was six hours' production. Why should we strain ourselves to make the same hourly rate we could make by coasting? We slowed down.

As I recall, our slowdown was undertaken without a single meeting among the three of us. (Our different shifts meant we were never all together, although each of us saw the other two every day.) One of us—I no longer remember who—simply announced one day to the operator coming after him, "I'm fed up with this. I gave them an hour and a half tonight and that's all I'm doing from now on." The next operator followed his lead, and it became standard practice on reporting for work to inquire of the departing operator how much he had turned out and to do the same or less. After a few weeks we had established our own norm, around three quarters of an hour each shift.

Of course the company did not like what was going on, but without assigning a foreman to observe each of us full-time, how were they to know when a tool burned up and needed replacing or how long the operator needed to wait for a new one to be ground when the tool crib was out of the required tool or when the coolant in the machine needed replenishing or when the crane was occupied or out of order or the crane operator was on break—or any of the mysteries of a horizontal boring mill operator's life, each faithfully recorded on a red card and entered into the computer that never lies?

Things went along for a while with us pretending to work and the company pretending to pay us, until one day the general foreman announced that since production on the horizontal mill was so low, the company was eliminating one of the three operators. Since I was the newest, the ax would fall on me. I was offered a choice: I could take a layoff or I could retrain on the tape-controlled machine. I chose the latter and was soon third-shift operator. The other two horizontal mill operators continued their slowdown without me. Shortly afterward, the company transferred them to another department and sold the machine to a salvage company for a fraction of its cost.

The episode was a small example of Marx's observation that the class struggle led either to a revolutionary reconstitution of the society or the common ruin of the contending classes. The three of us had destroyed that horizontal mill just as effectively as if we had taken a torch and sledgehammer to it. Although it remained physically intact and capable of performing the tasks for which it had been designed and built, it no longer existed as capital, the only form of value in a capitalist society.

———

The Tractor Works of the International Harvester Company was located across the street from the McCormick Reaper Works, the original plant of the Harvester Company and scene of the eight-hour-day strike of 1886 that led to the May First holiday. In 1940, when the Congress of Industrial Organizations finally forced Harvester to recognize it as the bargaining agent, Lucy Parsons—labor organizer and widow of Albert

Parsons, martyred in 1886—declared to assembled workers, "Now I know my husband didn't die in vain."

One of the products of the plant was earth-moving tractors. (Although foremen insisted that the proper term for that type of tractor was the generic "crawler," the workers perversely referred to them as "Caterpillars.") One of the customers was the government, which used them to fill bomb craters in Vietnam. The standard joke was that the soldiers drove them into the craters and shoveled dirt on top of them.

By 1968 the inmates were running the asylum. Wishing to recover the ability to plan production, Harvester launched a campaign against absenteeism, beginning by seeking to fire the worst offenders. They called in the chairman of the union grievance committee and showed him the record of one especially flagrant case showing seventeen dates over the span of a year.

"Why you bastards," yelled the committeeman, "you want to fire this guy and he's only missed seventeen days, and you don't even know what kind of problems he's been having . . ." and so on.

"Hold on, Bill," replied the personnel director. "These aren't the days he missed. These are the days he came to work last year."

What everyone in the plant knew, which never came out in the hearing, was that the guy had started up an ice cream parlor on the outside and was spending all his time there, hanging onto his job at Harvester for the health insurance. The most Harvester could get was a thirty-day suspension—like throwing Br'er Rabbit in the briar patch.

———

When I started in the steel mills, I was astonished at the extent to which the workers there had established control over the workday. In part, the power of the workers was a consequence of the way steel was produced: once the iron ore, coke, and limestone are in the furnace, they can't be drilled, or assembled, or stacked up, or any of the other things done on assembly lines. The technique is not the whole story, however, because the steel companies were always trying to combine jobs to make people work during the slack time dictated by the furnaces. The workers resisted them at every turn: In 1959 there was a three-month strike over job descriptions, just the visible tip of the ongoing war. At Harvester's subsidiary, Wisconsin Steel, the management tried for several years to replace the system whereby workers picked up their time cards at the mill entrance and handed them in to the foremen in their work areas to one in which they punched in at the entrance. The workers responded with several strikes, which appeared a mystery—why should people care where they hand in their cards? Talking to the workers revealed that many of them had private arrangements with their foremen which allowed them to hand in their cards and then disappear for the rest of their shift. Having to hand in their time cards at the entrance to plant guards they did not know would have interfered with these arrangements.

I remember at US Steel a foreman once came into a shanty where a bunch of maintenance workers were sitting around, some drinking coffee, some playing cards, some snoozing, and asked two of them to go out and see about a certain piece of equipment that was broken.

"Can't you see I'm busy?" said one of them as he picked up the cards for the next deal.

"We'll get it when the rain stops," said another.

The foreman exited, apparently satisfied that he had got the most he could from that group at that moment. That situation prevailed among maintenance more than production workers, and the line between them partly corresponded to the color line—but not entirely. I once asked a fellow worker, a black woman, why there were so few wildcat strikes in the steel mill compared to a nearby auto plant well known for their frequency. Without hesitating she said, "It's because people here are always on strike."[9]

Her answer stood out against the attitude of one of the more prominent left-wing trade unionists in the Calumet area, whom I visited shortly after I began work in the mill. I asked him about the movement of workers in the industry.

"What movement?" he replied. "There is no movement."

I knew that in his mill the workers in some departments were making their rates in half a shift and spending the other half in the tavern nearby. I asked him about it. "That's not a movement," he said. "They've been doing that for years. It doesn't mean anything."

To him "movement" meant the number of workers who attended union meetings, voted for the resolutions introduced by his caucus, and supported his slate at election time. The accumulation of shop-floor battles that had ripped half the day out of the hands of capital was not part of the class struggle as it existed in his mind.

C. L. R. James taught me to see otherwise. So did Marx, who devoted a chapter in *Capital* to the struggle over the length of the working day.

Of all the dogmas that hold sway among leftists, the most widespread and pernicious is the dogma of the backwardness of the working class. To adhere to it is to reject Marxism root and branch, for Marxism holds that the capitalist system revolutionizes the forces of production and that the working class is foremost among the forces of production.

A black woman I worked with told me that when she first started in a new position at the plant as a crane operator, she got no help from the others in the department, all white men. Contrary to their usual practice, whenever she was on the crane they would hook up the loads so that they were hard to move, and in general did what they could to make her job more difficult than necessary. After a few weeks she called them all together and delivered a speech: "Listen, you motherfuckers, I'm not asking for special consideration. I just want to be respected as a crane operator. I've got rent to pay and babies to feed just like you, so I don't care what you do, you're not running me out of here."

They changed their attitudes and became totally cooperative. Let no one think the victory was hers alone: she was a harbinger of the new society:

> [a] fully developed individual, fit for a variety of labors, ready to face any change of production, to whom the different social functions [s]he performs are but so many modes of giving free scope to [her] own natural and acquired powers.[10]

James's revolutionary optimism was inspired and sustained by his deep appreciation for the kinds of experiences I have recounted. Those experiences were hallmarks of the period when large numbers of workers were brought together in factories and where they had the opportunity, and took it, to impose some control over their work circumstances, taking advantage of the cover provided by a union and contract. Today, in the United States, the ability of workers to assert that kind of control in a single workplace is diminished. The situation may be different in India and China.

If James teaches us anything, he teaches us to look. I knew a radical in 1969 who took a job as a truck driver and after a few weeks reported that the chances of collective action among truck drivers were slim since their work dictated that they be isolated as individuals instead of being brought together in large concentrations. Then someone invented the CB radio, and the result was a national wildcat strike of owner operators. In part out of fear of working-class strength, capital broke up or greatly reduced in size the large centers of proletarian concentration, the River Rouges, the Gary Works, the FIAT Mirafiori works. Yet in pursuit of its own need to coordinate production (including research) and distribution on a world scale, capital gave us the internet, with the result that a man who sets himself on fire in Tunisia in protest against high prices touches off a wave of struggle that topples a government in Egypt, which in turn serves as an example to people in Madison, Wisconsin, which inspires the Occupy movement (which seems to have gone into fatal decline, to be surely followed by new struggles).

James has been criticized for failing to acknowledge or explain defeats in the class struggle. Like any person engaged in serious day-to-day politics, he found it necessary to take into account and adapt to setbacks.[11] But his overall outlook led him to seek out the future in the present. In this respect he brings to mind the abolitionist Wendell Phillips, who declared in a speech following John Brown's raid on Harpers Ferry, "What is defeat? Nothing but education—nothing but the first step to something better"—and was proven right within a few years.

———————————

It was James's custom to speak without notes, and there is every reason to believe that he delivered these lectures that way (although they may have been edited later for publication). He was able to do so because he had thoroughly mastered his subject matter. Like a great athlete who pulls off amazing feats on the court, his mastery was due to the countless hours he put in off the court or the lectern. In *Modern Politics* James stresses that philosophy must become proletarian, which is to be understood as the need for philosophers to embrace the proletariat and the proletariat to embrace philosophy. Whatever our disappointments and difficulties at the moment, his wisdom needs to be reaffirmed. Not long ago I took part in a two-person panel at a conference of mostly young activists. The panel was set up as a debate, and each of us circulated well in advance a five-page essay we believed would help the discussion.

When my turn came to speak, I asked that those who had not read the essays refrain from speaking in the discussion that would follow our opening remarks. I do not know how many of those who spoke had read the material we circulated, and I had no way of enforcing my request. Afterwards, one person, who had not spoken, came up to me and said she was offended, saying she felt "disempowered" by my request that she not take part. I replied that I had not asked her not to take part, merely not to speak, and that she was welcome to listen. My reply made no difference. I later learned that others shared her feelings; anti-intellectualism is widespread in radical circles, infecting many dedicated activists. I asked myself, what would C. L. R. James (or Malcolm X) have said?

James devotes part of the final lecture to what he calls "the undying vision," a survey of works of art he believes point the way toward the future. He names D. W. Griffith, Chaplin, and Picasso. All of them, he argues, were shaped by the need to serve a popular audience. Elsewhere he had said the same about the Greeks and Shakespeare. One of my teachers in high school, Dr. Gordon, told us that if we had gone up to someone on the street in London in 1605 and asked the names of the best poets, the answer would have been Marlowe or Donne or Jonson. If we had asked about Shakespeare, our informant would have slapped his upper leg and said, Will Shakespeare—why, he's the best playwright in town! Theater was seen as popular entertainment, not serious literature. Dr. Gordon would have shared James's view. If Shakespeare were alive today, he would be writing for the movies.

James concludes, "Anyone who tries to prevent you from knowing, from learning anything, is an enemy, an enemy of freedom, of equality, of democracy." His words were prophetic: Scarcely were the lectures published in book form than Prime Minister Williams ordered the books suppressed, placing them under guard in a warehouse in Port of Spain. In his Introduction to the 1973 edition of *Modern Politics*, Martin Glaberman provides the context; I won't repeat what he wrote. James left Trinidad. Later, when he reentered the country, Williams placed him under house arrest. Thus James joined the long and honorable list of those who were locked up for what they wrote.

One turns to C. L. R. James for many reasons. If pressed I would say *Mariners, Renegades and Castaways: The Story of Herman Melville and the World We Live In* is my favorite among his works.[12] Yet for comprehensiveness, integration of history, philosophy, culture, politics and method, as an introduction to Marxism and socialism for new readers, *Modern Politics* is in first place. John Bracey, who was part of the group that brought James back to the States in 1967, tells of the time James called his attention to a football game on television: "Look at that, Bracey," he said, "black people beating up white people on TV—capitalism is doomed." It is hard to imagine an anecdote that captures and brings together so many different facets of C. L. R. James. *Modern Politics* is that story elaborated over six lectures.

39

Alternative Institutions or Dual Power?

This essay was prepared for a talk Ignatiev gave at the Radical Book Pavilion at the Baltimore Book Fair in 2010. He explains the revolutionary strategy of dual power and how it differs from the effort to build alternative institutions on the margins of capitalist society.

Today I want to talk about strategy for revolution. As Malcolm X said, I want to have a conversation between you and me, us. On my way here I picked up a copy of the *Indypendent Reader*, which on its masthead carries the slogan "toward building a new society on the vacant lots of the old . . ." The paper contains good articles, some written by people I know to be revolutionaries. But I want to focus on the slogan, to use it to talk about strategy. It was obviously put forward with one eye on the old Industrial Workers of the World (IWW) slogan, Building the New Society within the Shell of the Old. The IWW sought to develop a counterpower. The Indy slogan means developing alternative institutions. The two are not the same.

What are alternative institutions? Infoshops, bookstores, free schools, coops, community gardens are all examples. These may be worthwhile projects, but they are not examples of counterpower because they do not represent a threat to capital. In fact, they are compatible with it.

Things are entirely different with counterpower.

One of the earliest expositions of its meaning, if not the earliest, was by Lenin when he returned to Russia in April 1917 shortly after the fall of the czar. I know many of you do not like to hear me quoting Lenin, but I urge you to pay attention. Whatever you think of the course Lenin followed once in power, you must admit he understood something about making a revolution, and therefore you can learn from him.

In "The Tasks of the Proletariat in Our Revolution," Lenin wrote:

> The main feature of our revolution, a feature that most imperatively demands thoughtful consideration, is the *dual power* which arose in the very first days after the triumph of the revolution.
>
> This dual power is evident in the existence of *two* governments: one is the main, the real, the actual government of the bourgeoisie, the "Provisional Government" . . . the other is a supplementary and parallel government . . . in the shape of the Petrograd Soviet of Workers' and Soldiers' Deputies . . .
>
> This remarkable feature . . . has led to the *interlocking of two* dictatorships: the dictatorship of the bourgeoisie . . . and the dictatorship of the proletariat and the peasantry (the Soviet of Workers' and Soldiers' Deputies).
>
> There is not the slightest doubt that such an "interlocking" cannot last long. Two powers *cannot exist* in a state. One of them is bound to pass away.[1]

In that situation Lenin put forward the slogan "No support to the provisional government. All Power to the Soviets."

Lenin and the Bolsheviks did not invent the Soviets (councils). They were invented by the workers and soldiers. In periods of upsurge ordinary people (people who do not normally spend their time thinking about how to make a revolution) do very revolutionary things, far more revolutionary than any individual or party could imagine. But they think of them in old ways.

Lenin and the Bolsheviks did what the workers could not do by themselves: recognize the soviets as the germ of the new society and pose them consciously against the institutions that integrate the workers and all the oppressed into official society.

No revolution has ever taken place without a period of dual power. The masses of ordinary people will not transfer their allegiance from the dominant institutions, an allegiance based largely on habit, to a new society unless the institutions of the new society already exist in tangible form. At the same time, every popular upheaval gives rise to institutions that prefigure the new society. The contending powers may be separated geographically, as in the US Civil War or the liberated zones in China, Vietnam, Cuba, and perhaps Chiapas, or by sphere, as they were in Russia.

The above were situations of general crisis. Do conditions prevail at present in the United States such that dual power is a relevant notion? Well, certainly no one would claim that the United States today is in the grip of an immediate crisis comparable to what existed in Russia between February and October 1917.

But it may be tomorrow. Every modern society, the United States included, no matter how stable it appears, is but one step away from a general breakdown in which the existing institutions collapse and the issue of power is posed. Consider the following nightmare scenario: a decline in public revenues due to the deepening financial crisis, such that public authorities are unable to pay public workers or are forced to pay them in worthless scrip. Bridges, roads, and rail-beds falling apart (that is already happening) so that the transport of food becomes unreliable, police and firemen on slowdown because they have not been paid, perhaps most important of all sanitation workers without wages. Under those circumstances, is an outbreak of plague inconceivable? If things reached that point, would it not fall upon the general population to take into their hands the task of maintaining order, collecting the garbage, purifying the drinking supply, etc.? That is the situation that prevailed in Germany at the end of World War II, and only the presence of the occupying armies prevented the German working people from taking power.

Every genuine struggle against entrenched power brings forward forms of dual power. Factory workers slowing down an assembly line by direct action, cubicle workers surfing the internet on company time or using the company's equipment to communicate with their friends, fast-food or grocery workers deliberately undercharging customers—most of the examples in daily life are too fragile, small in scale, and sporadic to take on political meaning, but all of them taken together represent the new society. At what point do revolutionaries transfer their attention from the institutions that represent the oppressed within the existing society to these admittedly weak and often barely visible elements of the new? I once asked a member of a socialist organization that claimed to uphold a strategy of dual power, at what point do we shift our attention from work within the unions and the various reform movements that seek to exert pressure on the government and give central place to the elements of the new society that spring up like mushrooms after a summer rain—drawing a line between them and the existing reform institutions, doing what we can to link them together, differentiate them from the old, and clarify their implications? Do we wait until they enjoy the support of 51 percent of the population? He was unable to answer.

For me, the answer is easy: the time is now. We revolutionaries are against representation and in favor of direct democracy. We are against the unions, which seek better terms in the sale of labor power, and in favor of abolishing the sale of labor power. Instead of reforming the economy we want to abolish the economy, and in its place put community. We are enemies of the nation-state, the family, the white race, and everything else that is respectable in the society. "We hate this rotten system more than any mortals do/ Our aim is not to patch it but to build it all anew." Our political intervention must reflect that sentiment, not leave it on the shelf to be hauled out for holiday speeches.

How to do that? I would be the first to admit that I am not flowing over with brilliant ideas. But for revolutionaries, it is the main question worth asking.

Can alternative institutions serve revolutionary strategy? In some ways and under certain circumstances, yes. They may provide valuable examples of what the new society might look like and space for people to mobilize to achieve it. The aim is not a food coop but rather the organization of the workers in agriculture and transport to convert the production of food into production for use instead of for profit. I doubt the Free School will ever replace Johns Hopkins or the public schools, but if it provides a space for students to organize to revolutionize the schools and the university, then it will have justified the sacrifices people are putting into it. I doubt that the *Indypendent* quarterly will ever replace the *Baltimore Sun*, but if it provides space and inspiration for workers at the *Baltimore Sun* to take over their place of employment and turn it into a public resource, then the *Indypendent* will have served a revolutionary function.

40
Race or Class?

In this incisive intervention, Ignatiev reminds revolutionaries considering race and class that the objective is not to prioritize one over the other but to specify how they intersect and interact in everyday life.

There are those who think that because something is about class it cannot also be about race. I am not one of them. There are those who think that because something is about race it cannot also be about class. I am not one of them, either. The task is to specify the relation of race and class.

There was a time when the task of subjugating black people was carried out by the mass of ordinary whites, in return for which they were socially defined as part of the dominant race. While "white" laborers did not in general receive a share of the profits extracted from the exploitation of black labor and were often cruelly exploited, they were the favored slaves of capital, holding a monopoly of the better jobs, standing at the front of the hiring line and the rear of the layoff line, and partaking in what Du Bois called a "public and psychological wage"—in other words, the privileges of whiteness. At that time the black "bourgeoisie" (such as it was) played little role in keeping the masses down, and class divisions within the black community were relatively unimportant. As a symbol of who enforced control, in 1940 there was not a single black policeman in any Deep South state, where more than half the black population lived, and few elsewhere.

The triumph of the civil rights movement gave rise to a layer of black people, north and south, whose job is to administer the misery of the black poor, often in the name of "Black Power." Black mayors, police chiefs, city councilmen, prison officials, superintendents of boards of education and welfare departments, and heads of foundations now do the job once done by whites, who as a consequence have lost a great deal of their social function and the status attached to it. I am not suggesting that the privileges of whiteness no longer exist; but changes in the economy and the decline of many institutions that used to guarantee them— in the first place, the unions—mean that they are no longer what they were. Some whites have accepted the changes without much fuss: two out of five voted for Barack Obama in 2012; whatever they thought they were voting for, clearly it was not traditional white supremacy. Of the three-fifths who did not vote for him, not all can be assumed to have voted for white supremacy, although some certainly did. Current battles over the Confederate flag reflect the unwillingness of some whites to accept the changes, but the direction of the wind is shown by the vote of the Memphis City Council to take down the statue of the number-one war criminal, Nathan Bedford Forrest, and disinter his remains and those of his wife, as part of a national wave of casting off Confederate icons since the massacre at the church in Charleston, South Carolina.

The changes in the mechanisms of control are not limited to high-level administrators: many of the police in the black neighborhoods are black, along with social workers, schoolteachers, corrections officers, etc. It used to be that poor black people who went to the Social Security office or the DMV were insulted and humiliated by white clerks; now they are insulted and humiliated by black clerks. Because of the peculiar history of America, in which white men have sought to protect their most precious property, their women, black progress is gendered; that is, while black professional women have unprecedented visibility in situations from which they were previously excluded, black men are seen as dangerous and still can't get a taxi in New York City. Many of these people themselves face racial oppression: Trayvon Martin's mother was a corrections officer, and it didn't save her son.

The immiseration of the black poor and the existence of a privileged layer of black professionals in previously white spheres appear to be in conflict: How could such progress exist alongside such misery? We've come a long way, say the pundits, but there is still a long way to go. That is a completely wrongheaded way to look at it. In fact, there is a necessary connection between the two phenomena: neither could exist without the other; that is, without black faces behind desks, no force could stop the masses of black poor from tearing the country apart; and on the other hand, without the threat of the black poor there would be no black faces behind desks. *To understand the relationship between black progress and black genocide is the heart of class analysis today.*

The supreme example of the interaction of class and race is President Obama. Is he the target of attacks that would not be directed at him if he were not black? He certainly is, and it is lucky for him that he is, because without those attacks the masses of black people and hopeful whites who looked to him to lead the country out of the mess would see him as "a child-murdering imperialist" instead of a *black* child-murdering imperialist in whom they still have lingering hopes. Do I acknowledge the racial element in the attacks on him? Yes, I do. Do I sympathize with him? Yes, I do, and with his wife and daughters, and after I have shed my tears for the young men in Baltimore he labeled as "thugs" and for their mothers who whack their sons around in public to keep the police from killing them, I will send him a sympathy card, which I hope he will read while awaiting trial by an international tribunal for his crimes, along with Biden and Kerry, Bush, Cheney and Rumsfeld and the Clintons. But who has done more harm to black people, the vicious Spokane County, Washington mayor who called Michelle Obama "gorilla-face," or the First Lady's husband who presides over the institutions that condemn millions around the world to endless night?

A big failing of US political life today, affecting radicals like Cornel West, Harry Belafonte, and many others and including most progressive whites, is the insistence on seeing President Obama, Supreme Court Justice Clarence Thomas, former Chief of Staff Colin Powell, et al. as traitors to their race or, more gently, brothers gone astray, instead of as the class enemy, and until people make that breakthrough they will continue to be disappointed.

41

Race and Occupy: Remarks Delivered at Occupy Boston

This talk was given at the Occupy Boston encampment in 2011. Ignatiev invites the audience to imagine radically how to engage more racially oppressed people to join the largely white Occupy movement. He proposes that the movement embrace the demand of prison abolition as a way to reimagine the restructuring of society.

Every revolution is a surprise, above all to the revolutionaries. If you had gone around Paris on July 1, 1789, and asked people if there would be a revolution in two weeks, they would have looked at you with puzzlement. They would not have been able to answer because they did not know. I read a talk Lenin gave to members of his party in January 1917 in which he said, "We of the older generation may not live to see the changes that are coming, it will be up to you young people to carry the fight." Ten months later he was running the country. Clearly he was surprised by the events that took place. I have been taking part in revolutionary politics for more than a half-century, and I was surprised by this movement.

I was asked to speak about race. I think my title is "Race and Occupy." I have written and thought about race for many years, and I am honored that you thought enough of my work to invite me to address you. I am humbled by the initiative and determination you have shown in building the movement. In the spirit of helping to strengthen it, I hope to say one or two things of value.

The United States, like every country in the world, is divided into masters and slaves. For a long time the problem here has been that many of the slaves think they are masters because they think they are white. By white, I am not referring to skin color, but to some people's belief that they are represented in the society. They may not get everything they want, but at least they are heard.

That belief persisted for a reason. During most of US history the white skin represented a badge of citizenship and social advantage. It brought with it the right to vote and serve on juries, to work in all spheres of the economy, to live wherever its owners could afford, and to spend freely whatever money they had managed to acquire. Even if all overt discrimination had ceased with the passage of the Civil Rights bills— which is not the case—the effects of past inequalities would still be felt. As a great writer said, the past is never dead, it's not even past. The person whose parents and grandparents had a college degree or a skilled job has an advantage in a competitive society over the person whose parents or grandparents walked behind a mule or a mop.

Of course the white skin never guaranteed freedom and dignity; it was the consolation some people got for the absence of freedom and dignity. Now the consolation is not working as well as it once did, and the tremendous turnout for the Occupy movement on the part of people who are nominally classified as white is testimony to the erosion of their confidence in the value of the white skin.

Yet problems remain. The Occupy movement here and in other places is not fully representative of those who suffer the most. It is whiter than the population as a whole, and especially of the downtrodden. That is a problem, but it should not lead persons of good will to oppose the movement or to turn their backs on it. It does need to be discussed, and that is what I propose to do here.

In the past, challenges to white supremacy have exercised an influence far beyond the ranks of those taking direct part in them. The Abolitionist Movement gave rise to the women's movement and a movement against the Mexican War. In the 1960s the black freedom struggle inspired and encouraged the student, women's, Chicano, anti-war, and other movements and the counterculture. Of course, all those movements developed out of their own needs and had their specific concerns.

So far the state has been able to deal with all-white movements by selective concessions and repression. It finds it easy to isolate and repress an all-black movement. For reasons rooted in American history, a movement that brings together black and white is the most dangerous to the existing order. The question facing the Occupy movement is how to transform itself into a solid movement embracing both the racially privileged and the racially oppressed.

The Civil War broke out with both sides fighting for slavery—the South to take it out of the Union, the North to keep it in. What did the slaves do? They watched and waited. They were waiting to see if the dispute was merely a family quarrel among whites, in which case it would have been foolish for them to take sides, or whether it was serious. Once they were convinced that the North was determined not to allow things to go back to the old way, they intervened, by withdrawing their labor power from the plantation and enlisting in the Union Army. Their intervention decided the outcome.

The situation today is similar to that at the outbreak of the Civil War. I have not been sent here with a mandate to speak on behalf of black America, but I do pay attention. A number of black observers have pointed out that the conditions the Occupy movement is fighting against are what black America has been suffering from for years if not centuries and that the repression the movement faces is far less than what black Americans have faced. I feel safe in saying that the majority of black Americans are in sympathy with the goals of the Occupy movement and are watching it, waiting to see where it goes.

If that is the case, then the way to enlist more black folk in the movement is not by adding specific demands aimed at them in particular, but by demonstrating seriousness and radical vision. Part of that demonstration will be by showing persistence, creativity, and resistance to repression, including by means other than those deemed acceptable according to the rules of conventional politics. The famous words of Malcolm X—By Any Means Necessary—must become our motto. Another part of the demonstration will be by projecting a vision of a new society, so different from what exists that it will overturn all existing social categories, including race.

One of the most harmful effects of whiteness is that it cripples the imagination. We are trying to expand the power of the imagination. Can we project a vision that ties together the issue of race with the general potential of this movement?

The prison is probably the most important institution in the lives of black Americans. You know the statistics—black folk going to prison at five to ten times the rate for whites, one of every four black men between the ages of sixteen and fifty is in prison, awaiting trial, on parole, etc., more black men caught up in the penal system now than were enslaved in 1850.

Can the Occupy movement embrace a vision of a world without prisons? I don't mean prison reform. After 200 years of reform, the prisons are worse than ever. The only solution is total and unconditional abolition of prisons and the immediate release of all those confined within them.

Every thoughtful person knows that prison is a bad institution. In addition to the 2.5 million people held in cages, there are probably an equal number directly or indirectly involved in putting and keeping them there. They, too, are imprisoned. Yet I am sure that some of you regard immediate abolition as an unrealistic demand. Even if it is agreed that most people in prison are there as a result of accidental and unfortunate circumstances, the largest number being held for a $5 high, nevertheless, it may be pointed out that there are some bad people in those places. Who would want them walking around or living next door?

Prisons cannot be abolished without restructuring the entire society. It is precisely for that reason that I propose the movement embrace abolition as a goal. To make the commitment to a world without prisons is to invite people to think about alternate ways of living together. I notice you have posted a sign declaring this encampment to be a drug- and alcohol-free zone and announcing that you will escort from the premises anyone found to violate that policy. You adopted that policy after full discussion, and you enforce it directly, without the state's courts, judges, police, or prisons. I ask you to think about that example and imagine how you might extend it throughout the entire society. Think about the words of the Scottish poet, Robert Burns:

> A fig for those by law protected,
> Liberty's a glorious feast.
> Courts for judges were erected,
> Churches built to please the priest.

The present discussion of prison abolition reminds me of the debate over slavery. Before the Civil War most people—at least most people in the North—knew that slavery was wrong. Nevertheless, few could envision the country without it: How could 4 million people who had been made dependent suddenly be turned loose in a modern society? What about the problem of labor competition?

The abolitionists refused to engage in those discussions, which always turned into excuses for the continued existence of slavery. They insisted on immediate, total, unconditional emancipation of the slaves in the land where they lived. That insistence was the true measure of their radicalism. Those radicals turned out to be the most realistic of all.

I am asking the Occupy movement to adopt their stance: Be realistic! Demand the impossible!

42
Defining *Hard Crackers*

The Hard Crackers *journal was Ignatiev's brainchild and his last political project before he died. Inspired by C. L. R. James's revolutionary optimism, the journal is dedicated to exploring the contradictions within everyday life and the possibility within them for building a new world free of oppression and domination. The following essay was published in 2016 as an editorial statement, outlining the project's mission.*

1. Modern American society is a ticking time bomb where an impending social explosion is hinted at by everyday violence of all kinds—the abuse of children; physical and sexual attacks by men against women, against other men, and against those who do not conform to conventional images of men and women; the mistreatment of animals; suicides; street shootings and occasional but frequent mass shootings in places like schools and entertainment events. The violence is accompanied by a widespread sense of dread that something awful may very well happen to all of us.

2. This state of affairs demands an explanation—not one about tormented minds or evil souls, but one that makes sense of the fact that many individuals are coming to grips or, perhaps more precisely, failing to come to grips with the real circumstances of their lives. Modern society in the United States more or less provides individuals, families, and communities with "enough" food to live and clothing to wear. It does not do nearly as well with providing them with places to live.

3. With good reason, some see themselves as much worse off than others; others see themselves as one paycheck away from being as badly off as the worst; and, not so surprisingly, others see all too many reasons to be miserable about their lives—hateful jobs, low pay, tyrannical bosses, bills that can't be paid, illnesses and inadequate health care, drugs for every occasion (including the occasion of overdosing and killing yourselves), kids who hate their schools and whose schools appear to hate them, water they can't drink or swim in, and (to add insult to injury) advertisements on a thousand television channels about how good sugar, diets, and prescription drugs of every kind really are; you get to decide how you consume the poison—cable, fios, or direct TV.

We concede that there are a good number of people who think they are doing just fine—their SUVs are getting sportier; their first and second houses are getting fancier; their pension funds are growing (until the market exacts its periodic revenges); their kids are getting into better colleges (except, of course, when those kids get murdered in a high-school shooting and they get into no college at all). They all too often believe that the good times are going to keep on coming, and they are inclined to pay little or no attention to the disasters that build up like hurricanes far off in the Atlantic Ocean. For the moment, our publication is not really for them.

And then there are the others, perhaps the great majority, who are concerned about where things are headed. But beyond what they do within their families and local neighborhoods, they don't really think there is much they can do about the larger state of affairs. So they focus on what they can—taking care of parents, children, neighbors; going to church or not; coaching kids on sports teams. Somewhat remarkably, when it comes to politics, individuals who may have all but identical everyday life experiences and who behave in much the same manner at work and at home come to diametrically opposed views about different politicians—Trump is a good example of this.

Life on the ground is never quite completely determined by the grand structures. In spite of it all, individuals and groups find their ways from one day to the next—they surprise with their ingenuity and generosity; they fail to do what they're assumed to want to do; they keep alive old memories and invent new cultural practices; they say one thing and do something else—and the doing is often more important than the saying.

4. It has been observed that every institution in modern society does the opposite of what it pretends: schools spread ignorance; hospitals spread disease; the justice system promotes anti-social behavior, and so forth. Nonetheless, people have ambivalent attitudes toward those institutions. Their attitudes reflect an odd combination of confidence and cynicism. They want FEMA to work in the aftermath of a disaster, but they are seldom surprised when it doesn't. As one friend of our project told us about a neighborhood man's reaction to the news that a local hospital would be closing (but that activists were trying to keep open), "It's about time they shut that place down. I wouldn't go there if my head was about to fall off." It may well be that the most revealing institution in current American society is the lottery in all its incarnations (Powerball, and so forth)—everybody plays and almost no one wins.

5. The goal of *Hard Crackers* is to help bring into existence in place of the existing society (disfigured by the hidden theft of human lifetime and freedom by the organization of production for the sake of production, the careless disregard of human needs, an absent-minded and frantic consumption of stuff that we mostly don't need, lives of quiet misery in the face of the absence of human community, pervasive violence, an almost willful ignorance of the consequences of what we do to the world within which we live, and an obliviousness to the devastating consequences of American world dominance) an association in which the free development of each is the condition for the free development of all.

6. *Hard Crackers* chronicles everyday life, both to demonstrate that a better world is possible and to examine the barriers to it, including the barriers that have been erected by those who must build it. It seeks to be a place where black people can express their bitterness at the prolonged oppressions they have suffered at the hand of whites; where whites who resent being blamed for a history they do not think is their fault can be heard; where women can share stories of the ways in which men have mistreated them and how they have resisted that mistreatment; where men can express their own frustrations about their experiences in what used to be called "the battle of the sexes," and where young people can express their dismay at the world they are to inherit.

7. *Hard Crackers* is not alone in its conviction that we need to be alert to the possibilities of "the beach under the pavement" or "the future in the present." Dramatic events that appear to have come from nowhere

often have much in common with earlier developments that have eaten away at the consensus of accommodation with misery that appears so often to be the norm. Of course, it's hard to know what will come of what goes on and some moments that appear to be full of future promise will turn out to have short lives. Nonetheless, it seems wise to carefully observe what people actually do in situations like natural/social disasters (of which we have way too many) or instances of official crimes that go without consequence (like murders by police officers) and to appreciate that the potentials may not be exhausted in the short run. Large, organized actions are more easily recognized but small, maybe almost invisible acts of individuals or communities also deserve attention. The significance of all those moments deserves to be explored and debated. For *Hard Crackers*, the explorations and debates will primarily be done through the stories our contributors have to tell.

8. *Hard Crackers* does not believe that a new society can be achieved without a dramatic rupture in the political landscape—to be precise, a revolution. We further believe that the US Civil War and Reconstruction, taken together, constituted a revolution as great as any in history, an event of global significance from which all those who seek a better world can learn. The lessons include the powerful model of insistent politics provided by the abolitionists; the heroic defiance of John Brown in Kansas and at Harpers Ferry; the exemplary solidarity of the English textile workers who refused to work with Southern cotton; the outstanding role played by the International Workingmen's Association in rallying support for the cause of emancipation of the slaves; the general strike of the slaves, which turned the Civil War into a revolutionary war and led to the Northern victory; the establishment of renegade islands of freedom such as the Free State of Jones; the passage of the 13th, 14th, and 15th Amendments to the Constitution, which provided an antidote of sorts to the evil that the initial Constitution had made sacred and that the Fugitive Slave Law and the Dred Scott decision had perpetuated; the establishment of the Reconstruction governments across the defeated Confederacy—governments that were so unlike other governments that W. E. B. Du Bois considered the Reconstruction government of South Carolina to be an instance of "the dictatorship of the proletariat."

To the everlasting shame of this country, the grand experiments in freedom were violently crushed and a cloud of reaction, initiated by terror, settled across the South—with convict labor for emancipated slaves, grinding sharecropping, Jim Crow laws restricting black lives at every turn, and the all but unimaginable crime of lynching. The reaction lasted for more than seventy years until its stranglehold was broken by the emergence of the civil rights movement. But the world that the segregationists made still casts a shadow over much of the country's political life. Once again, Trump is a good example.

It is not enough merely to celebrate the history of abolition, Civil War, and Reconstruction or to lament the savagery of the reaction. The great figures of that day—Lincoln and Douglass, Grant and Sherman, Brown and Tubman, Garrison and Phillips—made choices, and their doing some things foreclosed the possibilities of doing others. We believe one of the foremost intellectual tasks of *Hard Crackers* is to examine those choices and evaluate which we think were right and which were wrong, not with the certainty that we can ever know beyond doubt but with the conviction that whatever we learn will help us make our way through the contemporary tangle to which the Civil War experience is relevant.

9. *Hard Crackers* is internationalist; our country is the world, our countrymen and countrywomen all humankind. We recognize no national borders and welcome all who wish to come to this land.

10. *Hard Crackers* is political but not defined by party or program, literary but not pretentious, scholarly but not academic.

11. At present the *Hard Crackers* project consists of three parts: (a) the print journal, contents of which are determined by an editorial board that functions by consensus; (b) the website, which posts blogs on a variety of topics that fall broadly within the *Hard Crackers* purpose; and (c) gatherings at which writers and friends come together to do whatever they wish.

12. *Hard Crackers* is paid for entirely by its writers and readers. There is no fixed cover price; people pay what they can afford.

13. "Hard Crackers" was a song popular among Union soldiers, a takeoff on the Stephen Foster song "Hard Times." It referred to one of the staples of the soldiers' diet and expressed some of their mood. Our name reflects our desire to identify with the experience of those "on the ground."

43

Frederick Douglass, John Brown, and the Virtues of Impracticality

This is the final essay Ignatiev wrote. It was prepared for and published post-humously in the December 2019/January 2020 issue of the Brooklyn Rail. *Returning to a lifelong preoccupation, Ignatiev reflects on the differences between reformist and revolutionary strategies of abolitionism, as embodied in the historical figures of Frederick Douglass and John Brown.*

In a lengthy review in the *New Yorker* of David W. Blight's recent book, *Frederick Douglass: Prophet of Freedom*, Adam Gopnik calls Douglass "the progenitor of the 'pragmatic-progressive' strain in American thought that led to Martin Luther King and Barack Obama."[1] Douglass is an attractive figure, and it is easy to understand why he fills the need of American mainstream thought for a black political hero now that George Washington Carver (the one black figure in the textbooks when I went to grade school) no longer serves. But the notion of "pragmatic progressive" suggests an alternative tradition, which we might call "impractical revolutionary." Nat Turner, John Brown, and Malcolm X come to mind as exemplars.

Douglass made his first public appearance on an anti-slavery plat-form in 1841. For the next eight years he identified as a Garrisonian abolitionist, that is, a believer with William Lloyd Garrison in what was then called "nonresistance" (noncooperation with the government in any form, including a refusal to take part in electoral activity). Beginning in 1849 he began to rethink his position, soon breaking with Garrison and allying himself with the "political" abolitionists (at first with Gerrit Smith's Liberty Party and later with Free-Soil and Republicanism). Gopnik attributes Douglass's falling out with Garrison in large part to the latter's paternalism but admits that it was partly due to political differences, "with the irony that the white crusader was the more conventionally radical actor, and the Black ex-slave seemingly the more 'moderate.' "

The dispute between them initially took the form of a disagreement over whether the Constitution was in its essence proslavery. As Gopnik writes:

> Douglass came to believe that the Constitution was a good document gone wrong—that in its democratic premises, it breathed freedom, and that it needed only to be amended to be restored to its first purposes . . . The constitutional issue was, and remains, epic. All of American liberalism remains at stake in this choice.[2]

I agree. The dispute was not merely over the meaning of a text but reflected the difference between the revolutionary and the reformer. In my view, the verdict of history is in: as the Garrisonians foresaw, it was necessary to break up the Union in order to reconstitute it without slavery. However, if the sum of two-plus-two were of social significance, there would be no agreement on it yet. Those who think slavery was abolished through the Civil War will conclude that the Garrisonians were right; for those who think its demise came about through the electoral process, Douglass is vindicated.

If matters were that simple, modern readers would have little difficulty making up their minds: those who believe in "working within the system" would fall one way, those who believe that only revolution offers a solution would fall the other. However, matters were not that simple.

One problem is that Garrison rejected physical force of any kind, being committed to what he called "moral suasion," that is, winning over the slaveholders to voluntarily renounce their system. I don't intend to argue the question of political violence; people will believe what they want. But a few points are in order. First, Garrison stretched nonviolence to its limits: As C. L. R. James noted, "The violence of the polemic, the attack without bounds upon everything that stood in the way, the unceasing denunciations of slave property, the government, the

constitution, the laws, the church was in itself a repudiation of pacifism."
According to James, the abolitionists sought

> To tear up by the roots the foundation of the Southern economy and
> society, wreck Northern commerce, and disrupt the Union irretriev-
> ably . . . They renounced all traditional politics . . . They openly hoped
> for the defeat of their own country in the Mexican War . . . They
> preached and practiced Negro equality. They endorsed and fought for
> the equality of women.[3]

When, in 1849, Douglass made a speech calling for slave insurrection, Garrison published it in *The Liberator*. When anti-slavery forces
sent arms to free-state settlers in Kansas, Garrison asked, "If such men
are deserving of generous sympathy, and ought to be supplied with
arms, are not the crushed and bleeding slaves at the South a million
times more deserving of pity and succor? Why not, first of all, take
measures to furnish them with Sharp's rifles?" At a public meeting held
after Harpers Ferry, Garrison declared himself still a nonresistant and
asked how many others were in the audience of 3,000. Only one hand
went up. He then announced "as a peace man—an 'ultra' peace man—I
am prepared to say: 'Success to every slave insurrection at the South,
and in every slave country.'"[4]

Notwithstanding his nominal commitment to nonviolence, Garrison
adhered to the essence of a revolutionary strategy—dual power, the
belief that the existing institutions could not be transformed but had to
be destroyed and new ones created in their place. When he burned the
Constitution at a public meeting, his act was more than symbolic. He
was seeking to resist official authority, not merely oppose it, and to
thwart its operation. More than that, he viewed the resistance as not
peripheral but central to abolition.

When the Garrisonians, denouncing the Constitution as a "covenant
with death," began a campaign to get the North to secede from the
Union, it was not a quixotic effort to remain uncontaminated by association with slavery but the expression of a conscious strategy. The
abolitionists took seriously their assertion that the North, through its
military backing, was the true upholder of slavery. By taking it out of the
Union, they hoped to free it from the need to enforce the Fugitive Slave
Law. "All the slave asks of us," declared Wendell Phillips, "is to stand out

of his way, withdraw our pledge to keep the peace on the plantation; withdraw our pledge to return him . . . and he will right himself." The slogan "No Union with Slaveholders" translated itself at every abolitionist rally into a pledge never to send back the fugitive slave who set foot on free territory. Harpers Ferry was the expression of the dual-power strategy.

Douglass's adoption of an anti-slavery interpretation of the Constitution led him toward political, that is, electoral action. The abolitionists had always been political. They regularly interrogated candidates for public office as to their views on the internal slave trade and slavery in the District of Columbia and called upon those of their supporters who voted to vote accordingly. They sought to repeal the fugitive slave laws and to pass personal liberty laws. The immediate difference between them and those who became known as "political abolitionists" was that the latter called for a new, anti-slavery political party.

Garrison opposed this on principled and tactical grounds; most relevant here is that officeholders would be required to swear to uphold the Constitution, including the fugitive slave laws. "Thank God I'm not a citizen," declared Phillips. The split took place in 1840. Those who split with Garrison formed the Liberty Party in time for the 1840 elections. It drew fewer votes than the number of members of the two anti-slavery societies combined. Gerrit Smith used his personal fortune to keep the party alive, but it never amounted to more than a place for sectarians to cast a symbolic vote against slavery.

Far more important was the emergence of the Free-Soil Party in 1848 and the Republican Party in 1856. Free-Soil was the name given to the movement to exclude slavery from the territories newly conquered from Mexico. It was not "soft" abolitionism: it was the enemy of abolitionism. Many supported it because they did not wish to compete with black labor, slave or free. They could make their peace with slavery where it existed, so long as it was excluded from the West. The Free-Soil constitutions of Oregon and Kansas, for example, prohibited slavery but also prohibited the immigration of free black people.[5] Nevertheless, the demand for Free-Soil disrupted the coalition that had governed the country since its birth. The Free-Soil Party shrunk after the Compromise of 1850 but was reborn as the Republican Party after the Kansas–Nebraska Act of 1854.

From the time he broke with the Garrisonians until the outbreak of the Civil War, Douglass went back and forth between supporting Smith's Party (under various names) and being involved with Free-Soil and Republicanism; sometimes he did both simultaneously.[6] His policy (if it can be called that) reached its nadir in 1860, when he cast his ballot for Smith's Party (by then called the Radical Abolitionist Party) while working to carry New York for Lincoln. Lincoln carried the state by 50,000 votes, but the effort to overturn New York's discriminatory property qualification for black men, for which Douglass worked hard, lost by 140,000 votes. He was disheartened.

I find Douglass's electoral efforts uninteresting, just as I find uninteresting today's debates over whether socialists should take part in elections, whether they should limit their electoral efforts to socialist candidates, whether it is possible to be both a socialist and a Democrat, and so on. He was flailing, and he knew it.

But a strong case can be made for Douglass when we shift our ground from his electoral to his nonelectoral activities: what did he do when not electioneering?

In the first place he continued to identify with women's rights. This was no small thing, since one of the accusations made against Garrison by his conservative opponents was that he had brought discredit on the movement by his support for women's rights. Douglass was one of the few men present at the 1848 Seneca Falls Convention, and to his credit, identified to the end of his life as a women's right's man.

Second, he identified with the struggle for equal rights for black people everywhere—not as obvious a choice as it might seem, since a number of Garrison's opponents distanced themselves from the equal rights struggle: it was one thing to seek to exclude slavery from the territories, quite another to demand equal rights for the persecuted black people in the "free" states, where they competed directly with white labor.

Third, he promoted and took part in the rescue of fugitive slaves, going so far as to declare in a public speech that "two or three dead slaveholders will make [the Fugitive Slave Law] a dead letter."[7] These deeds explain why Gopnik can claim Douglass as "the father of the most militant strain of resistance," both "prophetic radical and political pragmatist."

In its classic period the Industrial Workers of the World (the Wobblies), consistent with its revolutionary outlook, refused to sign contracts with employers, believing that to do so would tie its members' hands. As a matter of principle it reserved the right to strike whenever conditions were favorable. Since the rise of the Congress of Industrial Organizations (CIO), however, the contract has been the centerpiece of labor-management relations. In a contract the company agrees to a certain standard of wages, working conditions, seniority, and so on in return for the union agreeing not to interrupt production while the contract is in force. Those experienced in the world of trade union politics will recognize that quite often reformist or even conservative union leaders show remarkable militancy in tactics; union officials who never question the private ownership of wealth or the company's right to manage its affairs often find themselves tolerating or even encouraging (with a wink) illegal acts, including sabotage, as a means of pushing the company to the bargaining table or, once there, persuading it to grant concessions to the union. Such instrumental illegality is a standard feature of every contract dispute in industries, like telephone and electric power, where the technical conditions make it difficult for the workers to interrupt service by the mere withdrawal of their labor power. Both management and the workers expect sabotage as a normal part of negotiations; neither regards it as a challenge to the existing social relations, and only some leftists take it seriously.

Under certain circumstances, thus, tactical militancy is compatible with reformist strategy. How to decide in Douglass's case whether what was involved was militant reformism, which may have included violence, or an embrace of a revolutionary strategy of dual power? The key lies in the figure of John Brown.

According to Douglass, he first met Brown in 1847 or early 1848. He had heard of him, especially from other black abolitionists whose voices, when speaking of Brown, "would lower to a whisper." At that meeting, Brown unfolded a large map of the United States and pointed to the Alleghenies. "These mountains are the basis of my plan . . . They were placed here for the emancipation of the Negro . . ."

The two met numerous times over the next ten years; Douglass seems to have believed that Brown's plan was

> to take 20 or 25 discreet men into the mountains, selecting secure and comfortable retreats where they could defend themselves in case of attack and subsist upon the country thereabout. They were to be well

armed but to avoid battle or violence, unless compelled by pursuit or self-defense.[8]

In fact, Brown had other ideas. In May 1858 he convened a conference in Chatham, Canada at which he presented a "Provisional Constitution" for an interim government that would operate in areas where his movement succeeded, an indication that he was thinking in grander terms than running off slaves.[9]

Brown and Douglass met for the last time at Chambersburg, PA, on the eve of Harpers Ferry. Here is the exchange between them, as recounted in Truman Nelson's *The Old Man*:

> Brown informed Douglass of his plan to make an attack on the arsenal at Harpers Ferry and to occupy it for a few hours to give the signal that the long-awaited attack on slavery had begun. Douglass argued that this would jeopardize the effort to run off slaves from nearby plantations, he further warned Brown that by occupying the Ferry "he was going into a perfect steel trap, and that once in, he would never get out alive."[10]
>
> "No," Brown calmly disagreed, "the Ferry itself is in a defile, from which a small number of men can stand off vastly greater numbers. Furthermore, the arsenal itself is entirely defended by civilian watchmen; there are no military guards and the northern operatives who make the guns are simply good craftsmen and mechanics who do their own work and appear to have no interests in the politics of either the North or the South."
>
> "But you are in the middle of slave country," Douglass protested. "The whites could raise a posse against you in that position in a matter of two or three hours."
>
> "I expect some of the whites there to join us," said the Old Man.
>
> With those words Brown showed himself an astute student of American life. He continued:
>
> "[Virginia] Governor Wise has recently come out with the astounding assertion that Virginia has no fear of the insurrection of the blacks, but of the poor whites. This statement was made as he was trying to put through his legislature a bill to restrict the slaves from learning the mechanic arts, with the design of restoring their trades to the poor whites. But this is merely a sop; the poor whites have nearly broken

away and made a separate state in the mountain regions . . . They nearly did it during the Nat Turner troubles and could again, with some slight encouragement."[11]

Karl Marx himself could not have provided a better class analysis—nor anticipated more accurately the course of events during the Civil War. Continuing from the account provided by Truman Nelson, Douglass

at once opposed the measure with all the arguments at my command. To me such a measure would be fatal to all engaged in doing so. It would be an attack upon the Federal Government, and would array the whole country against us." [Making war on the Federal Government was unacceptable to the person who believed the Constitution was an anti-slavery document.]

Brown replied: "What country? We have two countries here. Even Mr. Sanborn and the Massachusetts men, conservative as they are, feel the country is split apart beyond redemption . . . and that only an uprising of the slaves and the separation of the poor whites can unite the country again, without the slaveholders."

"Nothing short of an open recognition of the Negro's manhood and of his rights to have a country and to defend that country would move me into such a desperate scheme as this," said Douglass. To which Brown replied: "After occupying the arsenal, which will serve as notice to the slaves that their friends have come . . . we will move into the mountains, you will have your country, or at least a provisional state . . . This is why I need you, Frederick. You must take power, be the first president of the new provisional government."[12]

The exchange illustrates the difference between the reformer and the revolutionary.

As most readers know, Brown and his men captured the arsenal but could not hold it. It would appear that Douglass was right and Brown wrong. In my view, Brown's mistake was of the same order as Garrison's nonresistance: a tactical flaw within a sound strategy. I suggest that his plan might have worked had he withdrawn from the arsenal and waged a protracted war. There is some evidence that Brown was aware of such a possibility: he had visited battlefields where the Spanish resisted Napoleon during the Peninsular Campaign (the first place where the term "guerrilla" was employed) and Saint-Domingue, where the Haitians waged their War of Independence. For some reason he chose not to pursue that course; Russell Banks speculates in *Cloudsplitter* that Brown, aware that he was too old to start again and that word of his plan had leaked out, decided to go ahead. Who knows? W. E. B. Du Bois thought Brown's plan could have worked.[13]

When news of Harpers Ferry broke, Douglass was in Philadelphia. Afraid of being arrested and charged as a co-conspirator, he fled to Canada and then to Britain, and he did not return until the war broke out. Gerrit Smith had himself committed to an asylum for the mentally ill. I criticize neither man's behavior: even revolutionaries need to hide sometimes.

But someone has to explain and defend their actions. The public has a need to know. Only Wendell Phillips was willing to take upon himself the task of explaining and justifying Brown's actions. In a speech in Brooklyn two weeks after Harpers Ferry, he said, "The lesson of the hour is insurrection. Insurrection of thought always precedes the insurrection of arms." Five weeks later he said that Brown had "abolished slavery in Virginia. You may say this is too much . . . History will date Virginia Emancipation from Harpers Ferry. True, the slave is still there. So, when the tempest uproots a pine on your hills, it looks green for months—a year or two. Still, it is timber, not a tree." Brown, he said, had "startled the South into madness."[14]

The slaveholders indeed reacted with fury to the raid, imposing a boycott on northern manufactures and demanding new concessions from Washington. Their arrogance compelled the people of the North to resist. Lincoln was elected a year later. As Phillips said, "for the first time in our history the slave has chosen a President of the United States," adding, "John Brown was behind the curtain."[15] Lincoln's election brought Civil War, which led to slaves as "contraband," spies and soldiers—and the fall of the slaveocracy.

Today, when many place their hopes in a Green New Deal and other schemes which will never be achieved through the electoral system, or, consumed by the need to overturn Trump at any cost, are willing to go along with the maneuvers of the party that shares responsibility for the country's desperate condition, it is good to bear in mind Du Bois's words: "At last we know: John Brown was right . . . The cost of liberty is less than the price of repression."[16]

Down with crackpot realism! Be realistic! Demand the impossible!

Epilogue: My Dream

This short piece first appeared on Ignatiev's PM Press blog in 2019.

Telephone conversation with my best friend from high school. We had not seen each other or spoken since graduation in 1958 and only exchanged a couple of letters. We soon established that we were a couple of old guys. How did that happen, he asked—not the first to ask that question. He recalled my father fondly, the time he came back into the house after a bird had shit on his new hat, with the comment, For the rich, they sing. I dream of my father as a young man. We compete to see who can run an unspecified distance the fastest. I do it in 57 seconds. My father beats my time—56 seconds. I envision him as a beautiful young man. He had lost his trunks—that can happen in dreams—and I see him running into the distance, nude, in long, graceful strides. Freud says that every character in our dreams is us. If that is so, my dream is no mystery. My father wrote poetry. He worked hard at it. One of his poems read:

> Rampaging Time, hard-hoofed
> leaves us all behind
> gazing from the monster's rear
> Into its eternal mind.

Afterword: Noel Ignatiev, an Intellectual Biography

Noel Ignatin was born on December 27, 1940, in Philadelphia. His grandparents were Jewish immigrants from Eastern Europe, and the family had changed its last name before Noel was born. Noel changed it back to something closer to the original name in the 1980s. He graduated from Central High School in Philadelphia and attended the University of Pennsylvania, but he dropped out after his third year. He had a summer job in a small plant that made Philadelphia's street lamps, and he simply kept working when the fall semester started. He worked in a few other similar factories in Philadelphia and then in New York City. After he moved to Chicago, he worked in steel mills and other large plants.

While still a teenager, Noel joined an obscure group called the Provisional Organizing Committee to Reconstitute the Marxist-Leninist Communist Party (POC) that was on the "ultra-left" of the Communist Party meaning, for example, that it supported the Russian invasion of Hungary to stop the revolution in that country of 1956 and opposed the moves by the Russian Communist Party toward a policy of "peaceful co-existence" with the United States. Though small in number, it included celebrated radicals such as Harry Haywood (author of the "Black Belt Thesis" that first argued that black people in the United States constituted a national minority rooted in the territory of the Deep South), Ted Allen (who went on to author *The Invention of the White Race*), and Nelson Peery (veteran of World War II, the Watts riot, and later still the new communist movement) among its ranks. While the

POC initially recorded some successes in local organizing (especially around police brutality against black people), over time it became more cultlike and rather obsessed with its own internal purity. Noel was a diligent member and rising star of sorts in the Philadelphia branch before he was expelled in 1966. He was shocked and then thrilled at having been set free to develop his own views.

His first noteworthy contribution in writing occurred in 1967 with the publication of "White Blindspot," consisting of a critical letter from Noel to the Progressive Labor Party (PL) and a letter from Ted Allen corroborating Noel's analysis. PL was another group that had emerged from within the rapidly transformed Communist Party. Noel's arguments focused on PL's position that the black liberation struggle was outside the class struggle and advanced the principle that the struggle against white supremacy and the associated privileges provided to white workers was fundamental to the possibility of effective working-class solidarity. A close reading of "White Blindspot" reveals an independence of thought and spirit—Noel quotes George Bernard Shaw (as he would continue to do for decades) and Ted insists on the importance of the development of subjectivity (including an attentiveness to matters of morality) as an essential part of revolutionary class consciousness. And both Noel and Ted relied on W. E. B. Du Bois's *Black Reconstruction* as foundational.

Their arguments were especially convincing to members of Students for a Democratic Society (SDS), who, as their numbers were swelling in the fight against the war in Vietnam, were trying to defeat the efforts of PL to take over that organization. Soon after the publication of "White Blindspot," Noel was recruited to join SDS. He became a principal spokesperson of the short-lived Revolutionary Youth Movement II tendency within the now dying student organization. At the time, Noel still considered himself a Marxist-Leninist—which was the shorthand of the day for a Maoist opponent of the Communist Party of the Soviet Union—as did Ted Allen. Over the years, Noel retained an appreciation for Maoism because of the emphasis it had placed on the significance of individual and collective will in changing the course of history. Eventually, though, his restless intellect and his passionate commitments would lead him far beyond the classificatory schemes of his younger years.

In 1969, Noel was part of a small group that established the Sojourner

Truth Organization (STO) in Chicago. Noel later summarized the founding members' agreement that the central organizational task of the present period "was the building of a Marxist-Leninist party." In early 1970, they decided that the best way to build a party was to start acting like one. They had little in the way of unified positions but felt, on the basis of previous activity in common, that they would be close enough. They survived in this manner for three years without any splits and by 1972 had grown to about thirty members. Within the next two years, two significant splits occurred, and the group was reduced to a small fragment. They had not been able to avoid the recurrent plague that breaks up political sects. The organization lived to fight another day. It endured, in different incarnations, into the mid-1980s.

Arguably, STO was one of the most important political organizations of that moment. From the start, they embarked on a strategy that had few well-defined precedents; they had to learn by doing. Their work in the factories and mills seldom resembled that of more traditional left groups that were also placing members in them. They consistently attempted to promote the autonomy of all workers' activities with respect to the union (whether progressive or not); similarly, they promoted and supported the autonomous activity of black workers, especially when it came to opposing job and wage differentials that favored white workers. They did not try to organize rank and file caucuses with the goal of running for and becoming elected officials. They interpreted contracts as instruments that were designed to control workers and work processes. They paid close attention to what workers were doing and often relied on humor to highlight the absurdities of the conditions workers labored under. For these approaches, they earned a great deal of scorn from the high priests of the left, like the editors of the very popular newspaper of the "independent left," the *Guardian*.

At the same time that they were engaging in intense activity at work, they maintained an active program of internal education that was intended to help members "learn how to think" and not how to parrot a line developed by the organization's leaders. Nonetheless, it's worth noting that the organization was poorly prepared for the assault that was launched on the industrial workers of Chicago and other cities by the corporations' abandonment of enormous industrial capacity in the pursuit of lower wages and higher profits elsewhere and the consequent loss of hundreds of thousands of jobs. It may well have been the case that at the very moment that an intensification of work-based struggles would have been most significant, STO's withdrawal from the workplaces to focus on other areas of political activity was a significant error. This point has been forcefully argued by Dave Ranney. STO would not have been what it was without Noel's contributions; then again, Noel would not have become who he did without being part of the group.

For most of the 1970s, I was a taxi driver in New York City and a member of the Taxi Rank and File Coalition. The coalition had learned about STO through some of its writings in Radical America and realized that at least some of us had similar positions—although STO's views were much more developed. We established informal ties.

At first, I had a hard time figuring STO out—at times, it appeared to be yet another Marxist-Leninist group, but that description never quite fit. In any case, I was attracted by the group's lively internal debate, its understanding of the centrality of the "white" question in American politics, its concentration in factories and its embrace of an autonomous approach to workplace organizing and, perhaps most important, its appreciation of C. L. R. James.

In retrospect, Noel was an expression of what was a global tendency: a sort of generational rediscovery of a revolutionary communist politics, forged against the compromises and reformist drift of the official communist parties and other parties of the left opposition. In this sense, Noel joins a roster of other militant intellectuals who tried to theorize within and against the limits of inherited communist and Marxist-Leninist tradition, putting Marxism back into dialogue with the explosive movements of his day—for Noel, above all, the struggle against white supremacy. His work—organizational, agitational, theoretical—is of a peer with other heterodox Marxists at the outer edges of the communist movement: Mario Tronti, Stuart Hall, Alain Badiou, Antonio Negri, Paul Gilroy, Neville Alexander, John Bracey, Ferrucio Gambino, Peter Linebaugh, Marcus Rediker, Dave Roediger, and Staughton Lynd.

In 1976, Noel published "No Condescending Saviors," a pamphlet that would attempt to come to grips with the legacy of the Russian Revolution. As well as drawing from the analysis that James and his comrades had advanced many years earlier in *State Capitalism and World Revolution*, he relied on a favorable reading of Lenin's thinking about state capitalism. To be clear, the use of a state capitalism analysis may or may not be fully sufficient, but most of its later proponents, including Noel, had no interest in subscribing to such an analysis as an apologetics for what had become of the revolution.

After being laid off in 1984 and after a period of estrangement from at least some STO members, Noel applied to the Graduate School of Education at Harvard University and, despite his lack of an undergraduate degree, was accepted. He earned his master's degree from the Education School in 1985 and then applied for admission to the Graduate School of Arts and Sciences.

This shift thrust him into a new role—where he did longer term historical research, experimented with the prospect of an abolitionist revival, and reached for new coordinates of revolutionary politics.

In 1985, the two of us co-authored an unpublished paper entitled "The Peculiarities of the Americans." In brief, we couched our arguments as another approach to the age-old question of why there was no socialism in America. We began with a reaffirmation of W. E. B. Du Bois's claim that the black worker during Reconstruction should be seen as the "kernel of the labor movement." We also tipped our hats to Edward Thompson, the great English historian, and acknowledged the influence of his 1965 essay "The Peculiarities of the English." There he examined the defeat of Chartism and looked for the roots of the pulling apart of the working class and the absorption of its fragments into defining and limiting institutions—such as trade unions. In the case of the United States, the essential "defining and limiting" institution was the color line.

In 1994, Noel received his PhD in American Studies, working paradoxically with Stephen Thernstrom, the conservative historian and opponent of affirmative action, as his advisor. Noel insisted that Thernstrom's only concern was making his dissertation a better one. In 1995, it was published as *How the Irish Became White*, whose success launched Noel into a number of teaching and research jobs at various institutions, including Bowdoin College, the University of California, Riverside; the Massachusetts College of Art; and the American University of Beirut.

Around that time, in 1993, we launched *Race Traitor* and published sixteen issues over the course of twelve years. Rather than accepting the conventional commonsense view that race was grounded in biology, we understood the white race as a socio-historical formation designed for purposes of controlling the working class. We were, therefore,

committed to abolishing the white race in order to establish a new starting point for anti-capitalist revolution.

We emphasized that membership in the white race did not exempt its
working-class members from poverty or misery. We never endorsed or
promoted identity politics. We wanted nothing to do with the then
burgeoning academic field of "whiteness studies." We did, however, make
use of "privilege" as a way of describing the material advantages enjoyed
by white workers. In light of the political travesties around privilege that
have developed since, we might have found a better way of differentiating
ourselves from those who insist that the psychic battle against privilege
must be the terminal condition of any politics whatsoever.

Since that moment, material privileges have been eroded and the
protections once routinely afforded to white workers have become far
less universal. Many of the large preserves of protected white worker
privilege have been shut down and the white workers set adrift. Noel
spent a good deal of time and energy grappling with the significance of
those changes and probably never arrived at what to him was an adequate
interpretation. It seems to me that the key to a new understanding was
present all along in Noel's thinking—over the course of time, whiteness
mutated, a bit like a virus. That's why it was important to document how
the Irish became white. And it's still mutating—the emerging profile of
the Trump voting bloc and even of the far-right nationalists provides
ample evidence that individuals who were once assumed to be not white
by virtue of ancestry are ready, willing, and able to sign up for the non-
black citizenry. As Nell Irvin Painter has argued, the fundamental
dichotomy remains black and non-black. White may just be a shorthand
for non-black.

In 2016, Noel initiated the publication of *Hard Crackers*. In its original statement of purpose, he wrote:

> Attentiveness to daily lives is absolutely essential for those who would
> like to imagine how to act purposefully to change the world. *Hard
> Crackers* . . . is guided by one principle: that in the ordinary people of
> this country (and the world) there resides the capacity to escape from
> the mess we are in, and a commitment to documenting and examin-
> ing their strivings to do so.

"Hard Crackers" was a song popular among Union soldiers during
the Civil War, a takeoff on Stephen Foster's "Hard Times." The Civil

War and Reconstruction, viewed as a single event, was a revolution as great as any in human history, transforming property into strikers, soldiers, citizens, voters and legislators—a sequence unparalleled elsewhere. To get an idea of its radicalism, consider the following from Lincoln's Second Inaugural Address:

Fondly do we hope, fervently do we pray, that this mighty scourge of war may speedily pass away. Yet, if God wills that it continue until all the wealth piled by the bondsman's two hundred and fifty years of unrequited toil shall be sunk, and until every drop of blood drawn with the lash shall be paid by another drawn with the sword, as was said three thousand years ago, so still it must be said "the judgments of the Lord are true and righteous altogether."

Has any statement ever captured more succinctly the meaning of revolution? The Lincoln who spoke those words was not the moderate who came to office four years earlier seeking to maintain the Union at almost any cost. Revolution is a process, not a single event, and millions, including Lincoln, were changed by it. Although the leaders of that revolution undoubtedly made mistakes and did not realize all their hopes, neither did they disgrace with their own deeds the cause for which they had fought or leave a stench in the nostrils of later generations, as did many of the revolutionaries of the next century. *Hard Crackers* identifies with that history, and especially with the experience "on the ground" of those who made it.[1]

In Noel's mind, *Hard Crackers* was a continuation of *Race Traitor* but, at the same time, a transcendence of it—simultaneously an abolition and a preservation at a higher level—more adequate to new times. We needed to take seriously the erosion of privilege and, at the same time, take very seriously the ferocious efforts by many discontented whites to demand a return to the old order.

Noel never really stopped developing. Evidence for that claim is especially clear in the numerous blog posts he published on the website of PM Press (well represented in this collection). In one exemplary piece, he returned to where this reader begins, with his longtime collaboration with his former Provisional Organizing Committee comrade, in an essay titled "My Debt and Obligation to Ted Allen." Here, Noel worked through a complex critique of Ted's argument—one that Noel long shared—that the foundation of the white race was a conscious, instrumental political decision and strategy on the part of the ruling class:

> At first I accepted his explanation of the origin, but the more I thought about it, the less satisfying it became. While I do not doubt that elements in the dominant classes (and not only the dominant classes) conspire, I do not believe that great historic turns can be attributed to conspiracies. I was led initially to question Ted on this point by thinking about the origins of reformism in the labor movement, particularly during the rise of the Congress of Industrial Organizations (CIO). Like the seventeenth century, the period that produced the CIO also presented revolutionary possibilities, possibilities that were contained by the form of labor organization that emerged dominant. No doubt decisions made by capitalist institutions, especially the Roosevelt administration and its left-wing auxiliaries, played a role in pushing the labor movement along a certain path and not another, and that the path taken limited the possible outcomes, but the triumph of reformism cannot be blamed on bourgeois machinations; one must look instead to its roots within the working-class movement. Similarly with the origins of the white-skin privilege, which certainly functioned, as Ted said it did, to suppress the revolutionary possibilities in the period it arose and subsequently.

Noel was influenced and shaped by a number of outstanding thinkers, writers and activists born in the nineteenth century, including John Brown, Wendell Phillips, Karl Marx, Rosa Luxemburg, Vladimir Lenin, and W. E. B. Du Bois. In addition to Ted Allen, he was shaped by others born in the first decades of the twentieth century—C. L. R. James, Marty Glaberman, Herbert Hill, and George Rawick.

Noel became an embodiment of several grand traditions and was a creative interpreter and synthesizer of them. He played an outsized part in the long history of radical links across generations.

Noel had asked for Padraic Pearse's "The Fool" to be read at any memorial. It was the last reading at a memorial held in January 2020. In part, the poem reads:

O wise men, riddle me this, what if the dream come true?
What if the dream come true? And if millions unborn shall dwell
In the house that I shaped in my heart, the noble house of my thought?

It was a fitting end to the memorial and is a fitting end to this essay.

John Garvey
June 2021

Notes

Foreword

1 Noel Ignatiev, *Acceptable Men*, Chicago: Charles H. Kerr, 2021.
2 James Baldwin, "On Being 'White' . . . and Other Lies," *Essence*, April 1984.
3 Noel Ignatiev and John Garvey, eds., *Race Traitor*, Milton Park, UK: Routledge, 1996.
4 Noel Ignatiev, *How the Irish Became White*, Milton Park, UK: Routledge, 2012.
5 Noel Ignatiev, ed., *The Lesson of the Hour: Wendell Phillips on Abolition and Strategy*, Chicago: Charles H. Kerr, 2001.
6 Alexander Saxton, *The Rise and Fall of the White Republic: Class Politics and Mass Culture in Nineteenth-Century America*, New York: Verso, 2003.

Introduction: An American Revolutionary

1 Vincent Kelley "Hard Crackers: Come Again No More: An Interview with Noel Ignatiev," initially appeared in *Orchestrated Pulse*, January 2018.
2 W. E. B. Du Bois, *Black Reconstruction in America*, New York: Harcourt, Brace, and Howe, 1935.
3 Kristian Williams, "Interview with Noel Ignatiev," 2019, kristianwilliams.com.
4 "Without a Science of Navigation We Cannot Sail in Stormy Seas" (Excerpt), this volume, 86.
5 Noel Ignatiev, *How the Irish Became White*, London: Routledge, 1995, 178.
6 Angela Davis, *Abolition Democracy: Beyond Empire, Prisons and Torture*, Chico, CA: AK Press, 2005.
7 See Ignatiev's introduction to C. L. R. James, *A New Notion*, Oakland, CA: PM Press, 2010.

8 "The Backward Workers," this volume, 179–80.
9 Ignatiev, *How the Irish Became White*, 4.
10 Ibid., 3.
11 "Alternative Institutions or Dual Power, " this volume, 364–5.
12 Ibid., 365.
13 "Truth and Revolution: A Symposium on Sojourner Truth Organization," *Insurgent Notes*, October 15, 2012, insurgentnotes.com

1. Passing

1 E. P. Thompson, *The Making of the English Working Class*, London: Victor Golancz, 1963, 9.
2 Michael Staudenmaier, *Truth and Revolution: A History of the Sojourner Truth Organization, 1969–1986*, Oakland, CA: AK Press, 2012.

2. The POC: A Personal Memoir

1 The "ultra-left" broke with Foster very early in the factional struggle, largely over his willingness to sacrifice the total struggle against revisionism in the interests of formally preserving the party. It was the experience of observing him operate in the 1956-68 period that led the extreme left to reevaluate his alleged opposition to Browder over a decade earlier, an "opposition" that was tolerated only because it was kept a total secret from the rank and file. This appreciation of Foster's conciliatory role is shared by none of the more recent "anti-revisionist" groups, all of whom make him their hero and guiding star.
2 There were quite a few who were willing to meet with the caucus in their own local- ity but balked when it came to calling a national conference, with its implications of a formal break. Several of those who later founded Progressive Labor fell into this category. They argued that it was premature to break with the party, that it was still possible to wage struggle within. POC called this group the "conciliators of revision- ism"; when they did leave three years later, they took a smaller number with them than POC did, almost solidly white in composition.
3 In his autobiography, *A Long Journey*, George Charney refers to these comrades as "a rather motley group who lived on their past reputation" and "a shriveled semi-anarchist group that displayed its militancy in wordy battles within party meetings." A few pages later, he rhapsodizes over Seymour Martin Lipset, James Wechsler, Harrison Salisbury, Michael Harrington, Bayard Rustin, and Daniel Bell. Certainly none of these would ever "display all the frustration and instability of a 'seaman' cast on the beach for twenty years." George Charney, *A Long Journey*, Chicago: Quadrangle, 1968, 282.
4 This comrade, the late Ramon Acevedo, soon joined POC.
5 I have since learned that the POC leadership, in a criminal display of sectarianism, virtually sabotaged that defense effort. That youth—no longer a youth!—is still in prison, absolutely innocent.
6 Agron, a revolutionary figure in the prison movement, has recently escaped from jail.

7 For example, the April–May 1964 issue was eight pages long and carried five articles; part one of an analysis of the Suslov Report to the Communist Party of the Soviet Union Central Committee; a May Day article which dealt with the growth of the anti-revisionist movement in the world; an article entitled "Imperio-Revisionist Skin Game" about the crisis of neo-colonialism; a long anti-revisionist article from the Marxist-Leninists of New Zealand; and a plenum report which dealt with internal questions of "growth," cadre policy, education, and so on. This was not an exceptional issue.
8 Tom Scribner, the West Coast organizer, was included among this number, as were nearly all those who had come out of the Communist Party with the original group and who made up the middle leadership.

4. Meeting in Chicago

1 C. L. R. James, *Mariners, Renegades & Castaways: The Story of Herman Melville and the World We Live In*, Hanover, NH: University Press of New England, 1953.
2 C. L. R. James, "Dialectical Materialism and the Fate of Humanity," 1947.
3 Martin Glaberman, "Punching Out," Detroit: Our Times Publications, 1952.
4 Antonio Gramsci, "Workers' Democracy," 1919, *Selections from Political Writings (1921–1926)*, translated and edited by Quintin Hoare, London: Lawrence and Wishart, 1978.

5. The White Blindspot

1 Karl Marx, "Resolution on Relations Between the Irish and the English Working Classes," in Ralph Fox, *Marx, Engels and Lenin on Ireland*, New York: International Publishers, 1940, 41.
2 Karl Marx, Letter to Ludwig Kugelmann, November 29, 1869, *Marx-Engels Collected Works, Volume 43*, New York: International Publishers, 1988, 389.

6. Learn the Lessons of US History

1 W. J. Cash, *The Mind of the South*, New York: Knopf, 1941. Broadus Mitchell, *The Rise of Cotton Mills in the South*, Columbia: University of South Carolina Press, 2001.

8. Without a Science of Navigation We Cannot Sail in Stormy Seas (Excerpts)

1   W. E. B. Du Bois, *Black Reconstruction in America*, New York: The Free Press, 1992, 353.
2   Karl Marx, *Wage Labour and Capital*, New York: International Publishers, 1975.
3   "You Don't Need a Weatherman to Tell Which Way the Wind Blows, *New Left Notes*, June 18, 1969, vol. 4, no. 22, 3.
4   Vladimir Ilyich Lenin, "Imperialism, the Highest Stage of Capitalism", 1916, in Lenin's *Selected Works, Vol. 1*, Moscow: Progress Publishers, 1963, 667–766.
5   Vladimir Ilyich Lenin, "Imperialism and the Split in Socialism", 1916, in Lenin's *Collected Works, Vol. 23*, Moscow: Progress Publishers, 1964, 105–20.
6   Lenin, *Imperialism and the Split in Socialism*.
7   Lenin, *Imperialism and the Split in Socialism*.

9. My Debt and Obligation to Ted Allen

1   "In Memoriam: Theodore W. Allen," *Cultural Logic* 8, 2001.
2   Ted denounced the notion of an "unthinking decision." See "Summary of the Argument of *The Invention of the White Race,* by its author, Theodore W. Allen," elegantbrain.com/edu4/classes/readings/race-allen.html.
3   Engels, Letter to Bloch, September 21, 1890 (italics in original).
4   Theodore W. Allen, *The Invention of the White Race*, vol. 2, New York: Verso, 2012, 274.
5   Karl Marx, Preface to *Contribution to Critique of Political Economy*, *The Marx and Engels Reader*, New York: Norton, 1972, 4.
6   Barbara Jeanne Fields, "Slavery, Race and Ideology in the United States of America," *New Left Review* 181 (May–June 1990).
7   "Summary," no. 14 (italics in original). It is the most useful definition I have heard.
8   Fields, "Slavery, Race and Ideology."
9   Ted discussed this letter in "Summary," no. 84 and at greater length in volume 1 of *The Invention of the White Race*, New York: Verso, 1997, 424–45. I got the text of Gooch's letter from Lerone Bennett, Jr., *The Shaping of Black America*, Chicago: Johnson Publishing Company, 1975, 71.
10   "I had no need of that hypothesis." I have said nothing here about the Indians, who, while they were in some cases enslaved, were not the targets of a general policy of enslavement. I am sure that the explanation will be consistent with historical materialism, not "conscious decision."
11   *The Invention of the White Race*, vol. 2, 244, and "Summary," part 2.

10. Black Worker, White Worker

1 C. Vann Woodward, *Tom Watson: Agrarian Rebel*, New York: Oxford University Press, 1963, 222.

12. No Condescending Saviors: A Study of the Experience of Revolution in the Twentieth Century (Excerpts)

1 Karl Marx and Friedrich Engels, *The Marx-Engels Reader*, second edition, New York: W. W. Norton, 1978, 595.
2 Karl Marx, *Capital, Volume 1: A Critical Analysis of Capitalist Production*, New York: International Publishers, 1967, 715.
3 See the Sojourner Truth Organization pamphlet, "Towards a Revolutionary Party."
4 Marx and Engels, *The Marx-Engels Reader*, 5.
5 Karl Marx, *Communist Manifesto*, New York: Penguin Books, 1985, 105.

14. Are US Workers Paid above the Value of Their Labor Power?

1 Karl Marx, *Capital, Volume 1: A Critical Analysis of Capitalist Production*, New York: International Publishers, 1967, 168.
2 David L. Featherman, *Has Opportunity Declined in America?*, Institute for Research on Poverty no. 437, Madison: University of Wisconsin, 1977.

16. The Backward Workers

1 Karl Marx and Friedrich Engels, *The Marx-Engels Reader*, second edition, New York: W. W. Norton, 1978, 476.
2 To demonstrate to the world that they are not at all the "peculiar people" and that under different circumstances they are as capable of bellicose action as any other human tribe.
3 George Bernard Shaw, *Man and Superman*, Norwalk, Conn: Heritage Press, 1990, 85–6.
4 Humor is double-edged; in some circumstances it makes oppression bearable, in others unbearable. Consider the following characteristic tales: A black man was walking on the streets of Chicago, cursing to himself. God speaks to him and asks what the matter is. "The white folks took my land and ran me out of Mississippi," comes the reply. "Do you have a gun?" asks God. "You know I do," says the black man. "Do you know how to use it?" "Yes." "Well then," says God, "I want you to take your gun and go down to Mississippi and kill that white man who is on your land and take your land back." "Will you go with me, God?" asks the black man. "As far as Memphis," says God.
5 A poor Jew is surprised to hear God addressing him one day. God tells him he can

have anything he wants just for the asking. At first the poor Jew doesn't believe it is God talking to him, but he is finally convinced. "Anything at all?" he asks skeptically. "Anything!" comes the thundering response. "Well then, please God, if it's not too much trouble, could I please have every morning a hot roll with butter?"

6 The remark common among US proletarians, "the hours sure fly by when you're having a good time," was undoubtedly heard on the pyramids.

7 To forestall the critic who points out the evident contradiction between my referring to the workers' total attachment to reality and their elaborate mechanisms for denying reality—what the worker sees realistically is that portion of the world that touches on him and that he can do something about. For the rest, the worker's head is as likely to be filled with ignorance and nonsense as anyone else's. I have known people who believed the world was flat and who nevertheless knew to the minute how long it took to drive from Chicago to Detroit and what was the best route to take. It is a matter of what Hegel calls the first level of thought, empiricism, everyday common sense. I recall one conversation, at which I sat as a silent and pained observer, in which a leftist was propounding to a worker his opinions on world affairs. The leftist declared that he had "opposed" the Soviet intervention in Czechoslovakia. The worker quickly asked him, with a wink to me, "How did you oppose it?" The leftist responded, without the slightest embarrassment or awareness that he was being mocked, that he had spoken out against it and so on. The inability of the left to distinguish between various levels of thought is responsible for a lot of hand wringing, for instance, over the influence of the Catholic Church in Poland. The fact is that in no country—not in Poland, the United States, or Iran—does the problem lie in the influence of religion over workers' actions, in the sense they decide what to do based on its counsel. If workers support or do not support the Church or any other institution, it is because it says or does not say what they want to hear. The problem lies in their perception of what is possible and necessary.

8 This generalization does not apply to farm workers, hospital workers, and others who do not take for granted the minimum necessary for survival.

9 Shaw, *Man and Superman*, 86–7.

10 Lee Holstein, *Urgent Tasks*, no.9, Summer 1980, 18.

11 This writer goes further than I would, at least without clarification, when she writes that "This type of activity—revolutionary self-activity—does not develop revolutionary class-consciousness. It is revolutionary class-consciousness." Still, she is closer to reality than those who contemplate the working class and see only its hind end.

19. The American Intifada

1 G. W. F. Hegel, *Phenomenology of Mind*, New York: Cosimo Classics, 2005, 75.

2 The quote is from Midnight Notes Collective, *Midnight Oil: Work, Energy, War, 1972-1992*, New York: Autonomedia, 1992, 321.

20. Immigrants and Whites

1 David Brody, *Steelworkers in America: The Nonunion Era*, New York: Harper Torchbooks, 1969, 120. John Higham, *Strangers in the Land: Patterns of American Nativism 1860–1925*, New York: Atheneum,1963, 66, 173.

2 Richard Sennett and Jonathan Cobb, *The Hidden Injuries of Class*, New York: Random House, 1973.

3 Various scholars have explained the emergence of whiteness as a response to a problem of labor control in the seventeenth-century Chesapeake region. See especially Theodore Allen, "'They Would Have Destroyed Me': Slavery and the Origins of Racism," *Radical America* 9: 3, May–June 1975, 40–63, reissued as *Class Struggle and the Origins of Racial Slavery: The Invention of the White Race*, Hoboken, NJ: Hoboken Education Project, 1975. Lerone Bennett, Jr., *The Shaping of Black America* (Chicago: Johnson Publishing, 1975) is a popular account. Alden T. Vaughan, "Slavery and Racism in Seventeenth-Century Virginia," *Virginia Magazine of History and Biography* 97: 3, July 1989, 311–54, provides an introduction to the literature and debates on the relation between the appearance of slavery and the ideology of race. See also Richard Williams, *Hierarchical Structures and Social Value: The Creation of Black and Irish Identities in the United States*, New York: Cambridge University Press, 1990.

4 Reprinted in David R. Roediger, ed., *Black Writers on What It Means to be White*, New York: Schocken, 1998, 178–9.

5 Barbara J. Fields, "Ideology and Race in American History," in J. Morgan Kousser and James M. McPherson, eds., *Region, Race and Reconstruction: Essays in Honor of C. Vann Woodward*, New York: Oxford University Press, 1982.

6 Higham, *Strangers in the Land*, 169.

7 Albert Murray, *The Omni-Americans: New Perspectives on Black Experience and American Culture*, New York: Outerbridge & Dienstfrey, 1970.

8 Constance Rourke, *American Humor: A Study of National Character*, New York: New York Review Book, 1931, 98.

9 Murray, *The Omni-Americans*, 18, emphasis in original.

10 Murray, *The Omni-Americans*, 18.

11 Murray, *The Omni-Americans*, 20–4, emphasis in original.

12 Murray, *The Omni-Americans*, 21.

13 John Langston Gwaltney, *Drylongso: A Self-Portrait of Black America*, New York: New Press, 1990, xxiii.

21. The White Worker and the Labor Movement in Nineteenth-Century America

1 The best account of the riots is Iver Bernstein, *The New York City Draft Riots*, New York: Oxford University Press, 1990.

2 Orestes A. Brownson, *The Laboring Classes: An Article from the Boston Quarterly*, Boston: Benjamin H. Greene, 1840, 10.

3 John R. Commons and associates, *A Documentary History of American Industrial Society*, vol. 7, New York: Russell & Russell, 1958, 356, 361, 362.

4 Ibid., 217, 218, 219.
5 Luther spoke of his travels in the South in "An Address on the Origin and Progress of Avarice," Boston: 1834. For information on his life, see Carl Gersuny, "Seth Luther—The Road from Chepachet," *Rhode Island History* 33, May 1974, 47–55; Louis Hartz, "Seth Luther: Story of a Working-Class Rebel," *New England Quarterly* 13: 3, September 1940, 401–18; and Edward Pessen, *Most Uncommon Jacksonians*, Albany: State University of New York Press, 1967.
6 *Liberator*, August 26, 1842.
7 *Liberator*, October 29, 1841, and January 14 and August 7, 1842.
8 A modern history of the Dorr Rebellion is a book of that title by Marvin E. Gettleman (New York: Random House, 1973), which presents a brief for the Dorrites. *The Afro-Yankees* by Robert J. Cottrol (Westport, CT: Praeger, 1982) manages to provide a more balanced picture in just a few pages.
9 C. L. R. James, "Every Cook Can Govern: Democracy in Ancient Greece and Its Meaning for Today," *Correspondence*, vol. 2, no. 12, Detroit: Bewick/Ed, 1992, 20.
10 For a suggestion of a possible channel of information, see Frederick Douglass's account of his time in the Baltimore shipyard, working alongside and talking with white workers, while still in contact with the plantation.
11 The best discussion of slave resistance is George Rawick, *From Sundown to Sunup: The Making of the Black Community*, Westport, CT: Praeger, 1972.
12 W. E. B. Du Bois, in *Black Reconstruction in America* (New York: Atheneum, 1935), was the first to label the flight from the plantation a general strike. He noted explicitly (page 64) that it was a strike of black and white labor.
13 The Emancipation Proclamation declared slavery abolished in those areas of the country in rebel hands, that is, where Union authority did not reach. Hence, it freed literally not a single person; but it was important as a declaration of purpose, and it encouraged the flight of black labor from the plantation. See Joseph T. Glaathaar, "Black Glory: The African-American Role in Union Victory," in Gabor S. Boritt, ed., *Why the Confederacy Lost*, New York: Oxford University Press, 1992, 133–62.

24. Aux Armes! Formez Vos Bataillons!

1 Lydia Maria Child, "Dissolution of the Union," *Liberator*, May 20, 1842, as quoted in Aileen S. Kraditor, *Means and Ends in American Abolitionism, 1834–1850*, New York: Pantheon, 1969, 23.
2 President Abraham Lincoln's Second Inaugural Address (1865).

25. How the Irish Became White

1 For a consideration of these and other absurdities, see Barbara Fields, "Ideology and Race in American History," in J. Morgan Kousser and James M. McPherson, *Region, Race and Reconstruction*, New York: Oxford University Press, 1982, 143–77.
2 Ted Allen, *The Invention of the White Race, Vol. 1: Racial Oppression and Social Control*, New York: Verso, 1994, 28, 32.

27. Abolitionism and the White Studies Racket

1 *Boston Globe*, December 21, 1997.
2 Matt Wray and Annalee Newitz, eds., *White Trash: Race and Class in America*, New York: Routledge, 1997, 5, 6.
3 Ibid., 150, 149.
4 Ibid., 125.
5 Ibid., 148.
6 Ibid., 139, 137.
7 Howard Winant, "Behind Blue Eyes: Whiteness and Contemporary U.S. Racial Politics," in Michelle Fine, Lois Weiss, Linda C. Powell, and L. Mun Wong, *Off White: Readings on Race, Power, and Society*, New York: Routledge, 1997, 48.

28. Reality and the Future

1 C. L. R. James, Grace C. Lee, in collaboration with Cornelius Castoriadis, *Facing Reality*, Chicago: Charles H. Kerr, 2006.
2 C. L. R. James, *New Notions: Two Works by C. L. R. James*, edited with an introduction by Noel Ignatiev, Oakland: PM Press, 2010, 14.

29. Abolitionism and the Free Society

1 C. L. R. James, *American Civilization*, Cambridge: Blackwell Publishers, 1993, 209.
2 Ibid., 208.
3 Ibid., 206.

30. The American Blindspot

1 Eric Foner, *Reconstruction: America's Unfinished Revolution, 1863–1877*, New York: Harper and Row, 1988, xxi. W. E. B. Du Bois, *Black Reconstruction in America*, New York: Atheneum, 1935. Subsequent references to page number only. The germ idea for this essay I owe to Theodore Allen, who many years ago introduced me to Du Bois's book. I wish also to acknowledge contributions of Peter Coclanis, the late Nathan Huggins, and Peter Linebaugh.
2 In an earlier work, *Nothing But Freedom* (Baton Rouge: Louisiana State University Press, 1983); Foner commented on Du Bois's use of the term "worker" instead of "slave" (p. 5). His decision not to use the term in *Reconstruction* is, therefore, significant.
3 G. W. F. Hegel, *The Phenomenology of Mind*, New York: Harper and Row, 1967, 81–2.
4 Samuel Bernstein, *The First International in America*, New York: A. M. Kelley, 1962, 81–2.

5 James S. Allen, *Reconstruction: The Battle for Democracy, 1865–1876*, New York: International Publishers, 1937, 123–5; Robin D. G. Kelley, *Hammer and Hoe: Alabama Communists During the Great Depression*, Chapel Hill: University of North Carolina Press, 1990, 39.

6 In *Politics and Ideology in the Age of Civil War* (New York: 1980), Foner noted that "Du Bois referred to the Reconstruction regimes as the rule of the 'black proletariat.' The terminology is exaggerated, but Du Bois did have a point," he conceded (p. 120). In a review of *Reconstruction*, Vincent Harding notes that Foner's decision to condense the struggle of Afro-Americans against white hegemony within southern Republicanism "tends to undermine his own commitment to demonstrating the centrality of the black experience." *American Historical Review* 5, February 1990, 264–5.

7 Accounts of the march are given in Allen, *Reconstruction*, 178–9 and in Iver Bernstein, *The New York City Draft Riots* (New York: Oxford University Press, 1990), 233–4, and various other places, from reports in the *Times*, *Tribune*, *Herald*, and *Sun* of September 14, 1871.

8 Philip S. Foner, *The Great Labor Uprising of 1877*, New York: Pathfinder Press, 1977, 182; David Roediger, "'Not Only the Ruling Classes to Overcome, But Also the So-Called Mob:' The St. Louis General Strike of 1877," *Journal of Social History*, 19, Winter 1985, 225.

9 Charles and Mary Beard, *The Rise of American Civilization*, New York: The Macmillan Company, 1927.

10 Allen, *Reconstruction*, 18.

11 Wilson Record, *The Negro and the Communist Party*, New York: Atheneum, 1971, 92.

31. Whiteness and Class Struggle

1 Peter Kolchin, "Whiteness Studies: The New History of Race in America," *Journal of American History* 89: 1, 2002, 154.

2 W. E. B. Du Bois, *Crisis*, vol. 39, cited in W. E. B. Du Bois, *Black Reconstruction in America*, New York: Atheneum, 1969; W. E. B. Du Bois, *An ABC of Colour*, New York: International Publishers, 1963, 170.

3 Du Bois, *Black Reconstruction in America*, 30.

4 Du Bois, *Black Reconstruction in America*, 700.

5 For a compilation of black writers looking at whiteness, see David R. Roediger, *Black on White: Black Writers on What It Means to be White*, New York: Schocken, 1998.

6 Theodore Allen, *The Invention of the White Race, Vol. 1: Racial Oppression and Social Control*, London: Verso, 1994; Theodore Allen, *The Invention of the White Race, Vol. 2: The Origin of Racial Oppression in Anglo-America*, London: Verso, 1997. David Roediger, *The Wages of Whiteness: Race and the Making of the American Working Class*, New York: Verso, 2007. Noel Ignatiev, *How the Irish Became White*, London: Routledge, 1995.

7 Eric Arnesen, "Up From Exclusion: Black and White Workers, Race, and the State of Labor History," *Reviews in American History* 26, 1998, 151.

8 Eric Arnesen, "Whiteness and the Historians' Imagination," *International Labor and Working-Class History* 60, 2001, 11–12.

9 Alexander Saxton, *The Rise and Fall of the White Republic: Class Politics and Mass Culture in Nineteenth-Century America*, London: Verso, 2003.

10 For a critique of Roediger's psychoanalytic approach from a class-struggle stand-point, see Gregory Meyerson, "Marxism, Psychoanalysis and Labor Competition," *Cultural Logic* 1: 1, 1997.
11 Allen, *The Invention of the White Race*, vol. 2, 274.
12 Not all persons of African descent in the Chesapeake were slaves, but the hardening of the color line made the free Negro an anomaly. It was different in the West Indies, where *free person of colour* designated a recognized social station.
13 Allen, *The Invention of the White Race*, vol. 2, 244.
14 Vijay Prashad, *The Karma of Brown Folk*, Minneapolis: University of Minnesota Press, 2000, 91.
15 Joel Perlmann and Roger Waldinger, "Are the Children of Today's Immigrants Making It?" *Public Interest* 132, 1998, 86.

33. Palestine: A Race Traitor Analysis

1 Joseph Weitz, deputy chairman of the board of directors of the Jewish National Fund from 1951 to 1973, former chairman of the Israel Land Authority, quoted in Uri Davis, *Israel: Apartheid State*, London: Zed Books, 1987, 6.
2 Reported in *Ha'aretz*, April 4, 1969; Davis, *Israel*, 21.
3 Reported in *Associated Press*, December 23, 2003.
4 Greer Fay Cashman, "53% of Israelis Say Arabs Should Be Encouraged to Leave," *Jerusalem Post*, December 1, 2010, jpost.com.
5 *Ha'aretz*, July 18, 2004.
6 *Ha'aretz*, July 18, 2002.
7 Roger Garaudy, *The Case of Israel: A Study of Political Zionism*, London: Shorouk International, 1983, 139.
8 In his poem Baraka charged that the Israeli government knew in advance about the impending attacks and closed its offices in the World Trade Center two weeks before September 11, pulling out 2,000 Israeli workers. His charge was based on reports in a number of mainstream European and Israeli newspapers. He insisted later that his target was the Bush administration, which he accused of ignoring advance warnings, and that he did not mean to imply Israeli complicity in the attacks. I give no credence to the reports: the Israeli government has shown repeatedly that it doesn't give a damn for the lives of ordinary Jews and would have been happy to sacrifice 2,000 of its citizens in return for the sympathy of the American public.
9 *Guardian*, April 29, 2002.
10 *Guardian*, February 28, 2002.
11 *New York Times*, September 14, 2003. Readers interested in the idea of a single democratic secular state in the Middle East are referred to the Association for One Democratic State in Palestine/Israel, which brings together people of various ethnicities and creeds from around the world.
12 Michael Collins, *The Keepers of Truth*, London: Phoenix House, 2000, 205–6.

34. Zionism, Anti-Semitism, and the People of Palestine

1 Sir Mohammed Zafrullah Khan (Pakistan's representative to the UN), "Address to the 126th Plenary Meeting of the UN General Assembly, November 28, 1947, unispal.un.org.
2 Yoav Gelber, "Zionist Policy and the Fate of European Jewry (1932–1945)," *Yad Vashem Studies* 12, 199.
3 Lenni Brenner, *Zionism in the Age of the Dictators*, London: Croom Helm, 1983.
4 Menachem Begin, *The Revolt: The Story of Irgun*, New York: Henry Schuman, 1951, 164–5.
5 Joseph Weitz, deputy chairman of the board of directors of the Jewish National Fund from 1951 to 1973, former chairman of the Israel Land Authority, quoted in Uri Davis, *Israel: Apartheid State*, London: Zed Books, 1987, 5.
6 *Ha'aretz*, April 4, 1969, quoted in Davis, *Israel*, 21.
7 Associated Press, December 23, 2003.
8 Agence France-Presse, January 17, 2004.
9 *Ha'aretz*, July 18, 2002.
10 *Guardian*, April 29, 2002.
11 Ran HaCohen, "Abusing 'Anti-semitism,'" antiwar.com, September 29, 2003.
12 Matthew Engel, "Meet the New Zionists," *Guardian*, October 28, 2002.
13 *New York Times*, September 14, 2003.
14 Delivered by Rabbi Mordechi Weberman under the auspices of the Palestine Right of Return Coalition (Al-Awda NY/NJ), at the march in front of the Israeli Consulate, Friday, July 26, 2002.

35. Beyond the Spectacle: New Abolitionists Speak Out

1 Ralph Ellison, "The Little Man at Chehaw Station," *The American Scholar*, 1978.
2 C. L. R. James, "The Revolutionary Answer to the Negro Problem in the United States," in Scott McLemee, ed., *C. L. R. James on the "Negro Question,"* Jackson: University Press of Mississippi, 2008.
3 Nell Irvin Painter, *The History of White People*, New York: W. W. Norton, 2010, 396.

36. The Lesson of the Hour: Wendell Phillips on Abolition and Strategy

1 "To the Public," No. 1 (January 1831), quoted in Ellen H. Todras, *Voice of Abolition*, Linnet, 1999, 46.
2 C. L. R. James, "Stalinism and Negro History," *Fourth International*, vol. 10, no. 10, November 1949.
3 Francis Jackson Garrison, *William Lloyd Garrison, 1805–1879; The Story of His Life Told by his Children: Volume 3, 1841–1860*, New York: The Century Company, 1889, 324.

4 Ibid., 439.
5 C. L. R. James, "The Abolitionists" in *American Civilization*, edited by Anna Grimshaw and Keith Hart, Cambridge, MA: Blackwell, 1993, 89.
6 Walt Whitman, *Selected Journalism*, Iowa City: University of Iowa Press, 2015, 51.
7 James J. Green, *Wendell Phillips*, New York: International Publishers, 1945, 14.
8 Wendell Phillips, "Under the Flag," speech delivered at the Music Hall, Boston, April 12, 1861, as cited in *Friends' Intelligencer*, vol. 70, 1913, 552.
9 *The Life and Times of Frederick Douglass Written by Himself*, Boston: De Wolfe, Fiske and Co., 1895, 435.
10 Wendell Phillips, *Speeches, Lectures, and Letters*, Boston: Lee and Shepard, 1884, 420.

37. The World View of C. L. R. James

1 C. L. R. James, *Modern Politics*, edited with an introduction by Noel Ignatiev, Oakland: PM Press, 2013.
2 From Ignatiev's introduction to *A New Notion: Two Works by C. L. R. James*, Oakland: PM Press, 2010.
3 C. L. R. James, Raya Dunayevskaya, and Grace Lee Boggs, *State Capitalism and World Revolution*, Chicago: Charles H. Kerr, 1986 [1950], 43.
4 Ibid., 48.
5 C. L. R. James, "The Revolutionary Answer to the Negro Problem in the United States" (1948), *International Socialist Review*, no. 85, 2012, isreview.org.
6 C. L. R. James, *The Black Jacobins: Toussaint L'Ouverture and the San Domingo Revolution*, London: Secker and Warburg, 1938.
7 C. L. R. James, *Mariners, Renegades and Castaways: The Story of Herman Melville and the World We Live In*, Chicago: University of Chicago Press, 2001 [1953].
8 C. L. R. James, *Beyond a Boundary*, London: Hutchinson, 1963.
9 John Edgar Wideman, *Hoop Roots*, Boston: Mariner Books, 2003.
10 C. L. R. James, *Notes on Dialectics: Hegel, Marx, Lenin*, Westport, CT: Lawrence Hill, 1948.
11 C. L. R. James, *Nkrumah and the Ghana Revolution*, Westport, CT: Lawrence Hill, 1977.
12 Martin Glaberman, ed., *Marxism for Our Times: C. L. R. James on Revolutionary Organization*, Jackson: University Press of Mississippi, 1999.
13 C. L. R. James, Grace Boggs, and Cornelius Castoriadis, *Facing Reality*, Detroit, MI: Bewick Editions 1974, 151.
14 Ibid., 151.
15 C. L. R. James, F. Forest, and Ria Stone, *The Invading Socialist Society*, Isleham: Bewick Press, 1972.
16 C. L. R. James, "Every Cook Can Govern," *Correspondence*, vol. 2, no. 12, June 1956, marxists.org.
17 Stokely Carmichael with Ekwueme Michael Thelwell, *Ready for Revolution: The Life and Struggles of Stokely Carmichael (Kwame Ture)*, New York: Scribner, 2005.

38. *Modern Politics*

1 C. L. R. James, *Modern Politics*, Chicago: Charles H. Kerr, 1973 and San Francisco: PM Press, 2013. I am grateful to Geert Dhondt and John Garvey for their suggestions.
2 A fuller outline of James's life and thought can be found in my introduction to C. L. R. James, *A New Notion*, Oakland, CA: PM Press, 2010.
3 James explores this subject at greater length in "Every Cook Can Govern," reprinted in *A New Notion*, Oakland, CA: PM Press, 2010.
4 Ellen Meiksins Wood traces the devolution from direct to representative democracy in *Democracy Against Capitalism: Renewing Historical Materialism*, Cambridge: Cambridge University Press, 1995. She makes no reference to James.
5 James, *Modern Politics*, 35.
6 Eric Wolf, *Europe and the People Without History*, Berkeley: University of California Press, 1982, 5.
7 See Martin Bernal, *Black Athena: The Afroasiatic Roots of Classical Civilization*, New Brunswick, NJ: Rutgers University Press, 1987.
8 For more on this, see Archibald Robertson, *The Origins of Christianity*, New York: International Publishers, 1954, and the classic by Karl Kautsky, *Foundations of Christianity: A Study in Christian Origins*, New York: Monthly Review, 1972.
9 She made another comment I wish to record: "I've been in prison, I've been in a mental hospital, and I've been at US Steel. As far as I'm concerned, this is the strangest of them all: in those other places people knew something was wrong, and around here people think that what they do is normal."
10 Karl Marx, *Capital*, Volume I, Chapter 15. This was the only passage James quoted from Marx in these six lectures.
11 In a little-known address he delivered in London in 1967 on the death of Che Guevara, James predicted that if the capitalist system continued on the path of destroying the material elements of civilization, rendering impossible traditional means of struggle, then guerrilla warfare could become the only method open.
12 C. L. R. James, *Mariners, Renegades and Castaways: The Story of Herman Melville and the World We Live In*, Chicago: University of Chicago Press, 2001.

42. Defining *Hard Crackers*

1 V. I. Lenin, "The Tasks of the Preletariat in Our Revolution," in Lenin's, *Collected Works, Vol. 24*, Moscow: Progress Publishers, 1964, 55–92.

43. Frederick Douglass, John Brown, and the Virtues of Impracticality

1 David W. Blight, *Frederick Douglass: Prophet of Freedom*, New York: Simon and Schuster, 2018. Adam Gopnik, "The Prophetic Pragmatism of Frederick Douglass," *New Yorker*, October 15, 2018.

2 Gopnik, "The Prophetic Pragmatism of Frederick Douglass."

3 C. L. R. James, *American Civilization*, London: Blackwell, 1983, 89.

4 Wendell Phillips Garrison and Francis Jackson Garrison, *William Lloyd Garrison, 1805–1879: The Story of His Life Told by His Children*, Houghton Mifflin: 1894, 491.

5 See Albert Fried, *John Brown's Journey: Notes and Reflections on His America and Mine*, Norwell, MA: Anchor Books, 1978, especially chapters 5 and 6.

6 Like the Communist Party a century later, which formally ran its own candidates while supporting the Democratic Party.

7 Blight, *Frederick Douglass*, 240–5.

8 Frederick Douglass, *Life and Times of Frederick Douglass*, Hartford, Conn.: Park Publishing Co., 1881, 318–21.

9 The best biographies of Brown are W. E. B. Du Bois, *John Brown* (New York: Penguin, 2001 [1909] and David S. Reynolds, *John Brown: Abolitionist: The Man Who Killed Slavery, Sparked the Civil War, and Seeded Civil Rights* (New York: Vintage, 2006). Truman Nelson has written two fictional accounts of Brown: *The Surveyor* (New York: Doubleday, 1960) and *The Old Man* (Chicago: Haymarket, 2009). Du Bois credits Nelson with having dug more deeply into the sources than anyone else, and I have treated them as authoritative. Russell Banks's novel, *Cloudsplitter* (New York: HarperCollins, 1998) is great. *The Good Lord Bird* by James McBride (New York: Riverhead Books, 2013) treats Douglass without reverence. The account of Douglass's relations with Brown are based on Douglass's *Life and Times of Frederick Douglass*, Radford, VA: Wilder Publications, 2008 [1881]. As Blight notes (*Frederick Douglass*, 271), it contains "a touch of legend, creatively crafted." It is the only account we have.

10 Nelson, *The Old Man*, 50.

11 Ibid., 50–1.

12 Ibid., 51–2.

13 Du Bois, *John Brown*, 345.

14 Wendell Phillips, "The Lesson of the Hour," delivered at Brooklyn, NY, Tuesday, November 1, 1859.

15 A reference to a stage performance popular at the time, the subject of an essay by Edgar Allan Poe, "Maelzel's Chess Player."

16 Du Bois, *John Brown*, 338, 375.

Afterword: Noel Ignatiev, an Intellectual Biography

1 Abraham Lincoln, Second Inaugural Address, March 4, 1865.

Index